Thursday's Child

TRENDS AND PATTERNS IN CONTEMPORARY CHILDREN'S LITERATURE

Thursday's Child

TRENDS AND PATTERNS

IN CONTEMPORARY

CHILDREN'S LITERATURE

Sheila A. Egoff

AMERICAN LIBRARY ASSOCIATION   CHICAGO 1981

Acknowledgments

p. 227. "The Horseman" from *Peacock Pie* by Walter de la Mare. London: Constable, 1913. Reprinted by permission of the literary trustees of Walter de la Mare and the Society of Authors as their representative.

p. 228. Stanzas 1 and 4 from "The Wholly Family" in *Finding a Poem* by Eve Merriam. New York: Atheneum, 1970; Toronto: McClelland and Stewart, 1970. Copyright © 1970 by Eve Merriam. By permission of International Creative Management.

p. 229. Text excerpted from *Who Look at Me* by June Jordan. Copyright © 1969 by June Jordan. By permission of Thomas Y. Crowell, Publishers, and June Jordan.

p. 230. From "A March Calf" in *Season Songs* by Ted Hughes. Copyright © 1968 by Ted Hughes. Reprinted by permission of Faber and Faber Ltd. and Viking Penguin, Inc.

p. 230–31. Sixth stanza from "And Here's What Happened Next or Those Three" from *THE MONSTER DEN, or Look What Happened at My House—and to It*, written by John Ciardi. Text copyright © 1963, 1964, 1966 by John Ciardi. By permission of J. B. Lippincott, Publisher.

p. 231. First verse of "Alligator Pie" from *Alligator Pie* by Dennis Lee. Copyright © 1974 by Dennis Lee. Reprinted by permission of Macmillan of Canada and Dennis Lee.

p. 232. "German Song" from *The New Nutcracker Suite and Other Innocent Verses* by Ogden Nash. Boston: Little, Brown & Company, 1962. Copyright © 1961, 1962 by Ogden Nash. Reprinted by permission of Curtis Brown, Ltd.

p. 232. Lines from *The Hill of the Fairy Calf* by Charles Causley. London: Hodder & Stoughton, 1976. Text copyright © 1976 by Charles Causley. Reprinted by kind permission of David Higham Associates Limited.

p. 233. "The Sewing Basket" from *Ann at Highwood Hall* by Robert Graves. Copyright © 1964 by International Authors N.V. London: Cassell, 1964; New York: Doubleday, 1964. Reprinted by permission of Robert Graves.

p. 235. "My Papa's Waltz," copyright 1942 by Hearst Magazines, Inc., from the book *The Collected Poems of Theodore Roethke*. Reprinted by permission of Doubleday & Company, Inc., New York, and Faber and Faber, Ltd., London.

Library of Congress Cataloging in Publication Data

Egoff, Sheila A.
  Thursday's Child
  Includes bibliographies and index
  1. Children's literature—History and criticism.
I. Title.
PN1009.A1E32   809'.89282   81-8066
ISBN 0-8389-0327-4   AACR2

p. 235. "Markings: The Semicolon" from *Finding a Poem* by Eve Merriam. New York: Atheneum, 1970; Toronto: McClelland & Stewart, 1970. Copyright © 1970 by Eve Merriam. By permission of International Creative Management.

p. 236. "Sometimes" from *For Me to Say: Rhymes of the Never Was and Always Is* by David McCord. Copyright © 1970 by David McCord. By permission of Little, Brown and Company.

p. 237. From *More Cricket Songs: Japanese Haiku*, translated and copyright © 1971 by Harry Behn. Reprinted by permission of Harcourt Brace Jovanovich, Inc., and Curtis Brown, Ltd.

p. 238. Stanza from *Father Fox's Pennyrhmes* by Clyde Watson. Text copyright © 1971 by Clyde Watson. By permission of Thomas Y. Crowell Co., Publishers, and Curtis Brown, Ltd.

p. 238. Reprinted by permission of Macmillan Publishing Co., Inc., and Penguin Books, Ltd., from *A Bat Is Born: From the Bat-Poet* by Randall Jarrell. Copyright © Macmillan Publishing Co., Inc., 1963, 1964.

p. 239. "Mother to Son" from *Selected Poems of Langston Hughes*. Copyright © 1926 by Alfred A. Knopf, Inc., and renewed 1954 by Langston Hughes. Reprinted by permission of the publisher.

p. 242. Poem from *There's a Sound in the Sea . . . A Child's Eye View of the Whale*, comp. by Tamar Griggs. San Francisco: Scrimshaw Pr., 1975. Copyright © 1975 by Tamar Griggs. Reproduced by permission of Tamar Griggs.

Monday's child is fair of face,
Tuesday's child is full of grace,
Wednesday's child is full of woe,
Thursday's child has far to go,
Friday's child is loving and giving,
Saturday's child has to work for its living,
But a child that's born on the Sabbath day
Is fair and wise and good and gay.

——Anonymous Nursery Rhyme

Contents

Preface

The last twenty-five years have been a period of astonishing growth in the publication of children's books. In Britain and the United States alone over 100,000 titles have been issued since 1957—perhaps as many as in all the years preceding. It has also been a period when qualitative changes occurred at a similarly dizzying rate. Many of these changes were of such importance and sharpness as to occasion sharp debate and widespread public attention.

It seemed clear that new developments of this magnitude warranted some description and analysis. This book is therefore an attempt to identify and assess the main trends, features, and accomplishments of the last quarter century.

My basic design has been to approach the subject by time period and by literary genre. Since even the rampant changes of the recent past are part of the continuum of children's literature, I begin by examining that literature and assessing its growth. Chapter 2 pins down the necessarily broad generalizations of chapter 1 by applying them to specific books, those publications of the past which have retained their popularity. Since these "classics" are still read by present-day children, they should be considered part of contemporary children's literature and thus included alongside recent publications. More particularly, in attempting to account for the persistence of these books, one can discern those features which are of permanent consequence in children's literature, as distinguished from trends of the moment.

From this background I proceed to examine, genre by genre, the publications issued since the 1960s. Inasmuch as every genre (realistic fiction, fantasy, science fiction, etc.) constitutes in effect a separate body of literature, I believe it inappropriate to treat them in uniform fashion. Each chapter in this work thus varies according to the requirements of its particular subject matter. Indeed, in one instance—informational books—the genre's particular characteristics were such as to force its total exclusion from this study. Informational books are now so numerous, varied, and significant that they deserve a full treatment of their own. Consequently the present work is given over entirely to imaginative writings.

Another exclusion—in this instance, partial—is children's literature in foreign languages. This study is primarily limited to works written originally in English, but I have sought to give some consideration to books from other cultures. Not only have these been of considerable influence but also, insofar as they have been translated, they have become part of the common stock of English-language readings. The chapter on the European children's novel in translation deals with the material in this light.

The chapter on poetry was written by my colleague, Judith Saltman, an experienced children's librarian and lecturer in children's literature at the University of British Columbia. I consider this chapter a most valuable and essential contribution to the evaluation of children's literature. While there are many articles on the teaching of poetry to children, there are almost no studies that deal with children's poetry in terms of literary criticism.

Two final points. Some repetition will be noticeable from chapter to chapter. This has come about by design, not accident, since I intended that each genre, although dealt with separately, could also be seen as following the general pattern of contemporary children's literature. Also, in a relatively brief study such as this, I believe it advisable to concentrate on those individual books which represent achievement of one kind or another. So while I do not ignore the fact that a great deal of inferior writing has been produced and do give attention to the trends that have fostered such, I tend usually to single out for individual discussion only those titles I consider to be successful or markedly influential.

The last point relates to the matter of objectivity. Total objectivity is, of course, unattainable in any field, and in children's literature, where so much recent work has caused impassioned controversy, my biases must really show. I do claim, however, to have one advantage which I share with Lillian Smith, my mentor in children's literature. In her classic book on children's literature *The Unreluctant Years*, Lillian Smith showed herself to be notably free of nationalistic biases. This objectivity, I suggest, was in large part due to the fact that Lillian Smith was a Canadian and so stood outside both major "camps" of children's writing—Britain and the United States. As another

Canadian, I hope that I have evinced a similar capacity for dispassionate evenhandedness in my judgments. Canada is perhaps the most cosmopolitan country in the world when it comes to the reading of children's literature. Having relatively few works produced in Canada itself, we borrow liberally from every other country and in fact import more books than any other country. I hope that my investigation has paralleled the breadth and "openness" of Canadian children's reading.

In terms of acknowledgment, this book owes most to Lillian Smith's *The Unreluctant Years* in which she determined the essential character of children's literature and how it should be assessed. I have not restated these views and the subject matter contained herein is entirely my own, as is also, of course, the responsibility for the judgments offered. I would like, however, to express my large indebtedness to Lillian Smith for the way in which I learned to view children's literature.

This book also owes a great deal to my students at the School of Librarianship, the University of British Columbia, whose insights into children's literature, whether expressed in class or offered in papers, have been most valuable. And finally, I am most grateful to former students and now colleagues Judith Saltman, Sarah Ellis, and Corinne Durston (all practicing children's librarians) for keeping me in touch with the present-day interests of children and their reading and for their accumulated knowledge of children's literature and its significant role in the lives of children.

1. Children's Literature and How It Grew

Since several generations of critical commentaries have produced no consensus on a definition of children's literature, a clear and simple description becomes preferable to one that attempts to be all-embracing. Children's literature has two basic characteristics: it is writing *for* children (that is, people up to the early teens) and it is intended to be read as literature and not only for information and guidance.

The first characteristic excludes books that are read by children although originally intended for adults, such as *Gulliver's Travels* and *Robinson Crusoe*. Their authors cannot be said to have contemplated the problem of writing for a child audience. "Children's classics" though some have become, they stand outside the mainstream of children's literature because children usually read abridged versions, the cutting having been done either by an editor or by readers themselves in the form of "skipping."

The second characteristic presents more problems in clarification simply because, as Sir Arthur Quiller-Couch has noted, "Literature is not an abstract science, to which exact definition can be applied. It is an art, rather, the success of which depends on personal persuasiveness, on the author's skill to give as ours to receive."[1] Whether child or adult, this receiving ability varies since it is dependent not only on the motor skills of reading, but also upon psychological and emotional makeup and experience. A child's experience is obviously more limited than that of an adult, and although constantly expanding, much of it is nonetheless obtained indirectly. Owing to this innate

1. Sir Arthur Quiller-Couch, *The Art of Writing* (New York: Capricorn Books, 1961[pa]), p. 20.

limitation in children as audience, their literature cannot claim the stature of that for the literate and knowing adult. Still, it differs only from adult literature in that its audience imposes the necessity for certain techniques and emphases: the paring down of characterization, the condensation of plot and incident, a faster pace, minimal description, and a basically straightforward story line—all in all, a less intricate web of plot, character, and style.

All these attributes of children's literature, while perfectly accurate and appropriate, are often misconstrued. The most serious error in judging writing for children is to equate simplification with simplemindedness. The writer for children may paint on a smaller canvas, using fewer and stronger colors, but is an artist still, not merely a craftsman. An author must write *for* a children's audience, not *down* to it. The most important single fact then, that must be understood about children's literature is that it *is* literature, another branch of the parent stem.

Examples may help in clarification. George MacDonald's *At the Back of the North Wind*, with its intuitive and perceptive interpretation of innocence, its emotion impregnated with thought, its memorable style, is a piece of literature. Thomas Day's *Sandford and Merton* with its heavily pedagogic writing is only interesting today as an English expression of Rousseau's theory of childhood education in fictional form; it is literature in the most generic sense as a piece of writing.

It is true that the acceptance of children's literature as literature came neither early nor easily to writers for children. Because children require direction from adults and because they are much more open to influence than adults, fiction intended for them has often been invested with very strong moral and social values, along with heavy doses of information. Indeed the basic necessity for the transmission of mores and manners from one generation to the next tends to place emphasis upon such a utilitarian approach. From this viewpoint, what children read is too important in its potential for society's good or ill to be made a matter of purely aesthetic consideration. Thus writing for children has tended, more than most other branches of literature, to be very much a reflection (although in miniature) of the prevailing social concepts and conditions, and it is in the history of society itself that one must look for the roots of children's literature and its role in reflecting changing values.

Because these views rarely were subject to debate and individual variation in outlook in the past, the development of writing for children can be visualized as a series of waves, each of which derives from or parallels a particular period in society's attitudes to children and their books. As we approach our own time, the waves become

2

progressively larger and more frequent, just as the rate and dimensions of social change have steadily increased. So each period has coded into its children's literature what may be described as a public or consensual view of the young and therefore of their books.

The span of time we call the Middle Ages enters here by default, as it were. Quite aside from the relatively small number of children who were then taught to read, writing for them was not considered necessary because—as Philippe Aries has explained in his magisterial study *Centuries of Childhood*[2]—childhood was not valued as a separate, unique identity. To pick out just one major observation from Aries's account, a high percentage of children were not expected to survive infancy. So why lavish special attention on them, particularly the laboriously taught skills of reading and writing? Those children who survived were quickly absorbed into the adult milieu. There is scarcely a vestige of writing in the medieval era, aside from a few books of manners and instruction, that were designed specifically for children.

Since there were no distinctions in life, there were none in literature, and it can be presumed that those children who did read fell upon the romances, ballads, fables, and legends that were intended for their elders. This had the logical effect of eliminating books for children almost entirely. Yet a foreshadowing of the next major public view came in the sixteenth century when Roger Ascham, the otherwise enlightened tutor of Elizabeth I, felt compelled to issue a diatribe (in 1570) against Malory's *Morte d'Arthur* as reading for the young. It was doubly ironic that he denounced a genre of literature that probably will outlast most books deliberately written for children and that he so misunderstood the quality of literature itself. The passionate energy in *Morte d'Arthur* that illuminates life rather than dampening and restricting a reader's response was better understood by Malory's printer, Caxton, who left the final judgment to the reader:

> And for to pass the time this book shall be pleasant to read in; but for you to give faith and believe that all is true that is contained herein, ye be at your liberty.[3]

The vital drama and force of romance and legend personified by Malory is with us still, while Ascham lies moldering in his grave.

Then came the Puritans. Having decided that "since children were not too little to die, they were not too little to go to hell," the Puritans almost simultaneously discovered (or "invented," as

2. Philippe Aries, *Centuries of Childhood* (New York: Knopf, 1962).
3. Sir Thomas Malory, *Le Morte d'Arthur* (London: Dent, 1933), p. 3.

McLuhan says) both children and children's books. They were the first to realize that children are interested in other children and that their books should therefore have child characters who were, however, made to express adult values in every aspect of their carefully controlled lives and deaths.

As much as we criticize seventeenth-century religious tracts disguised as fiction, it can be supposed that children were delighted to have books with child characters, even if they did not always recognize themselves in them. The relentless pursuits of divine virtue for children transform even Bunyan's spirited prose in *Pilgrim's Progress* (1678) to the laborious, strained verse of his deliberate work for children, *A Book for Boys and Girls, or Country Rhimes for Children* (1686). In thus setting the scene, the Puritans created a well-intentioned straitjacket that only the foremost writers of children's books have been able to discard.

In the next one hundred and fifty years, until about 1850, the religious tone gradually softened and themes increased in variety and scope. Still the public image of children's books was clear and strong. Children were people in process—in process of becoming adults—and they had to be brought to adulthood through books that stressed religious morality and socially acceptable behavior. This is not to say that all children's books were simply instructional manuals in disguise. Some were more than that, because they were better than average for their period.

The anonymous author of *Goody Two-Shoes* (1765) who relates a "disadvantaged" child's rise to station and fortune with dramatic verve, and Maria Edgeworth in "The Purple Jar" (1801) display a sensitivity toward childhood that was far ahead of its time. At the end of the latter, Rosamond, who learns the bitter lesson that a jar of colored water is not as valuable as a pair of shoes, says:

> However, I am quite sure—no, not quite sure, but I hope I shall be wiser another time.[4]

With this childish confession, children's literature is displaying, for the first time, one of the most notable traits of literature itself, its link with life. Rosamond here is a real, honest-to-goodness child speaking in an authentic voice, rather than parroting the adults around her. Hers is an advanced voice in children's literature, one that disappears quite quickly, yet reappears to stay in the mischievous younger children of Catherine Sinclair's *Holiday House* (1839), which many critics believe, and quite legitimately, marks the beginning of true

4. From "The Purple Jar," a story in Marie Edgeworth's *Early Lessons* (London: J. Johnson, 1809), pt. 1, p. 28.

children's literature as a nondidactic medium. Still, the majority of the books published before 1850 offered little more than the banal message that a rather narrow, selfish, and complacent goodness was the key to happiness and material success.

With the later Victorians, the whole concept of childhood changed. For the first time a separate state called "childhood" was envisioned. Now the child was thought of as basically good and innocent, although quite often mischievous in a learning manner, and childhood was to be valued for its own sake. "Heaven," Wordsworth claimed, "lies about us in our infancy." This sentimental but revolutionary view of childhood was first uttered on behalf of the children of the new middle class created by the Industrial Revolution and who became the new wave of readers.

One of the major spokesmen of this new middle class was George MacDonald, Congregational minister and poet. He most clearly expressed the cultural perception: while children should be cherished for their innocence and clear-sightedness, they must also be trained in the manners and virtues of the day, fulfilling the maxim "As the twig is bent, so grows the tree." In MacDonald's *At the Back of the North Wind* (1871), *The Princess and the Goblin* (1872), and its sequel, *The Princess and Curdie* (1883), he introduces two concepts that were to become an integral part of children's literature up until the late 1950s. Gillian Avery has described these as "the doctrine of perception" and "the doctrine of good breeding." [5]

The former assumes the natural goodness of children and their ability, unique to childhood, to cut through the gray areas of a question and get to the heart of the matter. But in MacDonald's time this ability also involved an innate trust on the part of a child in God and His surrogates on earth. The second doctrine emphasizes the crucial role of manners. Behavior rather than birth turned little boys into gentlemen and little girls into princesses. But unlike the children of the past, these qualities of character rarely were achieved without a sustained struggle. The young protagonists in the best fantasy and realistic fiction of the time (MacDonald's works, Kingsley's *The Water-Babies* [1863], Annie Keary's *Father Phim* [1879], Mrs. Molesworth's *The Cuckoo Clock* [1877], Charlotte Yonge's historical writings) all had philosophical quandaries to resolve, rather than obvious faults to overcome.

Victorian writers, in spite of their common view of childhood as a state of innocence, were by no means saccharine. They could be as tough and uncompromising as Kingsley, who thought of a children's book as a perfectly appropriate vehicle for diatribes against Catholics,

5. Gillian Avery, *Nineteenth Century Children* (London: Hodder and Stoughton, 1965), p. 59.

5

uncleanliness, and schoolmasters, in ascending order of denigration! Their main achievement was to move from a narrowly religious and doctrinaire adherence to rules of conduct to an optimistic philosophy that spoke in childlike terms of broad moral standards and universal values. Of course even with this mellowed approach, writers such as MacDonald were still paramountly moralists. Indeed, given their backgrounds (MacDonald was a Congregational minister and Kingsley an Anglican clergyman), such a purpose was almost inevitable.

Still, these later Victorians dealt with morality in a new and happier way, taking delight in entertainment instead of suggesting, as did their predecessors, that such delights were somehow sinful. They created exciting plots; they portrayed interesting characters and depicted them in memorable language—all considerable and welcome innovations in children's literature. Endowing their writing with this enlargement of vision, they sent their books on a journey across time and space. The great Victorian classics still stir the hearts and minds of children who have scarcely heard of England and for whom the nineteenth century is utterly remote.

This is not to say that all the authors of such good writing necessarily meant to provide an aesthetic experience. "Art for art's sake" is a relatively new motive in the history of artistic endeavor and it is certain that, like Molière's "Bourgeois Gentilhomme" who was surprised to find out that he had always been talking prose, many of these writers produced works of literature without intending to do so.

It is important to remember, however, that what we think of as the "classics" were by no means representative of Victorian children's books as a whole. One result of the invention of the rotary press, which became a ravenous monster demanding to be fed continually (much like television today), was the production of cheap, sensational magazines and comics directed chiefly at boys. Such "penny dreadfuls" drew the wrath of the guardians of morality and education to an extent not known since Mrs. Trimmer had tried to wipe out *Cinderella* over fifty years before. In the words of one despairing critic, Edward Salmon,

> No element of sweetness and light ever finds its way into their columns and . . . they are filled with stories of blood and revenge, of passion and cruelty, as improbable and often impossible in plot as their literary execution is contemptible. . . . Is it surprising that "the pales and forts of reason" should fall before the vicious onslaught? [6]

6. Edward Salmon, *Juvenile Literature as It Is* (London: Henry J. Drane, 1888), pp. 184-89.

Whatever the merits of Salmon's criticism, it clearly establishes one important point: literature for children was by now seen as having its own identity. The public had come to see children as a separate group, and the literature that treated them as a separate group was now accepted. Children's literature had become a genre at last, one that appealed to many professional writers. In England in the 1890s the production of children's books was second only to that of the novel. More important, writing for children was attracting literary craftsmen —Verne in France, Collodi in Italy, Spyri in Switzerland, Alcott and Twain in the United States, writers from Carroll to Stevenson to Nesbit in England—who chose to write for children because it suited their aesthetic goals and preferences (as well as their pocketbooks) to do so. Assigning functions and limits to the genre, these writers exploited its conventions imaginatively. The fact that children were the audience was seen not as a drawback to treating themes in some depth but rather as a stimulus and an opportunity for imaginative play and exuberant fancy in the development of literary ideas. What book is more thoughtful and yet playful than Edith Nesbit's *The Treasure Seekers* (1899) or more serious and romantic than Robert Louis Stevenson's *Kidnapped* (1886)? This era, then, saw not only the first full development of children's literature but also its first "Golden Age."

The Edwardians who followed intensified the sense of difference and distance between childhood and adulthood. Nowhere is this more charmingly expressed than in Kenneth Grahame's account of his own childhood, *The Golden Age*, wherein children see themselves as the fortunate ones, and adults are "the Olympians," powerful but misguided. When adults have the power to do otherwise, how can they possibly wish to spend a lovely Sunday going to church and drinking tea on the lawn instead of climbing trees or digging for hidden treasure? Childhood is the ideal state. This assumption also is made in other books of the period, such as *The Wind in the Willows* (in which the animals are really children), the Nesbit books, and, most of all, Barrie's *Peter Pan* (produced first as a play in 1904). It was not that the children in these books wanted to evade maturity and responsibility; it was rather that childhood had its own special character and flavor, qualities that could not be given up without a sense of loss. Childhood was to be prolonged as long as possible.

Historically speaking, the Edwardian period ended in 1910, but in terms of the public image of children's books, it melded into the period after the First World War, indeed persisting until the 1930s. The complete separation of childhood and adulthood, crystallized in Edwardian thought, led to an idealization of the young that, in a literary sense, was translated into a highly sentimental school of writing. The tough moral quality and broad social conscience exhib-

7

ited by the late Victorian writers and their portrayal of youthful characters who were obliged to make moral decisions quite disappeared. The newer protagonists were stereotyped superheroes and heroines engaged in larger-than-life adventures. Only a few writers— Edith Nesbit in *The Treasure Seekers* (1899), Barrie in *Peter and Wendy* (1911), Grahame in *The Wind in the Willows* (1908), Burnett in *The Secret Garden* (1911), and Milne in *Winnie the Pooh* (1926)—managed, by virtue of style and an understanding of the child's imaginative and day-to-day worlds, to write books of sentiment rather than sentimentality. For this they have been rewarded by the affectionate readership of generations of children until the present. But most of the children's books of this period, which was also one of formidable publishing in terms of numbers, are completely forgettable.

In strong contrast to the books for boys (by such writers as R. M. Ballantyne, Frederick Marryat, and William Mayne Reid) of some sixty years before, with their outdoors adventures and consequent emphasis on manliness, there came at the turn of the century a flood of books, chiefly from North America, with girls as the chief protagonists. Mr. Salmon, who had wanted "sweetness and light," would have been delighted. To pick out some titles that are still remembered, there were from the United States *Elsie Dinsmore* (1867), *The Five Little Peppers* (1881), *A Girl of the Limberlost* (1909), *Pollyanna* (1913), and from Canada, L. M. Montgomery's *Anne of Green Gables* (1908), and Nellie McClung's *Sowing Seeds in Danny* (1908), a title to give one pause! Even in England, where comparison with the Victorian classics might have been expected to exert a sobering influence, writing for children reached a degree of sentimentality hitherto unknown. In these rhapsodic narratives, the angelic heroines solved not only their own problems but those of every adult with whom they came in contact. They were portrayed as goodness incarnate, or at the very least as full-fledged saviors.

This odd idea, that children could accomplish anything they willed while retaining their childlike innocence, was later reinforced by the appearance of the American commercialized series books, most of which began between 1907 and 1930, published by the Stratemeyer Syndicate: *Nancy Drew, The Hardy Boys, Tom Swift*, the *Bobbsey Twins*. It is of course of some significance in children's reading, as opposed to children's literature, that these repetitive and anonymous series books outlasted their contemporary competitors. Their perennial appeal seems to bear out Ford Madox Ford's observation that "only two classes of books are of universal appeal: the very best and the very worst."[7] All in all it was an age that caused George

7. Ford Madox Ford, *Joseph Conrad* (Boston: Little, 1924), p. 184.

Orwell, who was working in a London bookshop in the 1930s, to remark that "Modern books for children are rather horrible things, especially when you see them in the mass. Personally I would sooner give a child a copy of Petronius Arbiter than *Peter Pan*, but even Barrie seems manly and wholesome compared with some of his later imitators."[8] Children themselves have rescued *Peter Pan* from this acerbic condemnation, but any examination of children's books of this period will show barely one-tenth of one percent to be of any enduring value.

After the Second World War, the writing of children's books took an upward swing and mustered a remarkable roster of diverse talents. In England there were Arthur Ransome, C. S. Lewis, J. R. R. Tolkien (*The Hobbit*, although published in 1937, did not make its impact until after the Second World War), Rumer Godden, Eric Linklater, Beverley Nichols, Philippa Pearce, Lucy Boston, Rosemary Sutcliff, and William Mayne; in the United States, Eleanor Estes, Scott O'Dell, Laura Ingalls Wilder, William Pène du Bois, and E. B. White (to name but a few). In spite of the considerable variation of theme and intent in the works of these writers, they agreed so strongly on basic outlooks and values as to suggest that there was still a public view or consensus on the nature of children and their literature, although again differing from previous eras.

The medieval view of children as little adults, (so illuminatingly portrayed in Brueghel's peasant paintings of the sixteenth century in which the children are recognizable only by size), the long progression from the Puritan to the Victorian concept of the complete separation of the child from the adult, and the shorter period of idealization of the young, were all swept away in a new assurance about children and their literature. Childhood was now seen as an existence in tandem with adulthood in the sense that child characters were engaged in an almost unconscious preparation for adulthood. Their activities called for the development of self-reliance, generosity, friendship, imagination, integrity—qualities that were deemed vital for maturity. Almost all the books of the period show children at play without adult supervision (Travers's *Mary Poppins* [1934] being a strong exception), and there is a sense of the children pacing themselves—they enter only the adventures for which they are prepared.

Arthur Ransome's *Swallows and Amazons*, published in 1930, was a precursor of these books. It epitomizes both the independent children and their parents' willingness to allow them freedom within sensible restraint. Upon being asked for his permission to let his

8. George Orwell, *The Collected Essays, Journalism and Letters*, vol. 1 (London: Secker & Warburg, 1968), p. 244.

9

children go off alone on a sailing and camping expedition, Mr. Walker (in an alarming fashion for the period) telegraphed them: "Better drowned than duffers; if not duffers, won't drown." Ransome, however, did not strain adult credulity. Mr. Walker was a sea captain and his children had been well trained, so it was not dangerous for them to "mess about with boats."

Whatever the variations of style and theme between an Eleanor Estes in *Rufus M* or a C. S. Lewis in his "Narnia" Chronicles, the fine writers of the period all infused their books with a marvelous warmth of feeling—most vividly that of the children for one another and for the few adults who shared their play and concerns; more remotely in the children's attachment to their parents, who moved on the periphery of their adventures but were nonetheless there, always ready to offer support. It is this quality, along with the well-defined plot lines and the belief in the essential decency, good humor, and good sense of these child characters that have kept them remarkably popular with young readers.

Yet the phrase "in tandem" suggests, and indeed the books show, that some restraints were put upon childhood. Children who aped the dress and manners of adults were guilty of presumption and affectation. Thus in C. S. Lewis's *The Last Battle* (1956) Susan, once a queen in Narnia, is criticized for becoming interested in "nothing but nylons and lipstick and invitations. She was always a jolly sight too keen on being grown-up." Any attempt to leave childhood behind prematurely seemed a betrayal to another child and earned a loss of respect. All in all the general feeling of a society, in this case security, was clearly expressed in the books of the 1940s and 1950s, provided the child protagonists did not venture outside the given emotional and social boundaries.

So too the nature of children's literature was clear. It was, first of all, literature; that is, qualities of presentation and style were as important as what was said. There was no real difference between the best written for adults and the best written for children. "Best" was the operative word rather than "child" or "adult." Didacticism was shunned as both irrelevant (in departing from the main goal of literary merit) and insulting (in suggesting that the readers needed instruction more than enjoyment). Literature meant enrichment, both in the sense of giving pleasure and of broadening experience and developing taste. It could be light and even frivolous; the essential point was that, whatever its type, quality had to be present.

The high plateau of children's literature reached by the end of the 1950s was occasioned by writers who were practitioners of fine writing in the traditional style (many of them noted as writers for adults) and the era can be described as the "Second Golden Age of

10

Children's Literature." Moreover it could be expected that readers of such books would have no difficulty in making the transition from children's literature to adult literature, and that of the finest sort.

But was there a tarnish on the Second Golden Age? In retrospect it can be seen that the social outlook in these books (taken as a whole) was perhaps too safe, too tranquil, and too predictable. The books had a repetitive quality, no matter how interesting the plot, the action, and the characters. There were intimations of change in the more introspective works of such writers as Philippa Pearce, Lucy Boston, and Rosemary Sutcliff, but the writers of the forties and fifties, by and large, did not deal with the unusual child, the alienated child, the outsider. There were few fresh insights into childhood and certainly no exploration of the uncertainties or the dark corners of the child mind. "They were so bloody healthy and well adjusted," one critic has said of the Ransome children. In short, if idealism was not present, expectations were. The writers portrayed behavior that society hoped for from its children rather than how children—many of them at least—really behaved.

The serene and certain fifties turned into the restless and anxious sixties, a period of social convulsion, when the young disputed the wisdom of their elders, defied established authority, and discovered the word "relevance." The changes came thick and fast. Indeed, rapid change came to be regarded as both inevitable and desirable in itself. In particular the young (people up to about age 25) eagerly and aggressively confronted problems that had hitherto been the domain of their elders. There are two axioms that apply in this kind of situation. The first is that any alteration in society is likely to affect children more severely than any other segment of society. The effect upon children of one-parent families is an obvious proof here. The second is that changes affecting children and young people will be rapidly reflected in the books written for them.

Although social changes in the past came more slowly, they did alter children's books with a speed noticeable within their time. But even more importantly, the changes were assimilated without undue upheaval and held for a considerable period. Thus in 1818 Mrs. Sherwood in *The Fairchild Family* felt quite free to show a family of naughty children punished by a visit to a gibbet where a murderer hung rotting in chains. By 1839 Catherine Sinclair in *Holiday House* could leave that attitude behind with a rather loving look at children's inevitable mischievousness that led to the understanding of the special qualities of childhood, so much a part of the late Victorian era. Indeed, the later editions of *The Fairchild Family*, published up until the early 1900s, omitted the offensive passage even though, as Harvey Darton has pointed out, "the English is little short of majestic

11

in its economy and plainness." [9] It was thus fairly quickly established (within a relatively short twenty years) that children were not to be subjected, at least in their books, to cruel and unusual punishment. But once accepted, this viewpoint remained constant for 120 years.

In the sixties, the change of social attitude to children seemed to come with wrenching suddenness—or was it the wrench that made it seem so sudden? Its most obvious manifestation was that long-standing convictions about what children *were* and so how to treat them at last had faltered and failed. They no longer appeared to be special, or different, or even delicately balanced in their passage between childhood and adulthood, but were considered adult to an extent not known since the Middle Ages. The reasons for this dramatic about-face were multiple, but they all seemed to come at once. It is of considerable significance that adolescents had been steadily assuming more and more of the attributes, perquisites, and problems of their elders. Like adults, teenagers now had money, cars, and jobs together with drugs, liquor, sex, and the assorted difficulties arising therefrom.

Even if one accepts the simple theory that the youngest child in the family gets more freedom than the oldest in similar circumstances, it can be assumed that much of this newish adolescent freedom had "rubbed off" on children. Many of the children now had their own share of weighty responsibilities. The term "latch-key children" was coined during the Second World War to describe those children who had to let themselves in to empty houses or apartments because father was at war and mother was working in a munitions factory. By the 1960s, with the increasing incidence of one-parent families and mothers who worked for necessity or fulfillment, the numbers of such latch-key children increased to the point where the term disappeared. The social phenomenon was too ubiquitous to warrant a special name.

Another great change was the adult demand for openness in dealing with children. There were to be no more evasions. Indeed, children's rights became a battle cry. The American Library Association joined in with a resolution that age was no longer to constitute ground for special treatment in libraries. Children were to be liberated from the restrictions of childhood. To support this view, useful ammunition was found in the fields of physiology and psychology. It was plausibly claimed that children matured earlier, in a physical sense, than they once did. Freud's theories on the early sexuality of children became argument for greater frankness, and modern child

9. F. J. Harvey Darton, *Children's Books in England* (London: Cambridge Univ. Pr., 1958), p. 177.

psychology revealed that children too had fears and anxieties, suppressions and repressions as did their older counterparts.

Reflecting and contributing to such disorienting change was the great behemoth of television. While the traditional storytellers of the early ages of mankind addressed both young and old with stories of universal experience, and stories in which the audience could literally participate, even through song and dance, the electronic Mother Goose represents at best only a passive joining of the two audiences. Television, as Marshall McLuhan has pointed out, is a cool medium. But certainly the shared content of the screen drew children into the adult world, even if much of that world was an illusion.

What did all this ferment of change produce but a return to the Puritan thesis that children were not innately innocent, able to discern good and evil. Indeed they could even knowingly be cruelly savage, as well as evil, a point that William Golding made in his popular and influential *Lord of the Flies*, where his protagonist, Ralph, laments "the end of innocence." Those words were written in 1954, but by the sixties there were no more tears. The underlying position of adults seemed to be that childhood itself was no longer especially sacred and in need of protection and, as a result, it became fleeting and ephemeral, if not entirely eroded. Children might still be seen as the hope of the world but this did not exempt them from an early exposure to society's harsh problems or the follies of adulthood.

A second noteworthy characteristic of the sixties was that the publishing of books deliberately written for children increased to unprecedented levels. Between 1957 and 1979 about 112,000 were issued between Great Britain and the United States alone. Frances Clarke Sayers's reference to the "muchness" of children's publications as early as 1956 was well taken.[10] Paradoxically, the many new books for children appeared precisely when children themselves were being considered more adult. This increase was not philosophical but pragmatic: there were so many more children and so much more money available. And the books themselves were, not surprisingly, much less childlike than their predecessors in content and tone. But sheer numbers created a centrifugal instead of a bonding effect: diversity rather than commonality. No longer were a great many children reading the same few titles, a situation which resulted in a concomitant loss of shared childhood experience. The proliferation also had its own influence on the nature of books published, and by and large it was harmful. The size of the market encouraged much commercial mediocrity and sometimes the blatantly exploitive kind of cynicism that we associate with the mass media.

10. Frances Clarke Sayers, *Summoned by Books* (New York: Viking, 1965), p. 41-51.

A second market effect—also tending to push children's writing into new directions—was the growing influence of the United States. With a hugely expanded market, American publishers were moved to select books that reflected the new American manners and mores or that at least were not alien to them. And, it was in the 1960s that the United States came to exercise a dominant influence on writing for children, a position previously held by Great Britain. The new trends were being set in the United States, the issues were being fought there, and its publishers were exporting to the rest of the world an image of children and children's literature that was radically different from that of the recent past.

The most notable, debatable, obvious manifestation of this American influence was the appearance of what was very quickly named the "problem novel." While the problem novel became the penultimate expression of the "new freedom" and the "new morality," its ambitions overrode its intrinsic merit. As the name accurately suggests, problem novels are subject- rather than literature-oriented, with their interest residing in the topic rather than in values such as plot, characterization, and style. The topics, such as divorce, alcoholism, drugs, sex, racism, and particularly alienation, matched society's concerns in a narrow sense as did religion and morality in children's books from the Puritans to the middle of the nineteenth century.

The same kind of ethical imperative was implied in these books as in those offerings of the more distant past: children need to be informed; the time is too short to let them reach their own conclusions or to move at their own speed. Just as the earlier writers offered the rewards of goodness, the writers of the sixties for the most part offered the protagonists the satisfaction of coming to terms with themselves and the situation at hand. Religion was replaced by the doctrine of existentialism and morality by sociology and psychology.

The development of this post-Freudian outlook vastly extended the scope of children's literature. Writers were free, as never before, to attempt themes of almost any kind; but along with the heady, new freedom came some interdictions, too. The pressure to find subject matter of "social relevance" not only led to tedious repetition (almost carbon copies) but also to the loss of something that had formerly seemed the very essence of children's literature, the traditional literary values of imagination and style. The repetition of plot and theme was paralleled by an inevitable typecasting of character. Rather than the good child or the bad child, we now had the "problem novel" with the alienated child, the abused child, the retarded child, at any rate a child defined by the terminology of pain.

In their inception, these novels were emblems of the earliest intimations of social change, but as the decade progressed they became rapidly transforming mirrors reflecting constant upheaval within the social order. When Emily Neville's *It's Like This, Cat* was published in 1963 it was heralded (to the extent of winning an award) as a groundbreaking innovator in the "new realism." The fourteen-year-old protagonist's alienation from his family's life-style was startlingly iconoclastic for its time. Six years later, Paul Zindel's *My Darling, My Hamburger* (1969) reflected a quantum leap from mild alienation to explicit discussions of sex, abortion, and the cruel disregard of adults for the problems of the young.

The American problem books dominated the sixties, but were not the only vision accessible to children at that time. Although their popularity gave them precedence, another element of children's literature persisted in its triumphant expression of fine writing, enduring values, and original imaginative power. While linked to the best of literature that had gone before, these novels also exemplified the freedom of experimentation in style and content, in a variety of genres, that defined their own era. Writers such as Ivan Southall, Philippa Pearce, Hester Burton, Lucy Boston, William Mayne, Leon Garfield, Alan Garner, Ursula Le Guin, Eleanor Cameron, and Paula Fox wrote novels that were the very antithesis of the narrow problem novel. Rather, their works brought modern children into their own time through an enriched, broadening experience. These authors were a touchstone in a decade of turmoil, a small still eye in the center of the cyclone. For those fine writers such as Garfield and Garner, Jill Paton Walsh and Virginia Hamilton, this was a time of apprenticeship to their craft which one suspected would flower into maturity.

In spite of their innate power, the works of such writers became the minority literature of the decade in a curious reversal of the literature of the forties and fifties where the best was widely acknowledged. Swamped with the tidal flood of the problem novel, most genres of the sixties were reduced in number and achievement. The great exception was the picture book, which absorbed the messages and social concerns of the problem novels. Its numbers and new themes were also fostered by the rise of the small presses devoted to special interest groups in the vanguard of social change.

By the end of the sixties, children's literature had moved from precept to pleasure to a state perilously close to schizophrenia caught between social turmoil and the legitimate claims of experimentation and development. The basic premise of children's literature as writing for children intended to be read as literature and not only for information and guidance appeared to be under attack. It was now directed to "adult" children deemed very much in need of therapeutic guidance and information. On the threshold of the seventies

15

children's literature echoed the confusion and energy inherent in Yeats's lines in "The Second Coming":

> Things fall apart; the centre cannot hold;
> Mere anarchy is loosed upon the world,
> The blood-dimmed tide is loosed, and everywhere
> The ceremony of innocence is drowned.

Works Cited

Barrie, Sir James M. *Peter and Wendy*. Illus. by F. D. Bedford. London: Hodder & Stoughton, 1911. 267 pp.

Bunyan, John. *A Book for Boys and Girls, or Country Rhimes for Children*. London: Nathaniel Ponder, 1686. 79 pp.

——*The Pilgrim's Progress from this World to That Which Is to Come....* London: Nathaniel Ponder, 1678. 232 pp.

Burnett, Frances Hodgson. *The Secret Garden*. Illus. by Charles Robinson. London: William Heinemann, 1911. 306 pp.

Day, Thomas. *The History of Sanford and Merton: A Work Intended for Use of Children*. 3 vols. London: J. Stockdale, 1783-89.

Estes, Eleanor. *Rufus M.* Illus. by Louis Slobodkin. New York: Harcourt, 1943. 320 pp.

Finley, Martha. *Elsie Dinsmore*. New York: M. W. Dodd, 1867. 288 pp.

Grahame, Kenneth. *The Wind in the Willows*. London: Methuen, 1908. 302 pp.

The History of Little Goody Two-Shoes; Otherwise Called Miss Margery Two-Shoes. 3rd ed. London: J. Newbery, 1766.

Keary, Annie. *Father Phim*. London: Warne, 1879. 126 pp.

Kingsley, Charles. *The Water-Babies*. London and Cambridge: Macmillan, 1863. 350 pp.

Lewis, C. S. *The Last Battle*. Illus. by Pauline Baynes. London: The Bodley Head, 1956. 184 pp.

McClung, Nellie. *Sowing Seeds in Danny*. New York: Doubleday, Page & Co., 1908. 313 pp.

MacDonald, George. *At the Back of the North Wind*. London: Strahan & Co., 1871. 378 pp.

——*The Princess and Curdie*. London: Chatto & Windus, 1883. 255 pp.

——*The Princess and the Goblin*. London and Philadelphia: Lippincott, 1872. 203 pp.

Milne, A. A. *Winnie the Pooh*. Decorations by Ernest H. Shepard. London: Methuen, 1926. 158 pp.

Molesworth, Mary Louise. *The Cuckoo Clock*. Illus. by W. Crane. London: Macmillan & Co., 1877. 242 pp.

Montgomery, L. M. *Anne of Green Gables*. Illus. by M. A. and W. A. Claus. Boston: L. C. Page & Co., 1908. 429 pp.

Nesbit, Edith. *The Story of the Treasure Seekers: Being the Adventures of the Bastable Children in Search of a Fortune.* London: T. F. Unwin, 1899. 296 pp.

Neville, Emily. *It's Like This, Cat.* Pictures by Emil Weiss. New York: Harper, 1963. 180 pp.

Porter, Eleanor. *Pollyanna.* Illus. by Stockton Mulford. Boston: L. C. Page & Co., 1913. 310 pp.

Porter, Gene (Stratton). *A Girl of the Limberlost.* Illus. by Wladyslaw T. Benda. New York: Doubleday, Page & Co., 1909. 485 pp.

Ransome, Arthur. *Swallows and Amazons.* London: Jonathan Cape, 1930. 349 pp.

Sherwood, Mary Martha (Butt). *The History of the Fairchild Family.* London: J. Hatchard, 1818-1847. 3 pts.

Sidney, Margaret, pseud. *The Five Little Peppers and How They Grew.* Boston: Lothrop & Co., 1881. 410 pp.

Sinclair, Catherine. *Holiday House: A Series of Tales, etc.* Edinburgh: W. Whyte & Co., 1839. 354 pp.

Stevenson, Robert Louis. *Kidnapped: Being the Memoirs of the Adventures of David Balfour in the year 1751.* London: Cassell & Co., 1886. 311 pp.

Tolkien, J. R. R. *The Hobbit, or, There and Back Again.* London: Allen & Unwin, 1937. 310 pp.

Travers, Pamela L. *Mary Poppins.* Illus. by Mary Shepard. London: Gerald Howe, 1934. 206 pp.

Zindel, Paul. *My Darling, My Hamburger.* New York: Harper, 1969. 168 pp.

2. Survival of the Fittest: Natural Selection from the Golden Ages of Children's Literature

The sheer number of children's books published in the English language in the last two decades (over a hundred thousand) suggests that there are current books to suit the reading tastes of every child or adult. Moreover, since children's literature tends to follow trends in the society at large, it may be presumed that the newer writers appeal more closely to the interests of the modern child than do their predecessors. In this sense, Norma Klein's *Mom, the Man Wolf and Me* (1972), a story about a single-parent child adjusting to her mother's lover and eventual husband, may be deemed more "relevant" than L. M. Montgomery's *Anne of Green Gables* (1908), the story of a red-headed orphan who conquers all around her by her irrepressible vitality, amusing follies, and essential goodness.

Although by today's standards, Anne's adventures must seem very tame indeed, they are obviously still of interest to children, for the *Anne* books are read almost as widely as most contemporary publications. This fact raises the intriguing and important question: why, amidst the flood of publishing today, are there still so many books written in the century before 1960 that are not only widely read, but are constantly republished in new editions? An examination of at least some of the books of the past that have remained popular may lead to some useful conclusions about the books of our own time.

It is undeniably true that the longevity of children's books is significantly influenced by adult concerns, concerns that may be irrelevant to the intrinsic worth of the book itself. One such factor is a combination of publishing acumen and adult nostalgia. While new titles are in the majority, publishers continue to bring out each year a fair number of reprints and reissues of books from the past, particularly newly illustrated editions of traditional oral lore—folktales, myths, legends, and nursery rhymes—as well as literary "classics." Most of these reprints are also available in paperback; some, such as works by Frank Baum, Hugh Lofting, C. S. Lewis, and E. B. White, even being available in boxed sets. Then too, each year as Christmas approaches, department stores display piles of cheap (in price, as well as in format) reprints of *Heidi*, *Treasure Island*, *Tom Sawyer*, and the like, often in abridged versions, the diminution of which measures the proximity of Christmas Day. And since adults, unless they are librarians or teachers, generally are unaware of what is available in modern children's literature, they choose a favorite from their own childhood reading; or, frantic for a last-minute present for a niece, nephew, or grandchild, they select a "classic" because of a vague feeling that it is a safer or more respected gift than an unknown, new title. Thus the publishing community and the adult purchasing market, with its conservative buying traits, both groups frequently at several removes from children's current interests, play a role in deciding which children's books survive.

The academic community as well is a factor in the evolution of children's books. Many writers of the past have produced a body of literature among which their children's books are an important part. Since many of these writers are studied in English departments of universities, their children's books will always receive at least some passing recognition. Such writers include George MacDonald, Robert Louis Stevenson, Mark Twain, J. M. Barrie, Rudyard Kipling, and C. S. Lewis. C. S. Lewis provides perhaps the best example here, his works, both fictional and critical, having secured both scholarly status and popular appeal. Among the company of his works on Milton, the Elizabethans, medieval cosmology, the courtly love tradition, and Christian theology, the seven "Narnia" Chronicles he wrote for children gain certain scholarly notice.

The influence of television and movie versions of children's books is, of course, a familiar phenomenon to all working with children. As television sparked new interest in Trollope, by way of his Palliser series, and in Galsworthy through *The Forsyte Saga*, so filmmakers for children are also responsible for revivals of interest. They choose books for filming that already have had a long career of appeal, among them E. Nesbit's *The Railway Children*, Johanna Spyri's *Heidi*, Louisa M. Alcott's *Little Women*, and Frances Hodgson Burnett's *The Secret Garden*. The popular and artful television series, "Once Upon a Classic," as its title suggests, depended upon books of the past. Animated cartoon versions abound in the innumerable Disney popularizations and the serious productions of such works as Tolkien's *The Hobbit* and C. S. Lewis's *The Lion, The Witch and the Wardrobe.* The filmmakers may have discovered the simple fact that children are not as socially mature and sophisticated as many modern writers assume them to be. However, the choice of an older work may only reflect a practical concern with choosing books in the public domain where copyright and contracts are no longer a costly nuisance.

The influence of these adult and generally extraliterary factors in the survival and popularity of a children's book may be exemplified by the publication of *Jacob Two-Two Meets the Hooded Fang* (1975). By Mordecai Richler, a well-known Canadian writer of adult books, who had the advantage of a ready-made entrée to the publishing world when he wrote this, his first children's book, it was read in parts over the Canadian Broadcasting Corporation before publication and is to be filmed. The story's fast-paced, cartoon characters and general comic-book approach will make it ideal for an already planned television movie.

However, the suggestion that children's books survive only on the basis of a benevolent conspiracy by adults is simply not confirmed by how they actually make their way in the world. In contrast to the media "hype" which can control the success or failure of new adult books, books for children make their way slowly, since children are less conscious of the best-seller syndrome than their elders and to them any book they have just read for the first time is a new book, regardless of its publication date. As Isaac Bashevis Singer has pointed out, "children read books, not book reviews."

It should be noted, however, that most children—certainly the younger ones—do not browse much and thus are not so apt as are adults to discover books on their own. Children usually read books that other people, adults or other children, have told them about. Thus the older books still chosen by the children themselves, as opposed to being pushed on them by parents, teachers, and librarians, are made known to them by word of mouth. And so, over the years, by this slow process of transmission of reported delights from one age group to that lower, certain books collect an enduring audience. If adults agree that these enduring books are "good," they are called "classics"; if not, then analysts can employ their talents to determine what in the world *does* account for the children's choice of favorites.

Few such analyses concur with each other, for it is risky to generalize about the reading tastes of children. Factors such as geography, cultural inheritance, or the enthusiasm of a teacher, librarian, or parent for a particular book are unpredictable variables. One example is Arthur Ransome's *Swallows and Amazons* series (1930 to 1950), those stories of self-reliant, happy children "messing about with boats" and enjoying holiday life on the English Broads. In British Columbia, for example, these books are still read by children of English parentage residing in West Vancouver, while they are ignored by the multi-ethnic population of Vancouver's inner city.

More often than not, however, the reasons why children have decided whether a book is to last or not seem more intrinsic than extrinsic, and these reasons are rather mysterious, at that. For example, the choice is by no means invariably dictated by the simple constant of quality; some of the best written books, as well as the worst, have been put into limbo. Thus, among the best that are no longer widely read is Bunyan's *Pilgrim's Progress* (1678), which generations of children adopted and played out as a game until the turn of the century. Another seeming reject is George MacDonald's *At the Back of the North Wind* (1871), the most spiritual of his work, whether for adult or child. Perhaps the saddest of all discards is Walter de la Mare's animal fantasy, *The Three Mullah Mulgars* (1910), one of the most beautifully written and sensitive works in the whole field of children's literature.

On the other hand, children have shown extraordinary good sense in consigning to the wastepaper baskets or to the storage libraries all the religious and didactic works of the first two hundred and fifty years of children's literature; the sentimental books of the 1910s to 1920s such as Jean Webster's *Daddy Long-Legs* and Eleanor Porter's *Pollyanna*; the unrealistic superheroes of such series as *The Boy Allies*; and the gushing, hearty, stereotyped schoolgirls of Angela Brazil.

A similar range of good and bad is also represented among the "survivors." The very worst to retain their popularity are probably those scions of the Stratemeyer syndicate, the *Bobbsey Twins*, the *Hardy Boys*, and *Nancy Drew*. The latter two were, for a while, reinforced by the television series and all three have been undergoing the publisher's knife to remove overt racist and sexist stereotyping and old-fashioned words such as "roadsters," all to no avail since they remain very much products of their time and no rewriting can supply the slick James Bond melodrama of their TV alter egos.

But offsetting these unwelcome survivors is a group of books, chiefly from the later Victorian period and the era between 1940 and 1960, that can be described as "good," both in a literary and popular sense; that is, they hold their position without undue pressure from adults. These are the survivors from the "Golden Ages" of children's literature. They are markedly different from the best books of the

21

1960s and 1970s, yet they still form the core of children's collections in school and public libraries, serving as the remnants of a commonality in children's reading in English-speaking countries.

As a group they also offer differences in readership from the present. They are read by the best and the most mature readers as well as the slower readers, usually at a later age. They conform to Thomas C. Haliburton's definition of a good book as propounded by his philosophic traveling salesman, *Sam Slick*, "Some books are read in the parlour and some in the kitchen, but the test of a real genuine book is that it is read in both." [1]

The best of recent literature, books by such writers as Susan Cooper, Jill Paton Walsh, and Ivan Southall, is generally deemed appropriate only for the special mature reader. Those that are generally designated as "problem" novels remain the province of the poorer readers or of the good readers going through "a phase." In this sense, modern children's literature seems almost to have split its readership. True, children have always read for different purposes: for personal satisfaction and fulfillment, for relaxation, and for social peer approval. In the past the best books served all these purposes, but today it seems there is strong polarization in reading purpose and content. For example, the Judy Blumes and the Hardy Boys seem to be read largely because they are "in." They offer a kind of social glue. Conversely, those children who turn to the best of modern writers, perhaps to a Leon Garfield or a Virginia Hamilton, do so in response to an entirely different set of appeals.

At first reach into the survival kit there seems to be no link among the hardy perennials. What do *Heidi, Homer Price, Charlotte's Web,* and the "Narnia" Chronicles have in common?

Gradually patterns begin to emerge. The single factor that links the survivors together is a sense of play, a sense that has all but vanished from contemporary children's books and increasingly from contemporary children's lives. This sense of play can be seen most obviously in those books that are best described as books of invention, wit, and light, extravagant imagination—Astrid Lindgren's *Pippi Longstocking* (1950), Mary Norton's *The Borrowers* (1952), Richard Atwater's *Mr. Popper's Penguins* (1938), William Pène du Bois's *The Twenty-one Balloons* (1947), Pamela Travers's *Mary Poppins* (1934), Edward Eager's *Half-Magic* (1954), Robert McCloskey's *Homer Price* (1943)—all based on the working out of logical domestic detail predicated on an outlandish premise. How does even a superchild like Pippi cope without parents? What use can you make of a darning

---

1. T. C. Haliburton, *Sam Slick's Wise Saws and Modern Instances* (London: Hurst and Blackett, 1853), p. 221.

needle if you are only four inches tall? How do you manage your washing if you live in a balloon? What would it be like to have a Nanny who can slide up a bannister? How do you get what you want from a coin that only gives you half of what you wish for? What do you do with a runaway doughnut machine? Part of the lure of such books is their similarity to the ways children actually play, the sparking of an imaginative world based on some common household object or situation.

A more sophisticated sense of play is evident in surviving books for slightly older children. Here the writer plays, not with domestic ideas but with literary ones. Such books provide the child's first experience of the joys of parody. Fresh from the folktale where magic is childlike and taken for granted, a child is still delighted with a dragon who wants a quiet life, as does Kenneth Grahame's *The Reluctant Dragon* (1938), or with a magic psammead who is all too humanly grouchy, encountered in Edith Nesbit's *The Five Children and It* (1902). Even parody carried to the sophisticated degree of Carroll's *Alice's Adventures in Wonderland* (1865) still seems to appeal. The strong links of such stories with the folktale tradition go a long way toward explaining their continued popularity.

As such books play with the child's expectation of story, so other eminent survivors play with a child's expectation of language. Into this category fall the nonsense verses of Lewis Carroll and Edward Lear. Their verses have no "meaning" at all, but they are presented in a strictly logical, highly syntactical pattern. And the combination, an august formalism building up to a wonderfully empty conclusion, is irresistible. It should be noted also that Carroll and Lear gain considerably from their poetic form. Because their work is designed to be read aloud, it undoubtedly possesses some of the attributes (rhythm and repetition) that have made folktales of the oral tradition survive over the centuries. A different sense of play, that based on domestic nursery pleasures and securities, imbues and also helps perpetuate the spirited verse of Robert Louis Stevenson and A. A. Milne.

Such essentially happy, often whimsical books do not, however, account for all the surviving children's books from the "Golden Ages" of children's literature. A child's sense of play is not confined to the sunny aspects of his life. Nor is it trivial, time-filling activity. As Huizinga points out in *Homo Ludens*, "play cannot be denied." [2] Through it children rehearse, in a safe environment, for the unsafe things to come in adult life. It is with this understanding of children that writers of past ages often dealt with tragedy.

2. Johann Huizinga, *Homo Ludens: A Study of the Play Element in Culture* (Boston: Beacon Pr., 1955), p. 21.

Just such motivation seems to account for the many stories of sentiment that have continued to appeal to young readers. As children go to *Pippi Longstocking* for a good laugh, they go to many books of the past for a good cry. Johanna Spyri's *Heidi* (1880), Anna Sewell's *Black Beauty* (1877), Frances Hodgson Burnett's *The Secret Garden* (1911), Louisa May Alcott's *Little Women* (1868), Edith Nesbit's *The Railway Children* (1906), and E. B. White's *Charlotte's Web* (1952) seem to fill a need that no book of the last twenty years quite succeeds in doing. They all include, but are not dominated by, the basic and moving situations of illness or death. Illness is generally shown as conquerable. In *Heidi*, Clara is roused from her lethargy by Heidi's cheerful energy; Mary in *The Secret Garden* conquers her own stubborn temperament and in so doing helps the fretful invalid, Colin, to enjoy the fresh air to promote health. The children in Nesbit's *The Story of the Amulet* and *The Railway Children* and in Hilda Lewis's *The Ship That Flew* know what it means to have a mother ill. But they use their wits, initiative, and ingenuity to offer what assistance they can, sometimes by magic, and in so doing they help themselves. These books, being strongly plotted, with exciting events beyond the sadness of illness or death, give space for both the protagonist and the reader to have time for adjustment. The children in these stories have a chance also for action, courage, and nobility. As in children's play and in the folktale, the child has power and choice.

In recent books, by contrast, the child is impotent. Death occurs suddenly in such books as K. M. Paterson's *A Bridge to Terabithia* (1977), Alan Garner's *Tom Fobble's Day* (1977), Mollie Hunter's *A Sound of Chariots* (1972), leaving the children with an immediate sense of loss which leads to a quick alienation and just as quickly to a desperate fortitude. It is significant here that death is actually the subject of the writer's concern and is limited to books of realism. In an earlier age death was handled, more so than in the present, through works of fantasy, as is evident in George MacDonald's *At the Back of the North Wind*, Kingsley's *The Water-Babies*, and E. B. White's *Charlotte's Web*. Certainly no modern writer has shown the affiliation of love and sacrifice and death as has Oscar Wilde in "The Happy Prince," "The Selfish Giant," and his other parables. But in all these books the framework of fantasy, like the framework of play, allows the child to survive relatively unscathed. Conversely, in present-day books in which the mother dies after a long illness, Robert Cormier's *The Chocolate War* (1974) and Peggy Mann's *There Are Two Kinds of Terrible* (1977) are examples, the young are shown only in terms of a raging helplessness.

Does this contrast then mean books of sentiment are unrealistic and false? The earlier books *are* sentimental, but they are not maudlin and not, ultimately, unconvincing. In modern books the surface detail may be deemed more realistic because the children's reactions are so clearly described, but in a situation where there is simply nothing a child can do to change it, the ideal of simply doing what one can (as in *The Railway Children*) is a fine survival technique. And in such books as *At the Back of the North Wind* and *Charlotte's Web*, although written almost a hundred years apart, the delicate balance between realistic detail and the solace of the imagination is one that has not been achieved frequently in the books of the past twenty years.

The social situations and consequent literary conventions that made books of sentiment and whimsy possible was an underlying and resilient sense of security in society in general. In essence, all the survivors from the past are linked by this perception of security. It applies as much to such books of extravagant imagination as *The Twenty-one Balloons* and *Mary Poppins* as to the tales of sentiment. Only in a safe and hopeful world can we enjoy and believe in a Professor William Waterman Sherman taking off in a balloon simply for the enjoyment of it and not to surpass a world record (*The Twenty-one Balloons*). Only in a stable world can we fully appreciate a Mr. Wigg sitting on his ceiling (*Mary Poppins*) or a girl who sleeps with her feet on the pillow (*Pippi Longstocking*), and not see these eccentricities as "problems." In a fragmented, shifting world eccentricity is all too closely allied with madness or, at least, unsocial behavior. Similarly, only a secure world can afford the indulgence of sentiment. In one where there is no order, the death of a spider does not mean very much.

For the child, the pattern of a secure world is set by the microcosm of the family. And family stories are the other major group that have survived into the modern age. Frequently a child makes the transition from picture books to "real" books via the light, even slapstick *Henry Huggins* (1950) by Beverly Cleary, and Carolyn Haywood's the "Betsy" books (1940s and 1950s). These books are not "classics" in the old sense. Their characters are jauntily rather than finely drawn; but while they contain little depth in their portrayal of child life, they do offer fun and the secure family situation that makes such simple fun possible.

Other stories of child and family life provided the sturdy base underlying much of the successful children's literature of the past. The family story, like the family itself, provided the security essential to the books that were written and, to a great degree, that can be written no more. In most books that have lasted from the past, the family may be running without its full set of components, that is, without a father or a mother, but they are absent for reasons beyond

25

control—death, war, or family emergencies. But the sense of the family is omnipresent in such favorites as Louisa May Alcott's *Little Women* (1868), Eleanor Estes's *The Moffats* (1941) and its sequels, Laura Ingalls Wilder's *The Little House* series (1930s and 1940s), Eve Garnett's *The Family from One End Street* (1937), Elizabeth Enright's *Gone-Away Lake* (1957), Sydney Taylor's *All-of-a-Kind Family* (1951), Farley Mowat's *Owls in the Family* (1961), Philippa Pearce's *Minnow on the Say* (1955). These are books that have outlived their contemporaries because of their sense of integrity and their believability. Each is infused with the feeling that an actual childhood is being portrayed— as if their writers were recalling their own experiences but endowing these remembrances with the touch of genius that makes them part of all childhood experience.

Books of light fantasy, closely akin to the family story in audience and style, are also dependent on an implied security. It is the major part of the ordered world of A. A. Milne's *Winnie-the-Pooh* (1926) along with, of course, the opportunity for the younger reader to feel superior to Pooh's bumbling ways. Indeed, this quality of bolstering the child-reader's self-image is a strong component of all these earlier books that children still enjoy.

It could be conjectured that Lewis Carroll in *Alice* took great risks when he pushed Alice so far from her secure world. But despite the outward appearance of risks, what ensued is safe play. Underlying all the unreason, the threats, and the loneliness is the secure world of Victorian convention. Alice herself is serene, unflappable, and invariably polite. Such risks were always taken by the great writers of fantasy from the past, and it is the enduring fantasies, exemplified by such books as George MacDonald's *The Princess and the Goblin*, Kenneth Grahame's *The Wind in the Willows*, C. S. Lewis's "Narnia" Chronicles, Tolkien's *The Hobbit*, and E. B. White's *Charlotte's Web*, that speak most clearly for all survivors. In a particular sense these writers have created "an Other World, . . . another Nature—another Universe—somewhere you would never reach even if you travelled through the space of this universe for ever and ever—a world that could be reached only by Magic. . . . "[3] They stand in strong contrast to most modern fantasists who deliberately go to great lengths in the opposite direction, keeping us in our own world and thus, in a way, diluting the traditional magic of a story as a journey.

Still, for the older fantasists, for the subcreators of magical otherwheres, these journeys were not undertaken to escape reality, but to illuminate it, to transport us to worlds different from the real world, while demonstrating certain immutable truths that persist in

3. C. S. Lewis, *The Magician's Nephew* (London: Bodley Head, 1955), p. 25.

any and every possible world, real and imaginary. In Tolkien's *The Hobbit*, no other world exists but the eerie, often magical universe of Middle Earth. Yet central to the story is a familiar code of values. The hobbit is faced with a challenge to his courage and resolution; he must change, for better or for worse. His response to the challenge is a proper one in any world. What really happens is that the old universe is seen through new eyes.

These books of fantasy demonstrate the high serious play that is only possible in the mind of a writer with an inner security, the stability of convictions. There is little doubt that the tone of these earlier fantasies is Christian, even downright biblical. As transmitters of values they are frequently like St. Paul admonishing the Hebrews:

> For though by this time you ought to be teachers, you need some one to teach you again the first principles of God's word. You need milk, not solid food; for everyone who lives on milk is unskilled in the word of righteousness, for he is a child. But solid food is for the mature, for those who had their faculties trained by practice to distinguish good from evil.
>
> ——Heb. 5:12–14

But writers of serious fantasy provided more than milk for the soul; they supplied food for the imagination as well. In discussing his Narnia books and religion C. S. Lewis said:

> Why did one find it so hard to feel as one was told one ought to feel about God or about the sufferings of Christ? . . . But supposing that by casting all these things into an imaginary world, stripping them of their stained-glass and Sunday School associations, one could make them for the first time appear in their real potency? Could one not thus steal past those watchful dragons? I thought one could.[4]

They could of course, because they were masters of method as well as message.

But the writers of fantasy join all other fine writers of the past in taking childhood seriously which, in turn, allowed them to write with some playfulness, an uncondescending playfulness, for they wrote from the child that still lingered within themselves. The Canadian poet, Dennis Lee, whose books of crafted nonsense verse such as *Alligator Pie* (1974) have achieved wide popularity is in the Lewis tradition. "I write," he said memorably, "as a 35-year-old *children*."[5] This spirit was common to all the survivors,

4. C. S. Lewis, "Sometimes Fairy Stories May Say Best What's to Be Said." *New York Times Book Review* (18 Nov. 1956), p. 3.

5. Dennis Lee, "The Roots of Poetry," *Canadian Children's Literature* no. 4:32 (1976).

whether stories of high fantasy, family life, or fantastic invention.

Whatever the genre, it was intimate, warm, and invariably reflected an omniscient narrator with a penchant for authorial intervention. "You must not forget the suspenders, Best Beloved," recites the omnipresent Kipling to the children at his feet. These stylistic interventions, common from George MacDonald to C. S. Lewis, were undertaken with the best avuncular motives, to provide a resilient cushion of understanding and protection. And it is interesting to note that even in today's ordinary conversation of adult to child, although the subject matter may be more startling or direct than previously, this timeless tone creeps in. It is only modern writers who eschew this tone as condescending. They tend to avoid any forceful manipulation of readers' emotions or thoughts by presenting only bald dialogue and actions, so that the readers come to their own conclusions without authorial intrusion.

Much as some contemporary adults tend to distrust what they perceive as archaic values or a patronizing manner in these older books, children themselves do not appear to be affected by such scruples. They take delight and security in such old-fashioned idioms as carefully paced narratives; deep, but never complex, characterization; and a casual, storytelling style.

Perhaps the strongest appeal of these older books is in the ages of their protagonists. While writers of contemporary books concentrate on older children, earlier writers dealt with children young enough not to resent or question societal values and adult authority. This is reflected stylistically in the evocation of a tender, if subtle, didacticism, in sharp contrast to the acrid didacticism of recent years.

It is true that the times and traditions that gave these older books birth have receded into history, but perhaps there are certain needs that are part of the unchanging heart and every age cannot supply them all. This is true of adult books as well, of course, When one wants the delicate, clean, orderly, and stylistic feeling of Jane Austen, there is simply nobody in the twentieth century who will do. Similarly while children's books of the last two decades have ably, even masterfully, supplied the need for books that explore the dark undersides of things or books in which the surface realities accord with their own world, children still go to books of the past in search of security, morality, extravagant imagination, sentiment, or, for downright fun.

Works Cited

Alcott, Louisa May. *Little Women; or Meg, Jo, Beth and Amy.* Illus. by May Alcott. Boston: Roberts Brothers, 1868. 341 pp.

Atwater, Richard, and Atwater, Florence. *Mr. Popper's Penguins.* Illus. by Robert Lawson. Boston: Little, 1938. 138 pp.

Bunyan, John. *The Pilgrim's Progress from This World to That Which Is to Come . . . .* London: Nathaniel Ponder, 1678. 232 pp.

Burnett, Frances Hodgson. *The Secret Garden.* Illus. by Charles Robinson. London: Heinemann, 1911. 306 pp.

Carroll, Lewis. *Alice's Adventures in Wonderland.* Illus. by John Tenniel. London: Macmillan & Co., 1865. 192 pp.

Cormier, Robert. *The Chocolate War.* New York: Pantheon, 1974. 253 pp.

Cleary, Beverly. *Henry Huggins.* Illus. by Louis Darling. New York: Morrow, 1950. 155 pp.

De la Mare, Walter. *The Three Mullah Mulgars.* London: Duckworth & Co., 1910. 312 pp. (Later pub. as *The Three Royal Monkeys*)

Du Bois, William Pène. *The Twenty-one Balloons.* Illus. by the author. New York: Viking, 1947. 179 pp.

Eager, Edward. *Half-Magic.* Drawings by N. M. Bodecker. New York: Harcourt, 1954. 217 pp.

Enright, Elizabeth. *Gone-Away Lake.* Illus. by Beth and Joe Krush. New York: Harcourt, 1957. 192 pp.

Estes, Eleanor. *The Moffats.* Illus. by Louis Slobodkin. New York: Harcourt, 1941. 290 pp.

Garner, Alan. *Tom Fobble's Day.* Etchings by Michael Foreman. London: Collins, 1977. 72 pp.

Garnett, Eve. *The Family from One End Street, and Some of their Adventures.* Illus. by the author. London: Frederick Muller, 1937. 212 pp.

Grahame, Kenneth. *The Reluctant Dragon.* Illus. by Ernest H. Shepard. New York: Holiday House, 1938. 57 pp.

———*The Wind in the Willows.* London: Methuen & Co., 1908. 302 pp.

Haywood, Carolyn. *B Is for Betsy.* New York: Harcourt, 1939. 159 pp.

Hunter, Mollie. *A Sound of Chariots.* New York: Harper, 1972. 242 pp.

Kingsley, Charles. *The Water-Babies.* London and Cambridge: Macmillan and Co., 1863. 350 pp.

Klein, Norma. *Mom, the Wolf Man and Me.* New York: Pantheon, 1972. 128 pp.

Lee, Dennis. *Alligator Pie.* Illus. by Frank Newfeld. Toronto: Macmillan of Canada, 1974. 64 pp.

Lewis, C. S. *The Lion, the Witch and the Wardrobe.* Illus. by Pauline Baynes. London: Geoffrey Bles, 1950. 172 pp.

Lewis, Hilda. *The Ship That Flew.* London: Oxford Univ. Pr., 1939. 320 pp.

Lindgren, Astrid. *Pippi Longstocking.* Tr. by Florence Lamborn. Illus. by Louis S. Glanzman. New York: Viking, 1950. 158 pp.

McCloskey, Robert. *Homer Price.* New York: Viking, 1943. 149 pp.

MacDonald, George. *At the Back of the North Wind.* London: Strahan & Co., 1871. 378 pp.

——*The Princess and the Goblin*. London and Philadelphia: Lippincott, 1872.

Mann, Peggy. *There Are Two Kinds of Terrible*. New York: Doubleday, 1977. 132 pp.

Milne, A. A. *Winnie-the-Pooh*. Illus. by Ernest H. Shepard. London: Methuen, 1926. 158 pp.

Montgomery, L. M. *Anne of Green Gables*. Illus. by M. A. and W. A. Claus. Boston: L. C. Page & Co., 1908. 429 pp.

Mowat, Farley. *Owls in the Family*. Illus. by Robert Frankenberg. Boston: Little, 1961. 103 pp.

Nesbit, Edith. *The Five Children and It*. London: T. Fisher Unwin, 1902. 301 pp.

——*The Railway Children*. Drawings by C. E. Brock. London: Wells Gardner & Co., 1906. 309 pp.

——*The Story of the Amulet*. London: T. Fisher Unwin, 1906.

Norton, Mary. *The Borrowers*. Illus. by Diana Stanley. London: J. M. Dent & Sons, 1952. 159 pp.

Paterson, K. M. *Bridge to Terabithia*. Illus. by Donna Diamond. New York: Crowell, 1977. 128 pp.

Pearce, Philippa. *Minnow on the Say*. Illus. by Edward Ardizzone. London: Oxford Univ. Pr., 1955. 241 pp.

Porter, Eleanor. *Pollyana*. Illus. by Stockton Mulford. Boston: L. C. Page & Co., 1913. 310 pp.

Ransome, Arthur. "Swallows and Amazons" series. London, Jonathan Cape, 1930-1950.

Richler, Mordecai. *Jacob Two-Two Meets the Hooded Fang*. Illus. by Fritz Wegner. Toronto: McClelland & Stewart, 1975. 83 pp.

Sewell, Anna. *Black Beauty: His Grooms and Companions*. London: Jarrold and Sons, 1877. 247 pp.

Spyri, Johanna. *Heidi: Her Years of Wandering and Learning*. Tr. from the German by Louise Brooks. Boston: De Wolfe Fiske & Co., 1884. 2 vols. in 1. (First published in German, 1880)

Taylor, Sydney. *All-of-a-Kind Family*. Illus. by Helen Jane. Chicago: Follett, 1951. 192 pp.

Tolkien, J. R. R. *The Hobbit; or, There and Back Again*. London: Allen & Unwin, 1937. 310 pp.

Travers, Pamela L. *Mary Poppins.* Illus. by Mary Shepard. London: Gerald Howe, 1934. 206 pp.

Webster, Jean. *Daddy Long-Legs*. Illus. by the author. New York: The Century Co., 1912. 304 pp.

White, E. B. *Charlotte's Web*. Illus. by Garth Williams. New York: Harper, 1952. 184 pp.

Wilde, Oscar. *The Happy Prince and other Tales*. Illus. by Walter Crane and Jacob Hood. London: David Nutt, 1888. 116 pp.

Wilder, Laura Ingalls. *The Little House* series. New York: Harper, 1932-43.

3. *Realistic Fiction*

> *"Gran, you see, first we grow up and have a lot of worries. And then we die, and I don't see the point."*
> *Heavens! the things children say! They certainly come trailing clouds of metaphysics.*
> ———Jill Paton Walsh, *Unleaving*

Those remarkable people, the Puritans, who simultaneously "invented"[1] both children and children's books, also gave children's literature its first genre, realistic fiction, the realism and the fiction by-products of the pervasive didacticism that dominated all Puritan thinking. Intent on teaching children the lesson that one's actions, even in the very earliest years of one's life, had inescapable moral consequences, the Puritans hoped that by dramatizing this lesson in a narrative filled with realistic detail they could make their message both more interesting and more convincing. What could be more starkly realistic than the graphic portrayal of the act of dying itself? The prolonged death scene, vividly described in a manner to the point of relish, was the central feature in Puritan children's books.

Judging from the number of such deathbed stories, the Puritans must have been quite right in supposing that they attracted the reader's interest. Perhaps they were quite right, too, about the presumed effectiveness of combining incident with moral consequence. Their successors certainly thought so, for, since the time of the Puritans, almost every branch of children's literature has tended to employ much the same mixture of moralizing and realistic detail. By the Victorian era the proportions in the mixture had altered. The melodramatic elements had diminished and the emphasis was now a close observation of daily life. Such books became known and advertised in the trade as "stories of child and family life." While most were stock productions, at their best these offered more than mere

---

1. I am indebted to Marshall McLuhan's *The Medium and the Massage* (New York: Bantam Books, 1967) for prompting this concept.

verisimilitude. Here, for example, is how Mrs. Molesworth's Helena reminisces in *My New Home* (1894):

> Never once in my life do I remember going into the dining room to dinner without first meeting grandmamma in the drawing-room, when a glance would show her if my face and hands had been freshly washed and my hair brushed and my dress tidy, and upstairs again would I be sent in a twinkling if any of these matters were amiss.

Molesworth's depiction of the child as totally obedient to adult authority and limited in her activities to those few approved for "genteel girls" is amply supported and paralleled by memoirs of the period. Undoubtedly the better "stories of child and family life" rang far truer than did the adventure stories of the same period, which depended for their appeal on feats of "derring-do."

Over the long course of the Victorian era, the genre inevitably underwent some further alterations. The strongest influence came, as usual, from society itself. As children came to be allowed more freedom in their activities, the number of lessons and "don'ts" within the children's stories diminished commensurately. Some literary influences made for greater freedom too. When Louisa May Alcott's Jo March (*Little Women*, 1868) broke the static bonds of girlhood and Mark Twain's Huck Finn (*Huckleberry Finn*, 1884) went against the conventions of his society, children's realistic literature had new models and standards to which it could aspire. Of course the majority of writers had neither the gifts nor the vision to depict Alcott's and Twain's kind of individualistic, free-spirited characters. Society's basic and traditional assumptions about the young were simply too strongly held, and most of these persisted right up into the 1950s.

One of the most crucial was the belief that children were generic; what was good for one child was good for all. It was inevitable, therefore, that youthful protagonists remained "stock" characters. Although individualized by age, sex, and character traits, they were used by writers to symbolize childhood or, at least, a certain type of childhood. Such fiction placed no strain on credulity. The protagonists were drawn from social classes that broadly paralleled those of the readers themselves; the settings were recognizable, perhaps even familiar; the incidents that occurred were just barely unusual enough to qualify as "fiction."

Much depended on the building up of naturalistic detail; for example, most of the enjoyment of Eleanor Estes's *Rufus M* (1943) derives from her slow, deliberate use of "real" time in Rufus's drawn-out struggle to obtain a library card. The purpose of all this concentration on outward appearances was to engage readers by convincing them that they themselves might very well have had a part in the action. Getting readers to identify with the people they are reading about is, after all, one of the oldest and surest literary devices for eliciting interest.

All this is to suggest the very narrow range of themes and tone that the realistic tradition has utilized. Whether from its longtime association with the moralizing motive, or, more likely because of its emphasis on the believable and familiar, realistic fiction assiduously avoided shocking, puzzling, and powerful subjects. When subjects such as death, cruelty, or suffering did occur, it was the moral consequence thereof rather than the event itself that received chief attention. The moralizing provided a kind of buffering effect and thus cushioned the reader against feelings of shock or distaste.

Indeed, since fiction that depicted actuality (as opposed to fantasy or narratives set in far-off times or places) had only two sides, either that of the domesticated story or the suspenseful adventure, the term "realism" was rarely applied to such writing. Children's novels were so confined, both by their intended audience and limited subject matter, that definitions of realism as applied to adult novels seemed irrelevant or even ludicrous. It was a cozy little kind of storytelling.

It is easy to understand, then, the tremendous consternation aroused when Louise Fitzhugh's *Harriet the Spy* burst upon the scene in 1964. Its harshness and candor gave a new definition to realism. It was satirical and astringent in its portrayal of adult society and, even more shocking, it questioned what had heretofore been considered an inviolable tenet in a child's life: do not tell a lie. Perhaps most significantly *Harriet the Spy* heralded the disappearance of children in groups, now to be replaced by the single child, examined in some depth as a unique individual in a unique set of circumstances, a concept which the best authors were to incorporate into a larger statement about life.

It is probably not accidental that *Harriet the Spy* bears a considerable resemblance in its approach to Eveyln Waugh's adult novel *The Loved One*. Waugh clearly does not pretend to offer exact representation of life in contemporary southern California, yet the book, through its distortions, tells us a great deal about life there and indeed about contemporary life in general. So Harriet is the first child protagonist to use her notebook not only as a confessional, but also as a barbed depiction of the human condition. The people she spies upon and criticizes are all exaggerations, even caricatures, and yet they are real in the sense of being archetypes of the follies of contemporary society.

33

Fitzhugh's use of purposeful distortion led to some claims that she was not writing "realism" at all. Indeed her realism in no way resemble the small scenes of day-to-day childhood concerns reported from a protective adult viewpoint in such books as *The Moffats*, the *All-of-a-Kind-Family* series, and others of the past. When Harriet defied the societal values of privacy, honesty, and compassion she challenged not only the adults of her society but also seemed to thumb her nose at all the "nice," polite, well-adjusted child characters who preceded her.

With the publication of this innovative book the realistic story seemed no longer bound by the traditions and expectations that had stifled its development. The controversy that surrounded the publication of *Harriet* revealed that a watershed had been reached in the depiction of contemporary children's lives. Most writers of the time, and especially the new writers, crossed that watershed, abandoning the bland if charming reportage of everyday child affairs. The writers of the sixties, and even more strikingly those of the seventies, came to see realism not as a parallel to representational photography but rather as a kind of a subjective, personal painting that transcends verisimilitude. Indisputably, this new view of reality has prevailed, and the present-day realism that writers seek to depict deals with the inner core rather than the surface of existence.

One of the most attractive features of the new realism is that it permits, indeed encourages, so many different approaches. Diversity could almost be called its hallmark. Still, there is a high degree of consistency, a detectable pattern of features, most readily seen in the contrast between present and past.

The most obvious and profound change between contemporary writing and its predecessors comes in the ultimate fate of the young protagonists. In books of the past children were almost invariably what may be termed "safe survivors." The term conveys two meanings. Most obviously, the children were "safe" in the sense that their happy ending was assured. Whatever the degree of suspense, the reader could be wholly certain that the hero or heroine would safely survive all perils. The second meaning is rather more subtle: not only did the protagonists survive but they did so unscathed and unaltered. However saddening or trying their experiences might have been they were never really affected by what had happened. Their parents or other solicitous adults were there to protect them against any drastic consequence. Interestingly enough, this characteristic may be seen to hold true even of the Puritan tales, whose leading characters frequently did die, sometimes painfully. The point, of course, is that for the Puritans death was no hardship, at least for virtuous children. Protected by their unshakable belief in the happy hereafter to which they would certainly go, Puritan children were indeed "safe survivors."

In sharp contrast, most children in modern realistic fiction are "dangerous survivors." Their lives are no longer bounded by the protective walls of childhood but involve situations in which they live without adults. Open and vulnerable, they must struggle to survive and cope on their own, often in the face of disaster. And in the process, they change. They may gain a courageous independence, a self-reliance and resourcefulness, but they also suffer the loneliness of isolation and the heavy insecurity and responsibilities of that independence. This spirit of suffering applies no matter what the specific setting may be. Children may be faced with survival in various landscapes: outdoor wilderness, urban jungle, the theater of war, or in what Gerard Manley Hopkins has called "inscape" as opposed to landscape. Whatever the impetus for the events that involve them, the protagonists share the common pattern of internal struggle, ultimate catharsis, or even defeat.

In its earlier forms, "survival" literature was almost entirely limited to young males pitting their skills against the wilderness or the sea. At first stylized and hackneyed, the stories gradually achieved considerable depth. As ably represented in such books as Roderick Haig-Brown's *Starbuck Valley Winter* (1946) and Farley Mowat's *Lost in the Barrens* (1956), survival literature could offer a genuine "feel" for the physical environment, an affecting depiction of friendship, and a dramatic unfolding of plot, laced with exciting yet plausible events.

This type of straightforward yet sensitive adventure story came to a peak and in a sense to its end in 1960 with Scott O'Dell's *Island of the Blue Dolphins*, deservedly called a modern "classic" for its imagery, emotional quality, and poetic style. As a "Robinsonnade," its link to the past is obvious, but while Robinson Crusoe had his faith in his personal God to solace him, Karana, the Indian girl, is completely alone, except for her animal companions, and sustained only by her inward courage. Even so, Karana survives and we readers are never in any doubt that she will do so. Moreover her dangers only seem to add spice to the story; they do not traumatize and indeed appear to leave almost no mental or emotional residue.

It is because *Island of the Blue Dolphins* is so well written that it is interesting to compare it with another excellent book, Ivan Southall's *Ash Road* (1965), published a mere five years later. In it Southall shows much the same literary skills as does O'Dell, but he deploys them in rather different ways and with much different effects. An insight into this difference may be derived from the fact that of the two words in the term "realistic fiction," Southall strongly

35

emphasizes the noun. Indeed he maintains that he writes fantasy and in a sense he does, as Fitzhugh, in *Harriet the Spy*, could be said to write surrealism.

Southall's *Ash Road* came out of his experience in an Australian bush fire, but he conceived the plot by asking, "What if"? What if children were left on their own? What if adults couldn't or, even more terrifyingly, wouldn't help? What if the children had to help the adults? The children are changed by their experiences. Peter discovers that his grandmother has been left behind in a burning house:

> Peter ran now as he had never run, with elation. He knew without being able to frame the words that he was running into manhood and leaving childhood behind. He hated childhood. ... He was ready to prove himself a man; ready to be baptized a man with fire, whether he survived the ordeal or died from it.

In contrast to the focus on one character that characterized most books of the 1960s, Southall does portray a group of children in *Ash Road* and also in his later *To The Wild Sky* (1967). But his children, particularly those in the latter book, are given highly individualized temperaments; they are not the interchangeable family children of Arthur Ransome. Nor are their adventures any longer a form of play. Southall's children survive a crash landing of a plane on a remote and barren Australian island, and immediately the stresses and strains among them begin to erode what little chance for life they may have. Like most fine contemporary writers, Southall is an artist in characterization and the quickly sketched strokes with which each child is introduced gradually take on the detail, texture, and coloration of a full portrait. For example Carol, who is shown initially as viewing her mixed blood with secret shame, allows her unconscious ancestral skills to surface in her search for indigenous, primitive foods and thereby acquires a new dimension: dignity.

> He [Gerald] burst out, "Well, what's wrong with that? I don't know what you're getting at? You're not a black girl, are you? And I wouldn't care if you were."
> "I bet you would."
> He let her walk on, then, away from him, and made no effort to overtake her again. She was walking into the setting sun, a black silhouette crowned with gold.

Similarly Jan, who felt like a "gatecrasher" when beginning the weekend outing, ends as the one who succeeds in lighting a fire by rubbing sticks. Ultimately then, it is the growth of the children themselves and the increasing understanding toward one another which constitute the key elements in the book, rather than the events or even the suspense.

Southall's *Ash Road* and *To the Wild Sky* pioneered a trend that has had many followers, though not all of comparable artistry. One fine example is Jean George's *Julie of the Wolves* (1972). Superficially a physical survival story, its breathtaking scenario depicts an Eskimo girl living through an arctic winter because of her adoption by a family of wolves. The exotic elements are, however, deliberately played down. The wolves are depicted in much the plain, matter-of-fact terms that a naturalist would use, with the emphasis on Julie's inward emotional struggle. Julie survives her physical ordeal by her courage and resourcefulness and by reviving her traditional native skills. But she does not emerge unscathed. In fact the book leaves open the question of whether Julie will survive the emotional shock of discovering that her father has "sold out" his heritage by using his skills in the service of white sportsmen. In the end, as she "pointed her boots toward Kapugen," toward her father, the implication is that she has settled for second best.

Julie, like the children in Southall's *To the Wild Sky*, is important for what she is, rather than for what she does or even for what she represents. She is a single individual, a more somber and shaken Karana, whose inward resources have been depleted and whose emotional survival is far from assured. Indeed, Jean George's ending is even more unsettling than that of *To the Wild Sky*. But to George, as to Southall, it is the emotional journey that counts, not the arrival at a safe port.

Of course, there are still a good many safe survivors in contemporary realistic fiction, but they are to be found nowadays in the humdrum productions rather than in the books that count. Similarly, most other elements of traditional realism—the blandness, the moralizing, the concentration on the domestic scene—have been rejected by the leading writers of the present time. Only the accuracy of the settings remains. It is as though first-rate modern writers have calculatingly decided to strip traditional realistic fiction of all but its framework—that is, presenting settings actually seen or studied rather than "imagined"—to see what could be devised with such an old-new medium.

One particularly appropriate, and hence frequently employed, setting for this new approach is the war story. Many modern writers are of an age to have themselves experienced World War II as children. They thus already "know the territory" very well. Their interest lies not merely in depicting how the war involved children in certain stirring events but rather in exploring the deeper "subject" of the war that took place within the children themselves as they groped toward an understanding of maturity, responsibility, selflessness, and love. The war, a man-made tragedy, is thus used as a

37

metaphor and, in a sense, replaces the savage natural environment as a test of survival. It is interesting to note, however, that while the physical environment is always well described, the modern war novel hardly mentions a specific event. The children in such books as Jill Paton Walsh's *Fireweed* (1969), T. Degens's *Transport 7—41—R* (1974), Robert Westall's *The Machine-Gunners* (1975), Nina Bawden's *Carrie's War* (1973), and Penelope Lively's *Going Back* (1975) do not respond to the beat of war drums but react in various ways to the uncertainties caused by the adult world. Hester Burton's *In Spite of All Terror* (1968), with all its artistry, now seems to be a "bridge" book and a fairly simple war story compared with what was to come.

As Burton chose to tell her story, the actual events of Dunkirk overpower Liz's problems as an unhappy child evacuee. The personal note lessens steadily as the certainty increases that England will survive. In the final analysis, the interest centers on the narrative qualities and the skillful way in which a stirring piece of history is conveyed in fictional form.

By contrast, the mood and tone of Walsh's *Fireweed* are all doubt and darkness. Bill is a runaway evacuee who, in a London air-raid shelter, meets Julie, also a runaway, but from a ship taking children to Canada. Both have a fierce determination to fend for themselves and to survive the war free from adult interference and authority. In the chaos of a crumbling, burnt-out city they live a dangerous but somehow carefree life. Every day they walk a tightrope of disaster. They may be discovered by the authorities, they may die in a bombing, yet they are protected by the seeming immortality of youth and the strength of their newly discovered freedom and responsibility. Bill says:

> I thrilled with excitement, felt it tingling the length of my spine. I was free. Nobody was going to look after me; nobody was going to worry, or plan for me, or make me eat on time, or delouse me, or keep me safe from harm. They were all wrapped up in something else; they were all having the war. Well, I was going to have a war too; and mine was going to be just like theirs, staying in London, staying put.

From their position of tenuous stability Bill and Julie witness the destruction and paradoxical abiding survival of their world. It is a world where "familiar things seemed as exotic and unlikely as hothouse flowers." London is being knocked apart, but the leaves turn gold and fall off while German bombers rend the sky. It is this eye for the familiar and terrible in one, the vivid beauty of threatened life that gives *Fireweed* its moving quality. Realistic details, such as finding milk for an abandoned baby in war-torn London or fixing a cart in order to sell vegetables, provide the feeling of actual experience and involvement.

Autumn is the time that Bill and Julie spend together, the season that symbolically moves towards inevitable and irretrievable loss. At the end Bill's and Julie's fragile happiness falls apart. Only Bill's positive memories can come to his aid. He sees the fireweed flourishing in the pavements around St. Paul's and comments, "It is a strange plant; it has its own rugged sort of loveliness, and it grows only on the scars of ruin and flame."

Unlike the "plain Jane" style that served very well for the situations used by the writers of the past, the new school in keeping with the emotional dangers into which they plunge their characters makes considerable use of imagery, metaphor, and symbolism. The nameless thirteen-year-old girl in Degens's *Transport 7—41—R* is "Everychild" representing all the lost, alienated children of war. Even so, her struggle is highly individual and personal. While the war has caused much of her misery, it is her father's violent and irrational temper that is the immediate cause of her transportation from her home to a boarding school. Like Bill in *Fireweed*, she learns to survive and even to acquire a greater moral capacity, but all this is at a high cost. She has lost any innocence, security, or faith in the adult world that she once possessed. She must go it alone, both damaged and transformed.

Where Degens concentrates on one character, Robert Westall in *The Machine-Gunners* uses a group of children to make a less optimistic statement about disruption in children's lives. For his stage he has chosen not the anonymity of a huge city but a small, stable community. Still, here too the war intrudes and affects. The school is closed, fathers are in the Home Guard, and mothers are concerned about food shortages. Left more or less on their own, a group of children sets up its own warlike society, complete with a machine gun from a crashed German bomber and a captured German pilot. However, just as in the *Lord of the Flies*, when the children are removed from adults, fantasy and reality become indistinguishable. When the adult world finds them out, it is not the expected Germans who do so but their parents, neighbors, and the Home Guard:

> "Oh, God, what have we *done*?" wailed Clem.
> The world had two faces. Which was the true one? The world of the long night of waiting, of Stukas and Panzers, storm troopers and death? Or the world of day, of punishments, hidings and the magistrate's court? They couldn't decide. And the advancing horde gave them no time to decide.

As in *Fireweed* and *Transport 7—41—R*, the tragedy of the children's experience lies not so much in the hurts and havoc caused by direct military action as in their growing alienation from and distrust of the adult world. This view is borne out by their punishment, irrevocably separating or incarcerating them from each other in a physical sense, much as they had previously been separated from their parents in an emotional sense. Poignantly, the only adult who retains faith with the children is their prisoner and friend, the German Rudi, who, like Anton in Bette Greene's *Summer of My German Soldier* (1973), becomes the symbol of adult caring beyond the boundaries of age, family, and nationality.

While these books make large use of symbol and metaphor, they retain enough realistic detail for convincing verisimilitude. The young protagonists suffer pain on an almost cosmic scale, but they also have the temperaments and the insights that make it all credible. A reader genuinely cares what happens to them. And with that ceaseless rumble of war in the background, the history books, so to speak, add their measure of plausibility. One imagines a young reader saying: "These sorts of incidents really must have happened, because haven't I read about the war in school?"

This kind of persuasive conviction is adeptly conveyed in two gentler books with a war background: Nina Bawden's *Carrie's War* and Penelope Lively's *Going Back*. In them the narrators are adult, and the war and evacuation only memories. This aspect of recall, quite likely autobiographical, gives these books a sense of childhood not apparent in most modern realistic fiction, particularly that sense of childhood which is connected to a physical place—the houses and countrysides in which that childhood was enacted.

Reciting the story of her stay in the village to her eldest son, Carrie says: "Places change more than people, perhaps. You don't change, you know, growing older." Yet these two novels are not merely pieces of nostalgia for adults. Both are directed to children; both present real, vital experiences of child characters in their own world. As Carrie tells her story she becomes a young girl again. Her son recognizes this when he tells her to "get on with the *story*":

> "I'm *trying* to," Carrie said, so impatiently, that she sounded, he thought, more like a cross girl his own age than his mother.

Carrie's War offers a series of linked child memories that Carrie does not understand until she "goes back." Bawden has a flair for heightened emotion and color almost to the point of melodrama, but here it is contained within the bounds of a displaced child's authentic emotions.

Lively's brief but forceful *Going Back* is less strongly plotted than *Carrie's War*, but it has an even greater concern with time. Indeed, her fascination with human memory can be seen in several of her books, among them *A Stitch in Time* and *The Ghost of Thomas Kempe*. She is fast becoming the Proust of children's writers with such passages as Jane's adult musings in *Going Back*:

> Remembering is like that. There's what you know happened, and what you think happened. And then there's the business that what you know happened isn't always what you remember. Things are fudged by time: years fuse together.... There is time past, and time to come, and time that is continuous, in the head forever.

Lively also has an uncannily accurate and honest recall of what it is like to be a child in a world made for adults. She uses the clear, perceptive eye of childhood observation with its chilling remorselessness, patient detection, and striking sensuality to uncover the difficult, confusing truths and half-truths that typify the relationships between adults and children. This she accomplishes by blending the passionate immediacy of a child's experience with the bittersweet, ironic understanding of that experience from the vantage point of adult memory. All this Lively combines with adept portrayal of sympathetic and very real characters, intricate dialogue, and a poetic prose style. As she struggles with her personal view of memory and time, as she works through the eternal "you can't go home again" to discover her own truths, she provides the reader with unusual rewards in a kind of realistic fiction that is highly subtle and almost unique.

Subtlety is hardly a staple of children's literature and, whatever its authenticity, *Going Back* does raise the suspicion that many modern writers for children are writing for the adult in themselves rather than, as in former times, for the child within the adult. In a very real sense this approach matches society's current view of childhood, which seems to be that it is somehow injurious or at least condescending to children to treat them as children. It may be, also, that modern writers found their own childhood reading to be inconsistent with the reality they observed about them or remember. In either case, the conclusion derived is that contemporary children's books should deal with serious matters in a serious manner.

One corollary of this view has already been described: the children in children's books nowadays face real dangers and childhood is no longer synomymous with "the happy time." A second corollary is a fascination with the problems of "growing up." Growing up now tends to be visualized as a testing of soul and spirit, to be worked out through emotional "rites of passage" almost as patterned as the physical testing undergone by adolescents in primitive societies.

41

There is, however, one huge and sad difference. Our own society's young people must go through these tests without training for them, without experience, frequently without the assistance of family or friends, and certainly without religion. It is as though most modern writers of realism for children have espoused Sartre's view of existentialism that sees human beings as totally free and thus entirely and individually responsible for what they make of themselves.

A recurring theme used to express these traumatic rites of passage is death. It is, of course, not the death of the protagonists themselves, for then the story would end too soon; but it is very likely a death which causes them severe emotional damage, which comes very near to destroying their psyches.

In earlier books it was often the death of a child protagonist that stirred the emotions—Beth in *Little Women*, Nell in *The Old Curiosity Shop*, or Little Eva in *Uncle Tom's Cabin*. Death now appears as the alien who hurts the children through an attack on their loved ones. Jill Paton Walsh in *Unleaving* (1976) expresses something of the view of many modern writers who explore this theme:

> And Peter beside her is saying, "Gran! Gran!" trying to bring her attention back to his question. "Gran, will you mind dying?" "I shouldn't think so, dear," she says. "It isn't our own death that troubles us. We have enough to do surviving other people's."

So, too, in such books as Mollie Hunter's *A Sound of Chariots* (1972) and Katherine Paterson's *Bridge to Terabithia* (1977), both gentle, philosophical stories, is death seen as the symbolic end of childhood.

In *A Sound of Chariots*, Bridie McShane is only nine when her father's death sets off her period of struggle. So Bridie's journey is one from childhood into adolescence rather than the more usual passage from adolescence to adulthood. It is also an immensely complex treatment of the intellectual and emotional development of a child sensitive and perceptive beyond her years.

Bridie, as the title suggests, is haunted by the sound of Time's "winged chariot" and has to learn to conquer her fear of death. As she explains to her teacher,

> "even though I'm—you know—grown up. I still think about it all, about my father dying and Time catching up on me. I still feel alone. I'm still—afraid."

Bridie's fear of her own personal death becomes a heartbeat pounding furiously throughout the book; and Mollie Hunter skillfully makes this emotion serve as centerpiece and symbol for all those fears that can dominate a sensitive child's life. Bridie has indeed much to fear—her isolation from her mother and her sisters, the prejudices rampant in her own village, even her own "special-ness" as a gifted, articulate person.

Bridie is thus the classic "outsider" and it is this fact that gives the characterization its double dimension of generality and individuality. As her teacher explains, Bridie shares her fears and concerns with all mankind but the way she reacts to and "expresses" these emotions are for herself alone to work out:

> "All men are afraid of the passage of Time carrying them on to death, Bridie, but only to some in each generation is granted this awareness of each passing moment as a fragment of the totality of Life itself. And of those who are so aware, there are only a few who have the talent to express their awareness in some creative form."

It is important to note that the poetic and philosophic overtones of *A Sound of Chariots* are not allowed to overwhelm the "everyday" flavor of its realism. The story is set in what is obviously beloved and intimately familiar territory, a small Scottish village on the Firth of Forth in the years following World War I. Not in the slightest degree sentimentalized, it is a landscape that is filled with the awesome reality of the war. As Bridie observes the people from her own street and those who live in the War Veterans' houses, she finds there the firm realities upon and against which to build her inner life.

A Sound of Chariots covers seven years of Bridie's life, a long time-span in which Bridie (and vicariously the book's readers) can absorb her pain and consequent emotional growth and make them more truly their own.

In Paterson's *Bridge to Terabithia*, death comes with appalling suddenness into the life of a ten-year-old boy. Jess Aarons lives in impoverished, rural Virginia. Given scant attention or respect by his family, he finds refuge in his powerful visual imagination and in the friendship of a classmate. She is Leslie Burke who, with her writer parents, has come to live in the Perkins place from the city. Leslie introduces Jess to the world of books and a host of new perceptions and ideas. Viewed with distrust by the other children, the two outsiders create a sanctuary for themselves in the form of a secret fantasy kingdom, Terabithia, where they reign as king and queen. One day, when Jess has gone off on an excursion he did not wish to share even with Leslie, she is drowned in Terabithia. Jess responds to the shock of her death with rage, defiance, disbelief, and cold despair. But now he also finds unexpected support: his father shows under-standing and care, and his teacher sensitively shares his grief. Ultimately Jess can recognize that Leslie has left him lasting gifts and responsibilities:

> Now it was time for him to move out. She wasn't there, so he must go for both of them. It was up to him to pay back to the world in beauty and caring what Leslie had loaned him in vision and strength.

This is a moving story with finely controlled language that evokes the atmosphere of the poverty-stricken but beautiful countryside, the volatile busyness and understated affection of Jess's family life, the bitter social struggles, the southern Virginia dialect, and the humor within the children's closed subculture. Images of falling, drowning, and death are present throughout the book, moving toward the tragedy in an ominous build-up of suspense. Paterson's greatest triumph is her skillful creation of two real children and the exploration of both their ordinary and special qualities.

With all its virtues, *Bridge to Terabithia* does impose some strain on credibility. Jess's very quick acceptance of Leslie's death seems much more the reaction of an adult than of a ten-year-old; so is his ability to derive a "lesson for living" from that tragedy. One senses that in *Bridge to Terabithia* it is the adult Katherine Paterson commenting on death rather than a raw country boy experiencing it.

Much the same sense of the adult author's "intrusion" into the children's world is manifested in many realistic novels. Several books of the 1970s seem to have as their objective the stripping away of any hopes or illusions the reader may have about life. Stretched to this degree, the desire to "tell it like it is" comes very near to misanthropy.

A well-written, if hardly pleasurable, case in point is Robert Cormier's *The Chocolate War* (1974). Here there is no longer any trace of the happiness and simplicity that traditionally are associated with childhood. Jerry, the young "hero," has found nothing in life but cynicism and fear. The book is the most brutal exposé of youthful physical violence and of both adult and youthful psychological violence in recent literature. As the events take place in a private Catholic school for boys, the implication is surely meant to be that the Devil is in control rather than God. Jerry's emotional life has already been debilitated by the death of his mother and by his father's aloofness; he is less than prepared for the malevolence that descends upon him when he eventually decides to assert his individuality. His courage is swamped by clinical savagery with no redemption in sight.

William Corlett's *The Dark Side of the Moon* (1976) has much the same tone as *The Chocolate War*. Like many other recent children's novels, the former is so filled with nuances and images of modern society as to demand a sociological or psychological interpretation. Two young men kidnap David Mason, a young teenager unhappy over his parents' divorce, not for monetary reward but as a blow against society. They see it as the inevitable and necessary thing to do. "David Mason is our weapon," say the kidnappers. "We will care for him and instruct him and we will send him back changed." In a counterpoint to the kidnappers' despair of society is the experience of an astronaut, orbiting the moon, and finding space to be as futile and as alien to man's inner spirit as is life on Earth. David does succeed in escaping but in so doing kills one of the kidnappers who was actually trying to help him:

> "Is there any way of saying 'sorry' and making it all right?" David said to him [the police inspector]. "None, is there? It's always too late. They didn't hurt me, you know. Not really. They were hurting themselves."

In the end both David and the astronaut, Wayne Andrews, are seen as scarred for life by their experiences and left with a feeling of the hopelessness of existence:

> For David Mason it was a dead seagull and for Wayne Andrews it was a space within the heart and, between those two points, was only the paraphernalia that makes up fact or fiction.

Empty anguish is the dominant note in yet another of Cormier's Kafkaesque novels, *I Am the Cheese* (1977). A boy, David Farmer, like the protagonist in *The Dark Side of the Moon*, is held captive against his will by a nightmare government agency. He too loses all sense of life's purpose and value and retreats into outright catatonia.

The preoccupation of modern writers with personal traumas can be seen even more clearly in those novels that do not hinge upon a large theme such as the effects of war or death or man's inhumanity to man. Some, among them Ivan Southall in *Josh* (1971) and Jill Paton Walsh in *Goldengrove* (1972) and *Unleaving* (1976), build up a series of episodic but linked events that are used as a drill to bore into and unleash dormant emotions with the consequent pain such exposure brings. With this kind of concentration the characterization in their novels is immeasurably enriched. Not only do we know how the young have reached their initial state as the novel begins, but we sense intuitively what kind of adults they will become. Equally, in the richness of the creation there is a believable sense of a childhood world that frequently emerges as a subculture accompanied by a childlike set of rigid rules and taboos and a ruthless application of unspoken values.

In Southall's book, fourteen-year-old Josh carries the surname Plowman. On a brief visit to his elderly aunt in a small Australian village where the Plowman name is a byword, he meets the unfathomable resentment of the village children. Feeling threatened by his presence, they resort first to half-lies, setting the adult world against him, and finally to an act of physical violence. When the children discover that Josh is no threat to their dependence upon his aunt, they try to make amends. But Josh will have no interference in his life, particularly from his aunt, and when he decides to walk back home to Melbourne he is advancing toward his true, independent self, not away from it. Josh's development is brilliantly compressed into a time span of four days. Like most fine modern writers, Southall achieves his results through style, as instanced by his combination of a colloquial, third-person narrative and Josh's own inward musings on himself:

> "Now why didn't you say to those boys you'd play cricket on Tuesday? They wanted to know. That's why they asked."
> Longing to run away. Longing to get outside the range of her voice. Longing to be at home. . . . Her voice wasn't angry. It was only that awful arrogance that all the Plowmans had.

The titles of Walsh's *Goldengrove* and *Unleaving* are taken from Gerard Manley Hopkins's elegiac poem "Spring and Fall" and have, like all serious modern realism for children, its bittersweet tone, as the following lines indicate:

> Margaret are you grieving.
> Over Goldengrove unleaving?
> . . .
> It is the blight man was born for,
> It is Margaret you mourn for[2]

Through both books we follow the events that have turned Madge Fielding (Walsh's counterpart of Hopkins's Margaret) from a young teenager on holiday, visiting her grandmother in *Goldengrove* to an alternating picture of her as a young and as an old woman in *Unleaving*. Both books are infused with a sense of absolutes about living that demand to be discovered. Life is a metamorphosis, allegiances change, emotions are fractured. One can witness a mercy killing, see a man die trying to rescue a retarded child, experience rejection, and yet know that one can grow through it all. A recurring symbol is a lighthouse, Virginia Woolf's lighthouse, in fact, a symbol opposed to the embittered blindness of the man who rejects Madge's

2. Gerard Manley Hopkins, "Spring and Fall," in W. H. Gardner and N. H. Mackenzie, eds., *The Poems of Gerard Manley Hopkins* (London: Oxford Univ. Pr., 1967), pp. 88-89.

youthful attentions and to the darkness of mind of the retarded child who paradoxically brings light to everyone around her, with the exception of her intellectual father.

In *Unleaving* Madge, who has inherited Goldengrove from her grandmother, is persuaded to billet a group of philosophy students and professors for the summer. Among the party are Professor Tregeagle, his wife, and two children—Patrick, a boy Madge's age, and a young retarded girl. The atmosphere is purely intellectual. The continuing discussion concerns life, death, and ethical choice. Patrick, very sensitive and introspective, rebels against this, for he feels that people and emotions are what count, and that these intellectuals know nothing about people:

> They're not so clever, really. Only about *the subject*. About people, they seem rather stupid to me, usually.

Professor Tregeagle, to whom the intellect is all, finds his mongoloid daughter, Molly, somewhat repugnant. Patrick, who cares deeply for his sister, bitterly resents his father's attitude:

> "We're not allowed feelings in my family," says Patrick. "Only thoughts. So if one has any feelings, one has them alone. That's partly why my father can't do with Molly. She has feelings all right—simple ones. But she'll never have anything he would call a thought."

When Patrick pushes Molly over the cliff in a mercy killing, his action causes the death of one of the rescuing fishermen, a friend of Madge's and Patrick's. Patrick has to live with the guilt and Madge, who sees all, has to live with her silence.

Unlike the books of the past that frequently dealt with groups of children externalizing their problems, as the Nesbit children digging for treasure to "restore the fallen fortunes of the House of Bastable," Walsh's books and most of modern realistic fiction convey a sense of loneliness. The reader is locked inside Madge's mind, chiefly seeing the events from her highly sensitive point of view. Like Southall, Walsh achieves this through style, an intermeshing web of dialogue and interior monologue. Yet, as in most of the books which depend for their drama on personal relationships, the young people appear to be headed for adulthood with a consciousness raised but not embittered. Indeed when Walsh precedes *Unleaving* with a quote from Wittgenstein, "Not how the world is, is the mystical, but that it is," an adult, at least, is immediately aware of entering a story of the celebration of life. At the end of *Unleaving* we see Madge as a grandmother close to death. When asked by a grandchild what the point of living is when we are all going to die anyway, she replies with words from Yeats's "Sailing to Byzantium." They express the unity of the two books—their concepts of loneliness, compassion, and ultimate optimism:

> "Well, we all die, but first we all live, . . . Don't worry about what's the point. Just take your share. Take it two-handed and in full measure. You have to clap your hands and sing."

Madge has learned from everything that has happened to her—sight from the blind man, humanity from the fisherman, love for a brother whom she first believed to be a cousin, the balance between intellect and emotion:

> And, what shall we sing about? Madge asks herself. . . . To be alive is to be bodily present, to notice where and when one is. Here we are: like amateur actors on some magnificent stage, dwarfed by the cosmic grandeur of our setting, muffing our lines, but producing now and then a fitful gleam of our own, an act of mortal beauty.
>
> "What shall we clap?" she says to Peter. "The lifeboat in the storm. What shall we sing? The beauty of the world!"

Of all these skilled and sensitive writers, Walsh is the most formally literary. Her writing is studded with allusions to poetry, art, and philosophy that give it an intellectual framework unmatched in children's literature. While Patty in *Summer of My German Soldier* (1973), by the American writer Bette Greene, is content with the loving servant's reiteration that she is "a person," Margaret, in Walsh's *Unleaving*, asks "what is a person?" British children do come "trailing clouds of metaphysics," as can also be seen in the discussions of time between Keith and David in William Mayne's fantasy *Earthfasts* and in William Corlett's existential expression of life in *The Dark Side of the Moon*.

The intellectual tone of the British realistic novel is most evident when compared to the "problem novel,"[3] which has dominated the American scene for the last twenty years and which deliberately goes to great lengths in the opposite direction. Its sterility in this area is due more to its style than to its actual themes. The problems that the problem writers deal with are real enough; many children are adversely affected by adults who divorce, disappear, drink, or otherwise display little concern for their offspring. Equally, children do have specific problems of their own, some disruption in their lives, sibling rivalry, a lack of preparedness for contact with the realities of life such as death or sex. In its subject matter the problem novel can make a strong claim to be realistic. It can also make the

3. See chapter 1, pp. 14–15 and chapter 4.

same claim for its presentation which is couched, more frequently than not, in the half-formed speech of the young or bears a veneer of half-joking sophistication. In either case the language is stripped of allusion, metaphor, or imagery that in turn make the problems devoid of a wider application. The writers of the problem novel are naive realists, depending solely for their effects on a few physical, personal descriptions, rarely on deep emotion, and never on setting.

The sense of the continuity of time that British writers impart in their books also gives them a more congruent realism; the story lines move with more deliberation, organic growth, and development. Although the events themselves may come with a shock, they nonetheless seem integral to the whole fabric of the novel. Hunter's *A Sound of Chariots* covers seven years of Bridie's life, and in that time she comes to a slow realization that life is not fixed; there is change, flow, a process of maturation. The shorter time span and faster pace of such American books as *Bridge to Terabithia* and *Summer of My German Soldier* lead to more dramatic but, in the end, less credible novels giving the effect of a patchwork, despite their being skillfully put together. Such overall differences between British and American realistic novels may well stem from a differing concept of childhood. In the British books children are children for a longer period and they have (whether expressed implicitly or explicitly) some secure years before they are faced with saddening or startling events.

Bilgie in Jane Gardom's *Bilgewater* (1976) lives a happy if unusual life with her eccentric father and his equally eccentric friends. Yet, she has her own problems. She feels she is "Bilgewater the hideous, quaint and barmy," to those outside her home. Bilgie is seventeen before she is invited for a weekend as the date of Jack to whom she has been attracted. But early Sunday morning she experiences the first of several betrayals:

> I fastened my eyes steadfastly on the coffee and the distant draining board; and then beyond me in the kitchen which was very untidy and messy I saw Jack and Grace rolling about together in silence on the floor.
> They didn't see me.
> I went to church.

Bilgie is not ready for sexual experiences, but her upbringing, her education, and her ability to think things through cushions most of the shock for her and for the reader, who not only sees her as a child and an adolescent but as a woman who is happy, loved, and successful as the novel begins. The slower maturation process in most British novels also leads to a quality of emotional and social development, as well as intellectual, in the youthful characters. It is too simple to say that it is merely a matter of schooling—both American and British protagonists go to school. But what one often senses in the British books is an excitement toward learning, a growth of analytical thought, and so the protagonists' ability to make judgments.

For the most part, the best American children's novels are more deeply rooted in social realism than are the British. They follow Stendahl's view of realistic fiction—a mirror traveling along a highway and giving an accurate though miniaturized picture of what is happening on it. This emphasis on specific reflections of social and political environments is most evident in the realistic fiction of American black authors or in stories of black American life. William Armstrong's *Sounder* (1969), Mildred Taylor's *Roll of Thunder, Hear My Cry* (1976), and Virginia Hamilton's *The Planet of Junior Brown* (1971) are close to Steinbeck's *The Grapes of Wrath*, creating like it precise, deliberate social and historical images which convey the outrage of conscience and heart.

The events in Taylor's *Roll of Thunder, Hear My Cry* swirl around racial prejudice with terror, murder, and lynchings in one heavy, hot summer during the Depression. While it conveys the pain and fierce courage that enabled the blacks to survive, it is also a story of traditional family life. The children are involved in the small but essential dramas of their own lives as well as in the larger forces of adult society. The reader senses that it is a mirror of things that actually did happen.

The Logan family in *Roll of Thunder, Hear My Cry* inhabit a defined space in a defined place and time. The unnamed black family of William Armstrong's *Sounder* act out their drama in a place no more loosely guessed at than the South and in a time that could be spanned by a hundred years. Their very namelessness makes them symbolic of all the poor, oppressed people of every place and every time. The named dog, Sounder, is given his own symbolism. All through the book he is used as a focal point for the family's suffering. They, like the dog, cannot articulate that suffering; it is too far beyond what anyone can endure, and the dog's death at the end finally separates the boy from his childhood. Armstrong writes his terrible story in an almost dispassionate tone, but one in which one can almost experience the heat of the South, smell the physical fear the family experiences, and feel the roughness of the swampland trees. It is a long way from Taylor's naturalistic, conversational style which, almost of necessity, is touched by the didactic.

Perhaps the most timeless of the group will prove to be Virginia Hamilton's *The Planet of Junior Brown* because it is imbued with the fantastic. Everything seems larger and more surreal than life—Junior's obesity (he is a three-hundred-pound outsider), the underground world of the homeless New York children, and the selfishness and narrowmindedness of an adult society that makes a hell for children. It is both a psychological and humanist drama, both an allegory and a social dissertation, but most of all it is a statement about friendship and freedom.

Set in the black urban environment of New York City, the novel concerns the friendship between two black boys in the eighth grade. Buddy Clark is a tender-tough street boy with a brilliant mathematical mind and wise heart who lives a mysterious life in deserted tenements, removed from the world of adults as a lone child-survivor. Junior Brown, suffocated and overprotected by his asthmatic, neurotic mother, finds solace from his deep unhappiness in his remarkable musical and artistic talents, in his fantasies, and in his friendship with Buddy. Bored with their prisonlike school, both boys have been cutting classes, hiding in a secret basement room with their friend and advisor, Mr. Pool, the school janitor. Here they share a secret—a brilliant model of the solar system through which they study mathematics and feel connected with the universe and each other. The book's title, *The Planet of Junior Brown*, in part, refers to one of these planets: a large, powerful planet made by Buddy and named for Junior as a sign of his affection for him.

> The great planet...was brown. It was stupendous. The planet of Junior Brown had come to life right in the room, out of themselves and how they felt about one another.

But Buddy has for many years lived yet another existence, in a role beyond his years as a "Tomorrow Billy," a guide for groups of homeless street children hiding from the controls of adult society. He tells Mr. Pool about these shelters:

> "You see,...it's not just these planets here that we made.... You see, there are planets all over this city. I am Tomorrow Billy. Tomorrow Billy! There are Billys all over this town!"

He is as much a secret outsider as is Junior in his growing alienation and madness, which is caused by the discovery of their school hideaway, the destructive acts of his mother, and his tortured relationship with his music teacher. At the end of the novel, Junior has taken refuge in his new planet-underground home with Buddy and his new child family. He says, in surprise and self-esteem, to his fantasy oppressor: "Didn't know I had some brothers."

Hamilton portrays this communal sharing of love, friendship, and survival as socially unacceptable and heretical (almost early

Christian) in the eyes of the conventional society of school, welfare, and home. It is fascinating that she has reversed the traditional archetypes, giving the children's underground "Tomorrow Billy" planets and their precursor, the janitor's cellar room, the value of heaven, of the planetary system of light, power, and conscious love rather than the dark realm of shades, despair, and the unconscious that the symbol of underground life has always evoked (Hades, Hell, and the underworld).

The subculture of the children, in this instance their literally underground society cut off from adults with its own harsh rules, is now almost a convention in children's literature. They are frequently shown as consciously divorcing themselves from the adult world and hiding from authority as refugees by choice. This pattern can be seen in Jill Paton Walsh's *Fireweed*, Robert Westall's *The Machine-Gunners*, Ivan Southall's *What about Tomorrow*, and Felice Holman's *Slake's Limbo*, the latter an excellent novel of a misfit teenager's one hundred and twenty-one days of scavenging in the New York subway.

The Planet of Junior Brown is also a "dangerous" survival story, but one with a positive, inspirational thread of salvation running through it. The world of eccentrics, misfits, and madness is given a sympathetic treatment; characters, both adults and children, are memorable and with both positive and negative attributes. They are whole, authentic human beings. There is also a visionary, or messianic note of the possibility of a new human race, self-fulfilled, a more humane and compassionate people than exists in the world today. Mr. Pool has always dreamed of a new human race for which life must be made ready and discovering the planets of the children has given him renewed faith in his dream:

> "The human race is bound to come one time," he said. . . . He never was sure what he meant by always having to say that. But to his soul he knew Junior and Buddy were forerunners on the road down which the race would have to pass.

Hamilton writes with force. Her overall, imaginative theme and intricate plot line are joined to a natural and at times poetic prose with an appropriate use of black English that lends vitality to the dialogue. At the same time, her imagery is at times overpowering: there is that of music—the planetary music of the spheres and Junior's playing on the silenced keys of a piano; there is color—Junior's black vision of his spirit and sin, and the red of his paintings; there is the image of New York—Buddy's awareness of the darkness, danger, terror, even beauty of the city; there is the image of obesity—Junior's weight is seen as a metaphor for isolation and a Buddha-like abiding presence rather than as a physical problem.

Hamilton reverses her images in her later book *M. C. Higgins the Great* (1974), although in both she explores the tensions between individual freedom and responsibility and society's capacity for destroying those who are unusual, who are not easily molded. M. C. Higgins's achievement is to climb to the top of his majestic pole, viewing heaven and earth in brilliant, solitary isolation while Buddy's was to burrow into an underground world, creating a shared, cooperative venture for living in a group. *M. C. Higgins the Great* investigates light and love in a nuclear family, joy in song, and a struggle for the threatened countryside of West Virginia. The earlier book investigates darkness, despair, madness, music of instruments, the love of a family of peers, and urban survival. The concepts in both are intriguingly similar to those in Alan Garner's *The Stone Book* (1976), in which Mary ascends to the top of the steeple and descends into the caves of the earth, experiencing the wisdom that lies within the heights and depths of both heaven and earth. What Hamilton and Garner are exploring is the archetype of opposites, the duality of existence, and the discovery of the ancient prophecy: "as above, so below."

All the fine, modern realistic novels are emotionally explosive. Their protagonists have deep and subtle temperaments. They concentrate within themselves all the forces of change at a particular time; they bring certain influences to the point of action; and after a sharp and bitter experience they become the determining influence in their own lives. Their personal intensity spills over into a close relationship with another person but one that is rarely sexual. They are more apt to be a Bridie McShane, recovering from the shattering experience of her father's death (*A Sound of Chariots*), a Junior Brown, finally finding himself in Buddy's way of life (*The Planet of Junior Brown*), or a Bill, absorbing the strength of a bomb-shattered city (*Fireweed*). Even the books that end on a note of despair, Cormier's *The Chocolate War* or Corlett's *The Dark Side of the Moon*, are imbued with the sensitive and often polarized feelings of their youthful characters.

These writers represent the avant-garde in children's literature and in books such as Ivan Southall's *Josh* and *To the Wild Sky*, the works of Cormier, and those of Walsh and Hamilton, they are stylistically avant-garde as well. Yet, within the ordinary definition of realism, that of representing things as they really are, their novels could also be deemed unrealistic because they are outside the realm of common experience. After all, how many children have a loved cousin who turns out to be a brother? How many children weigh 300 pounds or know one who does? And how many have lived and survived on their own in the midst of destruction? But if such books do not reflect common experience, they do propound a deep and universal reality, one that is not based on mere verisimilitude.

Many realistic novelists, and fine ones at that, do not attempt to portray such profound dramas of emotion. Rather, like Jane Austen, they focus on the niceties and perplexities of a more ordinary, everyday existence, emphasizing realism in its more down-to-earth manifestations. They hold up a looking glass, not to the soul, but to the daily gestures, gestures that are sometimes dramatic, of the body social. If Nesbit or Ransome were writing today, their approach would most likely be of this detailed, consciously practical documentation of today's youthful society, for this is how they approached their own eras. Nesbit and Ransome have been replaced by such modern writers as John Rowe Townsend, K. M. Peyton, and William Mayne of Great Britain, and Paula Fox of the United States, all continuing the tradition of daily domestic and social verisimilitude. Their writing appears to lie between the new harsh realism of the problem novel and the charged emotion of a Jill Paton Walsh or a Virginia Hamilton.

Many, especially the British writers, concern themselves with the patterns of class life. John Rowe Townsend's *Gumble's Yard* (1961) deals exclusively with the children of the poor, showing their lives with a harshness quite missing in such earlier books about economically underprivileged children as Eve Garnett's *The Family from One End Street* (1950) or Eleanor Estes's *The Moffats* (1941). When Townsend's Sandra and Kevin are deserted by the two grown-ups in the household, their uncle and his common-law wife, they look after their young cousins and set up housekeeping in the attic of an abandoned cottage to avoid the welfare people who would send them to different foster homes. The children's housekeeping problems are wrenched apart by a gang of ruthless crooks whom the children get the better of, but at the end only, with adult support.

In its setting, the back streets of an English industrial city, and in its unidealized picture of the working class, *Gumble's Yard* belongs to the present. In terms of its plot and its ending, devoid of strong emotion and propounding the view that life is made up of facts that simply have to be faced, Townsend keeps a link with the earlier stories of child and family life. Because of his participation in momentous events, Kevin feels that his life should change. But, as the kindly young curate explains, he has only two choices: he can appeal to the local authorities who would undoubtedly spread the children among foster homes, or he can return to his uncle with the possibility of a slight reform in the home situation and the family remaining as a unit. There are no knights in shining armor to charge to a rescue. And Kevin is reconciled. At the end,

It was a fine spring day.... Next week perhaps we would be playing cricket after school. There was a dog in Mimosa Row that I was getting very friendly with. I was going to make a soap-box car for Harold. Life was full of interesting things to do.

This quality of reconciliation, of coming to terms with one's state, and even station, in life, is a strong motif in this type of British social realism. K. M. Peyton's Pennington, in *Pennington's Seventeenth Summer* (1970) and its sequels, is the kind of troubled, and in trouble, teenager who in the more avant-garde novels would suffer a traumatic experience prior to reaching a mature equilibrium. Peyton's treatment is to let him run through his trials with much humor, portraying him as having a tough survival quality, and a modest self-esteem. Not even a term in jail breaks Pennington, as one sequel, *The Beethoven Medal*, reveals. Pennington wins out by his willpower and his phlegmatism as much as by his extraordinary musical talent.

Peyton never allows Pennington's problems to dominate her precise social scene. She has an ear for dialogue, whether that of the contrasting speech of boys and masters in the large comprehensive high school or Pennington's own working-class home. So her Pennington books are "slices of life" in the best realistic sense. Pennington may be at odds with his parents, but he knows that they will defend him when it comes to a conflict with the school authorities over the length of his hair or trouble with the police. In a few strokes Peyton can portray for readers the working-class attitude toward authority:

> His father thought the story a huge joke and laughed like mad.
> "That's the way to show the beggars!" he kept saying. He got Penn some dry clothes, and rubbed his knee with winter-green. He poured out two cans of beer, and held one up to Penn, who lay back in the armchair and turned on the television.
> "Here's to us," he said. "Disaster to all coppers."
> Penn smiled.

Like most middle-of-the-road realists, Peyton deals lightly but deftly with character; while Pennington's is not revealed through emotional upheaval, he has a high credibility level. For all his musical talent, which his teachers decide he inherited from a forebear, he is still shown as the child of his parents and conditioned by them. His initial violent reaction to most situations is a reflection of his parents' attitudes; he is never pictured as an especially sensitive, alienated youth, and his world is shown as a pragmatic one

55

rather than Manichaean—here the forces of good are not in conflict with those of evil.

Realistic fiction often depends for its interest on topics that are in the news and gives the impression that it is mere reportage, as hastily put together as a newspaper's headline story rather than with the insight of a crafted novel. Peyton's firm grasp on reality, noticeable in all her earlier works, which include *The Plan for Birdsmarsh* (1966) or *Fly-by-Night* (1968), slips when she tackles a voguish subject, kidnapping, in her more recent *Prove Yourself a Hero* (1977), and links this action to a now standard lacerated young protagonist. After Jonathan Meredith is kidnapped he feels that he has to choose to act or not to act, the dilemma of the existentialist hero. When he is freed upon payment of the ransom his authentic ordeal really begins. His failure to make a break for freedom causes him great shame and this shame is reinforced by his mother's lack of understanding. Indeed, no adult in this story is sensible enough to say that a kidnapping is rarely a situation for heroics. Eventually Peyton's lack of care traps her into a loss of concentration, with the result that she writes several books in one: the kidnapping and a sequel which wanders into class distinctions, horse-racing details, Jonathan's alienation from his family, and his beginning romance.

Prove Yourself a Hero begs comparison with William Corlett's *The Dark Side of the Moon* in which David Mason is kidnapped for an ideal rather than ransom. It is David's comprehension of years of imprisonment and brainwashing that sparks his escape. Corlett sticks to his last. The experience of the astronaut, although remote from the plot, is seen as a powerful and symbolic counterpoint to the kidnappers' nihilistic view of life. As a consequence the book is all of a piece and its bleakness of spirit is much more haunting than the supercharged atmosphere of the Peyton book. Yet both are significant examples of a realism that deals with effects upon character rather than upon the exploration of a topic. Neither writer is concerned about the nexus of kidnapping, that a violent act breeds violence.

When compared with Robert Louis Stevenson's *Kidnapped* (1889), the two books also point up—but more forcefully because within a specific theme—the long road children's literature has traveled. David Balfour in Stevenson's classic is first shown as a somewhat callow, self-concerned youth, and his kidnapping is chiefly a conventional plot device of the time. But whereas Corlett and Peyton provide a highly internalized experience, Stevenson has his protagonist journey beyond himself into the interior of the Highlands and so into a national epic. The plight of the displaced Highlanders puts his own problems into proper proportion.

This enlargement of life and vision beyond oneself, as shown in *Kidnapped*, has not entirely disappeared from children's literature, although it has taken a different form. The British writer, William Mayne, for example, can present a sharp picture of a modern child's social milieu while conveying the sense of a family past. Books of this kind have a link with the past different from that of historical fiction, for their modern protagonists gain an insight into and a comfort from their own "roots." In this vein is one of Mayne's quietest, yet most haunting books, *The Jersey Shore* (1973). Here the grandfather, from the Fen country on the North Sea, has come to another shore, the Atlantic shore of New Jersey where he spends the rest of his life in solitude, estranged even from his daughter who lives up the road. He recounts his life to his grandson in the fatalistic tone that Tess of the D'Urbervilles might have used had she told her own story. He sums up his own life:

> Whatever I do I find the world did it first, and I didn't choose, I just threw the net over my own head. But I don't complain of what befell me, no, not at all.

The listening boy, Arthur, sees it all in his mind's eye. Mayne moves smoothly from the old man's tale to:

> Arthur saw. He saw directly, with the children pictured in his mind, each one clearly there, even if the names he had heard were forgotten. He saw them moving in and out of the growing places on the marsh.... He saw the children walk together into this place, staying with the man for a time and then finding new directions for themselves, things that each wanted to look at.

The boy is seeing the day his sleeping grandfather lost his six children to the treacherous marshes and tides. Contrasted to this somnolence is the sharp, pointed daily conversations of Arthur, his mother, and Aunt Deborah, the latter one of Mayne's best-drawn eccentrics. Arthur never forgets his grandfather; then while a World War II pilot he visits Osney and the family graves. "Now he had in him all his own history and his family's history."

Mayne is a prolific writer and all his books show in some measure his fondness for eccentricity; his mastery of dialogue and dialect; his belief in the generational link; and, in particular, his ability to create atmosphere based on place, as if geography (such as the Osney Fens) has a psychic impact upon those who inhabit certain boundaries of space. Whatever this space, it is generally narrow and well-defined: the Cathedral School in *A Swarm in May* (1955), still one of his most delightful books; the small English towns which form the settings for *Earthfasts* (1966) and *It* (1977); and the part of Yorkshire that binds and bounds the protagonists in *Ravensgill* (1970). Bob of *Ravensgill* is not so passive a character as Arthur in *The Jersey Shore*. Still, both boys want to know about their past as they live out lives that are not going to be dramatically changed by their knowledge. A sense of where they are and where they have come from simply enriches their lives.

Although Mayne is a countryman and an Englishman, his writing bears a strong resemblance to that of the American writer Paula Fox in her urban books such as *How Many Miles to Babylon?* (1967) and her story of a poor little rich boy, *Portrait of Ivan* (1969). Like Mayne's children, hers too have experiences that take them out of themselves without any deep changes in personality because there are no deep psychological shocks. They come through their adventures with the resiliency of those sturdy children of an earlier generation. Her books of moderate social realism succeed through the evocation of a child's everyday life with enough fiction thrown in to make a credible novel. Perhaps what is most refreshing about John Rowe Townsend, William Mayne, and Paula Fox is that in their books the themes of alienation and anger are almost nonexistent.

James Douglas in Fox's *How Many Miles to Babylon?* has an absent father and a mother who has been hospitalized for months. He not only misses her, but fantasizes about who he is—really a prince. He lives in an ugly tenement building in Brooklyn with his three aunts: "Aunt Grace who kept a towel around her head to keep off the dust, Aunt Althea who ate more than anyone else, Aunt Paul who had lost her own first name when her husband died and had taken his." They look after him, make him wash behind his ears, and pack him off to school every day. But when James Douglas gets home after all his adventures (he has been kidnapped by three older street boys) and finds his mother who says, "Hello Jimmy," his fantasies come to an end.

In *Portrait of Ivan*, Fox moves from the tenement life of a black family to the wealthy white class. But Ivan has problems too. His mother is dead and his father who loves him is too busy to pay much attention to him. But when he is sent to have his portrait painted, the artist, by means of a drawing gradually filled in, gives him a sense of his mother's past and so his own. The figures of the past have the faces of the friends he has made in the present, and he gains a quiet confidence thereby. Like Mayne, Fox has the ability to bring her characters to life very quickly, and, more importantly, to make the reader care about them.

The middle-stream writers also offer readers some reassurance about modern childhood and adolescence. They see the young as having, at least for a while, a state of their own, rather than always being on the road to someplace else. They arrest time for a moment, so that an adventure or some other unusual happening can occur, one that flows into the protagonist's life rather than wrenching it apart. They also provide the strongest link with the literature of the past. Paula Fox, John Rowe Townsend, William Mayne and K. M. Peyton are writers who do bring the young into the present, but they see their protagonists as fairly unsophisticated and certainly not emotionally falling apart.

While some few writers hold to this middle-of-the-road approach, an even smaller group has made inroads upon the humorous novel. The simple and yet funny exaggerations of old, of a *Mr. Popper's Penguins* or a *Homer Price*, seem to have quite disappeared, as has the light yet authentic tone typified by Farley Mowat's *Owls in the Family* in which oddball pets hold center stage. In the few newer works where humor is present it takes on an astringent quality that is close to parody and often combined with adult eccentricity. Much of this seems to be a legacy from Louise Fitzhugh's *Harriet the Spy* in which most of the characters are eccentric. Indeed Harriet's nurse, Ole Golly, is the parody of an eccentric. She has a fondness for inserting quotations from famous writers into any conversation, no matter how irrelevant the quotation may be. On one occasion, when Harriet asks her to explain a passage from Dostoevsky, Ole Golly's faltering reply indicates that she has only the most superficial idea of what it is all about. Yet it is Ole Golly's view of life that is the sustaining force in the book, as is the cool irony of Mrs. Frankweiler in E. L. Konigsburg's *From The Mixed-Up Files of Mrs. Basil E. Frankweiler* (1967). Her observations on the children's adventure in the Metropolitan Museum of Art gives an added dimension to what would otherwise have been simply a light, pleasant, and sometimes funny story. These adult eccentrics remain at a distance from a book's actual events, as does the millionaire in Ellen Raskin's *The Westing Game* (1978), who sets up his own murder to test his heirs, thus providing an amusing game of "find the clue."

When the eccentrics in these few lighter-hearted novels are added to the large number in the problem novels, as exemplified by the alcoholic Mrs. Woodfinn in Barbara Wersba's *The Dream Watcher* and the grandly obese foster mother in Katherine Paterson's *The Great Gilly Hopkins* (1978), it can almost be said that eccentricity itself is the star of much modern realistic fiction. These adults are philosophical people acting as a foil for the children's view of their own lives. They give a sense of relativity to situations showing that absurdities and lunacies are as much a part of life as seriousness. Through these older characters too, the writers penetrate the charm of the very old communicating with the very young and give significance to the exchange of values which often takes place between the two seemingly disparate ages.

Yet humor of the laugh-aloud kind is almost missing from the modern scene; the streaks of irony and satire are too deeply rooted in the ethos of modern writers. One welcome exception is Helen Cresswell's *The Bagthorpe Saga* (1977-1979) which does aim for a laugh rather than a view of life. Every member of the Bagthorpe family (even the dog Zero) is highly individualistic, even "zany." Like Lucretia Hale's *The Peterkin Papers* of several generations ago, it spills over with extravagant absurdities, any one of which is possible but as a total moves into cumulative farce and slapstick similar to the droll fables and noodlehead tales. The characters have a larger-than-life Dickensian quality: the four-year-old is a pyromaniac; the grandmother constantly mourns the demise of her insufferable cat; Mr. Bagthorpe tries frantically to exert his superiority over his brilliant, competitive children (who have several "Strings to their Bow"); and the normal housekeeper, driven to distraction, has to take refuge with her friends every day at the local pub.

In the Saga's first book, *Ordinary Jack*, Jack feels the outsider in his brilliant, wacky family. But he suffers no mental trauma; like Claudia in *From the Mixed-Up Files of Mrs. Basil E. Frankweiler*, he is only mildly unhappy. Unlike Claudia, however, he would have gone on his way of accepting his usual noncompetitive role in the family were it not for Uncle Parker who decides to make Jack "unordinary" by truly bizarre means. Unlike most recent fiction—even *The Mixed-Up Files*—there are no messages. The ending is simply:

> And, so gradually life in the Bagthorpe household returned to normal, or as near normal as it was ever likely to be, and Jack and Zero (who could now at least fetch sticks) lived happily for several weeks after. They lived, that is, more happily ever after, because Prophet and Phenomenon or not, Jack was not for the time being thought of as ordinary. He was an equal. And that made Zero equal too.

While *The Bagthorpe Saga* may herald a return of humor to children's literature, there is another noticeable lacuna in realistic fiction. This is the straightforward, lively adventure story with a warm, humanistic approach to life, such as Philippa Pearce's *Minnow on the Say* (1958). A modest classic, this is the story of two boys from different social classes in England who join forces for a treasure hunt to save the family home of the impoverished upper-class family. Pearce does not rely for effect on heightened emotion, irony, or social observation in this book, but stirs the reader's emotions by understatement, by the smallest of actions, and by the very briefest exchanges of dialogue. Yet the story is filled with perceptions of nature, of family life, and of a leisurely childhood. The two boys do not change but simply add to their perceptions of adult life through their experience. *Minnow on the Say* is far removed from *Harriet the Spy*, which was published six years later but which by contrast seems more like fifty-six years later. Fitzhugh's satirical outlook and her more stylized writing has lent itself to duplication, even to carbon-copied problem novels. Although another *Minnow on the Say* may never again be written, it is to be hoped that Pearce's sanguine look at childhood and her lucid style do not disappear in the seeming drive of modern writers to push the children's novel ever further into the adult milieu.

Realism may be as difficult to define as fantasy. It is certainly as multifaceted as the fine writers who choose it as their vehicle of expression. In a sense, any concept of childhood or the experience of maturing must reflect the author's biases, theories, memories, and imagination. Although it may be the child in the adult writing the book, it is certainly not the child alone. Therefore, most so-called realistic novels of childhood can only be a reflection of childhood. The differences between harsh, nihilistic realism and warm, support-ive stories of family life lie in the individual author's viewpoint. Whereas Calvin saw children as "a seedbed of sin," Wordsworth envisioned them as "trailing clouds of glory." Cormier's tortured children are of the same human family as the ultrasensitive characters of Jill Paton Walsh and Virginia Hamilton and the resourceful boys of Philippa Pearce, but they stand poles apart in their creators' perceptions of the world as it affects the child's nature.

When these innate differences are added to the sheer numbers of the realistic novel, the total effect seems at first that of patchwork. Yet, even with the diversity of adult memory and imagination, it appears that a broadened landscape of harsh reality has superseded the more simple joys of child and family life. This does not mean that the new realism is as rigidly limited as in the past. With the evidence provided over the span of some twenty years, it is notice-able that its austerity may swell into hope and even a celebration of life. The transformation has come chiefly in more serious themes, the individualization of the protagonists, an unleashing within the writers of raw emotions, a heightened social awareness, and a pas-sionate concern with the psychological manifestations of growing up. Most of this is expressed with painful sensitivity, wry wit, and linguistic experimentation.

In many ways, Ivan Southall's *What About Tomorrow?* (1977) epitomizes the best in modern realistic novels for children. Like most contemporary realistic novels it is not strongly plotted, but moves in a series of linked episodes that describe the terror and beauty of growing up. Fourteen-year-old Sam, a victim of crushing poverty in the Australia of the Depression years, helps his family by delivering papers on an old ramshackle bicycle. Its brakes fail and he falls under a tram:

> People were discussing a mishap. Sam was there somewhere.
> "Is he dead?"
> "How'd he get *in there?*"
> "Look at the bike he was riding. . . . Tied up with bits of wire. There ought to be a law against it."

His bicycle is destroyed, the newspapers he will have to pay for mangled and wet, and the meager earnings that mean so much to his family lost along with his job. Sam is physically unhurt but in such a state of despair that he runs away from the situation and from home. What follows does not bring regression into childhood but sets him on a determined plunge forward into adulthood. Sam's experiences along the Australian byways from Melbourne to Gippsland act as his rites of passage, his first experiences outside the family circle. The unconventional young married woman who helps him but steals his two shillings; the stationmaster who gives him good advice; the farm family who take him in but want to write to his parents; and Mary, the young girl at the end of the road who becomes his ally—at the end of each episode in his picaresque odyssey Sam runs away, but each time with an increasingly mature knowledge of human nature in general, and of his own nature in particular.

Such a story line and such a view of life are typical of recent realistic fiction; only the settings and the particular trauma vary. But *What About Tomorrow?* bears the individual stamp of a particularly perceptive and well-written work. There is only one Ivan Southall, as there is only one Jill Paton Walsh and one Virginia Hamilton. In depicting Sam's growth to sexual maturity, both physically and emotionally, Southall shows an earthy quality quite lacking either in the more refined works of Jane Gardam or the rougher Pennington books by K. M. Peyton. His controlled treatment of a natural sexuality would, in the hands of the writers of the problem novels, be turned into blatant sex.

Southall also achieves with success what many of the newer writers only attempt weakly: to project the protagonist's adult future as part of the unified treatment of character development, as Jane Gardam does to some slight extent in *Bilgewater* and Jill Paton Walsh to greater effect in *Unleaving*. Sam's youth and his future are bridged as we learn that he will return to his Mary, but die as a pilot in World War II. *What About Tomorrow?* is truly a whole life story.

As with other creators of fine realistic novels, Southall is notable for breaking new ground in the style appropriate to the genre. Sam's colloquial, boyish speech conveys the writer's interpretation of his sensitivity to experience. Later, stream-of-consciousness writing propels us into Sam's future. Finally, passages of pure lyricism lift this "realistic" novel from the boredom of realistic reportage:

> Oh, what a place to find at the end of a long, long road. And oh, the smell of it: cinnamon and salt and bread and apples and vinegar and cedar and linseed oil and cloth and cane and flour and honey and clean black iron and who knows, maybe even gold.
> Someone moved, but no one came.... Who would come? Hey? If he dared to call?... He said, "Is anyone there?"
> A head appeared around a tea chest—like a Punch and Judy show on its side. Oh my goodness. Oh my goodness. It was a girl.

What About Tomorrow? is not only a top-ranking example of present-day trends in realistic fiction, it is also perfectly named. In its willingness to undertake themes of genuine depth, its rigorous avoidance of didacticism, and its intuitive understanding of boyhood, this story contrasts strongly with the cheerful, homey, moralizing narratives that traditionally constituted the mainstream of realistic fiction. By expanding the scope and deepening the power of what used to be only a mild excursion into childhood, Southall inadvertently raises the question of what this genre is likely to be "tomorrow" or even whether it will continue to exist at all in recognizable form. With realistic fiction, as with the human nature it is so fond of exploring, true maturity may always mean change.

Works Cited

Alcott, Louisa May. *Little Women; or, Meg, Jo, Beth and Amy.* Illus. by May Alcott. Boston: Roberts Brothers, 1868. 341 pp.

Armstrong, William. *Sounder.* Illus. by James Barkley. New York: Harper, 1969. 116 pp.

Atwater, Richard, and Atwater, Florence. *Mr. Popper's Penguins.* Illus. by Robert Lawson. Boston: Little, 1938. 138 pp.

Bawden, Nina. *Carrie's War.* Philadelphia: Lippincott, 1973. 159 pp.

Burton, Hester. *In Spite of All Terror*. Illus. by Victor G. Ambrus. London: Oxford Univ. Pr., 1968. 183 pp.

Corlett, William. *The Dark Side of the Moon*. London: Hamish Hamilton, 1976. 159 pp.

Cormier, Robert. *The Chocolate War*. New York: Pantheon, 1974. 253 pp.

——*I Am the Cheese*. New York: Pantheon, 1977. 233 pp.

Cresswell, Helen. *Ordinary Jack: Being the First Part of the Bagthorpe Saga*. New York: Macmillan, 1977. 196 pp.

Degens, T. *Transport 7—41—R*. New York: Viking, 1974. 171 pp.

Estes, Eleanor. *The Moffats*. Illus. by Louis Slobodkin. New York: Harcourt, 1941. 290 pp.

——*Rufus M*. Illus. by Louis Slobodkin. New York: Harcourt, 1943. 320 pp.

Fitzhugh, Louise. *Harriet the Spy*. New York: Harper, 1964. 298 pp.

Fox, Paula. *How Many Miles to Babylon?* Illus. by Paul Giovanopoulos. New York: David White Co., 1967. 117 pp.

——*Portrait of Ivan*. Illus. by Saul Lambert. Englewood Cliffs, NJ: Bradbury, 1969. 131 pp.

Gardam, Jane. *Bilgewater*. London: Hamish Hamilton, 1976. 200 pp.

Garner, Alan. *The Stone Book*. Etchings by Michael Foreman. London: Collins, 1976. 61 pp.

Garnett, Eve. *The Family from One End Street, and Some of Their Adventures*. Illus. by the author. London: Frederick Muller, 1937. 212 pp.

George, Jean. *Julie of the Wolves*. Pictures by John Schoenherr. New York: Harper, 1972. 170 pp.

Greene, Bette. *Summer of My German Soldier*. New York: Dial, 1973. 230 pp.

Haig-Brown, Roderick. *Starbuck Valley Winter*. Illus. by Charles De Feo. New York: Morrow, 1946. 310 pp.

Hamilton, Virginia. *M. C. Higgins the Great*. New York: Macmillan, 1974. 278 pp.; paper ed., New York: Dell, 1976.

——*The Planet of Junior Brown*. New York: Macmillan, 1971. 210 pp.; paper ed., New York: Dell, 1978.

Holman, Felice. *Slake's Limbo*. New York: Scribner, 1974. 117 pp.

Hunter, Mollie. *A Sound of Chariots*. New York: Harper, 1972. 242 pp.; paper ed. titled *Sound of Chariots*. New York: Avon, 1975; Don Mills, Ont.: Armada, 1975.

Konigsburg, E. L. *From the Mixed-Up Files of Mrs. Basil E. Frankweiler*. New York: Atheneum, 1967. 162 pp.

Lively, Penelope. *The Ghost of Thomas Kempe*. Illus. by Antony Maitland. London: Heinemann, 1973. 153 pp.

——*Going Back*. London: Heinemann, 1975. 122 pp.

Mayne, William. *Earthfasts*. London: Hamish Hamilton, 1966. 154 pp.

——*It*. London: Hamish Hamilton, 1977. 189 pp.

——*The Jersey Shore*. London: Hamish Hamilton, 1973. 159 pp.

——*Ravensgill*. London: Hamish Hamilton, 1970. 174 pp.

——*A Swarm in May*. Illus. by C. Walter Hodges. London: Oxford Univ. Pr., 1955. 199 pp.

McCloskey, Robert. *Homer Price*. New York: Viking, 1943. 149 pp.

Molesworth, Mary Louisa. *My New Home*. London: Macmillan & Co., 1894. 207 pp.

Mowat, Farley. *Lost in the Barrens*. Drawings by Charles Geer. Boston: Little, 1956. 244 pp.

——*Owls in the Family*. Illus. by Robert Frankenberg. Boston: Little, 1961. 103 pp.

O'Dell, Scott. *Island of the Blue Dolphins*. Boston: Houghton, 1960. 184 pp.

Paterson, Katherine. *Bridge to Terabithia*. Illus. by Donna Diamond. New York: Crowell, 1977. 128 pp.

——*The Great Gilly Hopkins*. New York: Crowell, 1978. 192 pp.

Pearce, Philippa. *Minnow on the Say*. Illus. by Edward Ardizzone. London: Oxford Univ. Pr., 1955. 241 pp.

Peyton, K. M. *The Beethoven Medal*. London: Oxford Univ. Pr., 1971. 152 pp.

——*Fly-by-Night*. London: Oxford Univ. Pr., 1968. 163 pp.

——*Pennington's Seventeenth Summer*. London: Oxford Univ. Pr., 1970. 183 pp.; title of US ed., *Pennington's Last Term*. New York: Crowell, 1971. 216 pp.

——*The Plan for Birdsmarsh*. Illus. by Victor G. Ambrus. London: Oxford Univ. Pr., 1965. 172 pp.

——*Prove Yourself a Hero*. London: Oxford Univ. Pr., 1977. 137 pp.

Raskin, Ellen. *The Westing Game*. New York: Dutton, 1978. 185 pp.

Southall, Ivan. *Ash Road*. Illus. by Clem Seale. Sydney: Angus & Robertson, 1965. 154 pp.

——*Josh*. Sydney: Angus & Robertson, 1971. 179 pp.

——*To the Wild Sky*. Illus. by Jennifer Tuckwell. Sydney: Angus & Robertson, 1967. 184 pp.

——*What About Tomorrow?* New York: Macmillan, 1977. 168 pp.; Australian ed., Cremorne Junction: Angus & Robertson, 1977.

Stevenson, Robert Louis. *Kidnapped; Being the Memoirs of the Adventures of David Balfour, in the Year 1751*. London: Cassell & Co., 1886. 311 pp.

Taylor, Mildred. *Roll of Thunder, Hear My Cry*. Frontis. by Jerry Pinkney. New York: Dial, 1976. 276 pp.

Taylor, Sidney. *All-of-a-Kind-Family*. Illus. by Helen Jane. Chicago: Follett, 1951. 192 pp.

Townsend, John Rowe. *Gumble's Yard*. Illus. by Dick Hart. London: Hutchinson, 1961. 135 pp.

Twain, Mark. *The Adventures of Huckleberry Finn* (Tom Sawyer's Comrade). New York: Harper, 1884. 405 pp.

Walsh, Jill Paton. *Fireweed*. London: Macmillan, 1969. 140 pp.

——*Goldengrove*. London: Macmillan, 1972. 124 pp.

——*Unleaving*. London: Macmillan, 1976. 150 pp.

Wersba, Barbara. *The Dream Watcher*. New York: Atheneum, 1968. 171 pp.

Westall, Robert. *The Machine-Gunners*. London: Macmillan, 1975. 189 pp.; title of US ed., *The Machine Gunners*. New York: Greenwillow, 1976. 186 pp.

4. *The Problem Novel*

There has been more distinguished fiction written for children since 1960 than in any previous two decades, perhaps even in the whole history of children's literature. *A Sound of Chariots* by Mollie Hunter, *What about Tomorrow?* by Ivan Southall, and *The Planet of Junior Brown* by Virginia Hamilton exemplify the heights reached by modern realistic fiction for children. These novels compel belief by the extraordinary strength of their literary qualities: the logical flow of their narratives, the delicate complexity of their characterizations, their probing style, and the insights they convey about the conduct of life as their protagonists move from childhood to adolescence or from adolescence to adulthood. They provide an experience that transcends such objectives as entertainment, information, or catharsis. They touch both the imagination and the emotions.

In popularity, however, such books are quite overshadowed by the publications of a legion of writers, chiefly American, who have remodeled and narrowed realistic fiction to the extent that a new name has been coined for their creations: the "problem novel." While most of these books could be destroyed on literary grounds, or challenged as amateurish forays into the disciplines of psychology and sociology, as a group they are formidable in their popularity and influence. Just as the series novels (*The Hardy Boys, The Bobbsey Twins* et al.) swept North America sixty years ago, so problem novels are the great addictive publications of today's young readers.

Though a convenient handle, it does seem a bit of a misnomer because almost all realistic fiction written today deals with problems children face in a time of physical, psychological, intellectual, and emotional maturation. Taking the approach that maturity can be

66

attained only through a severe testing of soul and self, most recent novels feature some kind of shocking "rite of passage," such as the uprooting of a child's life by war, the death of a close friend or parent, or an encounter with sex. Realistic fiction and its subgenre, the problem novel, both use similar themes having to do with conflict and crisis in children's lives. But while the realistic novel may have conflict at its heart, conflict being integral to plot and characterization, its resolution has wide applications, and it grows out of the personal vision of the writer. In problem novels the conflict stems from the writer's social conscience: it is specific rather than universal, and narrow in its significance rather than far-reaching.

It is easy to recognize this genre of children's fiction:

Problem novels have to do with externals, with how things look rather than how things are. They differ from the realistic novel in their limited aim, which is to tell rather than show. Indeed, the titles alone often tell all—*My Dad Lives in a Downtown Hotel*; *My Name Is Davy, I'm an Alcoholic*; *Philip Hall Likes Me, I Reckon, Maybe*—and the narratives are simply elaborations of those titles. One- or two-word descriptions can be affixed to them—*Dinky Hocker Shoots Smack!* (obesity, not drugs), *Hey, Dummy* (mental retardation), *Grover* (death), *The Man without a Face* (homosexuality)—as if the writers had begun with the problem rather than with plot or characters.

The protagonist is laden with grievances and anxieties that grow out of some form of alienation from the adult world, to which he or she is usually hostile.

Partial or temporary relief from these anxieties is received from an association with an unconventional adult outside the family.

The narrative is almost always in the first person and its confessional tone is rigorously self-centered.

The vocabulary is limited and the observations are restricted by the pretence that an "ordinary" child is the narrator.

Sentences and paragraphs are short.

Locutions are colloquial and the language is flat, without nuance, and often emotionally numb.

There is an obligatory inclusion of expletives.

Sex is discussed openly.

The setting is urban, usually in New York City, New Jersey, or California.

In retrospect it can be seen that the problem-novel formula was established by Emily Neville's *It's Like This, Cat* (1963). The first-person narration by a young teenager is glibly confessional and features alienation from parents, a New York apartment setting, a refuge outside the home with an older person who is not a relative, and stereotyped characters that are almost caricatures—a stuffy New York lawyer-father, a helpless mother, and an eccentric recluse who lives with cats. The problem of alienation is resolved when the square father helps the boy's new-found friends. The basic formula was to be maintained even when everyday and relatively uncontentious family "problems" gave way to social topics such as drugs, alcoholism, contraception, abortion, and homosexuality.

It's Like This, Cat, and all subsequent problem novels, were seminally influenced by Salinger's *The Catcher in the Rye* (1951). Holden Caulfield is an intelligent, sensitive teenager trapped, as he feels, in the "phoniness" of the adult world, which he describes with irony and bitter humor. Though he suffers a breakdown, he does come to terms with the world, and there is assurance of his recovery. But while *The Catcher in the Rye* inspired many writers of juveniles, it was Holden's alienation from adult society and the glory he found in criticizing it with unrestrained frankness that attracted them, not the novel's depth and insight, its credible eccentricity, or its stylistic brilliance. The earthbound confessions and banal reflections that make up the problem novel bear little resemblance to Salinger's first-person narrative, which is not only incisive and sometimes poetic, but is also refreshingly colloquial. The Salinger book spawned thin fiction, without weight or resonance, whose total significance seems to be on the surface of the narrative.

Problem novels can be divided into two groups: those that deal with normal problems of family life—sibling rivalry, moving, adjusting to a stepfather—and those that focus on social or emotional topics like drugs, alcoholism, abortion, or sexual experimentation. The former are usually read by a younger age-group, seven- to ten-year-olds, though some "heavy" problems eventually filtered down into these junior books.

Among those who write for the younger group, Judy Blume is by far the most popular. One of her early books, *Are You There God? It's Me, Margaret* (1970), is typical in its childlike concern with the effect of an action on "me," rarely on "us," never on "them." It is about eleven-year-old Margaret, whose anxiety is aroused because her family moves from New York to a small community in New Jersey. An added "problem" is her decision to choose her friends from among classmates who belong either to the Y or to the Jewish community center. Yet another arises at home: her paternal grandmother wants her to be Jewish and her parents, partners in a mixed marriage, want her to decide about a religion when she is older (while wanting her to be like them, agnostic). Taking precedence over these worries, certainly where readers are concerned, is Margaret's concern over the fact that she is slower than some of her friends in her physical development. She has not begun to menstruate. She discusses these things casually and often with her confidant, God, as in the opening paragraph:

> Are you there God? It's me Margaret. We're moving today. I'm so scared God. I've never lived anywhere but here. Suppose I hate my new school? Suppose everybody there hates me? Please help me God. Don't let New Jersey be too horrible.

It might be thought that the problems dealt with are to be given a moral or ethical dimension, but this is not the case. Religion has provided the book with its arch title and little else. In Margaret's homework project on the subject, God's surrogates on earth are found wanting, and God Himself is chastised when He does not obey Margaret precisely and immediately, though He is given the credit when her physical development takes its natural course. But the possible significance of religion in her life is not confronted, nor need it be to satisfy readers. The novel's immense popularity with young girls (and some boys) has been gained solely by the reassurance it conveys about pubescence.[1]

The greatest problems in problem novels are adults, usually parents, who contribute to the problems, frequently cause them, but rarely offer a believable or loving solution. Parents, the main alienating presence in these books, which are essentially about alienation, are often viewed as "the enemy."

Generally speaking, between 1900 and 1960 parents were removed from children's books in any serious, participative way: the young were thus given a taste of freedom, but still within a secure family setting. However, in the problem novel, parents figure prominently, as in the days of the moral tale, but they do not necessarily interact with the child protagonists. They are usually objects in space, mercilessly described as confused, inept, insecure, self-centered, cynical, violent, sadistic, or otherwise unsympathetic or damaging to the child's psyche. "My mother's a dumb one. My father's a mean one," says a runaway girl in Paul Zindel's *I Never Loved Your Mind* (1970). In contrast to parents in nineteenth-century fiction who could do no wrong, parents in the modern problem novels can do no right.

Unlike books of the past, almost every problem novel gives ample external information about parents, prejudiced though it may be: their clothes, lovers, views of life, and temperaments. Yet in most

1. While boys do not disregard problem novels, particularly if word of sensational content has reached them, it is girls who read them voraciously.

cases these adults are significant for their well-documented absence. This is sometimes physical—they have died, deserted, divorced, or are kept away on business. But in many books their absence is psychological—parents are too busy with their own concerns to pay attention to their children. Not only do they not know what's going on in their children's lives, they don't care.

In Jeanette Eyerly's *Escape from Nowhere* (1969), Carla, whose businessman father is often absent and whose mother is an alcoholic, experiments with drugs. Lisa's parents in John Neufeld's *Lisa, Bright and Dark* (1969) refuse to acknowledge that she is mentally ill, though she and her friends come to see this. In S. E. Hinton's *Rumble Fish* (1975), Rusty-James's mother has deserted the father, a drunken ex-lawyer on welfare, and is living in a tree house with a movie producer. When Rusty-James is injured in a knife fight, his father says:

> "Are you ill?"
> "Got cut up in a knife fight," I told him.
> "Really?" He came over to take a look. "What strange lives you two lead."
> "I ain't so strange," I said.
> He gave me a ten-dollar bill.

In Paul Zindel's *My Darling, My Hamburger* (1969), teachers and parents fail miserably in every incident. The book opens with the female gym teacher telling Liz, Maggie, and their class that the way to stop a guy who wants to go all the way is to suggest going to get a hamburger. When Dennis feels destroyed because Maggie has broken a date to the prom, his parents spend the dinner hour talking about the correct way for him to handle the kitchen garbage. While Liz at various times considers suicide, abortion, or forcing Sean to marry her, her mother gives her long lectures on smiling or on being sweeter to her stepfather at the dinner table. In school Sean writes a story called "The Circus of Blackness" about a young circus couple who commit a ritualistic murder of their child in front of an audience. The teacher's comment: "You have a remarkable imagination."

Moreover, adults are shown to be insensitive and callous about anything outside the norm. In Kin Platt's *Hey, Dummy* (1971), not one adult shows even ordinary humanitarian concern for a retarded child. Neil wants to bring the boy to his house for dinner:

> "Brain-damaged, did you say?" my mom said. She threw herself into a grotesque pose, arms and hands at awkward angles, making her face look stupid and drooly. "One of those kind?"

As a result of the attitude of unconcern, even loathing, of adults towards the handicapped child, Neil develops an "altered personality." He prefers to withdraw psychologically rather than be part of the so-called real world.

As the sixties moved into the seventies, the sexual content became more explicit. John Donovan's *I'll Get There: It Better Be Worth the Trip* (1969) contains one suggested, quickly passed-over homosexual incident, but in Isabelle Holland's *The Man without a Face*, published three years later, there is no doubt about the homosexual relationship. And 1977 saw the publication of a problem novel by Judy Blume, *Forever*, that is as explicit as a sex manual. The treatment of such topics as abortion and contraception indicates that these subjects are no longer even controversial, much less taboo. In Paul Zindel's *My Darling, My Hamburger* Liz is quite upset at the idea of an abortion. But Norma Klein's *It's Not What You Expect* (1973), which appeared four years later, describes Ralph and Sara Lee nonchalantly arranging to have an abortion in New York. They return, according to Ralph, with "no problems." Sara Lee does not tell her mother and carries on as if nothing unusual has happened.

The matter-of-fact explicitness of problem novels is accompanied by unrestrained language. Back in 1959 Karl Bjarnhof, in an adult novel, would not have surprised readers by having one of his youthful characters remark: "But Hamsun. . . . He's the one who swears in his books. I don't mind people swearing, but in a book!"[2] By 1973 a child in John Neufeld's *Freddy's Book* could ask the librarian for "a book about fucking." In an article written in 1975 Norma Klein said she would "like to see four-letter words used as frequently in realistic books for children as they are in everyday lives of what I would consider respectable middle and upperclass people."[3]

The spirit of linguistic liberation does not extend to departing from a style that is undemanding and serviceable at best, one combining banality and flatness in an attempt to suggest the speech of children, with a certain narrative efficiency that bespeaks the adult writer, exemplified by the following:

> I walked into the lobby of my apartment building, thinking how good a big, cold drink would taste. I pushed the Up elevator button and waited. When the elevator got to the lobby Henry opened the gate and I stepped in. Just as he was about to take me upstairs Peter Hatcher and his dumb old dog came tearing down the hall.
> ——Judy Blume, *Otherwise Known as Sheila the Great* (1972), p. 1.

2. Karl Bjarnhof, *The Good Light*, tr. by Naomi Walford (London: Methuen, 1960), p. 157.
3. "More Realism for Children," *Top of the News* 31:309 (Apr. 1975).

"What do you think of Mom's new boy friend?" she asked
suddenly.
I thought for a second and shrugged. "He's okay, I guess."
Chloris frowned. . . . "He's not okay," she said angrily. "He's a
creep."
"How do you figure that?"
She pushed back her long brown hair and scowled. "You don't
have to figure it. A creep is a creep."
"Yes, but . . ."
———Kin Platt, *Chloris and the Creeps* (1973), p. 2.

I'd better begin this story by telling you that until a month ago I
was quite a mess. I mean, I was such a mess that my mother wanted
to send me to a psychiatrist but backed down when she discovered
that it would cost twenty-five dollars an hour.
———Barbara Wersba, *The Dream Watcher* (1968), p. 1.

After a book-length recital of grievances and "problems" in these
books, their resolution becomes a matter of some interest. A consideration of the endings alone strengthens the impression that it is
the problems themselves, or rather the cool, anecdotal explication of
them, that are the raison d'être of problem novels, for psychologically
convincing resolutions seem to be neither required by readers nor
demanded by the conventions of the genre. Reflecting the fatalism
and resignation of the young who see their lives as compounded of
one "problem" after another, none of them with any hope of resolution, some of these novels are almost existential in not having a
conclusion. "Then again, maybe I won't," Tony says, at the end of
Judy Blume's book of that title (1973), about whether he will cease his
practice of spying on a girl undressing. And Ox, in John Ney's *Ox,
The Story of a Kid at the Top* (1970), after a wild trip with his wealthy
father from whom he feels estranged, simply decides that "nothing
ever changes."
In novels for older children, the conclusions suggest that the
long road to recovery has not even started, or is only just beginning.
Sean, in Paul Zindel's *My Darling, My Hamburger*, deserts Liz, who is
pregnant, after a conversation with his crude and cynical father.
Roger, in Kin Platt's *The Boy Who Could Make Himself Disappear*
(1968), undergoes psychiatric treatment, the outcome of which is not
at all clear. And ten-year-old Fran Ellen, in Marilyn Sachs's *The Bears'
House* (1971), who has tried to take care of a younger brother and
newborn baby while hiding her mother's breakdown, appears in a
nebulous ending either to have strengthened her grasp on reality
through day-dreaming, or to have lost that grasp, to enter her
playhouse of refuge of the three bears—psychologically, at
least—never to emerge.

In books for younger children, the endings tend to be predicated on arbitrary and sudden psychological changes or to appear as Band-Aids applied to a serious wound rather than as genuine cures achieved through a more mature outlook or some kind of rehabilitation. Overweight Dinky in M. E. Kerr's *Dinky Hocker Shoots Smack!* (1972) is taken off to Europe by her parents to encourage her to stick to her diet, leaving the impression that her psyche and body will be put in shape without any major effort on her part. In Norma Klein's *Confessions of an Only Child* (1974), Antonia grudgingly comes to terms with having a baby sister, and in Klein's *Mom, the Wolf Man and Me* (1972), Brett, in an unexpected reversal, accepts the fact of her mother's marriage.

There is one event that turns up over and over again to effect a miraculous change in the outlook and circumstances of the troubled protagonist, and that is death. The preponderance of deaths, though not death scenes, is astonishing, considering that ninety-five percent of us reach adulthood without experiencing a family death.[4] The death is usually that of a deus ex machina, usually an older eccentric outside the family with whom the child has had a close relationship and the support that had not been forthcoming from parents. The janitor in Constance Greene's *A Girl Called Al* (1969), Mr. Pignati in *The Pigman*, the alcoholic schoolteacher in Barbara Wersba's *The Dream Watcher* (1968), the lonely, middle-aged homosexual in Isabel Holland's *The Man without a Face* (1972) all have to die in order that the children who have become attached to them may come to terms with themselves. Death is treated as a "soft," only moderately disturbing problem because the authors want merely to provide the denouement that resolves insecurities and self-doubts. The deaths are never intended to inspire fear, awe, shock, tears, or even a violent change in the young protagonists. Their egos and self-absorption are hardly affected by the experience. In *A Girl Called Al* the death of the janitor is portrayed as "a good death, a happy death." Al's feelings on the subject are not recorded at all, while even the more sensitively portrayed narrator only regrets that Mr. Richards will not be around to see the effects of his advice:

> Maybe what Mr. Richards said about Al and me being stunners some day will come true. I only wish he could be around to see it happen. That's the only thing I wish.

In other books the children are left by adults to bear their grief alone, as in Constance Green's *Beat the Turtle Drum* (1976), or they come to

4. *World Book Encyclopedia*, vol. 5, p. 53 (1979).

terms with death more quickly than adults, as Grover does in Vera and Bill Cleaver's *Grover* (1970).

In all fields of writing there are the good and the bad and the mediocre. A rare problem novel successfully avoids the landmines of a clichéd form to become something else: a novel that employs all the stylistic and thematic devices of the genre while maintaining an emotionally charged credibility. Ursula LeGuin's *Very Far Away from Anywhere Else* (1976) and M. E. Kerr's *Is That You, Miss Blue?* (1975) are two such novels. Both writers use a brief time span and a circumscribed setting: LeGuin, a few months of friendship in the closed world of two teenagers, and Kerr, a term in a girl's boarding school. These books succeed because the protagonists are intelligent, well educated, with an ardent curiosity about life, and their main thrust is not an unburdening of the soul but concern for another person. They are not exercises in egotism. In cleanly written, controlled prose LeGuin shows the friendship between Owen and Natalie, two teenagers, neither of whom has a terrible home life, and how they delicately adjust to a loving relationship without the pressure of sex. They genuinely care for one another. Owen says:

> And so the next time we met, it was entirely different. I had decided that I was in love with Natalie. I hadn't fallen in love with her, please notice that I didn't say that; I had *decided* that I was in love with her.

The ending is as low keyed as the relationship. Both go off to their respective colleges. But this novelette of only 94 pages still manages to convey a whole life story. One knows what kind of adults Owen and Natalie will become.

The "Miss Blue" of *Is That You, Miss Blue?* is an elderly, brilliant schoolteacher driven from her job because of her eccentricities—especially because she converses with Jesus. The group of teenaged girls in the Episcopal boarding school, with whom the story is concerned, have problems of their own, and they express them in the breezy, sophisticated terms that are typical of the problem novel with older protagonists. Carolyn Cardmaker explains why she is at Charles School:

> "A Preacher's Kid!" She was tracing the initials PK in the soot on the train window with her finger. "I'm a preacher's kid with a high I.Q., which means I won a scholarship. There are only four reasons why anyone is ever shipped off to Charles School, and I qualify as a Number One. Number One is Bright and Pitiful. I could be Bright and Black, or Bright and Oriental, or Bright and a Migrant Worker's daughter. But I'm worse than all of those because I'm bright and a preacher's kid, which means

that I'm practically a pauper. I'm even wearing a secondhand school blazer."

Flanders Brown, the fifteen-year-old narrator with recently divorced parents, also has adjustments to make in her life. But all the girls can see outside themselves. They have an affection for eccentricity and feel strongly for a person driven to pain and disgrace. And their realization that remarkable people, no matter how briefly known, can have an effect on one's life is made convincing.

Both books are closer than most other problem novels to the concepts imaginatively expressed in Salinger's *The Catcher in the Rye,* especially his bitter-sweet view of growing up. These novels are self-defining; they possess a tough clarity of thought and language. Most problem novels give their protagonists a voice that is too shrill and garrulous for enlightenment. They are merely laments, that are glib and self-centered, couched in the language of the day. One thinks of Aunt Susan's remark in Penelope Lively's *The House in Norham Gardens*:

'It is only those who have never listened who find themselves in trouble eventually.'
'Why?'
'Because it is extremely dull," said Aunt Susan tartly, "to grow old with nothing inside your head but your own voice. Tedious, to put it mildly.'

Another rare quality that gives dimension to problem novels is that of regionalism in setting and cultural voice. Both Kevin Major's *Hold Fast* (1978) and Vera and Bill Cleaver's *Where the Lilies Bloom* (1969) convey distinctive flavors of landscape and speech. Major's Newfoundland tale provides glimpses of squid-jigging, camping, and hunting, as well as the differences between a village and a town school system. The Cleavers paint an Appalachian setting with such local customs as "wild-crafting," home medicinal remedies, and hill music. These vivid settings and pungent dialects, musical in *Where the Lilies Bloom* and earthy in *Hold Fast*, add substance to stories that in respect of theme are conventional problem novels.

Alienation, hostility, egocentricity, the search for identity, the flouting of conventions—these are what have evoked instant interest and sympathy from the young since the sixties, that period of general reaction against authority. It expressed itself in protest movements and various forms of rebellion that focused on a multitude of injustices and inequalities and revealed a hitherto unexpected need for honesty and openness in relationships, instinctively and tacitly yearned for by young people, actively sought by adults. They brought into question power structures of all kinds: in government, in education, in the family itself. The stability of family life was taken for granted in children's literature until changes in life-styles and the liberated attitudes of the sixties made this convention seem mythical.

A society where roles and standards are clear and consistently supported offers a form of security for children. Autonomy, though stimulating, can bring with it insecurity, and this is the generating force behind problem novels. The reassurance they provide in dealing openly with issues that had heretofore been hidden is perhaps the main reason for their popularity. Another is the hostility to adults they reflect, for these stories play on frustrations and resentments, increased where there is lack of attention or sympathy, that every child feels throughout the process of socialization. Not only are the main characters impotent and often angry, but they feel alone in a hostile world; they rarely have the support of parents, relatives, teachers, or spiritual advisors. On the other hand, they consistently oppose their parents' values, when they have any, as being oppressive and archaic. Combine these ingredients with parents who are responsible for all injustices—reversing the childhood syndrome that anything bad that happens in the family is somehow the child's fault—and you have a mixture of fictional elements that is irresistible to the older child or early adolescent.

There are numerous secondary reasons for the popularity of these books. In instances where readers suffer from the very difficulties featured, it is presumably good for them to know that they are not alone in their anxieties. Conversely, for those children who cannot identify themselves with the protagonists, there is the appeal of the exotic in the sordid events described or of having one's curiosity and even prurience satisfied by matter-of-fact discussions of sensitive subjects. Another attraction is that the language and style, or rather the simple "with it" language and the absence of a "literary" style, make the content totally accessible.

Although problem novels because of their short sentences and simple language are already linguistically accessible, it may be that writers will stretch even further for reader accessibility. Patti Stren's *A Rainbow in My Closet* (1979) is a "picture-book novel," perhaps a new format which will appeal even more strongly to the reluctant reader through its effective use of visual elements. With the inclusion of the author-illustrator's witty, childlike drawings, this story of a young girl's growth as an artist becomes, for a novel, unique in format and concept. The incorporation of such "visual hooks" was pioneered by Paul Zindel in *My Darling, My Hamburger*; his reliance on cartoon drawings and letters in youthful script give to the book a tone of verisimilitude and touches of teenage humor.

Yet another factor is the conditioning provided by television, its mesmerizing delivery of words and pictures flooding the unselective viewer with both images of real life and facile simulations of it. Problem novels, with their clear-cut topical subjects, their lack of background and depth, and the prevalence of dialogue, require little adjustment from the inveterate TV watcher. Indeed, more than a few of this genre have been dramatized for television.[5]

Shallow and narrow though they may be, problem novels have made their influence felt in the more creative realm of imaginative fiction for children. In freeing children from an idealized conception of childhood, they have demythologized it, while probably creating a few myths of their own. These books confront children with problems that are not of their own making, unlike the crises that issued from the spirited adventure stories of the past, but with which they have to come to terms. And these concerns, both social and psychological, have individualized characters to a degree that was formerly unknown.

It was the writers of the 1960s who began to emphasize the way in which personality and the sense of self alter when a psychological chasm is reached. Some protagonists find a bridge and cross it; others fall in. In either case the characters are changed to an extent and with a finality quite different from the rather simple and lighthearted "growing up" that the children in earlier books experience. This approach of treating characters as individuals and making them sensitive to their environment colors all recent fiction for children. Thus, even a historical novel about the American Civil War, Betty Cummings's *Hew against the Grain* (1977), focuses not on external events but on the introspective main character and her personal problems, the consequences of war and rape. And Mollie Hunter's *A Sound of Chariots* (1972) is about a young girl's obsession with death. Such an atmosphere of bleakness pervades most recent fiction for children, yet another legacy of the problem novel.

Children's literature has always responded to changes in social attitudes and values, but the mass production of problem novels and their quick acceptance has greatly speeded up the process of change. What new trend will manifest itself for children today who, we are told, are much more accepting of their parents' middle-class values than were their immediate predecessors? However this shift in attitude is confronted by writers, we can be sure that in one-and-a-half decades the world of children's fiction has already changed fundamentally—and forever.

5. John Neufeld's *Lisa, Bright and Dark* (1969), Richard Peck's *Are You in the House Alone?* (1976), and *Go Ask Alice* (Anonymous, 1971) are three problem novels that have been adapted for television.

Works Cited

Blume, Judy. *Are You There God? It's Me, Margaret.* Englewood Cliffs, NJ: Bradbury, 1970. 149 pp.

————*Forever.* New York: Bradbury, 1975. 199 pp.

————*Otherwise Known as Sheila the Great.* New York: Dutton, 1972. 118 pp.

————*Then Again, Maybe I Won't.* New York: Bradbury, 1971. 164 pp.

Cleaver, Vera, and Cleaver, Bill. *Grover.* Illus. by Frederic Marvin. Philadelphia: Lippincott, 1970. 125 pp.

————*Where the Lilies Bloom.* Philadelphia: Lippincott, 1969. 174 pp.

Cummings, Betty Sue. *Hew against the Grain.* New York: Atheneum, 1978. 174 pp.

Donovan, John. *I'll Get There: It Better Be Worth the Trip.* New York: Harper, 1969. 189 pp.

Eyerly, Jeanette. *Escape from Nowhere.* Philadelphia: Lippincott, 1969. 187 pp.

Go Ask Alice. Englewood Cliffs, NJ: Prentice-Hall, 1971. 159 pp.

Greene, Bette. *Philip Hall Likes Me, I Reckon, Maybe.* Pictures by Charles Lilly. New York: Dial, 1974. 135 pp.

Greene, Constance. *Beat the Turtle Drum.* Illus. by Donna Diamond. New York: Viking, 1976. 119 pp.

————*A Girl Called Al.* Illus. by Byron Barton. New York: Viking, 1969. 127 pp.

Hamilton, Virginia. *The Planet of Junior Brown.* New York: Macmillan, 1971. 210 pp.

Hinton, S. E. *Rumble Fish.* New York: Delacorte, 1975. 122 pp.

Holland, Isabelle. *The Man without a Face.* Philadelphia: Lippincott, 1972. 159 pp.

Hunter, Mollie. *A Sound of Chariots.* London: Hamish Hamilton, 1972. 242 pp.

Kerr, M. E. *Dinky Hocker Shoots Smack.* New York: Harper, 1972. 198 pp.

————*Is That You, Miss Blue?* New York: Harper, 1975. 170 pp.

Klein, Norma. *Confessions of an Only Child.* Illus. by Richard Cuffari. New York: Pantheon, 1974. 93 pp.

————*It's Not What You Expect.* New York: Pantheon, 1973. 128 pp.

————*Mom, the Wolf Man and Me.* New York: Pantheon, 1972. 128 pp.

LeGuin, Ursula K. *Very Far Away from Anywhere Else.* New York: Atheneum, 1976. 89 pp.; English title, *A Very Long Way from Anywhere Else.* London: Gollancz, 1976. 94 pp.

Lively, Penelope. *The House in Norham Gardens.* London: Heinemann, 1974. 154 pp.

Major, Kevin. *Hold Fast.* Toronto: Clarke Irwin, 1978. 170 pp.

Mann, Peggy. *My Dad Lives in a Downtown Hotel.* Illus. by Richard Cuffari. New York: Doubleday, 1973. 92 pp.

Neufeld, John. *Freddy's Book.* New York: Random, 1973. 132 pp.

————*Lisa, Bright and Dark.* New York: S. G. Phillips, 1969. 125 pp.

Neville, Emily. *It's Like This, Cat.* Pictures by Emil Weiss. New York: Harper, 1963. 180 pp.

Ney, John. *Ox; The Story of a Kid at the Top.* Boston: Little, 1970. 140 pp.

Platt, Kin. *The Boy Who Could Make Himself Disappear.* Radnor, Pa.: Chilton, 1968. 216 pp.

———*Chloris and the Creeps.* Radnor, Pa.: Chilton, 1973. 146 pp.

———*Hey, Dummy.* Radnor, Pa.: Chilton, 1971. 169 pp.

Sachs, Marilyn. *The Bears' House.* Illus. by Louis Glanzman. New York: Doubleday, 1971. 81 pp.

Salinger, J. D. *The Catcher in the Rye.* Boston: Little, 1951. 277 pp.

Snyder, Anne. *My Name is Davy: I'm an Alcoholic.* New York: Holt, 1977. 128 pp.

Southall, Ivan. *What about Tomorrow?.* New York: Macmillan 1977. 168 pp.

Stren, Patti. *There's a Rainbow in My Closet.* New York: Harper, 1979. 136 pp.

Wersba, Barbara. *The Dream Watcher.* New York: Atheneum, 1968. 171 pp.

Zindel, Paul. *I Never Loved Your Mind.* New York: Harper, 1970. 181 pp.

———*My Darling, My Hamburger.* New York: Harper, 1969. 168 pp.

———*The Pigman.* New York: Harper, 1968. 182 pp.

5. The New Fantasy

Fantasy is a literature of paradox. It is the discovery of the real within the unreal, the credible within the incredible, the believable within the unbelievable. Yet the paradoxes have to be resolved. It is in the interstices between the two halves of the paradox, on the knife-edge of two worlds, that fantasists build their domain. The creators of fantasy may use the most fantastic, weird, and bizarre images and happenings but their basic concern is with the wholesomeness of the human soul or, to use a more contemporary term, the integrity of the self. This is the major theme of fantasy, although it is played out in many guises and always in a thoroughly undidactic manner.

Fantasists wrestle with the great complexities of existence—life, death, time, space, good and evil—and a child's struggle to find its place within these awesome concepts. Yet these are only one side of the fantasy. Fantasists also indulge in creative play and celebration. It is as if they themselves were children, albeit godlike ones, redesigning the universe to make its realities more apparent, just as everyday play, one of childhood's greatest learning experiences, helps children to deal with the everyday problems they will meet as adults. Fantasists do not purport to ape life as do the "naive realists" who, with the cry of "this is real" upon their lips, offer narrow, personal problems with quick solutions and frequently no genuine understanding of the issues raised. Fantasists see life as an evocative but continuous whole. The tenet of the fantasist is "there is another kind of real," one that is truer to the human spirit, demanding a pilgrim's progress to find it.

Perhaps the greatest paradox is that fantasy is firmly identified as a literature of escape. Although the premise is perfectly true, yet no literature could be less "escapist." For while the fantasists do have us retreat or escape from the ordinary world into a strange "secret garden," they force us at the same time to confront the "truths"—truths that are often awesome and even bitter. The proof of this assertion is the evident fact that fantasy, far from being "easy reading" as escapist writing invariably is, demands extra effort from its readers. E. M. Forster described the readers of fantasy as being asked to "pay a little extra" in order to move in a strange new world. Coleridge called for the "willing suspension of disbelief." Batman, Superman, and Wonder Woman share with Merlin, Parsifal, and Will Stanton the fact that they possess supernatural powers. But the first three operate on the level of mindless and repetitive gimmickry, while the latter heroes are seekers and thinkers as well as doers in the spirit of true fantasy.

There is nothing particularly distinctive about the thoughtful character of fantasy. In one way or another all good writing seeks to impose some kind of meaning on the myriad experiences of life. What distinguishes fine fantasy from other fine literature is not its framework but its inner core. The writer of fantasy goes beyond realism to reveal that we do not live entirely in a world of facts, that we also inhabit a universe of the mind and spirit where the creative imagination is permanently struggling to articulate meaning and values.

This extraterrestrial character of fantasy implies that it is relatively little affected by the particular circumstances of the time and place in which it is written and is the least local and temporal of literatures. That being the case, how *new* then is the "new fantasy"? It may well be argued that as a genre fantasy has remained its own self —steady, conservative, and eclectic—following a tradition that goes back to the *Odyssey*. Its chief dictates still hold; they are neither flouted nor overridden. Modern fantasists still reveal "universal truths"; they ask their readers for a "willing suspension of disbelief"; for after confronting their characters with the supernatural and the insights to be derived from it, they send them back to view their everyday lives with clearer eyes. In fantasy what is past is present and what is present is past.

But certain innovations herald some new rules for an old game. In the works of the major modern fantasists—Alan Garner, Susan Cooper, William Mayne, Ursula LeGuin, Penelope Lively, Richard Adams—there can be felt a powerful, even an awesome, seriousness together with an uncompromising perception of reality, a command of mythology, an emphasis upon the individual, a complex concept of time, an elliptical style, and a cinematic vision that separate them from the fantasists of an earlier period. There is also a sense in which

81

most writers of modern fantasy are the moral arbiters of our time, in strong contrast to most writers of contemporary realistic fiction.

In making such claims one must go gently. Not every fantasy mentioned breaks new ground on all these points. Modern fantasy in its totality is the richest and most varied of all the genres. It seems impossible to discuss, in the same breath as it were, such diverse works as Susan Cooper's conception of the great struggle between good and evil in her *The Dark Is Rising* quintet (1966–1977), Philippa Pearce's quieter but more complex *Tom's Midnight Garden* (1958), and Richard Adams's animal fantasy *Watership Down* (1972). Still, fantasies they all are by common consent and their diversity only illustrates how rich the possibilities of fantasy can be, for, like the best literature, it deals with the infinite scope of human life and imagination.

Susan Cooper's work represents the most dramatic perception in modern fantasy—the epic or heroic. This epic view should perhaps be seen, not so much as a new trend, but as a return of fantasy to its mythic roots. Earlier fantasies had evinced what could be done with touches of legendary material, as may be seen in George MacDonald's goblins, Beverly Nichols's witches, and the whole procession of legendary figures in Kipling's *Puck of Pook's Hill*. A generation or two later, Tolkien and C. S. Lewis exploited this vein even further. In the works since the 1960s by Susan Cooper, Alan Garner, William Mayne, Urusla LeGuin, Mollie Hunter, and others, the full possibilities of casting fantasy within the structure of legend have been realized.

Modern epic fantasies are distinguished by their close relationship to such heroic tales of old as King Arthur, Beowulf, and the Mabinogian. They are not in any way retellings but they employ much the same structures and themes. Like their prototypes, modern epic fantasy is chiefly concerned with the unending battle between good and evil which is fought out in wide but well-defined landscapes. This type of fantasy is not to be confused with "sword and sorcery"—those action-packed pulps with their muscular barbarians so luridly drawn in Robert Howard's *Conan*. Epic fantasy, like its forbears, is dominated by high purpose. There are worlds to be won or lost and the protagonists engage themselves in a deeply personal, almost religious battle for the common good.

Needless to say, not all contemporary fantasists employ the epic framework and themes. Fantasies such as *Tom's Midnight Garden* (Philippa Pearce), while in their way as profound as any, are quite distinct from the epic or heroic kinds. The tone is lighter and not so mythically charged as epic fantasy, even though in many instances a mythic image is at the heart of the matter. Such fantasies do have an enchantment about them, but their achievement lies not in heroic patterns but in the way in which they delicately transform reality. Their magic is gentle, but because it always rings so true and seems so real, it merits the term "enchanted realism," which, like most literary labels, is not entirely appropriate, for it is reality in its several dimensions, the kinds we are hard put to explain without recourse to naked formulas. Still, the term aptly suggests the subtlety and the mixture of naturalistic and supernatural that characterizes this type of writing. It can rest comfortably in the details of the domestic world, or surreptitiously slide into a magical domain. Its protagonists are pulled into another realm less often and with less dramatic surprise than those of epic fantasy.

The writers of enchanted realism are concerned more with human time than mythic time and with the personal development of the characters rather than with the primordial forces of good and evil. In *Tom's Midnight Garden* the struggle is that of Tom's endeavor to understand time and its relationship to himself rather than with mysteries outside his universe. Indeed, often in enchanted realism the protagonists finally comprehend the mysteries inside their universe, the mysteries that tend to be overlooked in everyday living. Then does the ordinary become the fabulous, as the smallest details of life are made radiant with meaning and power.

The beast tale or talking animal story, a third form of contemporary fantasy, is anything but new. Stories of talking animals are at least as old as Aesop and their appeal has remained constant. The fact that animals talk in these tales and yet act according to their species makes them at once the most totally alien and deeply credible of all fantasy, credible because they recall us to a time when humans were said to have understood the language of animals who were their teachers, brothers, and alter egos. They are also alien because we in no way experience any real communication with the animal world; what communication there is, is one way. We order them about. Stories of talking animals have two forms: the didactic beast tales, direct descendents of Aesop, exemplified by John Donovan's *Family*, and the more imaginative and poetic works which are closer to the mainstream of fantasy and may be termed animal fantasy, such as Randall Jarrell's *The Bat-Poet*.

Lightness, humor, and satire also find a place in the new fantasy. Rich in witty, shrewd perceptions of life this kind of fantasy follows the tradition of George MacDonald's playful *The Light Princess* and may itself be termed "light fantasy."

Most children's classics that have lasted from earlier times are fantasies, mainly because they are a literature least dependent upon the immediacy of time and surroundings. It is to be presumed that at least some of the modern fantasies will achieve a similar permanency in the literature of childhood. However, fantasists are trying for such heights and new perceptions that they expose themselves to greater chances of failure than do writers in other literary genres. All of the fantasies discussed here offer what Tolkien considered the most important effect in fantasy: "a catch of the breath, a beat and lifting of the heart . . . a tale that in any measure succeeds in this point has not wholly failed, whatever flaws it may possess, and whatever mixture or confusion of purpose." [1]

Epic and Heroic Fantasy

The most demonstrable change in epic fantasy is one of flow, but as if one were paddling upstream rather than down. From Victorian times until the present, fantasy worlds were seen as a place *to go to* and the protagonists were transported to them from their home environments. These worlds—Carroll's Wonderland and Looking-glass realms, Barrie's Never-Never Land, Baum's Oz, Lewis's Narnia —were often wholly and perfectly created. Some were worlds within worlds, such as MacDonald's *At the Back of the North Wind* and Rumer Godden's *The Doll's House*, or the natural world only lightly but believably touched with fantasy, as in the domestic forest of Beverley Nichols's *The Tree That Sat Down* and the seascape of Eric Linklater's *The Pirates in the Deep Green Sea*. Then there is Tolkien's Middle Earth, which exists from the first sentence of *The Hobbit*.

In all of these works the events are played out in a Secondary World, a retreat from our everyday surroundings. In most modern epic fantasy this process is reversed. The supernatural comes to the world as we know it, breaking into it and shattering the division between the real and the unreal. In William Mayne's *Earthfasts* (1966) a drummer boy of the eighteenth century suddenly comes drumming out of a cave into a sleepy English town, Stonehenge-like boulders move, wild boars run amok in the marketplace, and electrical forces cause one of the protagonists to disappear. In Alan Garner's *The Owl Service* (1967), a Welsh valley is invaded by the forces of a myth, and three modern young people are forced to replay an old tragedy. The classic depiction of the invasion of the real world by supernatural forces comes in Susan Cooper's *The Dark Is Rising*, which is almost a groundplan for modern epic fantasy.

1. J. R. R. Tolkien, *Tree and Leaf* (London: Unwin Books, 1964), p. 68.

> For the Dark, the Dark is rising. The Walker is abroad; the Rider
> is riding; they have woken; the Dark is rising.

The power which such a breakthrough by the supernatural into the
familiar can exercise is seen even in a bald summary of the events.

During the Twelve Days of Christmas in a Buckinghamshire
village of the present, the forces of evil (the Dark), which have been
latent for a while, rise with purposeful strength to put England in
jeopardy through an onslaught of snow and flood. These forces are
opposed by those of the Light (the "Old Ones"), whose ranks have
been strengthened by a new recruit, the youngest and last of the "Old
Ones." He is Will Stanton who celebrates his eleventh birthday just
before Christmas and who, because he is the seventh son of a seventh
son, is magic. Will is the quester, the gatherer of the talismans that
can help to conquer the Dark, the innocent, the link with the
everyday world.

Some of the "Old Ones" are legendary figures—Merriman Lyon
(Merlin), John Smith (Wayland Smith), King Arthur, all representing
good or High Magic. Eventually unleashed by the struggle is a more
primitive magic, the "Old Magic," here represented by Herne the
Hunter and his wild hounds. Since the "Old Magic" is objective and
amoral, no one knows which side it will take. It is only known that to
unleash it is dangerous. The Light wins, but only for a time. The
Dark will rise again. The struggle is unending.

This concept of the supernatural invading or breaking through
into the real world is an essential feature of recent fantasy. It is
apparent also in such different works as Lucy Boston's *An Enemy at
Green Knowe* (1964), where an alien evil enters the old house of Green
Knowe in the person of a powerful witch, Melanie Powers, or in
Robert Westall's *The Wind Eye* (1976), where the invader in the
present is an early Christian monk. Even in works that have a more
psychological tone an invasion usually takes place, although on a
different level, as in William Mayne's *A Game of Dark* (1971). Here the
unconscious mind of an unhappy boy, unable to cope with the reality
of his father's illness, is seized by the alien power of a gigantic worm:

> What had happened? Had it been only a dream? Had a girl
> shouted for him? What had been the urgency? Cold air fell from
> the window behind him, and he remembered another cold that
> had been on him, not long ago, and yet unreachably distant.

In Penelope Lively's *The House at Norham Gardens* (1974), a less
somber but just as forceful a work, which is on the edge of epic
fantasy, the dreams of a young girl, who has more responsibility than
she can always cope with, are entered by the forces of an aboriginal
dream-time. They come through time and space to demand her quest.

The juxtaposition of the real and the unreal in literature is not wholly new. The Iliad, with all its involvement with gods and goddesses, was set in an existing city. Lucian of Samosata in his *True Historie* (A.D. 200) writes of his trip to the moon with the authentic tone of a travelogue. The compilers of the medieval bestiaries described a manticore and a unicorn with the same attention to detail that they gave to a goat or a lion. In almost all early literature the factual and the visionary were seamlessly intertwined. The seams were torn apart in the eighteenth century with the Age of Reason and the rise of the natural sciences.

Modern fantasy does not fit the two worlds back together again, but, particularly in its epic form, it establishes fantasy as an "edge" literature: the protagonists and their worlds are poised on the edge of Darkness or Light, of dream, or memory, on the boundaries of time and space. In Garner's *Elidor* (1965), Malebron, the deus ex machina of the fantasy world, explains to the children the edge between the real world and its fantasy counterpart:

> "Wasteland and boundaries: places that are neither one thing nor the other, neither here nor there—these are the gates of Elidor."

That fantasy exists not beyond but on the edge of things is a concept borne out by image after image, such as the "spear-edge and shield-rim" of Elidor, or the prow of the ship *Ressure* in Westall's *The Wind Eye* which cuts its way back into time. And the edge is sharp, not blurry. If the story is to exist on boundaries, then all must be clear; mists and vagueness have no boundaries. It is these edges that give such fantasies their incredible suspense. The protagonists find themselves in precarious situations; there is danger in falling off the edge. They can lose not only their lives but their souls, as the Walker loses his in *The Dark Is Rising*. Here, too, Susan Cooper typifies the genre in the way she expresses the feeling of being poised between the known and the unknown. As Will Stanton goes to his bed on the first night of his adventure, the violence of the night invades the familiar comfort of his room; the feeling that he is hovering on the very edge of chaos is immediately shared by the reader.

Since the action is played out on the edge of things, there has come a change in the method of entry into the unreal. Or, more frequently there is no distinct entry, no linear narrative approach in real time. Thus the protagonists are no longer like Lucy, who can stand in Narnia and still look back to the reassuring light from the wardrobe door. Rather, like Will Stanton, they turn momentarily from a window and, upon looking back, find their familiar world transformed. Or, like Linda and Philip in Ruth Nichols's *The Marrow of the World* (1972), they look up and discover that a new, marvelous constellation has taken over the night sky. Modern fantasists are thus transformers and they engender a sense of wonder in readers, not so much by making us realize that the fantastic and the real can coexist, as by convincing us that they already do so. It is the shock of recognition that we experience, a feeling even more stirring perhaps than the thrill of discovery.

Although bridges between the worlds of reality and fantasy no longer seem necessary, physical objects may be employed to intensify the presence of the alien in the everyday world. In William Rayner's *Stag Boy* (1972), Jim is leading an ordinary boy's life until he finds an old antlered helmet, a shamanistic ritual headpiece, and upon putting it on is immediately seized by the power of the object. The precious blue stones in Jane Curry's *The Day Breakers* (1970) and the updated wardrobe in Penelope Farmer's *A Castle of Bone* (1972) are keys to the puzzles of the fantastic. Alan Garner's works too are imbued with these mythic totems. Susan's bracelet in *The Weirdstone of Brisingamen* (1960) holds Frigg's stone, the Brisingamen. The three physical objects in *Elidor* retain their power in the real world but change their shape. Alison, in *The Owl Service*, traces owls instead of flowers from a set of plates and in so doing releases the lock of an ancient, mythic tragedy. Susan Cooper, in *The Dark Is Rising* sequence, sends Will on a quest for the most ancient symbols of all:

> Wood, bronze, iron; water, fire, stone;
> Five will return, and one go alone.

It is imperative, however, to make clear that these physical objects are by no means used as "openers" to the fantasy world, in the way they were used in the older narratives. They do not parallel Carroll's rabbit hole or Mrs. Molesworth's cuckoo clock (*The Cuckoo Clock*, 1877), but rather they become integral parts of the plot.

Modern fantasists, in order to make the transition from the ordinary to the fabulous are far more likely to employ highly sophisticated techniques, often derived from cinematography: three-dimensional viewing; slow motion; fade-ins; superimposition; sharp, staccato dialogue; and fast-paced cutting from scene to scene. At times, the cuts are even from time period to time period, as in Alan Garner's *Red Shift* (1973), perhaps the apotheosis of this experimentation with cinematic style. With consummate skill Garner creates a totally new form heretofore alien to children's literature in his melding of so many groundbreaking themes and techniques. The dialogue of the teenage lovers in the modern time frame reads not as a novel but as a screen play:

"I'll not beg."
"You'll not what?"
"I'll not beg."
"You'll not take."
"No. But I'll not beg."
"Who talks like that?"
"What?"
"That's not how you talk."
"What?"
"Who?"
"What?"

Most writers use a more linear approach than does Garner in *Red Shift*. They do, however, incorporate compelling descriptions of physical feelings that transfer to literary form the cinematic experience of "sensurround." A change even can be effected through music alone. Will, in *The Dark Is Rising*, is

> woken by... delicate music, played by delicate instruments that he could not identify.... It had gone again. And when looked back through the window, he saw that his world had gone with it. In that flash, everything had changed.

In Joy Chant's *Red Moon and Black Mountain* (1970), an unseen piper in a tree (Pan) and the irrational behavior of the compass are the only indications that the inexplicable is about to occur. Chant's novel is fairly traditional in that the action takes place in the Other World of Vanderei, but the moment of passage is described briefly through the senses: of taste: "(Nicholas) tasted something bitter at the back of his throat, and would have cried out but he could find no voice"; touch: "All Nicholas could feel was Penelope's wrist in his hand, he could see nothing"; sound: "And instead of the singing silence there was the flutter of leaves, the rustle of grasses, and the song of birds"; smell: "The wind carried a strange scent to him, bitter-sweet, cold and wild." These physical sensations, which are not confined to initial moments of transformation, are recurring motifs. And as Donald, in Mayne's *A Game of Dark*, returns from his fantasy world he carries in his nose and throat the metallic odor of the worm which dominates that world:

> In his mouth and nostrils and throat there was a stench, metallic and rotten and piercing, the most foul he had ever known, and that was the worst thing and what made him feel so sick ... the stench was not only felt by the ordinary senses of taste and smell but sensed by the whole of his skin, and seemed to weigh in every bone.

Among the cinematic techniques, that of superimposition is

perhaps used most frequently. A real image becomes the basis for a fantastic image, the latter overlaying the former and on occasion enveloping it. In Cooper's *The Dark Is Rising*, the towering form of the Black Rider is superimposed upon that of a small island in the River Thames and later the same island crumbles and merges into the golden image of a magnificent Viking long ship.

Although this literary technique of superimposition is remarkably noticeable in the new epic fantasy, it is not confined to it. It also is used in fantasies that might be described as being midway between epic and "enchanted realism," fantasies such as Penelope Lively's *The House in Norham Gardens* (1974) and Penelope Farmer's *A Castle of Bone* (1972) in which the mythic sense is internalized rather than being based on external forces. Penelope Lively describes Clare's quasi-hallucinatory meeting with a primitive New Guinean tribe:

> Clare, going back across the lawn, could see herself in the kitchen window, a black figure advancing out of a blank white square.
>
> Except that the square wasn't quite blank. Somewhere at the back of it, behind her, there were those spiny things sticking straight up, massing together, quivering slightly, like a forest of spears, or bows and arrows, and behind them, hidden among them, shapes, forms?

Penelope Farmer, in *A Castle of Bone*, even uses the language of photography to express Hugh's perception of the land of the castle of bone:

> Instead he saw other images from that morning beside the river . . . there had been across the river a group of trees, and now in bed that image crowded out the nearer one. They were a group of willows and alders, dourer-looking than the pollarded willow trees.
>
> The group seemed to be closing in on him, rushing toward him through his head. In a moment he could focus on one tree only, in a moment more could see only an area of trunk quite close to him.

The passage is virtually a literary zoom lens, narrowing the picture from the general scene to a particular detail and thereby inviting the reader to follow Hugh's line of vision. The leisurely, gradual approach to the fantasy world rarely had a place in older fantasies; the invitation to enter was issued fairly quickly. Modern fantasists effect transition with the speed of a camera shutter and the invitation becomes almost a command.

In bringing the supernatural into the real world, modern fantasists have not only changed the form of fantasy but also its innermost core. Once magic is persuaded from legend into life—when it changes into, or is converted into, reality—it becomes more menacing. This has, in turn, changed the quality of the age-old struggle in fantasy between the good and the bad. While good remains much as it has always been, the opposing bad forces have been raised to the status of evil: evil implacable, evil unalloyed, evil for the sake of power, evil as opposed to good, evil existing simply because good exists. If, indeed, the key to life is the struggle between good and evil, then no modern literature expresses it as graphically or as wholeheartedly as the new epic fantasy.

Earlier writers tended to humanize the bad (evil rarely had a place). The bad characters had recognizable faults and deficiencies. Moreover they were reformable, capable of a redeeming self-awareness. With a little bit of help they could even achieve goodness. Thus Griselda, in Mrs. Molesworth's *The Cuckoo Clock* (1877), is somewhat grumbly and impatient but is gently corrected by the magical cuckoo. *Pinocchio* (1880) is boisterously naughty but conquers his faults with the help of the good fairy. To George MacDonald, evil was a perennial and strong force within us all, pushing our society into greed, selfishness, and immorality; but humankind had the capacity to redeem itself. Lewis's Narnia is a Christian land, with redemption possible for those who will learn. Eustace is saved from his ugly nature by Aslan's punishment of him; but in keeping with the concept of reward and punishment, the dwarfs in *The Last Battle*, who take no side in the war between good and bad out of selfish reasons, are refused entrance to "evangilium." Compared with the evil unleashed in modern epic fantasy, Lewis's White Witch, who made Narnia "always winter, but never Christmas," seems only a bored, petulant adult. The doll Marchpane in Rumer Godden's *The Doll's House* (1947) is perhaps the most forceful example of unreformable "bad" in these earlier books.

The forces of evil in the newer fantasies are rarely individualized, described, or even shown. For the most part they are *emanations* of evil—too big, too powerful, too pervasive to have shape or often even name. (Naming, of course, gives power to the namer in folklore and the new fantasists are very good folklorists). Some personification of the forces of "the Dark" in Susan Cooper's *The Dark Is Rising* quintet is given in the characters called the Rider, the Walker, and Mrs. Rowland, but these are only minions; the major threat is formless and incomprehensible. Will Stanton experiences it in a fear that came "As if some huge weight were pushing at his mind, threatening, trying to take him over, turn him into something he didn't want to be."

In some books the evil characters make only brief appearances, although their presence is felt throughout the story and, indeed, is the reason for it. Haggerak, whom we meet only at the end in Ruth Nichols's *A Walk Out of the World* (1968) and Ygerna in her *The Marrow of the World* (1972) exemplify such characters. More frequently evil is seen as an amorphous form, a shape-changer, as Death. Even in Lloyd Alexander's more comic approach to epic fantasy in his Prydain series, there is Arawin, the Death Lord, Master of Evil, the shape-changer who can only be seen in his fading shadow. The most awesome manifestation of epic evil comes in Joy Chant's *Red Moon and Black Mountain*. There are the subordinates—the black eagles, the Kunil-Bannoth, and Fendarl—whom Oliver meets in hand-to-hand combat. But the real evil is met only at the end: "the great enemy; He Whose Name is Taken Away, that Prince of Heaven whom he had always called Lucifer, Star of the Morning."

In a purely literary sense, this idea of the facelessness of evil may be a borrowing from Tolkien, as so much of modern fantasy is. Sauron, in *The Lord of the Rings*, never appears in any scene and yet he dominates the whole work. The modern concept of evil really derives more from philosophy than literature. Modern fantasists see evil in a metaphysical way; it must be battled with, but it will always abide. Ultimately this idea rests upon and reflects a basically different set of convictions about the nature of the world from those held by earlier fantasists. To the Greeks, the good was something that mankind chose naturally. To the Romans, evil *could* win; it was seductive and had to be resisted. The Victorians believed in progress, in the raising of mankind to the level of a superior human being. Evil could be overcome if one simply showed reason and common sense and, of course, one could count on a steady increase in these traits as education spread.

However, the early twentieth century experienced two world wars and Nazism. Until then it had probably never been seen so clearly that ordinary people could become agents of malevolence, caught up in a great awesome evil that seemed beyond the power of the individual to combat. It is perhaps no accident, that most of the practitioners of epic fantasy are British, having either been children or young people when those wars broke out. Nor can it be an accident that most of this fiction has a kind of battlefield setting, or at least takes its images from the idea of a titanic struggle.

The writers of epic fantasy do not neglect psychological evil, although it is frequently there by implication rather than statement. David, in *Earthfasts*, allows himself to be conquered by the power of the candle and suffers thereby; Donald Jackson in Mayne's *A Game of Dark* is struggling with his feelings for his father as he fights the worm of the folktale; Alan Garner, in *The Owl Service*, brilliantly

91

underpins the real world with the mythological one, but at the end the struggle is one for Alison's mind. Ursula LeGuin's *A Wizard of Earthsea* (1968), which is played out in a traditional Secondary World, is really a psychological struggle for wholeness; Ged must finally turn and embrace the evil in himself, his Jungian shadow. The image of the battlefield remains however, even when the struggle is one in the minds and hearts of the characters. Whatever form evil takes, it is certainly a far cry from earlier fantasies in which the protagonists are opposed to a cunning but physical presence. There are few contemporary counterparts to the ordinary nastiness of Shift, the ape, in C. S. Lewis's *The Last Battle*.

Good is still viewed as the norm, however, the stability and security of the everyday round. The representatives of this view are usually average, everyday children, the kids next door. Modern fantasists seem to be saying, "The good is what we have, so hold fast." Thus, once the children in Penelope Lively's *The Whispering Knights* (1971) have battled Morgan Le Fay to save the village from a freeway, all returns to normal, the children especially, to their everyday lives. Will, in *The Dark Is Rising* and Ged, in *A Wizard of Earthsea*, do have supernatural powers, but Will is helped by the unmagical Drew children and Ged is but one wizard among many in the magical world of Earthsea. On the surface at least, good is thus likely to be seen as dull alongside the stronger colors of Evil, which seems to flaunt itself and be more impressive, like Milton's Satan. No children's fantasist has as yet created a counterpart to the charismatic, yet vulnerable "good" characters of Charles Williams, the adult novelist, in his religious fantasies. Less superficially, however, both sides are balanced. There can be no Light without Darkness, no Darkness without Light.

To serve this cosmic approach to good and evil, modern epic fantasists use myth as a springboard. Myth is the literature that above all fuses reality and fantasy and makes large statements about life. The battle is always between black and white, right and wrong; there is no room for the gray or the in-between. Modern fantasy, in its desire for strength and intensity of conceptualization, borrows heavily from this older form of literature. Moreover, myth adds another important element, the high seriousness that comes from its religious origin. Indeed, the mythic element in modern fantasy gives a quasi-religious tone to the narrative; we are persuaded that we are concerned with major moral issues, that the very stability and continuity of our world is at stake. This is in contrast to the magical, almost capricious supernatural effects of older fantasies: Peter Pan can fly; Mary Poppins can slide *up* a bannister; the Nesbit children always have a talisman—and so the magic begins. Epic fantasy uses not only the figures from myth but also its comprehensive view of life. Explanations are not given because the suggestion is that, as implied in every mythology, this is simply the way things really are. The sense of the mythic world gradually commingles with the everyday one, since the one is as "real" as the other.

Actual use of the mythic material varies greatly. Alan Garner bases *The Owl Service* on a complete story from the *Mabinogion*, but gives it a modern setting. William Mayne in *Earthfasts* and Penelope Lively in *The Whispering Knights* introduce only a slight strain of the Arthurian legend, while Susan Cooper in *The Dark Is Rising* sequence and Alan Garner in *The Weirdstone of Brisingamen* and *The Moon of Gomrath* work in so much of Celtic and Norse myth that their narratives seem almost an extension of the original material. Patricia McKillip in *The Forgotten Beasts of Eld* (1974) plunges us into a medieval world of myth and Dahlov Ipcar in *The Queen of Spells* (1973) recreates the folktale world of the ballad of Tamlane.

There is even a group based on the Scottish myths of the Selkie, the singing seals, which includes such varied works as Mollie Hunter's *A Stranger Came Ashore* (1975), Rosemary Harris's *The Seal-Singing* (1971) and Ronald Lockley's *The Seal Woman* (1974). Mollie Hunter in both *The Haunted Mountain* (1972) and *The Wicked One* (1977) blends a whole world of Scottish folklore and legend into psychological dramas of man's struggle with the Other World.

Some writers eschew the familiar world of European myth for the fresher impact of indigenous material. Christie Harris's *Secret in the Stlalakum Wild* (1972) is based on Canadian Indian legend. Sheila Moon's *Knee-Deep in Thunder* (1967) reflects Navajo myth; Patricia Wrightson, in *The Nargun and the Stars* (1973) and *The Ice Is Coming* (1977), adeptly employs Australian aboriginal myths.

Considering the widespread use of mythic material, it is of considerable significance that Greek myths are not used. It is easy to see why. They exhibit little or no struggle between good and evil and the turn of events is frequently based on the petulance of a god's desire, thus making mortals simply chance victims. Overall, Greek myths are bathed in a golden pagan light. Norse and Celtic myths on the other hand contain the powerful element of Ragnarok, the struggle against great odds and the ultimate hope for recovery and redemption. They were, after all, written down in Christian times and so are a blend of the spiritual and the primitive, a contrast that is well used in epic fantasy.

For all the variety of mythic material that fantasists draw upon, certain themes or elements occur frequently. The "high" or good magic is often represented by a Merlin-figure: Merriman Lyon in *The Dark Is Rising*, Malebron in *Elidor*, Cardellin in *The Weirdstone of*

Brisingamen, the Archmage in *A Wizard of Earthsea.* Opposed to these are the often nameless and faceless forces of evil that seem to derive from the early Christian idea of Satan. On the fringes of the action are the forces of the oldest magic representing the old pagan worlds, the primitive, objective, amoral powers which it is dangerous to rouse. In Joy Chant's *Red Moon and Black Mountain* an inhabitant of the land of Vandarei explains the primitive earth mother to Nicholas, one of the three children to be seized from their own world to help save Vandarei:

> 'She is one of the oldest spirits of the earth. She knows no law but one, and it is better for all that she should be under the earth and not over it, Vir'Vachal she is. Vir'Vachal! Oh, Vir'Vachal! Deep have they delved indeed, to wake the earth magic.'

Related to this primitive magic is the primitive or primeval side of onself. Both these aspects are present even in the humorous and almost farcical kind of epic fantasy represented by works such as Mollie Hunter's *The Wicked One.* This book recounts the adventures of Colin Grant, a forester and crofter whose quick temper brought great trouble upon himself and his family. For it was Colin's temper that drew to him the mischievous Grollican, the Other World creature known as "the wicked one." Like the poltergeist, the Grollican will not willingly leave its victim, and thus begins the strange relationship between Colin and the world of Faery. His struggles to escape the Grollican take him from the haunted hills of Scotland to the new world of America, but ultimately it is with his own character, his uncontrollable temper, with which he must come to grips.

With the use of myth, and particularly the "old Magic," modern fantasists have not only brought the "dream-time" of the human race into the modern world but they have also brought us to the realization that myths are the dreams of society in an archetypal, Jungian sense. The individual fantasy is the individual dream of the writer. George MacDonald was one of the few of the older fantasists who understood this intuitively and his fantasies, although all written in the 1870s, seem very modern because of the mythic sense inherent in the presence of Irene's grandmother and in the caves of the goblins in his *The Princess and the Goblin,* and in the primitive objective portrayal of North Wind in his *At the Back of the North Wind.*

Lewis Carroll and John Ruskin and other, subsequent, writers up to the 1950s, although frequently employing allegory, did not draw upon mythic images and dreams. By contrast, C. S. Lewis tells us that his *The Lion, The Witch and the Wardrobe* began with the image of a faun carrying an umbrella, Ruth Nichols that *A Walk Out of the World* emerged with the dream of an Indian longhouse, and Susan Cooper that *The Dark Is Rising* came from translating the image of a New England winter landscape into that of the forces of the Dark and the Light. One senses that most writers of epic, mythic fantasy begin with a visual, symbolic image arising from myth or the archetypes of dream and the subconscious, rather than from the more formal structure of plot and story line.

This mythic sense also controls the settings of the fantasies these writers create. By and large their tales of epic fantasy are played out in open spaces and in real, recognizable settings. There is no need for elaborate maps. Whereas Tolkien's imaginary land of Middle Earth seemed to require a cartographer as well as a narrator, a simple county map of Cornwall or Buckinghamshire would serve to explicate Susan Cooper's topography or a coastal map of Northumbria for Robert Westall's *The Wind Eye*. Just so, all that the children have at their disposal in *Elidor* is a street map of Manchester.

Conversely, there are few domestic scenes in epic fantasy. When they occur they are mostly used as a contrast to the great outdoor adventures and as a means of keeping the protagonists poised on edge. The home is seen as the last bastion of security and normality and the terror increases if it is invaded, as is Will's living room by one of the minions of the Dark on Christmas Day in *The Dark Is Rising*. Inanimate objects such as the electrical appliances in Alan Garner's *Elidor*, may also be affected by the forces of evil. Here, indeed, Garner shows a brief but superb sense of domestic comedy. Anyone who has sat impatiently watching someone else try to adjust a television set, convinced that one can do it better oneself, will appreciate Garner's handling of just such a scene. There is more than a touch of irony between the fantasy world of Elidor and that of the television western implied in the following sentence, as the children return to their home in Manchester:

> The sittingroom door opened, and there stood Mrs. Watson, and behind her a thousand redskins bit the dust.

Another great change that can be identified in epic fantasy is the concept of children and childhood. Victorian fantasies, and those up to the 1950s, exhibit a fascination with childhood; children's feelings and lives are described with sympathy and accuracy. As late as 1954 most of the children were like Martha in Edward Eager's *Half Magic*, who says impatiently after reading Nesbit's *The Enchanted Castle*: "Why don't things like that ever happen to *us*?" Then, of course, they do. These were children with leisure; they could wait for things to happen. They were also children with imagination and curiosity and they sought adventure. Their attitude is perhaps best expressed by Lewis Carroll's Alice, who blithely followed the White Rabbit down the hole, "never once considering how in the world she was to get out again." Or by C. S. Lewis's Lucy who entered the world of Narnia feeling a little frightened, but "inquisitive and excited as well."

The children in present-day fantasies do not have a chance to express curiosity or to be enticed by wonder. After only a brief moment of hesitation they are seized by a supernatural force. They are drawn unwittingly and often unwillingly across the border between reality and fantasy. The moment of transition is one of fear as they are seized and shaken by the supernatural.

Will Stanton of *The Dark Is Rising* has had a strange day with events that he has not yet understood. But at night in bed:

> And then in a dreadful furious moment, horror seized him like a nightmare made real; there came a wrenching crash, with the howling of the wind suddenly much louder and closer and a great blast of cold; and the Feeling came hurtling against him with such force of dread that it flung him cowering away.

For Linda and Philip in Ruth Nichols's *The Marrow of the World* the fear begins when they go out in a rowboat at night on a lake:

> and at the same instant a figure of ghostly brightness came shimmering up from the depths of the lake and broke the surface not four feet from the rowboat. Linda's cry was stifled in her throat. . . . For an instant they were silent, trembling. "Let's get out of here," said Philip.

Oliver in Joy Chant's *Red Moon and Black Mountain* is co-opted into the Secondary World before his brother and sister:

> Then he heard the children call him, and turned.
> His skin faded to dead white, and stone cold. He shook all over and gave a hoarse cry.

Occasionally there is a moment of rebellion. Roland, the youngest of the four children in *Elidor*, refuses to help Malebron save Elidor, claiming, "I don't care! It's nothing to do with me!" But after hearing Malebron's explanation, he gives in. Most of the children in these books really have no choice; they have been singled out, fated for the work they have to do. Nicholas of *Red Moon and Black Mountain* realizes despairingly that "There's only me. Only me who's free and who knows. . . . It's up to me." When Susan in Garner's *The Weirdstone of Brisingamen* is asked if she will help to defeat the evil forces, she replies, "Of course I will. I've no choice, really."

It seems therefore that the carefree quality which one associates with children is frequently negated, not only by virtue of the forced entry of the children into the action, but also because of the awesome responsibility they carry in the mighty struggles that ensue. The children are not engaged in a happy, sunny adventure but in a "game of dark." There is evil to be overcome and a world to be saved. Of course the children still have some childlike qualities; in fact they have been chosen because they do have them. They have freshness; they are not yet flawed with mundane compromises; they have untested courage.

They are also still children in the sense that they are not usually alienated from their parents, as are many of the protagonists in realistic fiction. Nor do the parents play an active role in the events. This is usurped by a surrogate parent figure, generally the Merlin character from the supernatural world, or an older person from the real world, such as Mrs. Hepplewhite in Penelope Lively's *The Whispering Knights*, or Bess and Farmer Gower in Alan Garner's *The Weirdstone of Brisingamen*. However, this dependency is not overdone. Once the young protagonists have been instructed in the needs of the quest, they must complete it on their own. "Will wished, not for the first time, that Merriman were with him to ease such difficulties." But at this point the young hero of Cooper's *The Grey King* must "go it alone."

Because the children in epic fantasy are so often an instrument for the play of great powers, whether for good or evil, they are frequently presented as being nonrealistic, or rather suprarealistic, characters. Earlier fantasists frequently presented their protagonists as lonely or alienated children, exemplified by Jill and Eustace in C. S. Lewis's *The Silver Chair*, whose special sensitivity or troubles draw them into adventure. There are some modern counterparts, of course: Donald Jackson in Mayne's *A Game of Dark* and Ged in LeGuin's *A Wizard of Earthsea* are perhaps the most striking examples. But, for the most part, the protagonists of epic fantasy are rather featureless children whose interest lies in the part they play in the drama rather than in themselves as people.

This symbolic role is most evident in those frequent instances where the children are given names that evoke characters from myth and legend and therefore indicate what types the children are meant to represent. Sybel of Patricia McKillip's *The Forgotten Beasts of Eld* is indeed a sibyl; Roland of *Elidor* is "Childe Roland"; and Roger of Susan Cooper's *Over Sea and Under Stone*, the first book of her *The Dark Is Rising* sequence, is introduced as having an affinity for the King Arthur stories. Lacking individuality, the child characters in modern epic fantasy are thus closer to Hardy's portrayal of Tess in *Tess of the D'Urbervilles* than they are to George Moore's remarkably similar story of *Esther Waters*. Esther engages our sympathy because she is so realistically portrayed. But our perception of Tess's tragedy is somewhat more disturbing because it is both more remote and more cosmic. The flesh-and-blood part of Tess diminishes in proportion to our realization of the malevolent forces that are working their way through her life. The practitioners of modern epic fantasy are more inclined to create Tesses than Esthers.

Although all good fantasy takes itself seriously, there is an almost awesome seriousness to many of these modern books; they seek to convince us that the adventure has momentous consequences. This solemnity can best be seen when one compares an epic fantasy with a "magic story" of the less imposing kind. Compared to the compelling belief exhibited by the children in the epic fantasies, Patricia Wrightson's children are positively frivolous. *An Older Kind of Magic* (1972) deals with supernatural happenings, but at the end of the story the children are not really convinced that the supernatural has occurred:

> When it [the adventure] began, they hardly knew what to believe; they were poised between comet-magic and ordinary life. When the giggling was over, they had come down on the side of ordinary life. They would never forget this fantastic evening, but neither would they believe in it.

Bran and Will, upon conclusion of the adventures in Cooper's *Silver on the Tree*,

> saw the familiar tall figure, standing very erect, with the fierce-nosed profile and the springing shock of white hair, blowing a little now in the wind that had risen out of nowhere. It was an image that would flicker in and out of their dreams for the rest of their lives, even when they had forgotten all else.

Writers of epic fantasy have set themselves an incredibly hard task. If they have not actually revolutionized fantasy, they have turned it into one of the most innovative types of writing of our time and, indeed, have set high goals, not only for other types of fantasy but for the children's novel in general. Perhaps their greatest achievement has been to resolve the paradoxes of fantasy. Writers such as Cooper, Mayne, Garner, Lively, Farmer, LeGuin, Westall, Chant, Nichols, and Hunter move surefootedly through time and space and mingle myth and reality with ease and flair. They walk a tightrope, not like children showing off, but like skilled acrobats balancing without a net. They are craftsmen and stylists daring new types of narrative form, especially in the use of elliptical conversation and cinematic images. And they develop as writers. One need only compare the rather ordinary *Over Sea, Under Stone*, Susan Cooper's first fantasy, with *The Dark Is Rising*, which appeared nine years later;

The Weirdstone of Brisingamen, Alan Garner's first book, with *The Owl Service* or *Red Shift.* Nor, with few exceptions, do they confine themselves to this one genre. Almost all of them are equally at home in other forms of writing or other types of fantasy.

Perhaps their greatest achievement is to make us see our universe as a whole. Penelope Farmer, in an article on myth,[2] suggests that science is really only now catching up with myth. She notes that modern physicists are proclaiming that the universe is a paradox, that matter, energy, space, time are all one and interchangeable—as the myths, poets, and mystics have always proclaimed them to be. Modern epic fantasists have now joined this community and are deeply involved in bringing together the essence of this knowledge, along with their own personal visions.

Enchanted Realism

In contrast to the "Sturm und Drang" of epic fantasy, with its cosmic battles and invaders from the mythic past, such fantasies as *Tom's Midnight Garden* (1958), Lucy Boston's *Green Knowe* sequence (1954–1976), or Natalie Babbitt's *Tuck Everlasting* (1975) seem made of gossamer. But the seeming fragility of their narratives is only an illusion. Their organic structure is like that of last year's leaf, fine, yet surprisingly strong enough to retain its integrity, though the ravages of winter have reduced it to a webwork of veins. Take away the air of wonder, mystery, and strangeness—take away the fantasy—and a strong framework of realism remains. While epic fantasy keeps the protagonists and the readers poised on the edge of what one may call two worlds, "enchanted realism" gradually penetrates the imagination, blending fantasy and reality through a distortion of time and space.

The imagery in enchanted realism is more subtle than that of epic fantasy. In *Tom's Midnight Garden* the children's imaginative games and wanderings through the rich, intricate landscape of the garden are held in check by garden walls. But the walls are also there for climbing, to give an extensive view of the world outside, and they open out to the freedom and danger of skating on the river of ice. Just so, the sheltered security of childhood gives way to the open spaces of adulthood and maturity.

These books restore to children's literature the traditional picture

2. Penelope Farmer, "On the Effects of Collecting Myth for Children and Others," *Children's Literature in Education* 8, no. 4:176–85 (Winter 1977).

of childhood that had held from Victorian times until the 1960s. In them childhood is still seen as a state separate from adulthood and the adventures the children encounter are a product of their own devising, their own serious play and imaginings, from which they emerge more matured and ready to accept approaching adulthood. This is in strong contrast both to epic fantasy, where the characteristics demanded of the children are immediate responsibility, courage, and resourcefulness and in even stronger contrast to the "problem" novel where the children have to cope with adult problems.

Like all fantasies, the books of enchanted realism have to provide a mechanism and raison d'être for the departure from reality to enchantment. The usual means is to portray the child characters as highly sensitive persons who feel emotionally imprisoned by the ennui and tension imposed by their surroundings. They are looking for a way out and it comes by way of magic.

Tom, in *Tom's Midnight Garden*, is bored and restless, confined to the dull, gardenless flat of his aunt and uncle while his brother recovers from the measles at home. Under the spur of loneliness, he enters the dreams of an old woman, Mrs. Bartholomew, who lives alone at the top of the house, and discovers there a Victorian mansion, its garden, and the Victorian child Hatty, who is Mrs. Bartholomew as a child, with whom he plays. Zan, in Norma Fox Mazer's *Saturday, the Twelfth of October* (1975), is emotionally wrenched apart when her brother discovers her diary and reads it to his friends. She escapes to the primitive world of "The People," who are not only close to nature but to one another, everyone sharing, talking, and touching. In her own ugly city and crowded apartment there is no communication. Fourteen-year-old Clare Mayfield in Penelope Lively's *The House in Norham Gardens* (1974), has the chief responsibility for the welfare of her brilliant, kind, eccentric, elderly aunts, a burden which is at times too much for her. Her dreams are invaded by a primitive New Guinea tribe whose ways had been studied by her Victorian grandfather. Clare discovers the diary of his anthropological journeys and a ritual shield in the attic of the old Victorian mansion, and the dreams come closer to reality.

But not all the children escape into dreams because the everyday world presses upon them too closely. Young David in Randall Jarrell's *Fly by Night* (1976) lives an idyllic life in the country, playing in the forest and his tree house with his cat and dog. But there is a need to get beyond the everyday world, no matter how satisfying it may be. So at night David flies. His floating night journeys take him through the known world of parents and animals, home, farm, and forest.

Some of these books of enchanted realism are set in a time gone by, giving the illusion of a dream. William Mayne's *A Year and a Day* (1976) is set in a Cornish village of several centuries past, while Natalie Babbitt's *Tuck Everlasting* (1975) is contained within a small American town in 1880. In Lucy Boston's *Green Knowe* series the old house is so steeped in atmosphere that we know that anything strange and wonderful can happen.

Writers of enchanted realism are chiefly concerned with time, human time, not with mythic or primeval figures breaking in from the past. One might debate whether or not King Arthur and his knights really existed, but enchanted realism convinces readers that they have existed and do exist. The children go into various times and return and in so doing face the implacable cycle of life, time, birth, and death. Zan's teacher, in *Saturday, the Twelfth of October*, says: "Imagine time as a curving ribbon in space, an infinite curve without beginning or ending."

In *Tom's Midnight Garden* Tom and Hatty come together across boundaries of time and dreaming because of their need and desire for each other. Both the Victorian Hatty and the twentieth-century Tom had longed for someone to play with and for somewhere to play; and that great longing, beating about unhappily in the great house, made its entry into old Mrs. Bartholomew's dreaming mind and turned her back into the little Hatty of long ago. Going back in time, she is able to take Tom with her. The striking sense of a haunted beautiful dream, a desire so strong that it alters reality and transforms time and space, pervades the book. Metaphysical questions on the nature of time, reality, ghost-lives, and dreams hang heavy in the air. Tom eventually loses his garden and his child-friend, Hatty, with great pain, but rediscovers her as an old woman with joy and wonder:

> Afterwards, Aunt Gwen tried to describe to her husband that second parting between them. "He ran up to her, and they hugged each other as if they had known each other for years and years, instead of only having met for the first time this morning. There was something else, too, Alan, although I know you'll say it sounds even more absurd. . . . Of course, Mrs. Bartholomew's such a shrunken little old woman, she's hardly bigger than Tom, anyway: but, you know, he put his arms right round her and he hugged her good-bye as if she were a little girl."

In his newfound recognition of Time and its meaning, Tom has made a real friend more important than his dream one.

Natalie Babbitt's *Tuck Everlasting*, like *Tom's Midnight Garden*, strives to capture the essence of humanity's struggle with the mystery of time. The plot is based on one of humankind's greatest yearnings, the search for immortality and the Fountain of Youth. The

Tuck family have drunk from such a spring and have unwittingly become immortal, trapped in the same bodies and ages forever, eternal observers as the cycle of life and death passes them by. As Tuck says:

> dying's part of the whole wheel, right there next to being born. You can't pick out the pieces you like and leave the rest. Being part of the whole thing, that's the blessing. But it's passing us by, us Tucks. Living's heavy work, but off to one side, the way *we* are, it's useless too. It don't make sense. If I knowed how to climb back on the wheel, I'd do it in a minute. You can't have living without dying. So you can't call it living, what we got. We just *are*, we just *be*, like rocks beside the road.

Ten-year-old Winnie, who becomes involved with the Tucks' affairs, grows as an individual through an awareness of the patterns of life and death. She gains both the ability to love and to sacrifice something of herself for others, and her final decision to reject the temptations of immortality for human joys and cares is a measure of new understanding and maturity.

William Mayne's *A Year and a Day* is also a story of life, death, and time, but it is condensed, as its title suggests, into a brief span. In contrast to the earthiness of Natalie Babbitt's *Tuck Everlasting*, it is a quiet, luminous work evoking the symbolism of Blake's *Songs of Innocence* and *Songs of Experience*. But, like *Tuck Everlasting*, it is based on a myth related to time—in this instance not the Fountain of Youth, but the ancient sacrifices that were connected with the renewal of the seasons, particularly the midsummer rituals.

The plot of *A Year and a Day* is almost too delicate to describe. Like most books of its type, it is not governed by the kind of strong, overriding theme that characterizes epic fantasy. Here a lost fairy child is found on midsummer's day and adopted into a family with two young sisters. Adam, as the girls name him, is referred to throughout as sacred, holy, a "Pigsy," a fairy child. Like Diamond, in George MacDonald's *At the Back of the North Wind* (1871), the uncanny visitor is too pure for this mortal, flawed world. He speaks many tongues, sharing the language and knowledge of birds, bells, stones, fish, but never learning human speech. He is like an artist or animal in his heightened perceptions; his otherworldly awareness is so extreme that he cannot truly sleep until his deeper sleep of death. When Adam dies, he is replaced by a new male child, who also replaces a child lost earlier to the mother and father.

A Year and a Day is, in a way, a gentle story of the inevitableness of death, in the manner of E. B. White's *Charlotte's Web*. Like Wilbur in *Charlotte's Web*, the children, Sara and Becca, come into a greater maturity and understanding of life and death. As in most of Mayne's writing the prose is lucid, quick, and understated, with a precise attention to landscape details and to the warmth and humor of character, family, and village relationships.

Time is also seen as multidimensional in Penelope Lively's *The House in Norham Gardens*. The twentieth century is represented by Clare and by the working girl who rents a room in the house. The contrast in outlook between the two characters offers an interesting depiction of the range of views that characterizes our own time. The immediate past is contained in the aunts' recollections of their busy intellectual lives when younger. The more distant past comes through Clare's grandfather's diary, as he describes the life of the New Guinea tribe. Clare sees the tribesmen in her dreams.

> Rounding a corner, she came upon them quite suddenly, in a clearing where there were low round huts, thatched, and open fires. Small dark people they were, and there were children, squatting in the dust, and pig-like animals, and dogs.

Clare feels that the natives want their ritual shield returned to them, the shield taken away by her grandfather. It is their link with their past. But then she sees them in their modern stage:

> The men wore shirts and khaki shorts, and most of them had cigarette stubs in the corners of their mouths, or tucked behind an ear. The women had cotton dresses on.... In front of the shop a group of the men were clustered around something, huddled over it in silence. Going up to them, and leaning over them, she saw that it was a transistor radio.

It is too late to return the shield. This alien culture is further represented in Clare's real world by her friendship with John, an African student, who is able to make an immediate link with the ritual shield. To him it is not something alien from an alien time. But the book suggests more than just the continuum of time. We are to see that the individual holds the collective unconscious of mankind.

In Eleanor Cameron's faster-paced *The Court of the Stone Children* (1973), with its intriguing mystery from Napoleonic times, Nina steps into the past by way of reading a journal and dreams her way to the heart of the mystery. Dr. Patrick is asked his opinion of prophetic dreams:

> "I'm a physicist," he said, "who takes delight in the Uncertainty Principle ... somehow I'm convinced that in creation there's something strange in the proportion, something reasoning can never quite get at, and I hope it never will...."

Much of the atmosphere in *The Court of the Stone Children* comes from the museum where the girl from the past makes her presence felt:

> [Nina] was surrounded by vistas, by depths and airiness, distances along green-golden halls that ended in enormous windows through which could be seen boughs moving in the sun and the shadow. The whole place seemed mysteriously alive.

A great deal of enchanted realism takes its aura from a house or from a narrow space—a Victorian mansion, a quiet village, a garden. Even "The People" in the primitive world described in *Saturday, the Twelfth of October* do not move far from familiar ground and are always happiest and safest in their caves.

For Lucy Boston the manor house, Green Knowe, has been a presence since her own childhood and so it affects the sensibilities of her characters:

> Inside, partly because of the silence within the massive stone walls, partly because of the complexity of incurving shapes, you get a unique impression of time as a co-existent whole. I cannot tell you with what sense you know it. It is simply given.[3]

In *The Children of Green Knowe* (1954) the events are real enough: Tolly's visit to Green Knowe, his loneliness, the growth of his relationship with his grandmother, and the awakening of his imagination, sparked both by Mrs. Oldknow's personality and the profusion of mirrors: 'In this house,' said Tolly, 'everything is twice!' Eventually Mrs. Oldknow convinces Tolly and the reader that 'there isn't anything real except thoughts' and that there the past and the present are meshed:

> It was queer to hear the baby's sleepy whimper only in the next room, now, and so long ago. 'Come we'll sing it too,' said Mrs. Oldknow, going to the spinet. She played, but it was Tolly who sang alone, while, four hundred years ago, a baby went to sleep.

Although the writers of enchanted realism see time as Einstein's "river" or space as McLuhan's "global village," they also see childhood as a continuum. If the children go into time, they also return from it and are changed by the experience, but gently. They do not reject their experience, they want to hold on to it, sensing that they have been privileged. An example is Zan who, in *Saturday, the Twelfth of October* by Norma Mazer (1975), finally gives in to the

3. Lucy Boston, "A Message from Green Knowe," *Horn Book* 39:259 (June 1963).

school psychologist and admits that she has merely had a dream that lasted one day instead of the eleven months of her sojourn with "The People." But at the end, she says fiercely to herself: "Am I going to be like everyone else? Afraid. Forgetting everything. Oh, please don't let me forget! Please." Writers of enchanted realism do not offer solutions to specific dilemmas; they offer instead a gentle but courageous view of life as a whole. Issues of morality and values are suggested but lightly and obliquely. They take the ordinary world and add to it splinters or twists or auras of fantasy and, small though they are, the elements of enchantment change the entire focus, making it more real rather than more unreal.

In such works there is no place for sentimentality or flabbiness of writing, as might be expected. Each book has a highly individual style. Randall Jarrell in *Fly by Night* blends clear musical prose and poetry in a dream-like saga that is deeply satisfying in its peaceful, almost somnambulistic tone. Natalie Babbitt has a more down-to-earth tone in *Tuck Everlasting* with her adroitly drawn eccentric characters and with the music and pungencies of southern country dialect. William Mayne's *A Year and a Day* is quiet and luminous, while Eleanor Cameron's *The Court of the Stone Children* and Penelope Lively's *The House in Norham Gardens* are replete with the lively, everyday speech of the young. But all have a cleanness and certitude in their writing style.

In many ways these fantasies of enchanted realism resemble the older ones, *Peter Pan, The Hobbit, The Doll's House*, more than do the epic fantasies. In all of them the protagonists change inwardly because of their adventures. But in these new fantasies the inner landscape of the mind is explored much more deeply and sensitively.

Beast Tales and Animal Fantasy

The seventeenth-century philosopher John Locke wrote much about the young which could only be appreciated many years later, but his suggestion of an illustrated Aesop's *Fables* as the best book for enticing children to read was quickly taken up by educators of his day. [4] A pragmatist, Locke had probably observed children's fondness for animals and their unique ability to consider an animal as an equal. He was also concerned that education should consciously

4. From the *Osborne Catalogue of Early Children's Books*, Toronto Public Library, 1975, it can be seen that a Latin Aesop was being used as a schoolbook as early as 1582.

impart moral values. No wonder he recommended Aesop's *Fables*, with its animal characters depicting human traits, notably weaknesses, as the ideal introduction to reading. Would he have come to the same conclusion about today's stories of talking animals? These are, in general, as highly moralistic as Aesop's. Some of them, at least, are as easily readable and intelligent, if not touched with Aesop's comic wit and genius for the pithy. But Locke, the supreme fighter for human (even children's) rights of his time, might well be horrified at the misanthropy of much of today's writers.

Locke in all probability would not have considered animal tales to be fantasy, else he would have forbidden them. Nor did J. R. R. Tolkien who excluded such works as "Reynard the Fox," "Brer Rabbit," "The Three Little Pigs," and *The Wind in the Willows* from his definition of Faerie:

> In stories in which no human being is concerned; or in which the animals are the heroes and heroines, and men and women, if they appear, are mere adjuncts; and above all those in which the animal form is only a mask upon a human face, a device of the satirist or the preacher, in these we have beast-fable and not fairy-story.[5]

Tolkien's specific term "beast-fable" appears to have fallen out of favor and, just as any story set in the future is deemed science fiction, so any book that today uses talking animals as protagonists is labeled "animal fantasy." In such a book we are asked to suspend our disbelief chiefly in the matter of speech—the animals talk the language of humans—and, in that of plot and action, to remember that the characters are dressed in fur or feathers or scales rather than skin, often only as the "mask upon a human face." The paradox is that humanization can only be successful if something is preserved of the animal nature. All depends on the fact, although in different ways, that animals behave like themselves masquerading as humans; the animal nature must never masquerade. Briefly, the more animals are anthropomorphized, the less successful the book. Richard Adams in *Watership Down* (1972) quite consistently keeps his rabbits rabbit-like, while the failure of Niel Hancock's *Dragon Winter* (1978) can be largely ascribed to the human-like actions of his animals who live and act like humans, as Granny Badger with her "silver-handled tea mug."

Yet within these generalizations there appear to be two strains of the talking animal story. The strongest, with the most ancient lineage, is the beast tale, the direct descendant of Aesop, La Fontaine, and

5. J. R. R. Tolkien, *Tree and Leaf* (London: Unwin Books, 1964) p. 22

John Gay. Like folklore, the beast tale was at first the preserve of both adult and children. But because of its inherent moralizing framework, it fairly quickly played a large part in the early development of children's literature. Following Locke, although without his clear vision toward Aesop, were dozens of English books such as Catharine Parr Traill's *Little Downy* (1822), the story of a field mouse, in which it is presumed that faults and virtues would be made clearer to children if they were attributed to animals.

Almost simultaneously came stories of the prevention of cruelty to animals. In Dorothy Kilner's *The Rational Brutes; or, Talking Animals* (1799), the ass is made to remark, "Well, I think it would be the happiest thing for this nation that ever yet was thought of, if some plan could be contrived to destroy every boy upon this island." The Victorian era brought this kind of animal story to a culmination in such books as Anna Sewell's *Black Beauty* (1877) and the Canadian Marshall Saunders's *Beautiful Joe* (1894). In adult literature they were matched by such antivivisection novels as H. G. Wells's *The Island of Dr. Moreau.*

The primary strain of the beast tale, with its emphasis on moralistic parable, softened in the first half of the twentieth century, as children's literature in general softened, only to resurface in a harsh and misanthropic form in recent years. It is the thunder of the moralist that is most strongly heard in such talking-animal stories as Richard Adam's *The Plague Dogs* (1977), John Donovon's *The Family* (1976), Russell Hoban's *The Mouse and His Child* (1967), Alan Arkin's *The Lemming Condition* (1976), William Steig's *Abel's Island* (1976), and, to a lesser degree, Adams's *Watership Down* (1972), and Robert O'Brien's *Mrs. Frisby and the Rats of NIMH* (1971).

The secondary strain can more truly be called animal fantasy as opposed to the tradition of the beast tale. It is almost a parvenu, its genesis rooted in the Edwardian period and its characteristics akin to those of classic fantasy. Writers in this subgenre, who number only a few, have used animals to create another secondary reality and to comment broadly and compassionately on the human condition, as distinct from the specific pointed attack on humanity in the beast tales. The writing styles of the fantasists frequently reflect a poetic and imaginative vision of life, the language enriched with beautiful diction and subtle images. This is opposed to the more naturalistic, mundane style of the moralists.

Walter de la Mare's *The Three Mullah-Mulgars,* later titled *The Three Royal Monkeys* (1910), exhibits the characteristics of animal fantasy in its truest form. It is, in its own way, as unique as *Alice's Adventures in Wonderland,* both being works that cannot be imitated, much less duplicated. Nod, the little monkey in the sheepskin coat with nine ivory buttons, is not an ordinary monkey like the Banderlog in Kipling's *Jungle Books*; he has magic about him. De la Mare does not impute human speech to his monkeys. The Portuguese sailor tries to teach Nod human speech, which results in a kind of Mulgar-English, a linguistic tour-de-force that foreshadows Tolkien's use of linguistics in his fantasy. Nonetheless, Nod is a primitive in a primitive animal society. De la Mare makes this clear when the home of the three royal monkeys has been burned down. Thumb, the oldest of the three monkey brothers, takes the lead:

> Soon he began to tingle, and laughed out to cheer the others when he tumbled head over heels into a snowdrift. And they combed themselves, and stood up to their trouble, and thought stubbornly, as far as their monkey-wits would let them, only of the future (which is easier to manage than the past).

Nod really belongs to epic fantasy. He is the counterpart (as is Susan Cooper's Will Stanton) of a Sir Galahad or a Sir Gawaine. We enter with him into a world of fantasy where the spell is never broken, a world of astounding adventures, escapes, struggles, terror, evil, and even death—a world, in fact, which is universal. His is a spiritual odyssey and Nod reflects Walter de la Mare's basic philosophy that life is good and beautiful. It is through the beauty and refinement of de la Mare's thought and language that we see the universal in Nod's primitive nature.

This philosophical type of animal fantasy in which the writer is attempting a statement about life rather than portraying a human characteristic can also be seen in Randall Jarrell's mood piece, *The Bat-Poet* (1963), in which the little brown bat, in discovering poetry, asks questions he has never thought of before. When the mockingbird "can sound like anything. Which one's the mockingbird? which one's the world?" Of course these books were written by poets, not satirists.

Both Kenneth Grahame's *The Wind in the Willows* (1908) and E. B. White's *Charlotte's Web* (1952) are also an unfolding of "other worlds." The former, which has been described as a "minor Edwardian classic," [6] takes place in the closed world of an English riverbank and the latter, in the equally separate world of an American Midwest barnyard. Both writers link fantasy and reality, animal life and human life, in their evocation of friendship, love of home, spirit of adventure, and the cosmic cycle of birth and death. Grahame's animals are more highly anthropomorphized than those of E. B. White, but still his technique is that adopted by most animal fantasists. Grahame

6. By John Reeves in the introduction to "Four Is Company," a program of the Canadian Broadcasting Corporation, 1961.

takes the quite legitimate characteristics of a certain animal that have overtones of a certain type of human being (pompous Toad) who in turn exemplifies more general human characteristics often attributed to a certain type of animal. Thus there is a circular "feed-back" between animal and human. Of course, the wonder really is that the technique works so well.

E. B. White keeps his animals "in their place" to a greater extent than Grahame. The concerns of White's animals are far less philosophical and so more closely attuned to natural animal life. Knowing nothing more than the barnyard, they would not dream of a life beyond their own, as does Rat in *The Wind in the Willows*. But, like Walter de la Mare, White succeeds in creating a fantasy world that has universal applications. Grahame, with all his perception of small animals, their behavior, and their habitats, remains chiefly a commentator about his own time.

Most recent animal fantasies tend to be written for younger children. They are inventive, droll, and amusing. As in nonsense literature the world in these fantasies is tipped over and the children are let in on the tricks and the jokes. This is the world of Margery Sharp's white mouse, Miss Bianca, whether she is acting as the president of the Mouse Prisoners' Aid Society (*Miss Bianca* [1962]) or flying to India to save a little page boy from being trampled by an elephant because he had snivelled into the Ranee's sherbet (*Miss Bianca in the Orient* [1970]). In George Selden's *The Cricket in Times Square* (1960) a cat and a mouse and a cricket are the three New York musketeers and Chester Cricket gives concerts in perfect pitch to hundreds of people in Times Square Station. These writers create an artificial, miniature world brimming with gentleness and good humor. When they do comment on human behavior, it is to point out foibles rather than sins. Their animals represent charming and slyly perceptive child substitutes who are often engaged in mischievous adventures for which real children would expect a slap on the hand. The animals escape without recrimination or even an affectionate scolding, because basically they know their limits. Michael Bond's *A Bear Called Paddington* (1958) is both cute and pampered, but Bond also endows him with the good sense of children. When Paddington is offered first choice of any type of firecracker he wishes in *More About Paddington* (1962), he says:

> "I think I'll have one of those you hold in the paw, first. . . . I think I'll have a sparkler."

In the more philosophical stories that concern both animals and humans, such as Sendak's *Higglety Pigglety Pop* (1967) or Saint Exupéry's *The Little Prince* (1943), writers put their most memorable

109

remarks into the mouths of their animal protagonists so that they are the fonts of wisdom. Sendak's Jennie, the Sealyham terrier, opens *Higglety Pigglety Pop* with the main theme:

"I am discontented. I want something I do not have. There must be more to life than having everything!"

And it is the fox in *The Little Prince* who expresses Saint Exupéry's view of life:

"It is only with the heart that one can see rightly; what is essential is invisible to the eye."

Such symbolic and sophisticated fantasies are not widely read by children, but they have become cult books with great appeal for adults. It can even be pointed out that the World Mother Goose Theater in *Higglety Pigglety Pop* has the same tone and purpose as Herman Hesse's celebrated magic theater in *Steppenwolf*. Despite all their poetic sensibility and adult sophistication, these cult animal fantasies remain separated from the newer beast tales by a great divide, although they too are for older readers.

It is in the recent beast tales that the elements of Aesopic didacticism can be found combined with bleak and bitter satire. Such books as Russell Hoban's *The Mouse and His Child*, Robert O'Brien's *Mrs. Frisby and the Rats of NIMH*, Richard Adams's *Watership Down* and *The Plague Dogs*, and John Donovan's *Family* are passionate outcries on humankind's blind insensitivity and inhumanity to others and to the animals cohabiting this earth. All are a far, far cry from *The Wind in the Willows* with its atmosphere of an Edwardian gentlemen's club, its cozy human-type dwellings, and its pantheistic philosophy. No animal in *The Wind in the Willows* wants to escape, or run away; theirs is a magic, closed circle and when danger does come, it comes from animal villains who want to break into that circle.

The animals in the newer tales escape from a human environment. In *Mrs. Frisby and the Rats of NIMH*, *The Plague Dogs*, and *Family* they flee human experimentations on them; in *Watership Down* from the destruction of their environment; in *The Mouse and His Child* from oppression in the form of an authoritarian political system. The struggle between technology and the natural world is yet another of the major themes. The action is played out in natural surroundings, for the most part, where the dangers are intense and predators are many. At an extreme, the animals appear to suggest the most vulnerable and put-upon people—children. Richard Adams's Fiver (*Watership Down*) is a childlike visionary as are his Snitter in *The Plague Dogs* and Hoban's child mouse in *The Mouse and His Child*. In this respect these stories connect with such realistic stories of the persecution of children as Anne Holm's *I Am David* and Robert Cormier's *I Am the Cheese.*

In *Watership Down* and *The Plague Dogs*, Adams is an Old Testament prophet thundering out his disapproval of humans and their injustice, cruelty, dishonesty, manipulation, and blind hatreds, contrasted in a Manichaean manner with the goodness of the animal world. Although *The Plague Dogs* can be seen as the penultimate beast tale with its Swiftian, misanthropic vision toward the human race, *Watership Down* can be said to straddle the gulf between Aesop and de la Mare. It is both moral and mythic. Basically it is a survival story given epic proportions by means of the utilization of lapine history, language, and mythology. Adams has taken natural lore from R. M. Lockley's *The Private Life of the Rabbit* and does not stray from what rabbits can actually do in a physical or instinctive sense. When Hazel's heroic little band is escaping from an enemy warren they have to use a boat. Hazel gnaws the rope apart and holds the ends together with his teeth, he does not untie it. And the doeless band has to be persuaded that bucks can dig as well as does, that it is a matter of conditioning. Their thoughts and feelings are also circumscribed. After some of them have told of their terrible experiences:

> The story over, the demands of their own hard, rough lives began to re-assert themselves in their hearts, in their nerves, their blood and appetites. Would that the dead were not dead! But there is grass that must be eaten, pellets that must be chewed, hraka that must be passed, holes that must be dug, sleep that must be slept.

Adams has managed to anthropomorphize his animals to the least possible extent. They do have the power of speech, but since they do not converse with humans, one assumes that they are speaking "lapine" or, with other animals, the "lingua franca" of the animal world. To many readers this is no stranger than D'Artagnan speaking English. Occasionally the mood of the narrative shifts into a mythic sensibility somewhat akin to poetic animal fantasy, especially when it involves Fiver, the visionary young rabbit who first warns his friends of the impending destruction of their warren and on whose foretelling seizures they learn to take action:

> "Hrairoo," said Hazel one evening, "what would we have done without you? We'd none of us be here, would we?"
>
> "You're sure we *are* here, then?" asked Fiver.
>
> "That's too mysterious for me," replied Hazel. "What do you mean?"
>
> "Well, there's another place—another country, isn't there? We go there when we sleep; at other times, too; and when we

111

die. El-ahrairah comes and goes between the two as he wants, I suppose, but I could never quite make that out, from the tales."

Adams's greatest triumph is the creation of a complete rabbit society, all the more astounding since rabbits have not been considered in any way the intelligentsia of the animal world. Therefore his success in suspending the reader's disbelief is really a greater achievement than that of Tolkien's creation of Middle Earth. But despite the book's wholeness and its poetic vision, it is Adams's view of humanity that severs its link with animal fantasy, particularly of the past.

His view of animals is a reversal of that in Kipling's *Jungle Books*. While Mowgli could learn skills, manners, even wisdom from his animal friends, he was nonetheless innately superior to them. Adams, on the other hand, in envisioning humanity as inhumane, defines his major group of rabbits as superior in spiritual, social, and political systems. Hazel, the book's chief protagonist, has visited another warren to ask for some does. He tries to negotiate with a fascist rabbit society:

"Well, I'd rather say no more about the end of that meeting. Strawberry tried all he could to help me. He spoke very well about the decency and comradeship natural to animals. 'Animals don't behave like men,' he said. 'If they have to fight, they fight; and if they have to kill, they kill. But they don't sit down and set their wits to work to devise ways of spoiling other creatures' lives and hurting them. They have dignity and animality.' "

In *The Plague Dogs* Adams abandons any connection with the poetic tradition of animal fantasy. Speaking with the voice of doom, he writes from a sense of theology rather than story. More metaphysical in proportion and intent than *Watership Down*, this novel's only relationship to fantasy is that the animals are endowed with the power of logical thought and speech. It is a brutal account of two dogs, Snitter and Rowf, and their shared escape from the horror of an animal research station, an immense Auschwitz-like laboratory where scientific experiments and tests are conducted on suffering animals. The dogs experience little joy in their freedom as they enter a nightmare struggle for survival in the Lakeland District, rediscovering their primal nature as wild animals, learning, with the aid of a fox, to kill, thieve, run and hide, to live in constant hunger, fear, and a bleak certainty of ultimate, painful death.

'What end can there be to this?' said Rowf to Snitter. 'To run about loose until they find us—how long?'

'You said we'd become wild animals. That's what *they* do—live till they die.'

'Why ay. Run on till th' Dark comes doon.'

But the terrible simplicity of this fate is not theirs. The dogs soon become a pawn in a sordid manipulative game of exploitation by gutter journalism, dishonest, cynical government officials, the fears and angers of local residents, and the self-serving tactics of the research scientists. An hysterical witchhunt for the dogs, falsely claimed to be carriers of bubonic plague, leads to an unfortunately melodramatic denouement.

While *Watership Down* has a distinct unity of style and plot, *The Plague Dogs* is structurally fragmented. Here Adams is the omniscient author, constantly present and interrupting the plot to speculate on the fate of his characters. His voices range widely from those of the intimate, three-dismensional animals, the satiric one-dimensional parodies of human "types," to the sympathetic country characters. The philosophic asides and digressions have many echoes in literature. At times there is the musical eloquence and ruminations of a Sir Thomas Browne, the seventeenth-century sermons of a John Donne, and most of all, the biting wit and satire of a Swift. Adams mimics Sir Thomas Browne in an elaborate musing upon the contents of ration packages for the laboratory animals:

> It were, as Sir Thomas Brown says, an excellent quaere to consider, *privatim et seriatim*, what drugs, what charms, what conjuration and what mighty magic those packages contained. They were indeed miracles of rare device. . . . Some induced disease, madness, or mortification of specific parts of the body; others cured, alleviated, or failed either to cure or to alleviate, diseases already induced.

But the most compelling voice is that of the dogs, not only in the expression of their existential sufferings, but also in their animal dilemma—the dichotomy arising from the need to flee from human cruelty, while being constrained through affection and circumstances to rely on and remain with humans:

> 'A dog stands firm,' said Rowf sharply. 'A dog never refuses whatever a man requires of him. That's what a dog's for. So if they say the water—if they say go in the water, I'll—' He broke off, cowering . . . 'I can't stand that water any more.'

In its diatribe against cruelty to animals, *The Plague Dogs* is the *Black Beauty* of the 1970s. But while Anna Sewell shows cruelty as an aberrant individual characteristic, Adams shows the world in general as cruel and malevolent towards animals. Twentieth-century casual cruelty is, according to Adams, shared by an entire society; at its best it is an uncaring forgetfulness, and at its worst, a grey, bureaucratic evil. There are no highly colored individual villains, no Miltonic Satans, in these modern beast tales. The animals have to escape man's scientific world and return to their natural habitat even when, as Rowf says musingly and in existential terms, 'The tod was right; you'd wonder why we take so much trouble to stay alive.'

As in most works of sociological science fiction, the individual can make only a losing bid for hope and freedom, because the main protagonist is a corrupt society itself. Indeed many of the new beast fables could fit equally well in science fiction because of their use of scientific experimentation on animals, however quickly propounded.

The rats in Robert O'Brien's *Mrs. Frisby and the Rats of NIMH* are also struggling for survival after being exposed in the laboratory of NIMH (National Institute for Mental Health) to experiments that have increased their intelligence. The echoes of science fiction continue as the rats reject technology and return to a primitive, more natural way of life. This book belongs to the new wave of the beast tale, not least because of O'Brien's pessimistic view of the human race which he expressed in his Newbery Award acceptance speech:

> I had been, and still am, concerned over the seeming tendency of the human race to exterminate itself. . . . I have wondered: If we should vanish from the earth, who might survive us? . . . I began to speculate: rats are tough, highly adaptable and . . . prolific. . . . What would a rat civilization be like? . . . Once I got started, the rats took charge, and they turned out to be much saner and pleasanter than we are.[7]

Like Adams in *Watership Down*, O'Brien explores the dynamics of a social community, creating a utopian, technological society very different from the cruel, fascist totalitarianism of General Wormwort's warren. Mrs. Frisby herself seems a character from the earlier animal fantasies with her concern for her ailing son and her courage in crossing the dangerous field and barnyard to seek help. In many of its details, in its portrayal of a miniature world, and in its optimistic view of animal (human) nature, it sits more easily amid the earlier animal fantasies than the new bleak science fiction.

Such softness is not a part of John Donovan's *Family*. In the mainstream of "escape stories" it follows the experience of a group of apes fleeing the laboratory experiments in transplants for the betterment of the human race. As didactic as *The Plague Dogs*, it also touts the superiority of the apes over humans. Sasha, the commentator, says of humans:

7. Robert C. O'Brien, "Newbery Award Acceptance Speech," *Horn Book* 48:344 (June 1972).

They are taught at the youngest age to see progress in change. It is why they get their education, and subsequently set their minds to improving the world. I dearly love their innocence, it is so sweet and short-sighted. And their great intelligence, it makes them the most stupid of all animals. This is another sad truth that all apes know.

While *Family* has little to offer in stylistic achievement, it makes up for it with emotion, for the group of apes does become a "family." In the end they are defeated by hunters and the weather; and the two remaining have to return to the experimental station. Donovan's message is clear and simple.

By contrast, Russell Hoban's *The Mouse and His Child* is the most multidimensional, complex, and ambiguous of the new wave of either animal fantasy or beast tale. In one sense it is a reversion to the use of animals as complete parodies of human beings. The mouse and his child, toy wind-up animals, are modern pilgrims on a dangerous Odyssey-like search for the mouse child's dream of family and home. He asks his father: "We'll find the elephant and the seal, and we'll find the dollhouse, too, and have our own territory, won't we Papa?"

The mouse child's plaintive lament is one that runs through most of the modern beast tales: *Watership Down, The Plague Dogs,* and *Family* too are examples of the quest for home and security. Hoban explores social orders and stereotypes in greater depth in his utopian and anti-utopian political statement. Instead of the dangers of the experimental labs, the social problem Hoban here symbolizes is the fact that the mouse and his child are *wind-up* toys; they are not the cuddly, warm toys of a "Winnie-the-Pooh"-style animal fantasy but the products of a cold, technological society. The struggle for self-winding and autonomy in their lives is akin to the break for freedom the living animals make in the stories of Adams and Donovan and O'Brien. How unlike the present-day animal fantasy is Margery Williams's *Velveteen Rabbit,* published in 1926, who also wants to be released. But, in tune with his period, he is liberated through a child's love and so becomes a *real* rabbit.

Like Aesop, *The Mouse and His Child* is filled with stock characters of satire. There is sadistic Manny Rat, the prototypical fascistic leader of a cowed society; the crochety, wandering medicine-man bullfrog; Old Muskrat, a parody of the batty scholars of pure thought; C. Serpentina, the morose snapping turtle whose playwriting is a satire of the nihilism of Samuel Bechett; and most strikingly, the Tramp, a fate-like god of chance who reappears at times of crisis and who represents the author himself—knowingly laughing and crying at the absurdity, beauty, and horror of the world.

In many ways *The Mouse and His Child* parallels the adult

115

modern novel with its now almost boring theme of a quest for meaning and identity in an absurd, cruel, alienating, and existential world. Indeed the mouse and his child pass through experiences that, in number and ferocity, few adult novelists would dare inflict upon their characters. They experience abandonment in a trash can, slavery to the rat-king of a dump, involvement in murder, robbery, war, avant-garde theater, meditation upon despair and eternity in the mud at the bottom of a pond, recovery of their doll-house home from the villainous rat, and a final, idyllic, well-deserved peace.

Much of the tale's pictorial symbolism, such as the label on the ubiquitous cans of dog food showing the black-and-white spotted dog carrying a can of Bonzo Dog Food infinitely repeated and appearing in almost every scene, seems more than heavy for a children's book, as does the vague explanation expressed through the turtle's dictum:

> "an endlessness of little dogs, receding through progressive diminution to a revelation of the ultimate truth. . . . Beyond the last visible dog. . . . Each of us, sunk in the mud however deep, must rise on the propulsion of his own thought. Each of us must journey through the dog, beyond the dots, and to the truth, alone."

And how many children will grasp the point that the power of the mouse and his child appears to be their ability to express emotion in the face of mechanical stoicism, breaking the rules of their pre-ordained destiny as circular-dancing wind-up toys by the sheer force of their own will? That this book is about the juggling of free will and destiny?

In *The Mouse and His Child* Hoban displays his adult cleverness and in so doing gives a flawed view of a child's world. The incredible weight of the book, its formal, gamelike structure and complex imagery is only barely balanced by the gentler scenes of the binding love and courage of the mice and their friends. *Watership Down*, in spite of its length, its political commentary, and "put down" of humans, is a far more childlike book.

The didactic beast-fable tone has also infiltrated animal fantasy for young children and can be seen as pure parable and allegory in this shorter form of the genre. Alan Arkin's *The Lemming Condition* (1976) uses a young lemming to comment on the conflict between conformity, destiny, and individual free will. Bubber questions the most profound, habitual action of his species—the mysterious great march west and the leap into the sea. With the helpful proddings and testings of both his analytical friend Crow and an elderly, eccentric lemming-hermit, Bubber faces the awesome meaning of this suicidal drive with growing courage and self-reliance. As in much of modern children's literature, particularly the problem novel, the solution is existential. Bubber refuses to leap to his death but has to accept a solitary life of quest and struggle, not even knowing what he is. *The Lemming Condition* is as bleak a statement on the human condition as Orwell's *Animal Farm*.

William Steig's *Abel's Island* (1976), another condensed fable, is unique to the new wave in that the central protagonist wishes to remain in his present society but is forced out of it and finally reverts to his true animal nature. Abel is a dandified Edwardian mouse, who is so extremely self-centered that although "the sky was overcast . . . Abel didn't think it would be so inconsiderate as to rain when he and his lovely wife were in the mood for an outing."

Abel's placid life of privilege, comfort, and security is shattered when those very rains sweep him away to an uninhabited island. Thus begins Abel's rite of passage, wherein his determination and courage are tested. Like Odysseus, Abel eventually returns home to his Penoplope-like wife, Amanda, but in mythic fashion, his heroic trials and quests have made a better mouse of him. In a moment of revelation during a life-and-death conflict with a cat, "Abel realized that the cat had to do what she did. She was being a cat. It was up to him to be the mouse." Abel has discovered his true animal identity. What a long way from *Wind in the Willows*! If Toad had ever discovered his real animal nature, he would have sat out half the book under a rock.

Illustrations have played an important role in animal fantasy and in the early beast tales but are not a factor in the newer books for older readers. Aesop, of course, has had countless illustrators, each interpreting him according to the tenor of the times as well as through a personal vision and artistry. It is revealing that in this era of the misanthropic beast tale, Charles Bennett's bitter nineteenth-century illustrations with their overall view of cunning, greed, and dishonesty recently have been reissued. The notable lack of illustration in the books by Adams and Donovan almost surely suggests that most scenes would be too painful for pictorial interpretation, or perhaps editors realize it would take a Goya to do them justice. And it is probably not mere coincidence that the acerbic tone of Hoban's *Mouse and His Child* is considerably softened by Frances Hoban's loving depiction of the mouse father and son, although the illustrations are by no means distinguished.

Many earlier animal fantasies, on the other hand, are almost as famous for their illustrations as for their texts. Our image of Pooh and his friends and of Rat and his cronies is virtually controlled by the beguiling illustrations of Ernest H. Shepard; even Arthur Rackham's attempt to reillustrate *The Wind in the Willows* met with failure. E. B.

117

White's *Charlotte's Web* and Margery Sharp's *Miss Bianca* books now would seem inconceivable without the perceptive and loving vision of Garth Williams. Sendak, in *Higglety Pigglety Pop*, and Steig, in *Abel's Island*, are author-illustrators, capable of creating the exact visual images they desire to complement their stories. These and other children's book illustrators have been masters at creating the fur and feathers as well as the masks upon the human faces; they give their animal tales a joy and an intimacy not frequently offered by those in other genres, with the exception of the animal-fantasy picture book.

Few writers have skirted the boundaries of this difficult genre of animal fantasy with such success as Lucy Boston in her *A Stranger at Green Knowe* (1961), the story of the mystical bond between Hanno, the kingly escaped gorilla, and Ping, a lonely, orphaned Chinese refugee. Its setting should be familiar to readers of the "Green Knowe" books, the major site being a thicket next to Mrs. Oldknow's garden at the ancient house of Green Knowe. The story is almost completely realistic; Hanno never speaks a word and his death at the hands of the police and the zoo keepers seems always fated, even perhaps desirable in light of the great ape's hatred of captivity. It is, though, an oblique entry into animal fantasy as the boy and the gorilla, for a brief time, live a kind of joint life in their closed-off world. Boston's style, like that of Walter de la Mare and E. B. White, is a combination of the lyrical and the practical, perfectly meshed:

> Imagine a tropical forest so vast that you could roam in it all your life without ever finding out there was anything else.... It is in such a forest that this story must begin. It is a far flight, both in distance and in imagination, from the dewy meadow and long history of Green Knowe to this primeval and almost immortal forest in the Congo. The journey however can be made, but not in a hurry.

Randall Jarrell in *The Animal Family* (1965) too describes a similar bonding between animal and human life in a delicate haunting prose.

This unity between human and animal characterizes only genuine animal fantasy; it does not appear in the modern beast tale. The romantic pantheistic vision in Kenneth Grahame's *Wind in the Willows* chapter, "The Piper at the Gates of Dawn," is a symbol of a former holistic unity between animal and human. This unity has now been fractured.

Stylistically, these new beast tales sacrifice beauty of language for message. One can hardly expect John Donovan to write with delicacy when he is trying to explain the Scopes trial or the nature of animal experimentation. And since the message is all, the newer books give rise to the feeling that messages and animals could be exchanged from book to book with little disturbance of the total effect. The well-delineated, north of England setting of *The Plague Dogs* and the use of local dialect aside, its dogs and the apes of *Family* could be easily interchanged.

The harsh themes, the bleak tone, the lack of illustrations of these books suggest an adult rather than a child audience. In fact, with *Watership Down* Adams, single-handedly, has given the talking animal story back to an adult audience from which it has been divorced since Aesop. *Watership Down* is a book that finds its own audience among both adults and children.

But while bringing child and adult readership together in these new sermons, their writers have divorced us from two important aspects of the animal world. In earlier animal fantasy we did not pity the animals, but rather we liked them and even envied them. How wonderful to be like Wart in T. H. White's *The Sword in the Stone* and actually enter into their bodies and join in their lives and adventures! No one would want to be Sasha the Ape, Snitter and Rowf or Fiver and Hazel or even Mrs. Frisby with all her troubles. Nor do their authors give us a chance to appreciate the natural life of animals. Indeed they negate Whitman's envious view of them:

> I think I could turn and live with animals, they are so placid
>   and self-contain'd,
> I stand and look at them long and long.
> They do not sweat and whine about their condition,
> They do not lie awake in the dark and weep for their sins,
> They do not make me sick discussing their duty to God,
> Not one is dissatisfied, not one is demented with the mania of
>   owning things,
> Not one kneels to another, not to his kind that lived thousands
>   of years ago;
> Not one is respectable or unhappy over the whole earth.[8]

Light Fantasy

Modern epic fantasy, enchanted realism, and beast tales are devoid of humor. But fantasy, taken as an entire genre, also wears the

8. Walt Whitman, v. 32 from his *Song of Myself* in *The Poetry and Prose of Walt Whitman*, ed. by Louis Untermeyer (Inner Sanctum ed.; New York: Simon & Schuster, 1949), p. 119.

mask of comedy in order to balance the lofty, often close to tragic
dimension of serious fantasy. It wears it less frequently but with an
equal vigor as it reveals the absurd in the human condition. Children's delight in tongue-in-cheek fantasy can be first seen from their
borrowings from adult literature: Swift, Raspe, and versions of "the
Sorcerer's Apprentice."

In their own literature they have been served first by Hans
Christian Andersen who, in his fleshed-out folktales, gave his caustic
view of human nature full play. After the soldier in "The Tinderbox"
had spent all his money, he lived a lonely life in his attic, for his
friends claimed "there were far too many stairs to climb." Surprisingly, George MacDonald almost parodied his own serious romantic
work, as well as a traditional theme of folklore, in his extravagent
story of *The Light Princess* who, like most princesses suffered an evil,
here the loss of gravity. After its one deep and tender moment, when
the princess forgets her own interests and saves the prince, the story
regains its lighthearted spirit and its clever punning as the princess
finally achieves "gravity":

> "Is this the gravity you make so much of?" she said one day to
> the prince, as he raised her from the floor. "For my part, I was a
> great deal more comfortable without it."

One aspect of light fantasy explored by writers for children is
that of comic melodrama. Joan Aiken is one of the most original in
her interlinking series of fantastical histories set in a time that never
was, a British never-never land, rampant with wolves and melodramatic villains in the reign of the imaginary King James III at the
beginning of the nineteenth century. The tone of her *The Wolves of
Willoughby Chase* (1962), *Black Hearts in Battersea* (1964), *Night Birds on
Nantucket* (1966), and *The Cuckoo Tree* (1971) is humorously gothic
and Dickensian, and the wildly improbable, outrageous plots read
like tongue-in-cheek parodies of crypto-Victorian melodrama and
high adventure.

Aiken has a flair for bright, crisp dialogue, and the pungencies of
musical dialect; she writes with an affection for the profound and
nonsensical power of words, taking delight in the witty interaction of
language, dialogue, and character. There is a striking sense of childlike play inherent in her plots; they are rambunctious, rollicking, fast
paced to the point of a frantic race, and form magnificent stages for
the courageous derring-do of her various insouciant child
protagonists. Aiken deliberately makes use of stock characters,
themes, and plots from British and American eighteenth- and
nineteenth-century adult novels in a witty salute to the classics, with

a nod to the adult reader's appreciation of parody and as well to the child reader's love of drama and humor.

The quest story lends itself well to farcical high adventure. In Natalie Babbitt's *The Search for Delicious* (1969) everyone is satisfied with the prime minister's definitions of As, Bs, and Cs but, oh, the trouble over D.

> But then we got to 'Delicious is fried fish' and he [the king] said no, I'd have to change that. He doesn't care for fried fish. The General of the Armies was standing there and he said that, as far as he was concerned, Delicious is a mug of beer, and the Queen said no, Delicious is a Christmas pudding, and then the King said nonsense, everyone knew the most delicious thing is an apple, and they all began quarreling.

Vibrantly plotted and stylistically smooth, it moves quickly and refreshingly through its lighthearted events with just the right touch of seriousness that makes humor credible.

Lloyd Alexander too writes with tongue in cheek in *The Marvelous Misadventures of Sebastian* (1970), the saga of a young fiddler, a bumbling anti-hero and his wandering adventures through a Renaissance-style landscape. Replete with the costumes and props of medieval romance—peripatetic circus troops, magical violins, a fleeing princess disguised as a boy—it rambles along at a lively, suspenseful pace.

Helen Cresswell's *The Piemakers* (1967) also exists in a quasi-historical time that never was, although its setting of Danby Vale, on the border of Yorkshire and Derbyshire, is real enough. And if the gigantic pie was never made, still the descriptions of the herbs and the juices makes the mouth water. Cresswell's style gives touches of humor rather than an overall sense of parody or satire, and so the whole tale has a satisfying sense of reality. *The Piemakers* is an unclassifiable book, being simply a piece of perfection in its robust portrayal of the piemaking trade. Like a Brueghel painting, Cresswell works in small humorous details and warm bright colors:

> Gravella on her back in the pie-dish stared up at the sky and leaves. Gravella tip-toe on her box gazed down on the glinting water or watched the hilly moors unrolling hot and still beneath a glaring sun. Soon the walls of the pie-dish grew almost too hot to touch and she had to fold a handkerchief and lay it on the rim so that she could hold on.

These simpler light fantasies have no messages to offer, no axes to grind; all are heirs of the humorous tales of an earlier time, whether the tall tale of *Mr. Popper's Penguins*, the flamboyant *Great*

121

Geppy, the miniature humor of *The Borrowers*, or the hearty satire of Richard Hughes's short stories. What makes these books notable is their high-spirited frivolity, nonchalance, good-tempered chaff, and homely warmth of family and friends.

The foregoing wave of tenderness and lunacy crashes down with a jarring sharpness in the unusual combination of slapstick with the moral cautionary tale found in the works of Roald Dahl and Mordecai Richler. More stylized and satirically honed than the simpler light fantasies previously discussed, Dahl's *James and the Giant Peach* (1961), *Charlie and the Chocolate Factory* (1964), and Richler's *Jacob Two-Two Meets the Hooded Fang* (1975) are closer to the comic strip and to the animated cartoon adventure familiar to the Saturday-morning TV-viewing crowd.

Using elements of popular kid culture—word play and well-worn jokes—references to TV, games, and social commercialism fill their pages, for both writers take their cues from American pop culture. This is expressed by Dahl in such joke-book terms as "all the beans, cocoa, coffee, jelly beans and has beens," with some cautionary prods to observing parents like "stickjaw for talkative parents." Richler's approach is more indirect. His Jacob Two-Two dreams his fantasy of adult oppression and liberation through "child power." The popularity of both books with children may well lie in their broad humor and their put-down of oppressors of children. They are modern versions of Astrid Lindgren's similar, yet more gentle, spoof of the adult world in her still popular *Pippi Longstocking* (1950).

Satire emerges in a darker form in the more adult, surrealistic fantasies of John Gardner, Mary Norton, and Florence Parry Heide. Heide's picture book for older readers, *The Shrinking of Treehorn* (1971), with its ironic illustrations by Edward Gorey, continues in the vein of the Dahl and Richler accounts of oppressed, ignored children in the adult world. In this parody, perhaps of Swift's Gulliver or even Kafka's *Metamorphosis*, the small boy Treehorn begins to grow even smaller. His fantastical experiences while shrinking are a black-humored account of the impotence and insignificance of children.

Surrealism continues in John Gardner's *Dragon, Dragon and Other Tales* (1975) and *Gudgekin the Thistle Girl and Other Tales* (1976). Gardner is one of the most highly respected novelists in America today. As in his *Grendel* for adult readers, Gardner begins with the traditional folk form, but turns it wildly upside-down. In his children's books he gives folklore a hilarious good shaking-up, adding a dash of zesty, though somewhat bitter, spices, and offering his own unique brew for the modern child and a parent's bedtime dose of storytelling. Gardner has created a brilliant style that reads like a cross between Hans Christian Andersen, Kafka, and Woody Allen; unfortunately, his droll subtleties may be appreciated more by adults than children.

In *Dragon, Dragon* the fanciful tales include the traditional cast of dragons, kings, queens, cobblers' youngest sons, timid tailors, giants, chimney-girls, and fairy godmothers, but with a twist. With zany satire, Gardner sketches a series of cowardly and foolish anti-heroes and heroines and sets for these contemporary schlemiels serious trials and perilous quests from which they emerge ultimately triumphant. Gardner's stories bristle with the suspense and humor that appeal to children, but to adult sensibilities they can be seen as ironic parodies of the naive folktale genre. An example is the difficult dragon, who "tipped over fences and robbed graves and put frogs in people's drinking water and tore the last chapters out of novels and changed house numbers around so that people crawled into bed with their neighbors' wives."

There is an even starker vein of black humor in *Gudgekin the Thistle Girl*. Its stories are filled with bleakly farcical characters, amoral acts, and surrealistic, bizarre anticlimactic or trick endings in which good is not necessarily the winner. An example is the fate of the king in "The Seagulls":

> No one ever saw the king again. Most likely the wicked witch got him for gambling and scheming and weaseling out of his debts.

Like Gardner, Mary Norton parodies folk- and fairy tales. In *Are All the Giants Dead?* (1975) she takes readers on a self-conscious tour of the fairy-tale world of the old stories which strips away the veils of timeless enchantment to reveal sadly aging and disillusioned folklore characters. James, a contemporary London boy who prefers science fiction to fairy tales, goes off on a night journey to fairyland with Mildred, a North-Wind–Mary-Poppins figure who is mildly scatter-brained, but full of "nice certainties and sound common sense." She introduces James to an odd host of celebrities, including the middle-aged, querulous Boofy and Beau (Beauty and the Beast); an aging, insomniac card-playing Belle (Sleeping Beauty); a languid, society-conscious Pumpkin (Cinderella); an octogenarian "odd couple," Jack-of-the-Beanstalk and Jack-the-Giant-Killer, who live together as two eccentric bachelors; and Princess Dulcibel, a golden girl with a golden ball anxiously living under a spell that dooms her to that fate of the princess in "The Frog Prince" without the certainty that the toad will become a prince.

The identity of this decomposing lost Edenic kingdom and its inhabitants is a puzzle to James. He questions Mildred:

"Where are we exactly?" said James.

". . . I suppose," she said after a moment, "you could call it the Land of Cockayne. . . . And I suppose they do live on forever and ever after—in the hearts of little children."

"They don't in mine," said James.

Eventually Norton reaffirms the power and magnitude of the tales. After his adventures in this retirement home for fairy-tale characters, James returns to his own world a more mature individual, with greater compassion and courage, having experienced adventure, love, jealousy, loss, and a rediscovery of childhood faith. Norton's lucid writing style is enhanced by her lively, quicksilver storytelling; brisk, entertaining dialogue; and offhand, dry wit which satirizes adult nostalgia for lost childhood innocence while remaining true to the bittersweet human need for an eternal return to the archetypal paradisical time of legend and fairy tale. But Norton has a final adult laugh: "These people belong to no particular period: they belong—as one might say—to Time Immemorial. They were more or less what they like. In some cases, of course, they go by the illustrator."

This wit is the identifying mark of light fantasy, which often mildly pokes fun at its very substance and structure. Whether the humor is broadly cartoonlike, child-simple, or sophisticatedly adult, its presence removes the stories from the threatening struggles and tragic themes of serious fantasy. Rather, the sharp parody or good thunderous fun of much of the writing almost makes it a separate genre in children's literature.

Works Cited

Epic and Heroic Fantasy

Boston, Lucy. *An Enemy at Green Knowe.* Drawings by Peter Boston. London: Faber & Faber, 1964. 156 pp.

Chant, Joy. *Red Moon and Black Mountain: The End of the House of Kendrath.* London: Allen & Unwin, 1970. 277 pp.

Collodi, Carlo, pseud. *The Adventures of Pinocchio.* Tr. from the Italian by M. A. Murray. London: T. Fisher Unwin, 1892. (First pub. in Italy, 1880)

Cooper, Susan. *The Dark Is Rising.* Illus. by Alan E. Cober. New York: Atheneum, 1973. 216 pp.

———*The Grey King.* Illus. by Michael Heslop. New York: Atheneum, 1975. 208 pp.

———*Over Sea, Under Stone.* London: Jonathan Cape, 1965. 252 pp.

————*Silver on the Tree.* New York: Atheneum, 1977. 269 pp.

Curry, Jane. *The Daybreakers.* Illus. by Charles Robinson. New York: Harcourt, 1970. 191 pp.

Eager, Edward. *Half-Magic.* Drawings by N. M. Bodecker. New York: Harcourt, 1954. 217 pp.

Farmer, Penelope. *A Castle of Bone.* London: Chatto and Windus, 1972. 152 pp.; New York: Atheneum, 1972. 151 pp.

Garner, Alan. *Elidor.* Illus. by Charles Keeping. London: Collins, 1965. 160 pp.

————*The Moon of Gomrath.* London: Collins, 1963. 160 pp.

————*The Owl Service.* Illus. by Charles Keeping. London: Collins, 1967. 160 pp.

————*Red Shift.* London: Collins, 1973. 158 pp.

————*The Weirdstone of Brisingamen: A Tale of Alderley.* London: Collins, 1960. 224 pp.

Godden, Rumer. *The Doll's House.* Pictures by Dana Saintsbury. London: Michael Joseph, 1947. 112 pp.

Harris, Christie. *Secret in the Stlalakum Wild.* Illus. by Douglas Tait. New York: Atheneum, 1972. 186 pp.

Harris, Rosemary. *The Seal-Singing.* London: Faber & Faber, 1971. 224 pp.

Hunter, Mollie. *The Haunted Mountain.* Illus. by Laszlo Kubingi. New York: Harper, 1972. 125 pp.

————*A Stranger Came Ashore.* New York: Harper, 1975. 163 pp.

————*The Wicked One.* New York: Harper, 1977. 136 pp.

Ipcar, Dahlov. *The Queen of Spells.* New York: Viking, 1973. 155 pp.

LeGuin, Ursula. *A Wizard of Earthsea.* Drawings by Ruth Robbins. Berkeley, Calif.: Parnassus, 1968. 205 pp.

Lewis, C. S. *The Last Battle.* Illus. by Pauline Baynes. London: Bodley Head, 1956. 184 pp.

————*The Lion, the Witch and the Wardrobe.* Illus. by Pauline Baynes. London: Geoffrey Bles, 1950. 172 pp.

————*The Silver Chair.* Illus. by Pauline Baynes. London: Geoffrey Bles, 1953. 217 pp.

Linklater, Eric. *The Pirates in the Deep Green Sea: A Story for Children.* Illus. by William Reeves. London: Macmillan, 1949. 397 pp.

Lively, Penelope. *The House in Norham Gardens,* London: Heinemann, 1974. 154 pp.; New York: Dutton, 1974, 154 pp.

————*The Whispering Knights.* Illus. by Gareth Floyd. London: Heinemann, 1971. 149 pp.

Lockley, Ronald. *The Seal Woman.* London: Rex Collings, 1974. 154 pp.

MacDonald, George. *At the Back of the North Wind.* London: Strahan & Co., 1871. 378 pp.

————*The Princess and the Goblin.* London and Phildelphia: Lippincott, 1872.

McKillip, Patricia. *The Forgotten Beasts of Eld.* New York: Atheneum, 1974. 217 pp.

Mayne, William. *Earthfasts.* London: Hamish Hamilton, 1966. 154 pp.

————*A Game of Dark.* London: Hamish Hamilton, 1971. 143 pp.

Molesworth, Mary Louisa. *The Cuckoo Clock*. Illus. by W. Crane. London: Macmillan & Co., 1877. 242 pp.

Moon, Sheila. *Knee-deep in Thunder*. Drawings by Peter Parnall. New York: Atheneum, 1967. 307 pp.

Nichols, Beverley. *The Tree That Sat Down*. Illus. by Isobel and John Morton Sale. London: Jonathan Cape, 1945. 302 pp.

Nichols, Ruth. *The Marrow of the World*. Illus. by Trina Schart Hyman. Toronto: Macmillan of Canada, 1972. 168 pp.

———*A Walk Out of the World*. Illus. by Trina Schart Hyman. Don Mills, Ont: Longmans, 1969. 192 pp.

Rayner, William. *Stag Boy*. London: Collins, 1972. 160 pp.

Tolkien, J. R. R. *The Hobbit; or, There and Back Again*. London: Allen & Unwin, 1937. 310 pp.

———*The Lord of the Rings*. London: Allen & Unwin, 1954-1955. 3 pts.: 423, 352, 416 pp.

Westall, Robert. *The Wind Eye*. London: Macmillan, 1976. 212 pp.

Wrighton, Patricia. *The Ice Is Coming*. London: Hutchinson, 1977. 223 pp.

———*The Nargun and the Stars*. London: Hutchinson, 1973. 158 pp.

Wrightson, Patricia. *An Older Kind of Magic*. Illus. by Noela Young. New York: Harcourt, 1972. 186 pp.

Enchanted Realism

Babbitt, Natalie. *Tuck Everlasting*. New York: Farrar, 1975. 139 pp.

Barrie, Sir James M. *Peter and Wendy*. Illus. by F. D. Bedford. London: Hodder & Stoughton, 1911. 267 pp.

Boston, Lucy. *The Children of Green Knowe*. Illus. by Peter Boston. London: Faber & Faber, 1954. 157 pp.

Cameron, Eleanor. *The Court of the Stone Children*. New York: Dutton, 1973. 191 pp.

Godden, Rumer. *The Doll's House*. Illus. by Dana Saintsbury. London: Michael Joseph, 1947. 112 pp.

Jarrell, Randall. *Fly by Night*. Pictures by Maurice Sendak. New York: Farrar, 1976. 30 pp.

Lively, Penelope. *The House in Norham Gardens*. London: Heinemann, 1974. 154 pp; New York: Dutton, 1974. 154 pp.

MacDonald, George. *At the Back of the North Wind*. London: Strahan & Co., 1871. 378 pp.

Mayne, William. *A Year and a Day*. Illus. by Krystyna Turska. London: Hamish Hamilton, 1976. 96 pp.

Mazer, Norma Fox. *Saturday, the Twelfth of October*. New York: Delacorte, 1975. 247 pp.

Pearce, Philippa. *Tom's Midnight Garden*. Illus. by Susan Einzig. London: Oxford Univ. Pr., 1958. 229 pp.

Tolkien, J. R. R. *The Hobbit; or There and Back Again*. London: Allen & Unwin, 1937. 310 pp.

White, E. B. *Charlotte's Web*. Pictures by Garth Williams. New York: Harper, 1952. 184 pp.

Beast Tales and Animal Fantasy

Adams, Richard. *The Plague Dogs*. Illus. by A. Wainright. London: Allen Lane in association with Rex Collings, 1977. 461 pp.

——*Watership Down*. New York: Macmillan, 1972. 429 pp.

Arkin, Alan. *The Lemming Condition*. Illus. by Joan Sandin. New York: Harper, 1976. 57 pp.

Bianco, Margery Williams. *The Velveteen Rabbit; or, How Toys Become Real*. Illus. by William Nicholson. London: Heinemann, 1922. 19 pp.

Bond, Michael. *A Bear Called Paddington*. Illus. by Peggy Fortnum. London: Collins, 1958. 128 pp.

——*More about Paddington*. Drawings by Peggy Fortnum. London: Collins, 1959. 127 pp.

Boston, Lucy. *A Stranger at Green Knowe*. Illus. by Peter Boston. London: Faber & Faber, 1961. 158 pp.

Carroll, Lewis. *Alice's Adventures in Wonderland*. Illus. by John Tenniel. London: Macmillan & Co., 1865. 192 pp.

Cormier, Robert. *I Am the Cheese*. New York: Pantheon, 1977. 233 pp.

De la Mare, Walter. *The Three Mullah-Mulgars*. London: Duckworth & Co., 1910. 312 pp. (Later published as *The Three Royal Monkeys*)

Donovan, John. *Family*. New York: Harper, 1976. 116 pp.

Grahame, Kenneth. *The Wind in the Willows*. London: Methuen & Co., 1908. 302 pp.

Hancock, Niel. *Dragon Winter*. Toronto: Popular Library, 1978. 351 pp.

Hoban, Russell. *The Mouse and His Child*. Pictures by Lillian Hoban. New York: Harper, 1967. 182 pp.; Avon Books, 1976. 182 pp.

Holm, Anne. *I Am David*. Tr. from the Danish by L. W. Kingsland. London: Methuen, 1965. 190 pp.; US title, *North to Freedom*. New York: Harcourt, 1965.

Jarrell, Randall. *The Animal Family*. Decorations by Maurice Sendak. New York: Pantheon, 1965. 179 pp.

——*The Bat-Poet*. Pictures by Maurice Sendak. New York: Macmillan, 1964. 42 pp.

Kilner, Dorothy. *The Rational Brutes; or, Talking Animals*. London: Vernor and Hood, 1799.

Kipling, Rudyard. *The Jungle Book*. London: Macmillan & Co., 1894. 212 pp.

O'Brien, Robert C. *Mrs. Frisby and the Rats of NIMH*. Illus. by Zena Bernstein. New York: Atheneum, 1971. 233 pp.

Saint Exupéry, Antoine. *The Little Prince*. Illus. by the author. Tr. from the French by Katherine Woods. New York: Harcourt, 1943. 91 pp.

Saunders, Marshall. *Beautiful Joe*. Philadelphia: American Baptist Pub. Soc., 1894. 304 pp.

Selden, George, pseud. *The Cricket in Times Square*. Illus. by Garth Williams. New York: Ariel Books, 1960. 151 pp.

Sendak, Maurice. *Higglety Pigglety Pop! or, There Must Be More to Life*. Story and pictures by Maurice Sendak. New York: Harper, 1967. 69 pp.

Sewell, Anna. *Black Beauty: His Grooms and Companions.* London: Jarrold and Sons, 1877. 247 pp.

Sharp, Margery. *Miss Bianca.* Illus. by Garth Williams. London: Collins, 1962. 143 pp.

———*Miss Bianca in the Orient.* Illus. by Erik Blegvad. London: Heinemann, 1970. 121 pp.

Steig, William. *Abel's Island.* New York: Farrar, 1976. 177 pp.

Traill, Catharine Parr. *Little Downy; or The History of a Field-Mouse.* London: Dean and Munday, 1822. 48 pp.

White, E. B. *Charlotte's Web.* Pictures by Garth Williams. New York: Harper, 1952. 184 pp.

White, T. H. *The Sword in the Stone.* London: Collins, 1938. 338 pp.

Williams, Margery. *see* Bianco, Margery Williams.

Light Fantasy

Alexander, Lloyd. *The Marvelous Misadventures of Sebastian.* New York: Dutton, 1970. 204 pp.

Aiken, Joan. *Black Hearts in Battersea.* Illus. by Pat Marriott. London: Jonathan Cape, 1965. 191 pp.

———*The Cuckoo Tree.* London: Jonathan Cape, 1971. 251 pp.

———*Night Birds on Nantucket.* Illus. by Pat Marriott. London: Jonathan Cape, 1966. 179 pp.

———*The Wolves of Willoughby Chase.* Illus. by Pat Marriott. London: Jonathan Cape, 1962. 159 pp.

Atwater, Richard, and Atwater, Florence. *Mr. Popper's Penguins.* Illus. by Robert Lawson. Boston: Little, 1938. 138 pp.

Babbitt, Natalie. *Search for Delicious.* New York: Farrar, 1969. 167 pp.

Cresswell, Helen. *The Piemakers.* Illus. by V. H. Drummond. London: Faber & Faber, 1967. 150 pp.

Dahl, Roald. *Charlie and the Chocolate Factory.* Illus. by Joseph Schindelman, 1964. 162 pp.

———*James and the Giant Peach.* Illus. by Nancy Ekholm Burkert. New York: Knopf, 1961. 119 pp.

Du Bois, William Pène. *The Great Geppy.* With illus. by the author. New York: Viking, 1940. 92 pp.

Gardner, John C. *Dragon, Dragon and Other Tales.* Illus. by Charles Shields. New York: Knopf, 1975. 73 pp.

———*Gudgekin the Thistle Girl and Other Tales.* Illus. by Michael Sporn. New York: Alfred Knopf, 1976. 59 pp.

Heide, Florence Parry. *The Shrinking of Treehorn.* Drawings by Edward Gorey. New York: Holiday, 1971. 63 pp.

Lindgren, Astrid. *Pippi Longstocking.* Tr. by Florence Lamborn. Illus. by Louis S. Glanzman. New York, Viking, 1950. 158 pp.

MacDonald, George. *The Light Princess and Other Fairy Stories.* London: Blackie & Son, 1890. 192 pp.; US ed. Illus. by William Pène DuBois. New York: Crowell, 1962. 48 pp.

Norton, Mary. *Are All the Giants Dead?* Illus. by Brian Froud. London: Dent, 1975. 119 pp.; New York: Harcourt, 1975. 126 pp.

————*The Borrowers*. Illus. by Diane Stanley. London: Dent, 1952. 159 pp.

Richler, Mordecai. *Jacob Two-Two Meets the Hooded Fang*. Illus. by Fritz Wegner. Toronto: McClelland & Stewart, 1975. 83 pp.

6. Science Fiction

You can, if you wish, class all science-fiction together; but it is about as perceptive as classing the works of Ballantyne, Conrad and W. W. Jacobs together as "the sea story" and then criticising that.[1]

To the uninitiated the term "science fiction" simply means another form of the "adjectival" novel, the kind based on scientific fact. For most readers of science fiction, however, neither science nor fact has much to do with their appreciation of this, their favorite kind of fiction, and their reading gratification. That readers of the genre responded to it with enthusiasm was apparent in the past and is increasingly manifest in the present.

Children and adults who read science fiction today read a great deal of it, and with this exposure they come to accept certain ideas and premises that, by repetition, take on a guise of validity. Thus there appear in this literature many phenomena which have neither basis in fact nor in accepted scientific knowledge; yet its readers readily accept such fantastic occurrences as faster-than-light travel, anti-gravity, and time travel without question. Moreover its creators have even developed a new and imaginative vocabulary to express movement through space without the operation of the laws of science —"teleporting," "space warp," "tesseract" are examples.

The growing interest in parapsychology has also entered modern science fiction, especially in the area of nonverbal communication, and this has also led to the invention of such terms as "mind touch," "kything," "grokking," and "tracing." These too have developed into concepts that have come to constitute a body of science fiction conventions that are freely drawn upon by writers as self-explanatory. They are perhaps acceptable in the sense that we accept

1. C. S. Lewis, *An Experiment in Criticism* (Cambridge: Cambridge Univ. Pr., 1961), p. 109.

the conventions of the folktale. Yet the parallel is not perfect since the folktales were based on observable human behavior, while the suspension of the laws of science requires a quantum leap of the imagination for people who do not generally read science fiction.

From its beginnings science fiction has been linked with the fantastic. Lucian of Samosata in his *True Historie* (A.D. 200) had his travelers reach the moon by means of a waterspout, and in Bishop Godwin's *The Man in the Moone* (1638), the same journey is accomplished in a swan-drawn chariot. Pulp science fiction of the 1930s and 1940s was filled with attenuated Martians and "Bug-Eyed Monsters." It is doubtless this element that prompted Sam Moskowitz, one of its eminent critics, to define science fiction as "a branch of fantasy." Although he went on to point out that it "eases the willing suspension of disbelief . . . by utilizing the atmosphere of scientific credibility for its imaginative speculation in physical science, space time, social science and philosophy,"[2] it is "the branch of fantasy" that seems to have appealed to most writers rather than "scientific credibility."

Peter Dickinson exemplifies this sometimes fatal attraction in his children's novel, *The Weathermonger* (1968). When he portrays Merlin, forcibly addicted to morphine, as the unwitting instigator of changes in the English weather, so that, mirabile dictu, in turn, society is transformed, the difference between fantasy and science fiction becomes negligible.

Tolkien said of fantasy that it is "undefinable but not imperceptible"; that is, it is perceived by one's imagination and intuition rather than by one's rational faculties. However, science fiction may be undefinable and imperceptible simply because its parameters vary with the circumstances of its application. The aficionados of science fiction who reject the term in favor of the abbreviation S/F are perhaps taking the more sensible approach. S/F can stand for Science Fiction, Science Fantasy, Space Fantasy, Speculative Fiction, or even the grotesque "Schlock Fantasy." It may be the breadth of the genre that inspired Brian Aldiss to describe it as "a whacky sort of fiction that grabs and engulfs anything new or old for its subject matter, turning it into a shining and often unsubstantial wonder."[3] It certainly does grab and engulf, taking in fantasy, realistic fiction, historical fiction, and social fiction, melding them frequently into a potpourri. The foreword to Sylvia Engdahl's

2. Sam Moskowitz, *Explorers of the Infinite* (Westport, Conn.: Hyperion Pr., 1963), p. 11.
3. Brian W. Aldiss, *Billion Year Spree* (London: Weidenfeld & Nicolson, 1975), p. 2.

Enchantress from the Stars (1970) is exemplary of how the vagueness of some science fiction can make a mockery of sense:

> The locale of this story can be fixed neither in space nor in time. Perhaps it is the planet Earth—but then again, perhaps not. . . . This narrative is no more a prophecy than a history. Yet this, within the limits of its form, is how things *may* have been . . . or how they will be . . . or how they now are, somewhere.

The liberty expressed by Engdahl should perhaps make science fiction the most exciting form of writing today, but its very breadth, both in its totality and its mixture of genres even within one book, can negate its impact. Her *Enchantress from the Stars* is an ambitious failure in its strained attempt to meld folklore, space travel, and pseudoparapsychology. Realistic fiction, historical fiction, and fantasy have more precise limits and are strengthened thereby.

Even the once common criterion which attempted to define science fiction as novels of the future presents difficulties and ultimately fails to apply. The present has an uncanny habit of leaping ahead of itself and what seems to be the distant future today is suddenly commonplace tomorrow. Jules Verne's *Twenty Thousand Leagues under the Sea* now reads like a historical submarine novel and his *From the Earth to the Moon* a spoof on space travel. Moreover, many science fiction novels require only a moment's belief that we are in the future and then, after some appropriate catastrophe, they plunge us into a world that is actually primeval or medieval. Thus Conan Doyle's *The Lost World* and its Russian counterpart, V. A. Obruchev's *Plutonia*, both of which describe pockets of primitive forms that have continued on into the present, are considered science fiction.

Like realistic novels of the past whose details of the social scene tend to date them all too quickly, the majority of early adult science fiction novels are now remembered for their charm as period pieces, rather than for their accuracy as predictions of the future. The most outstanding of these linger in the mind for fairly specific reasons. Who can forget Wells's Martians in *The War of the Worlds,* so imaginatively described as to become stock characters in "pulp" S/F, and Walter Miller's *A Canticle for Leibowitz* with its ironic picture of a future isolated religious community cherishing the remnants of scientific papers as holy relics?

Whether difficult or not to define, adult science fiction does have some conspicuous examples of individual works that, by consensus, can be considered science fiction. The science fiction written for children, on the other hand, has no such touchstones by which it may be measured and judged. Thus the character of children's science fiction cannot be deduced from its "shining successes" in the way that the works of Hester Burton or Rosemary Sutcliff exemplify the best for historical fiction, Ivan Southall for realistic fiction, Susan Cooper for fantasy, and Leon Garfield for the novel of atmosphere. Children's science fiction, to date, simply has no such distinguished and defining practitioners.

In fact, it is interesting to note that fantasy written for children is far superior to that written for adults, while the reverse applies to children's science fiction which tends to ape, in diminishing and diminutive detail, its adult counterpart. The qualities of imaginative invention and universal morality that make children's fantasy credible and purposeful are almost totally missing in children's science fiction.

These uncertainties, together with the absence of definitive boundaries, in children's science fiction in particular, may explain the lack of so essential a component as the "willing suspension of disbelief." While credibility is a necessity in all literary genres, in science fiction a novel tends to be criticized primarily for its scientific or technological failings, rather than for its weakness in imaginative elements. Is one to fault a writer such as David Craigie in *The Voyage of the Luna I* (1948) for putting vegetation on the moon or to praise him for breaking the laws of known fact, just as the laws of rationality are broken in fantasy? In this instance and in most others, the absence of imaginative inventiveness turns improbable science to absurdity, to spurious farce.

The flawed character of the Craigie book and of all other early books of children's science fiction, few though they were, is partially explainable by the late appearance of the genre in children's literature. Victor Appleton's *Tom Swift* books (whose forerunners were Roy Rockwood's *The Great Marvel* series) began appearing in 1910, but these crude relics of a less sophisticated time are only barely on the fringes of science fiction. The term itself was not coined until 1926 to provide a more pronounceable substitute for Hugo Gernsback's "scientification"; besides, the *Tom Swift* books at best were really only stories of inventions quite in tune with the then prevailing American passion for gadgetry. They had neither the seriousness nor the soundly based scientific background of the books written by Jules Verne who, according to his biographer, worked very closely with scientists. Even the second, contemporary series of *Tom Swift* books hardly promotes respect for their science content. When his makeshift and untested machine devised to foil the enemy and obtain the valuable undersea commercial lode of "neo-aurum" blows up,

133

Tom is "embarrassed and worried" because a direct hit "would have killed any one of us." Testing is not the young inventor's strong point.

The first clearly identifiable work of science fiction for children is Robert A. Heinlein's *Rocket Ship Galileo* (1947). The decades of the 1940s and 1950s were the heyday of the science fiction "pulps" in adult literature, the "space operas," an image that still calls forth disparagement of the genre. Heinlein has the dubious distinction of introducing the "space opera" to children's science fiction. Three high-school boys and a scientist, aged about 40, go to the moon in a do-it-yourself, made-in-the-backyard rocket. As the year is 1947, perhaps one should not be surprised that they find a nest of Nazis on the moon preparing for world conquest. *Rocket Ship Galileo* is an example of the transposed plot; put "cloak and dagger" on the moon and it becomes science fiction.

Heinlein did much the same in *Podkayne of Mars* (1963), an old-hat earth plot that combines kidnapping, terrorism and violence, and the United Nations. In describing travel from Mars to Venus, Heinlein does give what one assumes to be a scientific explanation of the "take-off" in a space ship with fact and fiction so mixed up that probably only his heroine Poddy, with her I.Q. of 148, can understand it. Other aspects are cloudily treated. In speaking of the space-port Deimos, we get this information:

> (Well, I admit that mother didn't exactly build Deimos; the Martians did that, starting with a spare asteroid that they happened to have handy. But some millions of years back they grew tired of space travel and devoted all their time to the whichness of what and how to unscrew the inscrutable.)

Heinlein has himself condemned a lack of invention based on realistic detail:

> It is not enough to say, "With a blast the space ship took off for Mars." Oh, it may do for comic books and for pulp magazines aimed at ten-year-olds, but not for serious literature. [4]

And while maintaining that "Science and science fiction do interact," [5] he is guilty of at least a gross improbability when he has his young hero in *Farmer in the Sky* (1950) save a starship that a meteor has struck by plugging the hole with his jacket.

Perhaps such improbabilities are acceptable simply because science fiction moves so uneasily between realism and fantasy. Inter-

4. Robert A. Heinlein, "Science fiction: its nature, faults, and virtues," in Basil Davenport et al, *The Science Fiction Novel* (2nd ed.; Chicago: Advent, 1964), p. 48.
5. Ibid., p. 36.

stellar flight is an example. In fact, to reach a typical galaxy situated near the limits of telescopic observation would take fifty years' time measured by flight crews and six billion years in earth reckoning. [6] If one can find plausible such a journey within brief human time, to cavil at minor details is perhaps to "strain at a gnat and swallow a camel." Yet *The Twenty-One Balloons* (1947) by William Pène DuBois serves as a reminder that books can cross lines and still be completely satisfying. This account of Professor Sherman's adventurous balloon trip with its stopover on the island of Krakatoa, landing on a diamond mine, and visit to a utopian society built on food- and labor-saving devices can be said to have elements of science fiction. It fits just as happily though into the extravagant and humorously inventive "tall tale" along with Atwater's *Mr. Popper's Penguins*. In the final analysis it is the book's artistry that counts and not the genre to which it is consigned.

Although the scientific and technological advances occasioned by World War II had an explosive effect upon science fiction for adults, curiously enough, that for children was almost unaffected. There were the popular *Mushroom Planet* fantasies by Eleanor Cameron and Heinlein's planetary adventure stories such as *The Red Planet* (1949), *Farmer in the Sky* (1950), and *The Rolling Stones* (1952), the latter being more satisfying in its portrayal of youthful energy and ingenuity than in its depiction of other worlds. Genuine scientific extrapolation was evident in only a few books, particularly Arthur C. Clarke's *Islands in the Sky* (1952) which is an interesting prophecy of Skylab. Clarke is a renowned physicist and his expertise in this book is obvious. Yet his story reads like a textbook, rather than a piece of crafted fiction and is now out of date. Science has, of course, also caught up with Jules Verne, but *Twenty Thousand Leagues under the Sea* remains a fascinating story.

With the advent of the 1960s, the vestigial remains of the adjectival power of the word "science" in science fiction vanished, seeming to surrender to the rising interest in sociology and psychology. While major writers for adults had quite consistently hewed to science fiction's traditional role of giving warnings about the future based on present realities, this sociological aspect had been less noticeable in that written for children. But it soon became a major stream, defining earth's present and imminent future, as opposed to exotic, alternative planetary worlds. With this alliance to adult science fiction of the period, children's science fiction too became earthbound, gaining a credibility in its everyday details and chillingly

6. Frederick I. Ordway, 3rd, *Life in Other Solar Systems* (New York: Dutton, 1965), p. 82.

convincing interpretations of future environmental and social collapse. While so doing, it lost its emphasis on technological gadgetry, and, more importantly, any naive, idealistic view of the future.

While the sociological works of science fiction for children became earthbound, another development, that of science-fiction fantasy, began to make itself apparent. Such tales of fantasy commonly swirled around other planets, portraying their protagonists as having or developing their psychic powers. Upon becoming confluent with pure fantasy, it only became distinguishable as science fiction by the fact that events either emanated from or took place on a planet other than Earth. Some writers, of course, made use of both streams, usually to their detriment.

With the appearance of John Christopher's *The White Mountains* (1967) and its sequels, *The City of Gold and Lead* (1967) and *The Pool of Fire* (1968), the "message" science fiction for children became firmly established. Not surprisingly, the plot of Christopher's trilogy bears a strong resemblance to *The War of the Worlds* (1898) by H. G. Wells, considered the father of social science fiction, just as Jules Verne is considered the father of scientific science fiction. Wells's Martians, who were encased in metal in order to cope with Earth's atmosphere, are by Christopher called Tripods and encased in gigantic walking towers for the same reason. They are defeated by much the same means, too—the Martians succumbing accidentally to our germs and the Tripods to our atmosphere.

However, Christopher's social message is presented more simply and strongly than that of Wells, who generally envisioned the future as a jungle through which humanity must fight its way, always on guard against aliens. Christopher is more specific about the inability of the human race to learn a lesson. At the end, the representatives of the remnants of Earth's varied governments meet in a United Nations-type conclave. National divisions are immediately apparent and the planet's peoples revert to their old narrow boundaries, presumably in the future to be again so divided that they will once more be an easy conquest for invaders from space.

In the ruins of the technological age that Christopher describes, only a few of the ramifications of science and technology are noticeable and, aside from the domed city of the Tripods, only at their most destructive: "mind-capping," the Tripods' method of mind control, as well as the old-fashioned airplane and balloon armaments that end the third book, *The Pool of Fire*. The absence of scientific progress is even more noticeable in his second trilogy—*The Prince in Waiting* (1970), *Beyond the Burning Lands* (1971), and *The Sword of the Spirits* (1972). These books are also typical of their decade, showing an even greater disillusionment with science and technology than those of the

1960s. Again the setting is a future Earth. Science and machines have been blamed for a volcanic upheaval that plunges England into a feudal society. Humanity's climb is a return to trains, roads, electricity, and cannon—the world of the late nineteenth century. The cyclic message that society will rise, only to decline, is repeated.

For his time, Christopher's works exhibit most of the characteristics of science fiction in general. In making society itself the main character, as it were, there is a corresponding de-emphasis on individual characters; they are representative of a type, fashioned of cardboard rather than flesh and blood. In placing emphasis upon social doctrine, writers seemed almost afraid to allow their readers to become anthropocentric, to enjoy identification with a strong protagonist. In the *White Mountains* trilogy, Will is the impetuous, but brave boy; Beanpole, the budding scientist; and Julius the wise old leader, while the other characters are identifiable only by what they do.

Basically, Christopher tells rather than shows. His style is clear, straightforwardly devoid of allusions and imagery, and unmemorable, yet less pedestrian than was customary. It does allow for concentration on the plot—the urge to turn the pages to find out "what happens next"—and in this sense science fiction for children still follows the tradition of the average adventure story, but without its romance. The mystic city of Rider Haggard's *She* (1887), which could also be considered science fiction, has been replaced by the clearer outlines of the city of the Tripods, much as the fascinating curlicues of Victorian furniture have been exchanged for the clean, unimaginative, but utilitarian lines of its modern Scandinavian counterpart.

With the imaginative ruminations of scientific surmise taken out of science fiction, writers tended not only to keep their stories earthbound but to cast them in future agricultural or medieval societies, thereby giving their stories a quasi-historical sense. The advantages are obvious. Although earthbound imaginatively, the writers can convince by plausible, and indeed, accurate details. Such a technique can be seen in Peter Dickinson's trilogy about a weather change in England that caused a revulsion against machines and technology and a reversion to an agricultural society: *The Weathermonger* (1968), *Heartsease* (1969), and *The Devil's Children* (1970). These are, first of all, solidly based in the topography of England; the setting and the journeys of the children, different in each book, can almost be mapped. Therefore, actual rivers, canals, bridges, and rights of way provide a convincing context for hunts and chases.

All the details, some of them most memorable, are skillfully woven into the plots and do not strain credulity. In *The Weathermonger*, the children, having escaped from England to France, are ordered to return, to try to uncover the secret of the weather change. They need transportation while in England and a Rolls Royce, a "Silver Ghost," which was left carefully covered up, is available to them. Mechanics and fuel are sent with them. The adult mechanics, being more subject to the effects of the changes than the children, have to leave England as soon as the car is in running order. This kind of realistic touch is absent in poorer science fiction, such as Andre Norton's *Star Man's Son* (1952), in which an automobile starts after 200 years of standing idle. Norton valiantly tries to bolster her plot action by noting that the car had a "sealed" engine, but ignoring the fact that any fuel is highly volatile. As opposed to Norton's vagueness in both topography and incident, Dickinson's work is strengthened by precision. Even the shock of the sudden introduction of Merlin into *The Weathermonger* is cushioned by the practicality of the children. They face Merlin's problem not only with the aplomb of Alice in Wonderland, but with some childlike culinary and medicinal knowledge.

Still, when writer after writer seeks to convince by homely, familiar details, they seem to be admitting that a vision of a new future world is beyond their art. Rather than presenting a superscientific or technological vision, they have turned to a version of the past, a future time when the world has either fallen into chaos or is being rebuilt in the image of an old, simpler order. They take as their models today's prevalent pessimistic theories of social collapse into a new feudalism or agricultural state—a new Dark Age. The signs of slowing economic and technological growth leading to instability and fearful collapse, as prophesied in such sociological works as Roberto Vacca's *The Coming Dark Age* (1973), have been eagerly seized upon by recent science fiction writers.

Economic collapse is the theme of John Rowe Townsend's *Noah's Castle* (1975). The title quite effectively suggests a survival story and convinces through our present knowledge of the problems besetting society: high unemployment, runaway inflation, shortages, and hoarding. The father of the Mortimer family buys Noah's Castle because it is large, isolated, and has plenty of storage space for the food he has hoarded. The Mortimer family lives very well indeed. Like Christopher's, Townsend's style is undistinguished, but in presenting the different reactions of the three children to their father's supposed care, Townsend asks the traditional question of science fiction, and one that gives the genre its greatest power: "What would *you* do in such a situation?"

While presenting a realistic picture of a close extrapolation of society's present ills, Townsend joins the feudalists in describing the results of a collapse rather than giving the reasons for it. In Christopher's *The White Mountains* there is the sudden invasion of the aliens; in his *Prince in Waiting* a volcanic explosion caused by a technological overload; in Robert O'Brien's *Z for Zachariah* (1975) an atomic holocaust takes place; in Rosemary Harris's *A Quest for Orion* (1978) it is the rise of a neofascist world order.

Elisabeth Mace, in *Ransome Revisited* (1975), is equally unspecific about the particular disaster that plunges England into a primitive society, but the effects upon a group of children who are condemned to labor in a mine, much like the sweated labor of children in the factories of the nineteenth century, are most graphically described. In true biblical fashion, Mace makes it very clear that the sins of the fathers are visited upon the children. Finding and reading an old, tattered book about a group of children called the "Swallows and Amazons," Susanna and Leven can hardly credit the life of these children of the past:

> She read until it was too dark to see.
> Most of it made very little sense to him: old children doing things he couldn't understand, for *play*. But their talk was alive, and he could see the places the book described. . . .
> "I wonder what chocolate was?" Leven muttered.
> "I don't know. Something nice."

Ransome's *Swallowdale* bolsters the children's escape and provides a continuity to the story much as do the remnants of scientific papers in Walter Miller's adult novel, *A Canticle for Leibowitz.*

But the ending of *Ransome Revisited* differs markedly from this adult counterpart. The scientific optimism of the 1950s called for an escape in a space ship while earth prepared for a second atomic disaster. Conversely, Susanna and Leven have to find refuge with different groups of people struggling for a livelihood on earth. One of the chief characters, Will, who believed in the stories that his ancestors had reached the stars and who wanted to reach a colony, presumably of scientists, is not considered by Elisabeth Mace to have necessarily the true answer to present conditions. As the book ends:

> Never mind death and the stars, Will; never mind the glory and the forever, this will do the rest of my life. He walked the length of the School Room, a little boy in Class 3, and it was a muddy yard leading to a thick stone farmhouse; an old man, a stinking dog, and Swallowdale sheep waiting like white stars for his hands, on the green universe, the mountain.

Mace's style is in a large measure based on conversation, that of children who are not the products of a sophisticated education and the flatness this engenders has its own artful quality.

These stories of survival in a future-past society indicate very clearly that the "Robinson Crusoe" theme is endlessly reusable. The drive for survival is shown most effectively in Robert O'Brien's *Z for Zachariah* (1975), which is premised on an atomic disaster. A fourteen-year-old American girl survives and lives alone, coping in true pioneer fashion. An older man finds his way to her secluded valley, and although she nurses and feeds him, he attempts to attack her sexually. He is a psychopath who has already killed to save his own life. Robert O'Brien concentrates on the everyday routine that one has to observe in order to survive: the search for water, for food, and for heat. He avoids the usual temptation of offering great messages, but one point comes through clearly: humankind's greatest drive is the need to survive.

While the foregoing future–past survival stories show some optimism regarding the toughness of the individual human spirit, if not in society, those that deal with future technological societies show them as crushing the individual; in them technology is equated with authoritarianism. Indeed, John Christopher's message in *The Guardians* (1970) is to abandon hope for any type of society; there are always "the guardians." Two future societies are contrasted. London, with sixty million inhabitants, is a Conurb, where people are crowded into dingy apartments, hold routine jobs, and, as in Rome of old, are fed on bread and circuses. The latter are actually spectator sports watched on holovision—three-dimensional television. The games played are extremely dangerous, frequently to the point of death, which the Conurban crowds love.

Beyond the Conurb is the County where the gentry live, much as they did in the eighteenth and early nineteenth centuries, with fox-hunts, balls, servants, and plenty of space.

A young boy, Rob, who escapes from Conurb to the County, finds that any talk of changing either situation is frowned upon:

> "What it seems to boil down to is this: ninety-nine percent or more are happy with the way things are. The Conurbans are happy, the Commuters are happy, our servants are happy, and most of us aren't complaining. *You* want us to go out and bust everything up. Why? So that we can go into the Conurbs? Hands up those who want crowds, street rioting and mass living in general.... So that the Conurbans can come over here? With no holovision? They'd go mad inside a couple of days. All right, say it's true we're kept apart. We can't go there and they can't come here. But neither of us wants to. Are you

going to launch a revolution to force us to do what we don't
want to do?"

A minor revolution occurs, but it is quickly suppressed, for the
government is always prepared. Rob discovers that people are
watched and lobotomized just for showing more spirit than the
society requires. He escapes to join the revolutionaries, and the reader
is meant to think that the human spirit cannot be downed. Yet the
implication that it can triumph only through force, as so much
science fiction suggests, makes even the slight hope of victory less
than wholly desirable.

The society envisioned in Simon Watson's *No Man's Land* (1975)
is also of this authoritarian and conformist character. On the surface
everyone is looked after, but the countryside is being turned into
food farms run only by machines, the population crowded into
underground cities, and the elderly forced into cold, antiseptic centers
where they have nothing to do but wait for death. The triggering
event of the plot comes when the village of Hamerbrugh is being
evacuated because its existence can no longer be "justified." But two
elderly people hide out, helped by thirteen-year-old Alan, who defies
his parents and eventually the authorities to help them. The symbol
of a freer past is seen in a 900-year-old Keep, which is to be destroyed
by Giant, a huge robot so scientifically advanced that it has some
terrible power of thought and emotions that not even its makers can
control. In this Keep the old General and Alan determine to make a
stand. But:

> "We've lost then," said Alan, still unbelieving.
> "Oh! yes, we've lost. We lost long ago. We lost the day
> somebody somewhere put his mind to inventing Giant, con-
> vinced that the world would be better for it; the day somebody
> preferred a penny in his pocket to a butterfly in the field. There
> is no winning this war, Alan. You can make an isolated little
> stand for a while as Mrs. Arbuthnot and I did, but they find you
> out sooner or later. You can make a gesture such as we're going
> to make tomorrow but waving a bright sword stops no bullets.
> You, Alan must go back to the world or go to Kilda—there's
> nowhere to live in between. Outlaws are heroes for a while, but
> outlaws never die of old age."

None of these in-the-near-future societies are depicted as particularly welcome places in which to live. Victories come grudgingly and
only on an individual level; that is, the protagonists make a
tremendous effort for a slight amount of personal freedom. The
society as a whole does not change, nor does anyone in power or

authority admit to any flaws in the system. The philosophy is "the greatest good for the greatest number"; down with the individual.

How far one fights for one's own survival is the theme of William Sleator's Kafka-like novel, *House of Stairs* (1974). In a bare, white, antiseptic environment, filled only with stairs—like an Escher print come alive—five teenagers, all sixteen years old, and all without homes or families, are subjected to a terrifying experiment for control of their minds. What will they do to get food? Played out in this narrow setting—a closed society not unlike a barbaric school situation—and in a brief time span, the story is one of the most brutal in science fiction, all the more sickeningly compelling because of its finely controlled, stark writing.

The governmental authorities in this totalitarian world are looking for servants of the state to respond automatically to stimuli, like Pavlov's dogs. Two of the five children try to hang on to honor and decency, without any help against adult technology, in a struggle that owes much to Orwell's *1984*.

This pessimistic view of the future may be directly linked to the decline of faith in science and a parallel feeling of victimization by technology through pollution, nuclear energy, and dependence on oil. Gone at any rate is the tradition of the humanistic scientist, who not only saw as his interest the entire natural world but who also saw no division between the sciences and the humanities, the kind of tradition exemplified in Darwin's grandfather who expressed his botanical research in poetry, although it is to be hoped that his botanical knowledge was better than his verse![7] Gone too, then, is the resulting positive, romantic view of the future that such a humanistic science fostered in the seminal period of the nineteenth century.

The older concept of science as simply being a disinterested, pure, and neutral pursuit of knowledge only for its own sake has been replaced in popular culture by the view of science as technology, utilitarian and often suspect in its motives and goals. Therefore it is not surprising that most science fiction is antitechnological and, by extension, confusedly antiscientific. Perhaps too, contemporary science fiction writers are overwhelmed by the magnitude of scientific development and distressed by witnessing "lofty" science transformed into a dangerous, even destructive technology as it compromises itself by collusion with governments in the form of military-industrial complexes. Today, we are actually living in the science fiction age depicted by many writers only fifty years ago. So great have been the strides of industrialized society that if a person

7. Wyndham Lewis, ed., *The Stuffed Owl: An Anthology of Bad Verse* (New York: Capricorn Books, 1962), p. 108.

from the year 1900 could be transported to 1980, the cultural shock would be more enormous than that of a fourth-century Greek traveling to England in the eighteenth century.

This emphasis on the ambivalent repercussions of technology has almost eclipsed the use of space and alien beings that were the mainstay of earlier children's science fiction. Even the few survivors that continue the tradition do so against an earthly background. John Christopher's invaders from space in *The White Mountains* trilogy resurface in such books for younger children as Nicholas Fisk's *Trillions* (1971) and *Grinny* (1973).

In *Grinny*, Beth, aged 8, is the first to sense that Great-Aunt Emma (Grinny) is not who she pretends to be. She is an alien who has mind-control over the adults in the family. The children lay traps for her; they throw her off balance by playing "Eyes Right," that is speaking to a person over their shoulder and refusing to look directly into their eyes. It is this silly, childlike quality that gives the book most of its appeal. The plot to overthrow Earth and enslave its people is defeated by the children's sense of responsibility, but the conflict is more basic than that between earthling and alien. It is really the age-old tension between child and adult.

Trillions makes an attempt, however brief, to give a young reader some concept of the mystery of space. The *Trillions* are symmetrical, hard, bright objects that first fall from the sky on the village of Harbourtown West:

> You can imagine a group of children squatting on the ground, scraping together heaps of brightly coloured, mysterious grit that had fallen from the sky . . .
> 'I've got millions!'
> 'I've got billions!'
> 'I've got *trillions!*'
> Trillions it was from then on. The name fitted perfectly.

The Trillions are frightening because they can mimic, imitate, and build human artifacts. A Dr. Strangelove-style general prepares, insanely, to fight them with atomic weapons. The situation develops to the point where a curious boy with a microscope and determination is more effective than all the scientists or soldiers who are called in to deal with the phenomenon. The plot veers close to fantasy as the boy, Scott, visits the home planet of the Trillions in his dreams, and so learns to control them and carry the responsibility for doing so, an ending similar to that of Will and Bran's responsibility in Susan Cooper's fantasy *Silver on the Tree*, although more lightly handled. But *Trillions* has a moment of terror when a space commander, scarred both physically and mentally by his experience, tries to explain to the children the loneliness of space:

> 'They tell you that space is emptiness, nothingness—the void. They suggest that space, empty space, is something negative. I found out that it's not! Space *lives*. . . . Nothingness, emptiness, has a life all its own. . . . [It's] Alone, Apart, Foreign. Unlike anything known to man. Alien.'

It is rather surprising that space, either its beauty or its terror, plays such a minor role in modern children's science fiction. Both aspects of space have been best described and their effect upon an individual most frighteningly depicted in William Corlett's realistic novel *The Dark Side of the Moon* (1976). Here two young men kidnap a teenager to express the futility of life. While the kidnap plot is unfolding, an astronaut faces his first experience of the dark side of the moon and finds his journey as futile as do the young men on earth. The astronaut thinks:

> A machine is programmed—and before that a machine is put together.
> *Who put me together?*
> Don't give me that bilge about eggs and sperms. Who put me together; or the cat or the rat or the bat or the good red herring?
> We have become as machines and believe that we know all the answers.
> *We don't know nothing.*
> Here I am orbiting the moon, prior to Mars, prior to *WHAT*?
> Where are we going?
> *Nowhere.*
> Space is nowhere; nothing; void.
> What are we playing at?
> I am the whole universe; and beyond; I am infinity.

Corlett's existential view of space is far removed from the earthbound approach of most science fiction writers. They seem to strain first for a "handle," usually an atomic disaster or its consequences, which they hope will appear novel or exotic, then for a plot line that will sustain an entire novel, and finally for some little characterization. To do the writers justice, they may well feel that children's lack of self-knowledge may leave them unprepared for excursions into the future. Conversely, making them familiar with where they have come from, without the stigma of the word "historical," may bring them to a more acute sense of their present. Whatever the reason, the mystery of space, of a universe of infinite wonder, of peoples and events worth exploring on their terms rather than ours, is not often sought and even more rarely communicated.

The title of Sylvia Engdahl's *Enchantress from the Stars* (1970) promises at least the excitement of a journey through space, but the story unfolds entirely after the space ship lands on earth. Engdahl's use of aliens in the plot again distracts the reader from the real question of where they are from and how they achieved their exalted position. Her aliens are a superrace of almost maddeningly superior beings who are trying to save Andrecia, an Earth-type planet in a feudal, almost prototechnological stage, from an invasion by aliens with a more developed culture. Thus there are two groups of aliens involved, one at its imperialistic space-flight stage, representing present-day Earth; the other, an anthropological team from the more culturally advanced Federation, who are not only endowed with powers of mental telepathy and psychokinesis but who have passed beyond wars and materialism and are trying to protect the cultures of "Youngling" worlds from interference.

In many ways, the book is typical science fiction in its pomposity and didacticism. Its lessons for us come through the leader of this "field trip" who is also the father of the young heroine Elana. In spite of her superior education, Elana is probably meant to be the questioning teenager who has to experience rather than be told, and the three worlds are meant to represent where we have come from, what we are now—the imperialists with space technology but little else—and what we may become. The agents of the Interplanetary Federation, of course, travel through space with as much casualness as we hop on a jet flight to another city, but the setting is Earth.

In Engdahl's second book, *The Far Side of Evil* (1971), the parallels are even more obvious: Earth on the verge of World War III. The violence inherent in serious science fiction is again obvious as Elana is tortured by Gestapo-like agents. Although she is protected by her "mind-control" powers, nonetheless the horror has the power to penetrate that of the reader.

The focus on sociological issues and societal structures in the mainstream of science fiction does not entirely disappear in science-fiction fantasy but is rather transposed into a more abstract, experimental sphere of imagination. These works are less successful, caught as they are between the two major genres—science fiction and fantasy—and much of it therefore becomes what best might be described as pseudofantasy. After all, sociological science fiction is primarily based upon extrapolation from an actual social reality. In general, however, science-fiction fantasy, like fantasy itself, eschews the known world for an imaginary, secondary reality and is therefore often confused with pure fantasy. These "other worlds" are rarely well delineated. There is no counterpart to Lewis's "Narnia," Tolkien's "Middle Earth," or LeGuin's "Earthsea." This failure in the

"inner consistency of reality" undermines the attempts at construct-
ing any imaginary subworld. And, of course, since the willing suspension of scientific and technological disbelief is not called for, the
differences between science fiction and fantasy are irrelevant. It
becomes simply a question of what succeeds and what does not.

The formlessness and confusion inherent in science-fiction
fantasy are well exemplified in Anne McCaffrey's *Dragonsong* (1976),
which in the paperback edition is billed "as an enchanting classic of
fantasy and imagination." While *Dragonsong* is by no means a classic,
it is easy to see how it could be considered a fantasy. The elements of
fable and myth in McCaffrey's works far outweigh those traditionally
identified with science fiction, with the single exception of place, an
invented planet rather than an imaginary otherworld.

Dragons are, logically enough, the focal point in McCaffrey's
books *Dragonsong* (1976) and *Dragonsinger* (1977), both based on her
adult novels *Dragonflight* and *Dragonquest*. Even the lack of originality
in the titles suggests the eventual monotony of the plots. All the
books are set on the planet Pern which orbits around the sun Rukbat.
The planet is inhabited by humans from Earth, although this is not
made clear until a later adult book, *The White Dragon*. The planet
supports a society that is reminiscent of Earth's Middle Ages and its
populace engages in cottage industries that flourish in "Holds." There
are even the equivalents of the medieval harpists and jongleurs to
further the parallel with Earth. The young heroine Menolly wishes to
become a harpist, but this is an occupation reserved for men. Pern's
nobility is represented by the Weyrmen and Weyrwomen, who
nurture and ride the dragons that protect Pern from the dreadful
"Threads" that fall from Rukbat destroying all they touch.

McCaffrey's simple, descriptive dragonlore begs comparison
with that of Ursula LeGuin's in *A Wizard of Earthsea*, which has a
profound mythic connotation. Still, McCaffrey, like many science
fiction writers, brings some special knowledge to her works. Hers is a
knowledge of equestrian skills which she translates to the riding of
dragons with the result that the passages describing this activity are
so convincing and absorbing in their factual authenticity that the
reader is engaged to an extent not actually justified by the stories
themselves.

Although the background draws considerable strength from its
medieval flavor, McCaffrey's work exhibits many of the faults of
science-fiction fantasy in its pretentiousness of language. For example, to control the dragons, (or fire-lizards), one "impresses" them,
which seems only to mean love at first sight. The other irritant,
which unfortunately has become a staple in science-fiction fantasy is
the use of contracted proper names, probably for their presumed

146

exotic appeal. Thus McCaffrey's roll call includes F'lar, N'ton, T'gellan, T'gran, T'sel and F'nor, none a happy choice.

Similar to *Dragonsong* in tone and spirit, but far stronger in style, characterization, and plot is Lawrence Yep's *Sweetwater* (1973). Like McCaffrey, Yep writes of a feudal society on another planet inhabited by humans originally from Earth. The colonists who live on the planet Harmony are divided. The people in the city of Old Sion are descendants of the crews of the starships who had brought the colonists. Living almost entirely on the water, much as do the Venetians of today, they exist as a kind of primitive sea society, lighting their homes with luminescent mosses and taking their food from the sea. They are called "Silkies" by the inhabitants of New Sion, who have imported their so-called advanced civilization from Earth.

Yep has created a dimension beyond that of McCaffrey in his portrayal of the original inhabitants imbued with dignity and a poetic wisdom, although "alien" in appearance:

> He looked very much like a four-foot-high Earth spider, though you would never suggest that to an Argan. They hate to be reminded of their resemblance to their Earth cousins the way humans hate to be reminded that they look like apes.

The young Silkie boy Ty has made friends with an old Argan, Amadeus, because of their shared love of music. When the Silkies' way of life is threatened by both the crass materialists from New Sion and the Seadragons, the Argans come to their rescue. The story is a struggle among three ways of life and at the end the Argans retreat forever from human contact.

The planet of Yep's devising is little different from Earth, even to the playing of the old hymn "Sweetwater," which gives the book its title. But while tourists are as crass and demanding as they are anywhere else and the grim landlord calls for eviction in true "East Lynn" style, the story remains memorable for its evocation of a different mode of life, but one that encompasses familiar human qualities such as loyalty, friendship, and the healing power of music.

Sweetwater bears a marked resemblance to Ray Bradbury's adult novel *The Martian Chronicles* in its portrayal of an advanced alien life retreating before the technology of the supposedly advanced human beings, much as the Indians and Inuits gave in to the advance of European civilization.

McCaffrey and Yep are prototypical examples of the best science-fiction fantasy, combining, with reasonable success, qualities of both genres. Madeline L'Engle's *A Wrinkle in Time* (1962) is less definable, which is not in itself a fault. In this instance the confusion arises from writing that is eclectic rather than selective, innovative rather than original, and ultimately muddy in purpose and style. Although beginning with an Earth family environment, the action quickly moves into space, not by means of scientific technology but by "tesseracting" (kitty-cornering through space). Hailed as science fiction, it is similar in many ways to modern world-swapping fantasies based in Christian theology, such as C. S. Lewis's *Narnia Chronicles* or Ruth Nichols's *A Walk Out of the World*. L'Engle, too, attempts the conflict of good versus evil inherent in most major contemporary fantasies, but her pseudometaphysics and doctrinaire messages have neither the urgency of sociological science fiction nor the grandeur of the best fantasy. Without its space-opera costume, *A Wrinkle in Time* would simply be uninspired fantasy.

Both the plot and the characters of *A Wrinkle in Time* are strained. Meg and her five-year-old brother Charles William can communicate mentally with one another and in a vague location in space they battle for the survival of civilization itself, fighting for genius, individualism, and human excellence in the face of an antihuman brain, which unfortunately rings too many bells with Dorothy's confrontation with the bogus great brain in *The Wizard of Oz*.

This kind of American pop history continues in the latent imperialism of L'Engle's subsequent book, *A Swiftly Tilting Planet* (1978). In this sequel to *A Wrinkle in Time*, Charles William, now fifteen years old, travels, in his mind, on a unicorn through time and space, entering other people's minds and bodies in an effort to alter human destiny and free human will in a noncredible attempt to save world peace. Crammed with characters from different periods, the narrative is difficult to follow. One can only hold on to the thread that the president of a small South American state may or may not loose an atomic bomb upon the world because of the color of his eyes. They have to be blue!

Tampering with free will and history have been generally considered antithetical to the tradition of dramatic conflict. Unfortunately L'Engle ignores this canon. The ill effects thereof may be seen in a comparison with Alison Uttley's historical fantasy, *A Traveller in Time* (1939). In Uttley's book, Penelope Taberner goes back in time to the period of Mary, Queen of Scots, and finds herself caught up in the Babington plot to rescue the Queen. Penelope knows the end result and realizes the inevitability of historic destiny. The plot thus gains an extra dimension of tragedy as well as a greater understanding of the human condition. Both these elements are notably absent in L'Engle's works. Her constant vision of shortcuts through space seems to head her into a similar kind of casual disregard of the complexities of human life.

L'Engle also illustrates the propensity for overwriting so

148

prevalent in much of science-fiction fantasy. Presumably in the attempt to create the imagery of first-rate fantasy, the writer's style often becomes overladen to the point of muddiness. Thus, in *A Wrinkle in Time* there are three good, witchlike characters reminiscent of Charles Kingsley's Mrs. Doasyouwouldbedoneby in *The Water Babies*. However, her writing makes these characters seem like parodies of Kingsley's clear-cut approach:

> "We cannot come to you now," Mrs. Who's voice blew to them like the wind. *"Allwissend bin ich nicht; doch viel ist mir bewisst.* [sic] Goethe. *I do not know everything; still many things I understand.* That is for you, Charles. Remember that you do not know everything." . . .
>
> "Tto alll tthreee off yyou I ggive mmy ccommandd," Mrs. Which said. "Ggo ddownn innttoo tthee ttownn. Ggo ttogetherr."

L'Engle's strained writing and imagination falters even more when she moves outside of the domestic lives of her scientist family, as, for instance, when she has the mother making a meal on her Bunsen burner. In these deficiencies she is akin to that ubiquitous writer of science-fiction fantasy Andre Norton who, in such books as *Forerunner Foray* (1973) and *No Night without Stars* (1975) presents only vaguely described other planets. Both have either forgotten or are unfamiliar with Tolkien's dictum that:

> Anyone inheriting the fantastic device of human language can say *the green sun*. Many can then imagine or picture it. But that is not enough. . . . To make a Secondary World inside which the green sun will be credible, commanding Secondary Belief, will probably require labour and thought, and will certainly demand a special skill.[8]

Neither L'Engle nor Norton possess this "special skill."

L'Engle and Norton also are alike in their constant reliance on parapsychological ploys. The claims and counterclaims for the validity of extrasensory perception (ESP) are only of concern here as affecting literary skill in the commanding of belief. The two authors seek to convince by mere force of repetition, rather than by bolstering this imaginative concept with a base in reality. The works of both swarm with ill-defined characters and events.

A more persuasive melding of the intangible to the tangible, and the incredible to the credible are the marks of such writers as K. M. Peyton in *A Pattern of Roses* (1972), Peter Dickinson in *The Gift* (1973), John Rowe Townsend in *The Xanadu Manuscript* (1977), and

8. J. R. R. Tolkien, *Tree and Leaf* (London: Unwin Books, 1964) p. 51.

especially Virginia Hamilton in *Justice and Her Brothers* (1978). The change in actual human development due to the expansion of the human mind that has already been used in such adult science fiction as Arthur C. Clarke's *Childhood's End* and John Wyndham's *The Chrsyalids* is encountered in these children's books as well. In them the children's newly developed powers also signal a change in society. Like Clarke and Wyndham, these writers for children keep their plots firmly rooted on present-day Earth and moreover portray the family life of their young protagonists realistically.

These writers also use the idea of the expansion of mental powers in somewhat different ways. Peyton limits *A Pattern of Roses* to one individual, a boy of the 1970s who can empathize with a boy of 1910, even to struggling within his body. She uses the ESP device not only to illustrate the past, which is extremely well done, but to give drama to a boy's problems of "growing up." In Dickinson's *The Gift*, the young protagonist has inherited a family trait and the plot is worked out more as a serious family story. In Townsend's *The Xanadu Manuscript*, the power of mental time-shifting belongs to our descendants of the year 2149, who return as tourists to their past and our present. Townsend gives us only a glimpse of the perfect future society our descendants have made for themselves, but he says much in little space about the boredom of perfection. The future-father who has discovered the pleasures of the past's pubs and race courses says:

> 'I'm not sure that I wouldn't rather die of drink than of boredom. I'm not sure that a few months in this lively twentieth-century mess wouldn't be preferable to a lifetime of reliable good behaviour in our own day.'

Townsend's casual tongue-in-cheek approach, both to the drawbacks of a utopia and the questionable use of parapsychology, differs from that of Peyton and Dickinson, who confer the capacity for extrasensory perception upon their individualized protagonists.

A far more serious, even mystical, comprehension of transformation in human spirit and powers is seen in Virginia Hamilton's *Justice and Her Brothers*. While she concentrates on three children in one family, two of them identical twins, the effects of their psychic discoveries and manipulations are meant to show a fundamental change in the human race. Like most science fiction writers, Hamilton shies away from concrete, rational explanations:

> Their alteration must have been an accident. The difference in one chromosome was enough to alter a few inherited characteristics. Into existence could come sensory and physical changes, the release of genetic information far beyond the ordinary.

However, she does offer an arresting, strongly physical treatment of Justice's initiation into her heretofore unsuspected powers by a next-door-neighbor, whose slatternly country persona is a disguise for secret pursuits as a medium. As does Don Juan to Carlos Castaneda, she escorts Justice along the mystical path of psychic knowledge.

While this exploration of the onset of newly developing human capabilities is almost earth-shaking in children's science fiction, it is the more human intimacy of family and sibling life that gives the novel its sense of naturalness and credibility. The family is composed of eleven-year-old Justice, her twin older brothers, Thomas and Levi, her skilled workman father and her loving mother, torn between studying at college and staying home to look after her family, all moving towards a crisis in summer days of almost unbearable heat. It erupts in the incredible mental power struggle among the children for dominance—that of Tom over Levi, and the final ascendance of the newly aroused Justice who will be "The Watcher." Justice knows that, "Our place isn't here. . . . Our time isn't now, but in the future." Having shown us both normal and supernatural children in strife and play, Hamilton reassures us with the abiding nature of childhood at the end:

> They were on their bikes, Thomas in the lead. Instantly, they raced in a flurry of shining, spinning wheels and glinting metal. . . . They had nothing more on their minds than beating the heat across town. Fresh cold drinks of water. Of getting home.
> Kids.

Yet the implication that children have the fate of the world in their hands is as strong in this children's story as it is in Doris Lessing's adult novel, *The Four-Gated City*, in which, after the collapse of western society, the exploration of ESP by two women leads to its discovery and development in a group of children.

While adult authors, from John Wyndham to Clarke to Lessing, have indicated through "childhood's end" a changing human consciousness, Virginia Hamilton is the first writer for children to see such transformation toward a new human race as a mystical necessity, a view that has its roots in her earlier novel, *The Planet of Junior Brown*. Hamilton's work underlines the fact that ESP and other psychological and psychic traits, increasingly to be found in fiction, really have little to do with either science fiction or fantasy in their classic forms. Since there does not seem to be any strong reason to expand the definitions of science fiction or fantasy, perhaps what Hamilton is offering is in fact a new genre. Is it too early to suggest that what we have here is the emergence of the parapsychological novel?

Science fiction, more than any of the genres of children's literature, is rife with these multiple subgenres and adjectival classifications. Few novelists have succeeded in creating a unity or melding among them. One who has is Rosemary Harris, a writer already noted for her unclassifiable novels, exemplified by her humorous extrapolation of the biblical flood story, *The Moon in the Cloud* (1968).

Harris's *A Quest for Orion* (1978), the first of a projected trilogy, is an intrepid saga set in the final year of the twentieth century, when Britain and Western Europe are in the iron grip of a neo-Stalinist organization of technological, militaristic dictatorships, known to their enemies as the "Freaks." The Freak-States have destroyed and enslaved many democratic nations by means of satellite bombardment and virus warfare, transporting their population to Europe as slaves. A new barbarism has swept the world, as frightening and cruel as any historical memory of pillage, rape, and destruction. But small pockets of guerrilla resistance have formed throughout Western Europe, isolated and scattered but emotionally dedicated to survival and, with some luck and courage in this David and Goliath situation, to the overthrow of the enemy.

The novel is more than just a fast-paced science fiction adventure. Any comparison with John Christopher's *The White Mountains* trilogy fails, because its mythic, romantic, and fantasy strains are more reminiscent of William Mayne's *Earthfasts* or Susan Cooper's *The Dark Is Rising* quintet. The power of the ancient hero-myths and legends resonates throughout the book. The mythical protectors of Europe—the Matter of Britain and France—hover in the air:

> "Plague, sword, exodus," said Bill abruptly. "Book of Revelation come to life, that's what it is. Sword: that's what *we* need, though—where's Arthur's, or whatsisname's. Roland's?"
> "What Europe needed was another Charlemagne, Matt said," murmured Jan, rousing herself to speak of him.

The novel is the legends come to life: the sleeping kings, Arthur and Charlemagne, who are in some way returning in symbol or spirit to aid their desperate people.

There are many characters in *A Quest for Orion*, and they are vividly sketched, leaving a taste of authentically delineated individuals. For although this is a story of plot and adventure, it is also one of character growth and formation. The characters are teenagers in a tale of survival and defeat, and the effects of struggle and suffering on the individual young people are made manifest in their character development. But even in character development, Harris maintains a

152

mystic quality. Alastair, like Fiver in *Watership Down*, is a physically weak, psychically powerful person, half victim, half prophet, who becomes a kind of priest-king to a tribe of teenage boys led by his wild protector, Wolf, a slum kid whose natural survival skills and uncanny sense of leadership inspire fervent allegiance.

Wolf and Alastair are in some sense the two parts of the Arthur legend—the rough but honorable chieftain and the visionary king. One may also see in them a kind of restatement of Launcelot–Merlin–Arthur. However aligned, they do embody the essential legend of Britain. There is a harsh loyalty and emotional link between the two boys that sparks the insane jealousy of Alastair's brother, Tom, an embittered, Mordred-figure, who ultimately betrays the entire clan.

The novel's science fiction elements are observable only at the beginning (future time) and toward the end of this first book when Alastair and Walther, another of the protagonists, receive a song–chant–message from what appears to be the constellation Orion. Walther, in an astronomical observatory with his captors, notices the image of the northern hemisphere constellations beginning to circle:

> The giddy dance went on. He saw Orion's familiar belt of stars, closer and closer . . . he grew conscious of sound waves beating against his eardrums, growing in volume, high, hypnotic, meaning somehow conveyed through the rhythms of a wordless song.
>
> "You are still too far away—You must hold to the Great King's treasure. Hidden are the ways— . . . "Not flinch before . . . Deliverance . . . do you understand?"

As in all "high fantasy," the primeval struggle of good and evil is here engaged, and the striking presence of unknown, extraterrestrial powers from the constellation Orion and of the mythic legendary kings is akin to Susan Cooper's forces of Light. In this mesh of science fiction, fantasy, and psychic phenomena, the unknown beings from Orion seem to be communicating through "mind touch" rather than advanced technology. *A Quest for Orion* may be breaking new ground or it may turn out to be what Brian Aldiss called "a shining but unsubstantial wonder."[9] Since the trilogy is not complete, judgment must be suspended.

Yet it is clear that Rosemary Harris, like Hamilton, has enriched science fiction by her emphasis on character development, so lacking in children's science fiction until the 1970s. While no character in

9. Aldiss, *Billion Dollar Spree*, p. 12.

present-day writing has reached the status of a Huck Finn or a Jo March, the overall improvement is considerable and most welcome. Characters now talk to one another rather than deliver an address and the conversations add to or advance the plot. The children in particular are far less wooden. The younger ones, such as those in Fisk's *Grinny* or Dickinson's *The Changes* trilogy, are recognizable as children who might be encountered in any good children's book. They are curious, resourceful, and courageous; their previous training supports them in time of crises, as is evident in Dickinson's *The Devil's Children*:

> She'd done what she'd always been told to, if ever she was lost —waited where she'd last seen Mummy and Daddy, waited for a day and a night and another day.

While it is still true that very few characters in science fiction are remembered as individuals, at least the genre's child protagonists are no longer message-bearing stereotypes. Logically enough, the more science fiction encompasses the dramatic tensions of realistic family and peer involvements, the more natural and unique the characters have become. Along with Mace, Hamilton, and Harris, Lawrence Yep in *Sweetwater* has created two fresh characters in fourteen-year-old Ty who is studious, sensitive, and musical, but who can do a man's work and in his blind sister Caley who can yet see with an inner eye.

While there has been an increase in the general memorability of individual characters as opposed to those in earlier works, the larger and more important character, society itself, has decreased in attractiveness. Whereas earlier writers gave us utopias, modern ones create dystopias. Society has become an anti-hero, the metaphor of the ideal humanistic dream turned sour.

If, as many of its critics claim it to be, modern science fiction represents a new mythology, it certainly can be seen that the Minotaur of our time has burst from its labyrinth; it has not yet been slain. Our technology is capable of taking us to the moon, but it also threatens us with the escaped Minotaur of nuclear holocaust and annihilation. In this new mythology there are no grand heroes, certain of their tasks. Its writers apparently lack confidence in values and ideals and thus almost none depicts a society in which one would want to live. Their works are generally negative in tone, gloomy in outlook, and nostalgic for a pretechnological age of presumed human innocence.

Quite gone is the cheerful, inventive spirit of earlier children's books that were concerned with invention or technology, such as Frank Baum's *The Master Key* (1901), a remarkable romp concerning the future of electricity, the Tom Swift books, and, in a later and better vein William Pène Du Bois's *The Twenty-One Balloons* and *Peter Graves*. In most of these works the tone is lighthearted and plots concentrate on frolicsome exploration, discovery, and invention. Inventors, after all, are people who have faith in the future.

The current depletion of science in science fiction and the loss of optimism has been accompanied by the greater loss of a sense of wonder, a quality that Einstein praised in science:

> The fairest thing we can experience is the mysterious. It is the fundamental emotion that stands at the cradle of science. He who knows it not and can no longer wonder, no longer feel amazement is as good as dead.[10]

Stories of space and other planets and scientific or technological advances would seem almost ready-made as good subjects, enlarging our sense of wonder as they take us into the future. But inevitably, in contemporary science fiction, the sense of wonder is muted by the repetitive choices of futures that are either cold, austere technocracies or feudal societies in a new guise. Like the children in Mace's *Ransome Revisited* who do not understand why they have to live as they do, writers make us feel with A. E. Housman: "I a stranger and afraid/In a world I never made." [11]

The missing wonder has been appropriated in some degree by the movies and television. Children's science fiction now has a new and serious rival in such flamboyant, spectacular presentations as "Star Wars," "Star Trek," "Battleship Galactica," and the like. These films continue the tradition of new-world exploration with outstanding movie technology that no novel can duplicate. "Special effects" are offered as visually satisfying thrills, which may be immediately appealing. Even so, none are true substitutes for the deep sense of Einstein's "wonder" which has always been essential to children's perception of the world.

Writers of children's science fiction may be following the self-named "new wave" writers in adult science fiction, exemplified by J. G. Ballard and Thomas Disch. They have shifted ground even from the serious human drama of survival on earth to an exploration of their protagonists' inner survival, from the depleted resources of outer space to the never-ending wonder of inner space. Left far behind is the optimism of such earlier writers as William Morris in *News from Nowhere* (1890) or Edward Bellamy's *Looking Backward* (1888) which were set against a backdrop of socialistic democratic ideals. Even the recent adult novel *Ecotopia* (1975) by Ernest Cal-

10. From "The Talk of the Town," *The New Yorker* (May 28, 1979), p. 27.
11. A. E. Housman, [no.]XII, in *Last Poems* (London: Grant Richards, 1922), p. 28.

lenbach is only a quasi-utopia, marred by a subtle authoritarianism despite its picture of a pristine ecological environment. Such outer-directed works have also been replaced in children's science fiction by the mystical search for wonder in such inner-directed works as Harris's *A Quest for Orion* and Hamilton's *Justice and Her Brothers.*

Curiously enough, the traditional role of science fiction as prophecy has also been eroded. Most often, predictions and prophecies have come to pass before the stories begin, and the dramatic tension in the narratives is thereby lessened. With the removal of science, optimism, prophecy, and wonder, science fiction appears to have thrown away the baby with the bath water. In terms of sheer quantity, however, the genre is certainly flourishing as never before. The number of science fiction books published has quadrupled in the 1970s, and their readership has similarly increased. Both children and adults still turn to science fiction for qualities not found in other forms of writing. It has always been a literature of change and ideas, and in this sense the best of science fiction can give children an intellectual awareness about the present and the future. Now, in addition, it can sometimes offer the aesthetic and personal emotional experiences which were once the prerogatives of fantasy and realistic fiction. Perhaps the only thing old-fashioned about science fiction is its name.

Works Cited

Adams, Richard. *Watership Down.* London: Rex Collings, 1972; New York: Macmillan, 1972. 413 pp.

Appleton, Victor. "Tom Swift series." New York: Grosset, 1910-1941.

Atwater, Richard, and Atwater, Florence. *Mr. Popper's Penguins.* Illus. by Robert Lawson. Boston: Little, 1938. 138 pp.

Baum, Frank. *The Master Key; An Electrical Fairy Tale Founded upon the Mysteries of Electricity and the Optimism of Its Development.* Illus. by F. Y. Cory. Indianapolis: The Bowen-Merrill Co., 1901. 245 pp.

————*The Wonderful Wizard of Oz.* Pictures by W. W. Denslow. Chicago; New York: G. M. Hill Co., 1900. 259 pp.

Cameron, Eleanor. *The Wonderful Flight to the Mushroom Planet.* Illus. by Robert Henneberger. Boston: Little, 1954. 214 pp.

Christopher, John. *Beyond the Burning Lands.* London: Hamish Hamilton, 1971. 159 pp.

————*The City of Gold and Lead.* London: Hamish Hamilton, 1967. 185 pp.

————*The Guardians.* New York: Macmillan, 1970. 168 pp.; London: Hamish Hamilton, 1970. 156 pp.

————*The Pool of Fire.* London: Hamish Hamilton, 1968. 178 pp.

———*The Prince in Waiting.* London: Hamish Hamilton, 1970. 160 pp.

———*The Sword of the Spirits.* London: Hamish Hamilton, 1972. 159 pp.

———*The White Mountains.* London: Hamish Hamilton, 1967. 151 pp.

Clarke, Arthur C. *Islands in the Sky.* London: Sidgwick & Jackson, 1952. 190 pp.

Corlett, William. *The Dark Side of the Moon.* London: Hamish Hamilton, 1976. 159 pp.

Craigie, David. *The Voyage of the Luna I.* Illus. by Dorothy Craigie. London: Eyre & Spottiswoode, 1948. 272 pp.

Dickinson, Peter. *The Devil's Children.* Illus. by Robert Hales. London: Gollancz, 1970. 158 pp.

———*The Gift.* Illus. by Gareth Floyd. London: Gollancz, 1973. 173 pp.

———*Heartsease.* Illus. by Robert Hales. London: Gollancz, 1969. 189 pp.

———*The Weathermonger.* London: Gollancz, 1968. 160 pp.

Doyle, Sir Arthur Conan. *The Lost World: Being an Account of the Recent Amazing Adventures of Professor George E. Challenger, Lord John Roxton, Professor Summerlee and Mr. E. D. Malone of the "Daily Gazette."* London: Hodder & Stoughton, 1912. 369 pp.

DuBois, William Pène. *Peter Graves.* New York: Viking, 1950. 168 pp.

———*The Twenty-One Balloons.* Illus. by the author. New York: Viking, 1947. 179 pp.

Engdahl, Sylvia. *Enchantress from the Stars.* Drawings by Rodney Shackell. New York: Atheneum, 1970. 275 pp.

———*The Far Side of Evil.* Drawings by Richard Cuffari. New York: Atheneum, 1971. 292 pp.

Fisk, Nicholas. *Grinny.* London: Heinemann, 1973. 96 pp.

———*Trillions.* London: Puffin Books/Hamish Hamilton, 1973. 119 pp.

Hamilton, Virginia. *Justice and Her Brothers.* New York: Greenwillow, 1978. 217 pp.

———*The Planet of Junior Brown.* New York: Macmillan, 1971. 210 pp.

Harris, Rosemary. *The Moon in the Cloud.* London: Faber & Faber, 1968. 176 pp.

———*A Quest for Orion.* London: Faber & Faber, 1978. 233 pp.

Heinlein, Robert A. *Farmer in the Sky.* Illus. by Clifford Geary. New York: Scribner, 1950. 216 pp.

———*Podkayne of Mars: Her Life and Times.* New York: Putnam, 1963. 191 pp.

———*The Red Planet, A Colonial Boy on Mars.* Illus. by Clifford Geary. New York: Scribner, 1949. 211 pp.

———*Rocket Ship Galileo.* Illus. by Thomas W. Voter. New York: Scribner, 1947. 212 pp.

———*The Rolling Stones.* Illus. by Clifford Geary. New York: Scribner, 1952. 276 pp.

Kingsley, Charles. *The Water Babies.* London and Cambridge: Macmillan, 1863. 350 pp.

LeGuin, Ursula. *The Wizard of Earthsea.* Drawings by Ruth Robbins. Berkeley, Calif.: Parnassus, 1968. 205 pp.

L'Engle, Madeline. *A Swiftly Tilting Planet*. New York: Farrar, 1978. 278 pp.

———*A Wrinkle in Time*. New York: Farrar, 1962. 211 pp.

Mace, Elisabeth. *Ransome Revisited*. London: Andre Deutsch, 1975. 139 pp.; U.S. title: *Out There*. New York: Greenwillow, 1978.

Mayne, William. *Earthfasts*. London: Hamish Hamilton, 1966. 154 pp.

Mazer, Norma. *Saturday, the Twelfth of October*. Delacorte, 1975.

McCaffrey, Anne. *Dragonsinger*. New York: Atheneum, 1977. 264 pp.

———*Dragonsong*. New York: Atheneum, 1976. 202 pp.

Nichols, Ruth. *A Walk Out of the World*. Illus. by Trina Schart Hyman. Don Mills, Ont.: Longmans, 1969. 192 pp.

Norton, Andre. *Forerunner Foray*. New York: Viking, 1973. 286 pp.

———*No Night without Stars*. New York: Atheneum, 1975. 246 pp.

———*Star Man's Son*. Illus. by Nicolas Mordvinoff. New York: Harcourt, 1952. 248 pp.

O'Brien, Robert. *Z for Zachariah*. New York: Atheneum, 1975. 249 pp.

Obruchev, Vladimir Afanas'evich. *Plutonia*. Moscow: 1937. 318 pp.

Peyton, K. M. *A Pattern of Roses*. Illus. by the author. London: Oxford Univ. Pr., 1972. 132 pp.

Ransome, Arthur. *Swallowdale*. Illus. by Clifford Webb. London: Jonathan Cape, 1931. 453 pp.

Sleator, William. *House of Stairs*. New York: Dutton, 1974. 166 pp.

Townsend, John Rowe. *Noah's Castle*. London: Oxford Univ. Pr., 1975. 180 pp.

———*The Xanadu Manuscript*. Illus. by Paul Ritchie. Oxford: Oxford Univ. Pr., 1977. 170 pp.

Uttley, Alison. *A Traveller in Time*. London: Faber & Faber, 1939. 331 pp.

Verne, Jules. *From the Earth to the Moon Direct in 97 Hours 20 Minutes, and a Trip Round It*. Tr. from the French by Louis Mercier and Eleanor E. King. London: S. Low, Marston, Low & Sear Co., 1873. 323 pp.

———*Twenty Thousand Leagues under the Sea*. London: S. Low, Marston, Low & Sear Co., 1873. 303 pp.

Watson, Simon. *No Man's Land*. London: Gollancz, 1975. 190 pp.

Yep, Lawrence. *Sweetwater*. Pictures by Julia Noonan. New York: Harper, 1973. 201 pp.

7. Historical Fiction

The man without a past is a fiction; even willful ignorance cannot erase our history. Only in eternal night will man be shadowless, and the past not follow the present into the future. . . . Knowledge of the past—of history—gives perspective to our world. Without that knowledge our loneliness would be harder to bear and sorrow would easily crush us.[1]

For most adults over fifty years of age, childhood reading is almost synonymous with historical romance. Stories of swashbuckling adventure, flamboyant heroes, and spirited heroines were the staple fare of generations of children who, probably because of their own confinement to home and hearth, succumbed completely to the enchantment of distant times and places and high adventure. And as with folklore in an earlier time, children shared their books with adults, both groups absorbed by works of such writers as Sir Walter Scott, Alexandre Dumas, Robert Louis Stevenson, and, later on, Jeffrey Farnol and Raphael Sabatini.

Modern-day children, by common consent, are not interested in the past. To them, even the tales and memories of their parents and grandparents seem like prehistory, and how much can distant places mean to someone for whom the airplane is a routine means of transportation? Moreover, there is an almost calculated discouragement of the reading of history when school curricula jumble up history and geography and lump them together under the unappealing term of "socials" or social science. The result of all this seems to be a depreciation of the past, an ignorance of geography, and an unconcern for people other than themselves. The lengths to which such narcissistic insularity may go can be seen in Joyce Maynard's *Looking Back* in which, at age eighteen, she chronicles her life and

1. Erik Christian Haugaard, *The Rider and His Horse* (Boston: Houghton, 1968), p. [ix] (opening page of preface).

that of her friends when they were sixteen. The book is appropriately subtitled: "A Chronicle of Growing Old in the Sixties."

There are some hard data to support the general opinion that it is indeed the present that counts with today's children. Publishing statistics indicate that the number of contemporary-scene novels published each year far outnumber any other kind, particularly historical fiction. Moreover, those who write exclusively or mostly in this category—Rosemary Sutcliff, Leon Garfield, Barbara Willard, and Hester Burton—account to a large extent for a feeling of substance in the genre.

Having thus carefully noted factors unfavorable to the development of historical fiction, one then finds that, illogically enough, it continues to be written and even to flourish. Although the readership is in decline, its production relative to publishing in general, has increased, particularly since 1970. Moreover historical fiction has had the vitality to change so considerably in style and approach as to develop in effect new forms.

The revival of historical fiction is not easily explained. Undoubtedly the sheer strength of its traditional place in children's literature has something to do with it. It may be that its intrinsic interest is so powerful among writers of children's books that they go on writing it, publishers keep on publishing it, and adults keep buying it, even though the children themselves no longer care for it. Another possibility is the factor of nationality. The modern, established, prolific authors in this field are chiefly British—Rosemary Sutcliff, Hester Burton, Barbara Willard, and Leon Garfield—and it may be that British children enjoy reading about the past more than do their North American counterparts.

Perhaps the best explanation lies in the sheer power of talent. Whether by force of circumstance or simple coincidence, this group of writers and some others share a commitment to history and an excitement in expressing it. They have produced fiction that is every bit as convincing as the modern realistic novel, at the same time describing past societies with the knowledge and integrity of the scholar.

The new writers are not interested in historical romance, that is, a story in which sentiment takes precedence over historical sense and plot over historical events. History itself can almost be said to be their subject, with the actual events playing a dominant role in the lives of their characters. They have saved the genre, but they also have changed it.

The dimensions of this change may be seen by some examination of the road which historical fiction has traveled. The historical

160

novel, whether for adults or children, appeared late in literature. It was sparked by the "Romantic Revival" of the nineteenth century and given form by Scott's *Ivanhoe* (1820) and *The Talisman* (1825), which had settings in the distant past as opposed to his "Waverly" novels which dealt with the contemporary life of the people of the Scottish Highlands. Historical fiction written especially for children came later. Marryat's *The Children of the New Forest* (1847) described the adventures of a family of children in the days of the Cavaliers and the Roundheads; Charlotte Yonge in *The Little Duke* (1854) and *The Dove in the Eagle's Nest* (1866) and Howard Pyle in *Otto of the Silver Hand* (1888) and *Men of Iron* (1891) looked back to medieval days.

These nineteenth-century novels set the guidelines for the historical novel. The period dealt with was to be "beyond the memory of those living." The novel was also to be "rendered historical by the introduction of dates, personages, or events to which identification can be readily given."[2] Typically, then, Charlotte Yonge's *The Little Duke* introduces Richard of Normandy as a young boy and in Pyle's *Otto of the Silver Hand* we are given a picture of the devastating feuds of the German barons who are finally brought under control by Otto, the Holy Roman Emperor whom the child Otto meets at the end of the story.

But guidelines seldom can cover all cases and certainly not for all time. Thus some fiction has become "historical" although it was never designed as such. For example, Jane Austen's *Pride and Prejudice* (1813) or Louisa May Alcott's *Little Women* (1868) can now be read as novels which give us insights into the family and social life of past eras. Moreover, what is historical to an adult is not so to children. For them Mildred Taylor's *Roll of Thunder, Hear My Cry* (1976), the story of a Mississippi black family during the Depression, or Penelope Lively's *Going Back* (1975), with its World War II setting, are certainly outside of their memory. These books of the recent past, which of late have been appearing in fair numbers, are not concerned with momentous, significant, historical events, but depend on small details to recreate a feeling for a particular era—books about World War II, for example, usually are remote from military events.

In Francine Pascal's *Hangin' Out with Cici* (1977), the young protagonist suddenly realizes that she is out of her own time, back into 1944, by noticing the difference between the clothes she is wearing and Cici's clothes—full skirt, white socks, and loafers—by

2. Alfred T. Sheppard, *The Art & Practice of Historical Fiction* (London: H. Toulmin, 1930), p. 3.

sensing that no one seems afraid of strangers, and by observing that a movie costs only seventeen cents, and that Woolworth's is really a "five and dime store." Although the book has an aura of fantasy—Victoria suffers a bump on the head—and, one presumes, dreams that she is in the past where her mother is her age and her friend—the selective details emphasizing the difference between 1977 and 1944 give the book some claim to be considered a historical novel.

The larger view of what is historical depends then ultimately on the reader or when the book is read. Since this larger view would in effect eventually subsume *all* writing, this chapter will concentrate on those novels that follow the traditional definition of historical fiction. Even in this narrower approach the historical novel poses many questions. What balance of history and fiction results in a fine historical novel? How has it changed? Should the writer of today impose modern concepts upon the past?

Any formula for definitive proportions of fiction and history seems elusive. The story is told of Charles Dickens that when he decided to write a novel based on the French Revolution he went to his friend Carlyle for help and was nonplussed when afterwards a cartload of books drew up at his door. We are not told what use Dickens made of the research material provided by the great historian of the French Revolution, but we do know that *A Tale of Two Cities* (1859) has never been considered an outstanding historical novel, even by the most ardent admirers of Dickens. Many of the novelists of the past were indeed historians with an almost passionate love of historical minutiae. This brings to mind Bulwer-Lytton's *The Last Days of Pompeii* (1834) wherein the minutiae develop into pedantry; Bulwer-Lytton even felt constrained to explain in a footnote the difference in amounts of Roman money between the sester*tii* and the sester*tia!* Harrison Ainsworth in *The Tower of London* (1840) proved his knowledge of the tower to the point of boredom. Since neither *The Last Days of Pompeii* nor *The Tower of London* is hardly read nowadays, it is obvious that the gratuitous dispensing of information, however historically accurate, will not bring success to a writer.

Many earlier writers also leave the impression that they became enamored with a historical period and then fitted in characters to suit. For instance, Robert Louis Stevenson's *The Black Arrow* (1888), set in the turbulent era of the Wars of the Roses, features two young protagonists who seem borrowed from some Gothic novel. It is not Stevenson's portrayal of character but rather the romantic plot that holds the reader's interest. Such emphasis on fast-paced events was also characteristic of much later historical fiction for children, particularly of the works of Geoffrey Trease. In his *Cue for Treason* (1940) two young people are pursued across England, meet Shakespeare and act in his plays, and foil a plot against Queen Elizabeth I. Like *The Black Arrow*, it is replete with disguises, villainous rogues, and incredible coincidences.

A stronger historical background is given in the works of Cynthia Harnett who shows the value of rejecting extremes but still runs the risks that compromise inevitably brings. In fact she gives almost precisely equal shares to fact and fiction, as though the mixture were made by formula. In her *The Wool-Pack* (1951), for example, Nicholas and his friends unmask a group of Lombard merchants who are bent on ruining the English wool trade and injuring Nicholas's father in particular. Harnett does not presuppose some knowledge by the reader of the medieval wool trade. Instead, she writes in separate streams—one of history and one of fiction. The action is frequently stopped for instruction:

> The wool trade, England's most important industry, was governed by three hundred leading wool merchants, known as the Fellowship of Merchants of the Wool Staple, and it was at Calais that they had their headquarters.

These numerous explanatory interruptions make the book more a social studies text than an integrated historical novel.

Harnett's method should not be taken to imply that a large admixture of history is necessarily inimical to success in historical fiction. Indeed, in the hands of a skillful writer, the very reverse may be true. That history with only a slight dose of fiction can be exciting is proved by Walter Hodges's *The Namesake* (1964). Here, the word "history" takes on its original meaning of "a story," for there is hardly any plot beyond the dramatic events of Alfred's reign as he fights against the Vikings to save Wessex. The narrator is an old man who recalls his boyhood days with Alfred and his personal struggle to overcome the disability of having only one leg. Aside from this fictional element, and of course the dialogue, *The Namesake* is a triumph of the fascination of history itself, and not just the romance of history.

A virtually perfect mesh of history and fiction can be found in the writing of Rosemary Sutcliff. She seems to work from no recipe for mixing fact and imagination and thus, like fantasy, which it also resembles in its magic qualities, her writing defies neat categorization. Still, what cannot be defined can be observed. Thus what one perceives is that Sutcliff begins with a very well stored mind and an affinity for a given period in the distant past that she sets forth as if it were something she herself had once experienced, richly remembers, and recounts—much as some ordinary person talks about the memories of childhood or a trip. Sutcliff easily, unobtrusively, and naturally seems able to supply just the right detail at just the right time to make both setting and plot utterly convincing. Her persuasion is so compelling that readers are imperceptibly led back into the past with such subtlety they feel they are living side by side with her characters.

A good example of Sutcliff's special skill is *Outcast* (1955). In this book her hero, Beric, experiences two civilizations—the primitive, "closed" tribal life of the small, dark people who live beyond the Roman Wall and the luxury and majesty of Rome with its class society, gladiatorial arenas, and galley ships. There are in Sutcliff's works no vague, untrustworthy generalizations but neither are there pedantic, pointless details. A case in point: Beric's time as a galley slave is far more briefly described than the similar passage in Lew Wallace's *Ben Hur*, but Sutcliff's description is at least as accurate historically and far more memorable.

With her first major novel, *The Eagle of the Ninth* (1954), Sutcliff brought a new dimension into historical fiction for children, indeed into children's literature. As she does with Beric, who is in search of his identity and who yearns for love and security, she gives all her characters universal, human problems while making them vital and recognizable in their own time. And with all this she also tells a great story.

This emphasis on character is not entirely new, of course. It is certainly evident as far back as Esther Forbes's *Johnny Tremain* (1943), wherein Johnny, although involved with Paul Revere, also has to come to terms with himself and, doing so, grows up in the process. But nowadays, thanks partly to Sutcliff's influence, such emphasis is the rule rather than the exception and the attention to character is greater than ever. Such recent writers as Hester Burton, Barbara Willard, and Katherine Paterson appear to *begin* with young people in crisis, ordinary young people who are caught in the net of history and whose lives are altered by its forces. Their protagonists face the rough edges of the world, its challenges, dangers, tasks, difficulties, and possibilities of real failure and severe loss. Hester Burton has perhaps expressed the feelings of most modern writers when she said, "As a novelist, I am primarily interested in one kind of story; it is the story of young people thrown into some terrible predicament or danger and scrambling out of it, unaided."[3]

Because of this approach, most modern writers do not feel the need to concoct a strong separate plot. The events themselves, the Battle of Trafalgar or the American Civil War, do not simply provide

3. Margaret Meek, Aidan Warlow, and Griselda Barton, eds., *The Cool Web: The Pattern of Children's Reading* (London: Bodley Head, 1977), p. 161.

a stage for the characters but mold their lives. The historical events do not move to a climax but end with a formative period in the protagonists' lives. They have changed and matured and that is the point of the story. Such novels, then, have a looser construction than the older historical romances, history cannot be bent to manufacture a plot and the new writers are very good historians.

Hester Burton's novels exemplify the above approach with near precision. *Castors Away* (1962) zooms in on the year 1805 and its culminating event, the Battle of Trafalgar. The 28th Regiment of Foot is wrecked off the Suffolk coast and a young soldier is washed up on its shores. At first presumed dead, he is restored to life by the combined efforts of Dr. Henchman and his children in a surprising, but documented medical triumph. To the children's horror, the soldier is to be punished upon his recovery; he will receive 500 lashes for being drunk at the time of the shipwreck. Burton does not make this authenticated incident part of a strong plot. She uses it as a step in increasing the emotional sensitivity of her characters. The children are changed by both experiences; they have gained a new respect for life and so they are repelled by a society that would deliberately take away a life so recently won from death. When the oldest boy, Tom, has the opportunity to join a ship in Nelson's fleet, his father tries to explain to a distraught aunt why he is not too young to fight:

> 'Here in this beautiful home, Susan, protected and loved by us both, my children have seen the very worst that life has to offer us.'
> 'Pain? Death?'
> 'No. No, my dear. Man's inhumanity to man. Senseless, heartless, cold-blooded cruelty. What more has Simon's naval engagement to teach Tom? Nothing. Nothing so bitter.'

Tom, initially caught up in the excitement of battle, soon perceives its harsh realities:

> A shot roared through an open gun port and tore off the leg of a powder monkey waiting among his gun crew. The boy screamed. His blood was spattered all over the berth. Tom felt sick. He had never expected it would be like this.

Instead of dwelling on Nelson's glorious victory, Burton describes the stench of the wounded and dying leaving Nelson's ship, a picture of the suffering sailors that is matched only in Hardy's *The Trumpet Major*. Nell, the Henchman daughter, also suffers. She has the anguish of watching her brother go off to battle, not knowing when or if he would return. In addition, her Aunt Julia is set on stamping out any signs of unladylike behavior. Nell is frustrated by 'the indignity of being a girl.' She is miserable with nothing to look

165

forward to for years and years 'and then it'll only be a husband who'll give me a bunch of keys to jangle round his house.' Her life takes a turn for the better when the intellectual M. Armand becomes her tutor and mentor and she meets her brother's friend, John Paston, a champion of 'Women's Rights.' The societal indoctrination of women as inferior to men is clearly shown in the nursemaid's stance: 'It's against the Bible,' and later on 'Our brains are smaller.'

For Burton background always has a direct relationship to her characters; it is more than a mere backdrop. Edmund Henchman does not only observe the state of medicine in the first years of the nineteenth century, he is to become a doctor. Like Sutcliff, Burton can also have child speak to child across the years as Nell in a realistically yet movingly described scene has her first experience of death.

It perhaps could be argued that *Castors Away* is too episodic a novel, with too many themes to make it compelling. But life itself is not one-stranded, and in its diversity within its period the story has a feeling of naturalness, especially when daily events are expressed in a conversational style and with a feeling for family life. As the Henchmans pack up to go to the seaside: 'What a scramble it *always* was!'

The great figures of the time do not appear in Burton's novels; they appear rarely, if at all, in most of the "new wave" historical fiction. The young people are not involved in high deeds in high places but with the daily social, religious, and political events that affect the lives of ordinary people, particularly the poor, the dispossessed, and the persecuted. Unlike the depiction of the young in many a modern realistic novel, Burton's protagonists are not whiners. They reach maturity by trying to help others as well as themselves. They have little time for their own inward considerations.

In Burton's *No Beat of Drum* (1966), mechanization comes to rural communities in England, but, in contrast to modern times, there is no state authority to feed those dispossessed of their jobs by the threshing machine and no labor union to fight their battles. The young girl Mary and the young farm laborers who take part in the protest are exiled to 'Demon's Land.' Burton makes it clear how terrible an injustice has been perpetrated, but even so her reasoned look at events never fails. In *No Beat of Drum* she shows that a mob, such as the farm laborers burning the ricks, even with right on its side, can become dangerously crazed. More important, however vividly Burton depicts the dreadful conditions of the past, she, as do Hardy and Conrad, affirms life's essential worth. She shows the nobler side of human nature, and in the end good always triumphs. So, in *Thomas* (1969), which portrays the persecution of the Puritans, we see the friendship and loyalty of the three young people surviving their religious and political differences. In *No Beat of Drum*, Mary and her

Joe, after all their sufferings, are rewarded by love and prosperity in Australia.

Burton's happy endings are not merely the reassuring contrivances that figure in so much writing for children. If her characters win happiness, it is because they have earned it. Her girls particularly are strong, vibrant characters who act with courage and good sense. Nell (*Castors Away*), Margaret (*Time of Trial*), Lucy (*Riders of the Storm*), Mary (*No Beat of Drum*), Richenda (*Thomas*), and many more are not just people whom events involve. Even in the then severe bondage of being female, they resolve, they act, they achieve. The status of women is, of course, an evocative indicator of the past and Burton is always subtly working to make the reader understand that the past is not a strange and exotic period.

She also makes use of nature and landscape. With their timeless qualities, these provide a means of linking past and present, of making clear which aspects of life change and which do not. Here, for example, is Stephen in *The Rebel*, just after he has left his uncle's house in disgrace:

> From this vantage-point, he watched the morning grow, bathing his native hills with an unpromised splendour. The November sunlight glowed in the tawny bracken farther down the slopes, glinted in every stream and runlet, and caught in every droplet hanging from every grass blade close at hand, so that each way he turned he was dazzled and enchanted by the million refractions of its rays. The artist in him that could not draw and the poet in him that was wordless were swept with joy. For a magic moment, he forgot the injustices of life.

Often in these stories we are made aware of the weather. The author seems to be saying, "Yes, they had weather in olden times too." Such a simple idea, but Burton senses that it may be occurring for the first time in the mind of the child reader. However, on a deeper level, such scenes express the continuity of the natural world in tandem with the human lives that inhabit it.

The result is that more than any other historical writer for children, Hester Burton's themes evoke parallels with modern times. They may not always be as prominent as that of freedom of press and speech in her *Time of Trial*; still, great issues are always in evidence and being great they have connotative value even for our own era. Thus *To Ravensrigg* (1977) begins with young Emily Heskett's first experience of slavery and her response is to help a young, runaway West Indian boy. Technical advances and their effects upon the laboring poor is the main theme of *No Beat of Drum*; religious persecution of a group provides the deep moral sense of *Thomas*.

167

Because her protagonists are young, intelligent, and sensitive, Burton leaves her readers with some sense of hope on a personal level, but still most young readers will understand that many of the issues Burton raises are still unresolved today.

Paradoxically enough, this very modernity sometimes operates against Burton as a historical novelist. Although her historical sense is impeccable and her treatment of details is of unquestionable accuracy, she lacks the power of the old-fashioned historical novelist to "transport" readers, to carry them away into distant times and places.

The capacity to provide escape belongs in greater degree to Barbara Willard, who has not thereby demonstrated a greater skill but rather a different style and purpose. Willard largely achieves a rapport with the past by concentrating on one place and basically one family, although different branches of it, in different periods of time. Her Mantlemass novels are family sagas, "romans fleuves," and one sinks into each succeeding novel with a feeling of familiarity and comfort—very like picking up another Trollope novel. There will be no great surprises.

The place that raises such steadfast devotion is the manor house of Mantlemass and its surrounding forests of Sussex, where the various families struggle with their destinies from the time of the Plantagenets to Cromwell. The Mantlemass novels are filled with great historical events, but we only see them as they affect the families.

Thus there is only one recognizable historical figure, Richard III, who is shown on the eve of the Battle of Bosworth in *A Sprig of Broom* (1971). He has sent for his illegitimate son, Richard, who has no knowledge of his father. In the wrenching change from Plantagenet to Tudor rule, the boy Richard of Plantagenet descent becomes Dick Plashet the forester, and the secret is kept for generations, only occasionally suspected by some members of the family. Lilias in *The Iron Lily* (1973), set in the time of Mary Tudor, has a crooked shoulder, as of course did Richard III. So Richard III, without figuring directly in the action of more than one of the novels, somehow takes part in them all. It is a telling demonstration of how a skillful writer can effectively use history in fiction without being subservient to it.

Because so few of the Mantlemass people actually participate in the battles of the time and because the taking of sides is a dominant theme in only the last book, *Harrow and Harvest* (1974), the result is that the Mantlemass narratives portray a kind of buffer between day-to-day living and the great events of wars and kingdoms and catastrophe. It is history as the passage of time, history as ebb and flow that seems to be the main character in the series and even in each individual book.

The impact of specific great events is seen far more immediately in two American novels, *My Brother Sam Is Dead* (1974) by James Lincoln Collier with Christopher Collier (the Revolution) and *Hew Against the Grain* (1977) by Betty Sue Cummings (the War between the States). Both books are closer to Hester Burton's concern with major social and ethical issues than to Barbara Willard's deliberate detachment from grand events. War—conflict as huge and convulsive —is the centerpiece in the Collier and Cummings novels and war affects every character, even those who would prefer to remain neutral and removed. Both *My Brother Sam Is Dead* and *Hew Against the Grain* raise specific questions: *Is war really necessary* in resolving differences? Are the disruption and outright destruction of lives too high a price to pay for patriotism, no matter which side one is on? The questions are not resolved in any overt way that affects the outcome of the events themselves, rather they are the focus for the voicing of the feelings of ordinary people caught in and victimized by the snares of the war. Most seriously both books raise Erik Haugaard's concept of evil—it is not so much a question of evil as it is the evil that good can do.

The Meeker family in *My Brother Sam Is Dead* live in the Tory town of Redding, Connecticut, at the time of the Revolution. The Meekers wish to remain neutral but in a period of confused, conflicting loyalties this proves impossible. Sam, the oldest son does commit himself to the Revolutionary forces but is executed by his own side on false charges of cattle-stealing. In war, it is more important to make an example than to establish the truth. Sam's brother Tim recalls the events in his old age:

> Free of British domination, the nation has prospered and I along with it. Perhaps on some other anniversary of the United States somebody will read this and see what the cost has been . . . even fifty years later, I keep thinking that there might have been another way, besides war, to achieve the same end.

The devastating side effects of the violence of war on one family is also the theme of *Hew Against the Grain*. With the advent of the Civil War, the Hume family is split as is the state of Virginia where they live. There is no "good" side or "bad" side in such a situation and both groups commit acts of violence outside the range of battle. As in *My Brother Sam Is Dead*, there is a final act of outrage. The burning of the Hume home, the raiding of the stock, the rape of Matilda, are violations by the Union soldiers who have no actual

169

reason for the raid beyond their need for supplies. What strength Matilda can muster comes from her grandfather:

> "It's like the world is coming apart, Grandpa Hume. Tell me how to live," she begged.
> "I tell you, honey, this is what life is—a building-up and then a dwindling. Sometimes the dwindling comes fast, like now with Jason's death and Sarah's leaving you. The thing to do is to get a hold on the dwindling and slow it down so you can *bear* it."

As this passage so clearly indicates, the most frequent message of modern historical fiction is that the individual has to find an inner strength; there is no outer help for the resolution of problems, even in the ending of war.

In the midst of these newer, more sensitive and complex novels the more traditional approach is still employed, but so rarely as to seem almost an anachronism. A good example is Anne Finlayson's *Rebecca's War*—i.e., the American Revolution—which, in spite of its recent date (1972) now seems to be old-fashioned historical fiction. Rebecca is a superchild, aged fourteen, who not only looks after her younger brother and sister but also copes with British officers billeted in her house, arranges the sale of smuggled brandy to feed American prisoners, and holds the secret of the gold cache on which the fate of the revolutionaries so much depends. The plot is also traditional in that Rebecca has dealings with Joseph Galloway, James Ogilvie, and just misses meeting General Howe, although she does abscond with his carriage and his driver. Rebecca is the larger-than-life heroine who is embroiled in events but not really touched by them.

What is compelling about *Rebecca's War* and what links it with the more modern works of the Colliers and Cummings is the attitude toward war. War is no longer the mere theatrical device it once was in historical fiction, a convenient raison d'être for depicting derring-do. The war that Rebecca sees retains many elements of romance, but it is also a harsh reality and Finlayson makes sure that the child reader does not ignore that second dimension.

The same viewpoint can be applied to many other events and aspects of history and in the case of conditions such as slavery and the treatment of native peoples, their authors' sense of social outrage can be fully as strong as in any anti-war novel. Paula Fox's *The Slave Dancer* (1973) illustrates how this rather new (for children's literature) viewpoint can transfuse and alter a very traditional story line.

What happens to a boy who has been "shanghaied" is a standard plot in children's fiction. In *The Slave Dancer*, however, the kidnapping of Jessie Boller is not accidental nor are his experiences merely adventurous. He is taken aboard an American slave ship in the year 1841 to be "the slave dancer,"—to play his flute while the African slaves are ordered to shuffle around the deck. They must be kept as healthy as possible for the auction block which Jessie knows about since one is near his home in New Orleans. But on the voyage:

> I thought of my home. If ever I got back, I would not, I told myself silently, ever go to the slave market on St. Louis and Chartres Streets again.

Paula Fox's opportunity for sensationalism was great, but she restrained it in favor of an emotionalism, all the stronger for its understatement. A fourteen-year-old boy (who tells the story) would not have the language to express the horror he witnesses on board the ship as he sees the slaves starved, beaten, packed into a small space, and, finally, thrown overboard. The story is therefore told as a boy's simple chronicle of happenings, the meaning of which is inferred rather than expounded. In the ending, *The Slave Dancer* reaffirms the best in the human spirit as Jessie and the one surviving black boy, Ras, join forces and escape from the foundering ship.

Scott O'Dell's *Sing Down the Moon* (1970) works in the same vein. Here the historical component is the Long March of the Navaho Indians to prison at Fort Sumner in 1864. Like the blacks on board the ship in *The Slave Dancer*, the human spirit in the Indians is broken under shock and degrading treatment. But Bright Morning, who is surely one of the most sensitive and spirited heroines in modern children's literature, persuades her husband finally to escape and they return to their valley home. In spite of all the misery they have endured, Bright Morning wants no revenge:

> I took my son from his carrying board and held him up so that he could see the lamb. He wanted to touch it, but with both hands he was grasping a toy which his father had given him, a willow spear tipped with stone. Tall Boy had made up a song about the Long Knives and how the spear would kill many of them. Every night he sang this song to his son.
> I took the spear and dropped it in the grass and stepped upon it, hearing it snap beneath my foot.

Sing Down the Moon, concludes then, just as did the works by Burton, Collier, Cummings, and Fox, in a kind of emotional "defense"—sometimes fierce, sometimes gentle—of the human spirit in time of trial. Is it just a coincidence that these books are also linked by virtue of the fact that they are set in the nineteenth century? Furthermore, no event is changed or even modified by the intervention of the protagonists in these novels. Rather it is they themselves

171

who have changed as they now look upon the world with wiser, more penetrating, and more sorrowful eyes.

This set of similarities seems to suggest that the traditional view of history as a series of great events diminishes as the setting nears our own time. So too, apparently, does the concern with plot and even character. The few writers who to date have chosen the era of the early twentieth century, as have K. M. Peyton in her *Flambards* trilogy (1967–69) and Marjorie Darke in *A Question of Courage* (1975), stress even more than Burton the effects of a static and compartmentalized society upon the individual. This is accomplished at some cost. Peyton's and Darke's protagonists appear to be symbols of a drive for equality and democracy rather than young people with a personal view of events. Character, and therefore intensity, are subordinated to the social message.

Peyton's *Flambards* has some of the attributes of a Virginia Holt Gothic romance. A twelve-year-old wealthy orphan, Christina, is sent to live with her uncle and his two sons. It is planned that she marry the elder son and live in the country estate of Flambards, the atmosphere of which has "the unhappy place of a tomb." But this is 1908 and matters such as marriage and family are no longer subject to dictation. *Flambards* (1967) and particularly the sequels, *The Edge of the Cloud* (1969) and *Flambards in Summer* (1969) chart the changes in social structure and outlook brought about by technology and war. Two societies are in conflict—the fox-hunting, high society represented by the elder Flambards son Mark, and the newer, more classless society represented by the younger son William, whom Christina finally chooses:

> on the aerodrome everyone was taken for granted if they were interested in the machines. There was no distinction of class or underdog.
>
> ——*The Edge of the Cloud*, p. 62

Emily, in Marjorie Darke's *A Question of Courage* (1975), also finds a new life, and presumably happiness, in a new social order, that embodied in the Women's Movement. Marjorie Darke gives a realistic picture of the lives of both the wealthy and the poor in the early 1900s, especially the latter in the sweated dressmaking trade. She notes the difference between the various women's groups at the time, the Suffragettes were deemed the extremists, and moves from charming vignettes of women's meetings, bicycle rides, and picnics to harrowing scenes of the harrassment, prison life, and forced feeding to which members of the Women's Movement were subjected. The book ends with the coming of World War I and the cessation of the Movement for the time being.

172

Neither the Flambards trilogy nor *A Question of Courage* has the emotional impact of Rosemary Sutcliff's works or the individual books of historical fiction by Paula Fox and Scott O'Dell. The reason for this is only partly a matter of lesser skill in sheer style. Rather it is their attitude toward their subjects that accounts for the relative "flatness" of the novels of Peyton and Darke. They themselves seem not to have, nor do they require from their readers, an avid interest in a given period and what it represents in the way of symbolism and parallels.

Both Peyton and Darke do, however, offer good, straightforward, competently written narratives, with themes that are immediately recognizable as linked to the present. Being set so close to our own time—less than a step away, really—their novels have a sense of immediacy closely akin to that of the realistic or problem novel. They therefore appeal to many children who might not otherwise be attracted to historical fiction. Moreover, both are astute enough writers to give us young protagonists who are not victims of events beyond their control, but who with determination join the struggle for social change. Such books remind us in how great a degree human progress depends upon the individual and that human society is not totally antlike. If in their broad optimism they are infused with a sense of steady advance toward social betterment, they are not so naive as to suggest that such progress is inevitable or easy. Gains are not assured; they have been very hard won.

Of course, changing socioeconomic conditions in the recent past are not what everyone would deem as the stuff of an historical novel. Many writers still prefer to find their inspiration in the distant past and in a foreign land. Jill Paton Walsh's *The Emperor's Winding Sheet* (1974) illustrates the continuing appeal of remoteness. While the chief figure is the last emperor of Byzantium, Constantine, we see the novel's events through the eyes of a young English boy who is co-opted into the emperor's service. He serves Constantine at first reluctantly, then with admiration, and finally with love, refusing his freedom and ministering to him at the end as his only servant. The use of a young protagonist as guide, observer, and commentator has almost disappeared as a literary device, but here it is used most successfully.

Another fine novelist who prefers the distant locale and a remote time is Katherine Paterson who makes feudal Japan her setting in *The Sign of the Chrysanthemum* (1973) and *Of Nightingales That Weep* (1974), and eighteenth-century Japan in *The Master Puppeteer* (1975). All three are somewhat brief as historical novels go, but Paterson, like the medieval Japanese painters of the long scrolls, finds room for the

173

specific observations and convincing details which convey authenticity.

Of the three novels, *The Master Puppeteer* (1976) is the most childlike in that it shows that the boys will be boys even in the harsh discipline of the Bunraku puppet theater class and in a city where famine reigns and bands of marauders roam the streets. It is also worth noting that, although replete with marvelous lore of puppetry, the book retains a strong narrative quality. The plot, which concerns the search for Saburo, the Robin Hood helper of the poor, is handled with suspense and verve. Despite their far-away and long-ago settings, Paterson's novels are very much of the present in their concentration on the protagonists' growth to maturity.

In both *The Sign of the Chrysanthemum* and *Of Nightingales That Weep* the crises through which the protagonists must pass are devastating. Both novels deal with the Civil War between the Heike and the Genji, and both have a number of authentic historical figures. *The Sign of the Chrysanthemum* is almost a traditional *Bildungsroman*—the story of one boy searching for a dream, his name, his father, his identity. At age thirteen the novel's protagonist is called Muna, which means "no-name." But as the two clans are warring, so are the two parts of Muna's character—his desire for respect and a name at any price, and a desire for truth and a moral life. As the capital city Heiankyo erupts into civil war, Muna comes to terms with himself:

> At one time it had been almost an obsession, the name that would replace "No Name" once and for all. But he had not thought of it now for a long time. It belonged to his daydream world of many months before, before Takanobu had reappeared and Kawaki had died. Before he had let go of his phantom of a father. . . . Before he knew that he himself could lie and steal and betray.

But the greatest character of all in the book is the city itself and its many levels of life—the subculture of thieves, beggars, renegades, and prostitutes; the stable, humble life of the artisans and merchants; the dazzling nobility and dignity of the court officials and samurai warriors—all of which form a cross-section of the life of the city and give a true feeling for the era.

In *Nightingales That Weep* there is a formal, stately, almost Arthurian tone to the scenes of the court. This formality is retained even in the battle scenes—which are described only through the eyes of the court women—and is applied with telling effect to the portrayal of the heroine. As a girl of feudal Japan, Takiko is, of course, very closely bound by the commandments of custom and ceremony, and Paterson is careful not to gloss that central fact in Takiko's life.

174

Within those constraints, however, she is depicted in very much modern terms: she strives to live her life for herself and the great decision in her life, when she chooses to become the wife of an artisan, is a resolution of her own making. For both Muna and Takiko their conquests over their own nature have radically altered their lives.

These links with present-day attitudes, which are so desirable in establishing a rapport between narrative and reader, are obviously difficult to establish when the historical milieu is so clearly and specifically defined as to set it off sharply from our own. It is therefore not surprising that it is often those writers who, because they move farthest back in time, succeed best in relating their characters to the present. Perhaps the haze of the very distant past is what blurs the perception of period. Such writers as Stephen Rayson in *The Crows of War* (1975), Roderick L. Haig-Brown in *The Whale People* (1962), and Rosemary Sutcliff in much of her work appear to be establishing a strong link between those who preceded us in the distant past and ourselves, thereby almost suggesting that the farther back we go, the closer the bond. These writers imbue their works with a primitive quality that brings them very near the universal quality of myth.

Stephen Rayson's *The Crows of War* is just such a book. Set in 43 AD, it describes the conflict between the Roman legions and the defending Celtic tribes as simultaneously a brutal physical battle and a profound psychological struggle of clashing cultures and minds. In a panorama of huge sweep we are able to see how such epic collisons affect the lives of ordinary people caught in historical events beyond their understanding or control.

At the hub of this wheel of destiny and history is Airmid, teenage daughter of a Celtic chieftain. When the Celts lose the battle, Airmid loses both her freedom and her eyesight. The novel continues in a brutally honest portrayal of her life as a blind woman wrestler at the mercy of sadistic soldiers. Then her tragedy takes on an epic dimension; she descends into madness as her mind is used as a symbolic battleground by two Celtic goddesses in their eternal struggle of "summer against winter, warmth pitted against the cold. Light and darkness, life, death." Nevertheless, the novel ends on a note of hope. Not only does Airmid's blindness give her access to prophetic vision, but also the two contending cultures begin to reach growing respect for one another.

The Crows of War is thus far Rayson's only attempt to handle themes of such magnitude and it is impossible to predict whether he can sustain work at this level of passion and grandeur. One writer who can indisputably do so is Rosemary Sutcliff. In her long career she has shown herself as consistently able to represent the strong emotions of primal times. She unleashes not only the dark sides of earlier civilizations, but the dark side of human life in most of her works. Her novels are filled with images of war, cruelty, blood, sacrifice, suffering, deformity, accompanied by an almost physical smell of fear.

Sutcliff is a "hot" novelist in strong contrast to the cooler, more cerebral, and lucid approach of a Hester Burton or a Barbara Willard. Like all modern writers she does not open her books with long descriptive passages to set the period but thrusts the reader immediately into the stir and terror of great, grim events. Thus *The Shield Ring* (1956) begins:

> The thing happened with the appalling swiftness of a hawk swooping out of a quiet sky, on a day late in spring, when Frytha was not quite five.

She creates a brooding atmosphere in *The Eagle of the Ninth* which holds even when her style has a marching rhythm like that of the Roman legions she so loves to describe:

> 'I had never seen such a sight before,' he said. 'Like a shining serpent of men winding across the hills; a grey serpent, hackled with the scarlet cloaks and crests of the officers. There were queer tales about that Legion; men said that it was accursed, but it looked stronger than any curse, stronger and more deadly. And I remember how the Eagle flashed in the sun as it came by —a great golden Eagle with its wings arched back as I have seen them often swoop on a screaming hare among the heather.

Sutcliff's perennial theme is that of personal responsibility, particularly if the protagonist is in a position of leadership. Her characters frequently resemble Beowulf, the King of the Geats, facing the dragon alone in his last battle. Most of her major novels have this epic quality. In *The Mark of the Horse Lord* (1965) the young gladiator who is chosen to be a substitute for the blinded real king gradually comes to feel that he is the real chief and in the end dies voluntarily that the tribe may be saved. So does Lubrin in *Sun Horse, Moon Horse* (1977). In order to free his people, Lubrin of the Horse People agrees to carve a huge horse on what is now the Berkshire Downs so as to honor and placate Cradoc, the conquering chief. But the achievement of this artistic work will not be enough:

> In that split moment of time, the unspoken, unthought thing between him and Cradoc came out of the dark, and he looked it in the face, and found that he had always known it. It was the last sealing of the bargain between them. It was his own death. His blood, his life to quicken the god-horse of his making; just

as the Old People shed the life of a man into the furrows every seven years to quicken the seed-corn to harvest.

In such novels, the incidents are of Sutcliff's own contrivance but the sense of passion and sacrifice seem drawn from the most ancient myths.

Like the myths, Sutcliff's works are by no means monochromatic. Her works are filled with images of light as well as dark. Amidst the clang and clash of war, the horrors of a slave ship or arena, or in the picture of the dark people who live beyond the Roman Wall in Britain, she also imparts a sense of the necessity for and the profundity of a culture. Above all, even in depicting the most harrowing tragedies, she suggests that these may be the steps we've been taking on our slow, hard climb to real humanity. The ending of *The Lantern Bearers* (1959) is a summation of her philosophy:

> 'I sometimes think that we stand at sunset,' Eugenus said after a pause. 'It may be that the night will close over us in the end, but I believe that morning will come again. Morning always grows again out of the darkness, though maybe not for the people who saw the sun go down. We are the Lantern Bearers, my friend; for us to keep something burning, to carry what light we can forward into the darkness and the wind.'

Not surprisingly, the importance of a culture is most movingly seen in those books like Sutcliff's *Sun Horse, Moon Horse* and Haig-Brown's *The Whale People* that depict a preliterate people. This may be because such peoples did live wholeheartedly by rigid standards and ritual observances. *The Whale People* are the Hotsath tribe of the west coast of Vancouver Island who hunt the whale from dugout canoes with weapons of wood and bone and horn. Atlin, a boy of the tribe and the son of its chief, receives both practical and spiritual training to prepare him to take his father's place as the whale chief. Upon his father's death he subjects himself to even more severe discipline in order to receive the spiritual insight—the appearance of his "tumanos" or particular spirit—that will confirm his leadership. In dealing with the ethos of a race, *The Whale People* has a simple strength, dignity, and even starkness that are akin to the great northern myths. But there is nothing stark about Haig-Brown's view of life. Like Sutcliff he sees his hero, purified by trial, leading his people to a better way of life.

Because the major writers of historical fiction deal with serious and profound themes, they very rarely indulge in the light touch. There is one outstanding exception, Leon Garfield, whose works serve to remind us that the comic side of life persists, even amid portentous events. His *The Prisoners of September* (1975) is based on a truly tragic incident in the French Revolution, the September massacre. It is also a story of friendship, that between Richard Mortimer, a young English aristocrat who goes off to Paris to join the Revolutionaries, and Lewis Boston, the son of a nouveau riche wine merchant who stumbles into the opposite side on a business trip to Paris.

The humor in this work appears chiefly in the doings of the friendly, rather bumbling Boston family who are almost puppyish in their efforts to please everyone. Young Lewis Boston has rescued a French emigré countess from a runaway team of horses and his father, dedicated to parties, gives one of his famous fêtes in the countess's honor. Lewis is head over heels in love with her but fears Richard as a rival. He prepares a surprise for his countess—an air balloon which circles the crowded room bearing the countess's coat of arms:

> "Look, look, my queen!" breathed Lewis ecstatically. "I've put a moon in the sky for you! I've dressed it in your livery! Your moon, your sky! What more can love do?"
>
> It was indeed the countess's moon, and would have been even more so if Mr. Boston hadn't seen fit to have painted round the lower half: *A. Boston and Son. Importers of Fine Wines.* But still, thought Lewis, it was an added tribute. Match that, if you can, Richard Mortimer!

The scene ends in an episode of near burlesque. The balloon catches fire and in turn sets the countess on fire. Lewis, devoted and brave but hopelessly clumsy, attempts to rescue her and tears her dress in the process, thereby revealing the mark of a thief on her breast. Out of place in a serious novel? Unbelievable? No, simply comic, as Leon Garfield does it.

The eighteenth century, which is Garfield's specialty, lends itself particularly well to his often larger-than-life approach. His novels revolve around swashbuckling highwaymen and captains; eccentric doctors, teachers, and lords; a gentle, mad girl, and a Lillith-like general's daughter. Through them move his young heroes on a journey from innocence to experience. Other than *The Prisoners of September* his novels are not, strictly speaking, historical fiction, since *Jack Holborn* (1964), *Smith* (1967), *Black Jack* (1968), *The Sound of Coaches* (1974) are completely fictional. *The Drummer Boy* (1970) does open with a battle scene (one of the most magnificent descriptions in children's literature), but we know neither where, when nor why the battle has taken place and it does not matter.

But Garfield's details are not fictional. When, at the beginning of *Black Jack* (1968) we read of the metal tube that the criminal inserted down his throat to prevent the suffocation of the hangman's noose, we know the scene to be accurate. When, in *The Sound of Coaches* (1974) we learn of the tradition of naming a coachman by the road on which he traveled (Mr. Dover, because of the Dover Road), its historicity can be accepted because Leon Garfield's name is on the title page. Whether he is describing an eighteenth-century asylum, Newgate Prison, or a sailing ship, the details are completely convincing.

They do much more than carry conviction, they create atmosphere and it is perhaps Garfield's ability to create atmosphere that has led many critics to reach for comparisons of his work with Dickens and Fielding. Atmosphere is of course indefinable, but it is easily sensed, especially when it is created with the remarkable swiftness and economy that Garfield displays. Here for example is the first paragraph of *Smith* (1967):

> He was called Smith and was twelve years old. Which, in itself, was a marvel; for it seemed as if the smallpox, the consumption, brain-fever, gaol-fever and even the hangman's rope had given him a wide berth for fear of catching something. Or else they weren't quick enough.
>
> Smith had a turn of speed that was remarkable, and a neatness in nipping down an alley or vanishing in a court that had to be seen to be believed. Not that it was often seen . . . the most his thousand victims ever got of him was the powerful whiff of his passing and a cold draught in their dexterously emptied pockets.

In these few lines we find ourselves rooted in the mean life of eighteenth-century London, in "the tumbledown mazes about fat St. Paul's." When Garfield's atmosphere moves into the macabre, which it does frequently, the spine actually tingles, the hair rises on the head, and one looks to see if the doors are firmly locked and the curtains drawn. He has provided many unforgettable episodes, one of the most notable being the first chapter of *Black Jack* in which Tolly, an orphan boy, is left alone in a locked, candle-lit room watching the hanged highwayman come back to life and forcing himself to participate in the resuscitation.

Although Garfield's plots are of the kind that keeps the reader turning the pages in the best tradition of storytelling, deeper themes do underly his work. He treats life as it comes—which is more often rough and uneven than smooth—and he is not afraid to describe plainly that which is ugly and grotesque. Usually however, Garfield is not so direct and plain in his treatment of evil, or of good. For to him the two are intermingled or disguised. Perhaps the most frequent and important choice his protagonists have to make is that between good and evil when neither is all that clear. Slowly, subtly,

179

they must learn to unmask apparent good as evil or apparent evil as good. Thus in *The Drummer Boy*, the drummer boy's love for the General's daughter, Sophia, turns out to be destructive, whereas he finds real courage and humanity in the rascally Mr. Shaw, whom we meet first robbing the bodies of the dead on the battlefield.

At the same time, Garfield's overall optimistic view of life has given us some of the tenderest passages in children's literature. *Black Jack* presents a macabre plot of a hanged man revived, his kidnapping of Tolly, the orphan boy, and the hold-up of a coach from which an insane girl escapes. It is also the story of the moving relationship between Tolly and the defective girl, Belle. Belle has never seen the sea:

> "Tell me about the sea," she begged. . . .
> "Water, Belle—as far as the eye can see . . ."
> "What noise does it make?"
> "It sighs and whispers and slaps and sometimes roars."
> "What's under the sea, Tolly?"
> "Green darkness—like a great forest. Strange flowers and weeds and fish and sunken ships and treasures."

It is probably the same delight in parodox that accounts for Garfield's sharp eye for the vulnerability even of villainy. *Black Jack* is at first presented as a terrible villain whose great bulk seems not to have a weak spot in it. But Tolly discovers:

> "That was her—eh?" he muttered. "That was the lunatic?"
> Of a sudden, Tolly suspected a strange thing. He suspected that this mighty ruffian, this vast, murdering felon who feared neither God nor the Devil nor even the hangman, was struck with dread by skinny, mad Belle!

Among the many other interesting features of Garfield's work, not the least noteworthy is his unusual willingness, for these days, at least, to depart from the conventional novel format. His "Apprentice Series" offers twelve (one for each month of the year) vignettes of something fewer than fifty pages each, and it is a very real treat to see how adeptly he makes the short narrative form work for him. The apprentices are young teenagers who are both literally and figuratively in the apprentice stages of their lives, involved in learning the secrets and powers of a craft. They are also all linked by a symbol, that of light, both physical light and the figurative light of enlightenment, and the young people themselves and those who become involved with them eventually "see the light." The progress of Garfield's apprentices is the reverse of Hogarth's "The Rake's Progress." His characters are not only searching for the truths their individual craft might yield, but they also are struggling toward maturity. In their "rites of passage" they are initiated into the Vanity Fair of the London street life with its colorful characters, painful truths, and sordid ironies. Eventually the apprentices win through to a revelation of the good and an unmasking of the tawdry.

On one level the stories are straightforward, exciting, and, at times, comic narratives, the apprentice rivalry in *The Enemy* (1978) being a particularly good example of the latter quality. There are as well other levels of meaning—highly symbolical, often allegorical— and these are sometimes elusive. Thus *The Lamplighter's Funeral* (1976) is radiant with imagery of light that balances and transcends the raucous, dangerous, brutally jostling and mean-spirited street life that lies at the core of the story. The central character, Pallcat, is an irritable, curmudgeonly lamplighter with a passionate belief in his work. In explaining his mission he says fervently, "Issa sacred dooty. ... Issa Christian office to lighten our darkness."

The dour isolation of Pallcat's existence is broken by the chance entry into his life of an impoverished urchin called Possul. The boy saves Pallcat from disgrace in his brotherhood by carrying his funeral light after he had fallen drunk by the wayside. Possul is an enigmatic figure with his "weirdly transparent face, ... angelic countenance and soft manners." Although he is a real child, he functions also as a wonderchild or Christ child, whose innocence and courage holds the light of conscience in the darkness of man's spiritual night. When Possul goes forth alone with his torch without Pallcat's guidance, he takes his customers to whom he is giving safe passage through the darkness on journeys of metaphysical dimension as his torchlight shines on the pain, misfortune, and degradation of society's outcasts:

> Men crying in corners, dead children, thieves lit up in sudden, horrible terror.... Human beings everywhere abandoning themselves to a despair that the darkness should have hid, abruptly seen in their crude nakedness.

The motifs of light and dark, or friendship and love, not romantic love, but the divine love of compassion, forgiveness, and rebirth, are creatively varied and skillfully interwoven very much like the contrapuntal lines of an eighteenth-century fugue.

In *The Enemy* a natural, comic, boyish rivalry is the surface theme, but both "enemies" as in other books, come to acts of extraordinary generosity. *Mirror, Mirror* (1976) is replete with a wealth of imaginative, inventive metaphors in which the daughter of the master carver of mirror frames uses her mirrors to visit ghastly, ghoulish torments on the poor apprentice. But once again, there is Garfield's perennial wit and good humor to lighten and vary the tone. The result is a story that has a medieval flavor, an eighteenth-century equivalent of some of the wry, whimsical, and sentimental anecdotes of Chaucer or the amorous jests of Boccaccio.

In format the "Apprentice" books appear designed to attract young readers, age nine or ten. They are not only brief, they have large type, a spacious look, and are perfectly illustrated by either Anthony Maitland or Faith Jacques. The stories also have been issued in a combined one-volume edition, but lack the illustrations. The latter edition is probably intended for adults and if so, this publishing venture makes great good sense: Garfield is, for child or adult, a great storyteller.

The format of Garfield's "Apprentice" books has been adopted by Alan Garner in his "Quartet," a grouping of well-illustrated, "long-short stories." As the name suggests, the "Quartet" is composed of four linked narratives: *The Stone Book* (1976), *Tom Fobble's Day* (1977), *Granny Reardun* (1977), and *The Aimer Gate* (1978). Chronologically, the series begins with *The Stone Book*, and ends with *Tom Fobble's Day*—stories that are extraordinary miniatures which can be enjoyed in their directness and simplicity by younger children, but certainly their levels of metaphor will also touch the older child and adults. Garner's overall theme is the continuity of time and, like Garfield in the "Apprentices," he is fascinated by the skill of the artisan. However, unlike Garfield, he makes powerful use of the classical unities of time, place, and action. The events in each book take place in a single day; all four books are concerned with the same family, although in different generations.

The Stone Book moves in a series of small, symbolic acts, all of which are unfolded to Mary, the daughter of a stone mason in a small Victorian village. Mary's father gives her a vision of height and light as she rides the golden weathercock on top of the church he is building. Then comes the sense of depth and darkness in a cave with a prehistoric painting, "the most secret place she had ever seen." She is not alone there. All about her in that small place under the hill that led nowhere were the footprints of people who had been there before her. Mary's father, as they arrive home, says "once you've seen it, you're changed for the rest of your days." Mary has wanted to learn to read but her father makes her a "stone" book symbolic of the deeper and wider understanding of the natural world that can surpass the knowledge found in booklearning. "And Mary sat by the fire and read the stone book that had in it all the stories of the world and the flowers of the flood." Thus *The Stone Book* pursues the themes of initiation and growth of understanding: the older generation sharing its worldly and spiritual wisdom with the young; how meaning is conveyed through iconic elements of the natural world— iron, wood, or stone; the roots of love between family members; the sharing of common, small details as the family carries on its day-to-day life in their home and chosen craft or work.

Tom Fobble's Day—"Tom Fobbling" is the old childhood ritual of borrowing, lending, and claiming—employs the same themes in a very different setting, that of World War II. William's grandfather makes him a new sledge to replace the one that has been "Tom Fobbled" away from him. The grandfather makes that sledge from the iron and ash of his forge and the oak of the grandmother's loom, and he does all this on the day he dies. William takes his grandfather's horseshoe, one that symbolized his marriage, in a Tom-Fobbling ritual and enters a service as passionate and as fiercely mourning as Dylan Thomas's prayer-poem to his dying father, "Do Not Go Gentle into That Goodnight." William takes his sledge to the field where the children of the village do their sledding, a dangerous place scattered with shrapnel from the German night bombers and the British fighters, and the sledge was good:

> The line did hold. Through hand and eye, block, forge and loom to the hill and all that he owned, he sledged sledged sledged for the black and glittering night and the sky flying on fire and the expectation of snow.

The four stories of the "Quartet" grow into one another, even though each is told in its own time and place. They are linked together not only by the fact that they deal with the same family over the years but also, as with Garfield, by the homely details of craft and artifacts that one generation inherits from another. Thus the pipe which Mary's father buried is found by William on the day of his grandfather's death.

Alan Garner's several parallels with Garfield should not be taken as too meaningful, for there is no question here of direct influences or any "school" of contemporary historical fiction. Nevertheless, comparisons between individual writers are inescapable, and so indeed is some overall description and judgment of current trends and features in historical fiction as contrasted with those of previous periods and other genres.

Such a general assessment may properly begin with an analysis of characterization as being the central feature of almost every form of prose fiction. Here historical fiction has always presented some special considerations and requirements. Seemingly children develop an awareness of an interest in history only after they become conscious of their own personal history, their own passage through themselves. It follows then that not only are the readers of historical fiction somewhat older than those for other genres but that the characters in historical fiction are older as well. This is not simply the usual matter of the reader preferring characters with whom he can closely identify; it is also that the characters must be old enough and mature enough to grasp, and hence impart, the nature of the often awesome events in which they find themselves.

For much the same reason adults play a far more important role in historical novels than they do in other types of children's fiction. In narratives with a present-day setting, for example, the adult characters are often shadowy, mere accessories so to speak, for the child protagonists. This criticism applies with particular force to the depiction of parents, who are often shown as stereotypes with no real individuality. In historical fiction, however, the adult characters are *needed* if the narrative is to portray with any credibility the central characters as taking an active, prominent role in the unfolding of the events, let alone affecting their outcome. After all, even the unsophisticated Henty had to let Wolfe, rather than his boy companion, capture Quebec! The result is that in most recent historical fiction there are relatively few child figures; they are more likely to be adolescents. In Barbara Willard's *Harrow and Harvest*, the only young child we encounter is a half-witted boy and his is a minor role. Rosemary Sutcliff's *Song for a Dark Queen* (1977) has a completely adult cast except for Queen Boducca's two daughters, who are symbols rather than characters.

All this suggests that the writing of historical fiction for younger children presents very large difficulties—which may explain the relatively few successes. In addition to the problem of creating believable young child characters, the writer has also to condense dramatic time. Since younger children cannot easily grasp the concept of developments occurring over a long period of time, authors must pack more drama into a shorter period. They thus represent the past in a kind of reversal of dimension in which a small detail can loom so very large and significant. As D. H. Lawrence put it, on imagining a prehistoric hummingbird, "We look at him through the wrong end of the long telescope of time."[4] Writers generally use Lawrence's end-of-the-telescope technique to enlarge a moment of social history through the lives of young children. It is characteristic that many books of historical fiction for children are produced in a publisher's series with outstanding writers of the day such as the Hamish Hamilton "Antelope Books" and the Heinemann "Long Ago Books."

Almost all these novels of historical fiction are very brief. Although that classic example of historical fiction for younger children, Howard Pyle's *Otto of the Silver Hand* (1888), is almost 200 pages

4. D. H. Lawrence, "Humming-bird," in his *Complete Poems*, 2 vols. (London: Heinemann, 1964), vol. 1, p. 372.

in length, those of today rarely reach half that. The difference, moreover, is not merely a matter of scope. Modern writers emulate Pyle's basic technique of emphasizing the child rather than events but they do so in a more sharply focused manner. When they have achieved success, it is because they have so well absorbed the material of their period that they can render it with the utmost economy— providing just enough of the right detail to make the historical setting colorful and evocative, while superimposing upon that setting the relevant activity of the child characters.

Rosemary Sutcliff, for example, is so much at home in ancient history that when she writes of the friendship between an Athenian boy and a Spartan boy at the Olympic Games in *The Truce of the Games* (1971), a brief book of fewer than 85 pages, her background details of the rivalry between the two city-states are given briefly and precisely, but the rivalry between the two boys, complicated by their friendship, takes center stage. Similarly, Leon Garfield, in his *The Boy and the Monkey* (1969), uses his usual, rapid, knowing strokes to describe some eighteenth-century London streets, a jail, and a courtroom with a marvelously touching and funny cast of eccentrics, including a most perspicacious monkey. And all within only 47 pages! It is to be noted that in tune with modern children's literature in general, even these small books have a serious tone, most resembling Gillian Avery's *Ellen's Birthday* (1971), which gives a vivid picture of the English country poor in the year 1852.

It is usually only in family stories of the past that the lighter touch can be perceived and these are few in number. Nina Bawden's *The Peppermint Pig* (1975) follows in the tradition of books such as Carol Brink's *Caddie Woodlawn* (1935) and Laura Ingalls Wilder's "The Little House" series in that it is social history rather than an account of great events. The appeal of all such books derives more from nostalgia than from romance. Like the families in these earlier books, Bawden's Greengrass family has its ups and downs, many of them amusing. It is an evocative, perceptive, good-humored picture of family life at the turn of the century that is somewhat reminiscent too of Edith Nesbit's *The Railway Children*, in which father comes home, his name cleared of having stolen from his employer.

Another family narrative that offers a rare and, on the whole, successful attempt at broad humor is John D. Fitzgerald's *The Great Brain* (1967) and its sequels. In these stories Fitzgerald has created a kind of minor Tom Sawyer. They are set in Adenville, "a typical Utah town" in 1896. The young heroes, especially Tom the "great brain," are inventive and tricky, with the corners not yet knocked off them. Fitzgerald's boy protagonists have funny yet plausible adventures matching the ebullient spirit that opened up the American West.

It should be noted that these humorous books invariably have a setting in the recent past. In this, their authors gain at least one large advantage; they lessen for themselves the problem of vocabulary. Vocabulary is a constant difficulty for writers of historical fiction, a difficulty which intensifies as the writer reaches further back into history. The solutions vary. Barbara Willard sails neatly between the Scylla of "prithee" and the Charybdis of "okay," by employing a heightened version of standard English, a sort of timeless noble language that is difficult to achieve and maintain. She does use some dialect and archaic words—"suent," "sponky," and "sworly" are examples—but introduces them so naturally and with so clear a meaning that only a coloration of the text is noticeable. Generally her style is as smooth and literate and simple as these opening lines of *The Lark and The Laurel* attest:

> Cecily had been brought to Mantlemass at dusk. Already bitterly fatigued by the long ride from London, by the haste and surprise and fear of it all, she had clung to her father as if she were drowning and only he of all the world could save her. Her own misery, loud and ugly, clamoured in her ears and she could not stop it in spite of the distaste and anger she saw in her father's face.

Hester Burton, whose nineteenth-century characters seem almost as modern as those portrayed in contemporary-scene fiction, actually uses more dialect and archaic words than Barbara Willard, but she too makes the context clear. "Now don't you cruckle, lass," said Farmer Moore in Burton's *Time of Trial*, but we know that he is attempting to comfort Margaret as she is on her way to Ipswich Gaol to see her father. Stephen, on the road to Manchester in her *Riders of the Storm*, meets an old woman who says, "Is it clemmed thaw art?" He shook his head. "My sister put a pasty and bread and cheese in my pack!"

Garfield's mastery with eighteenth-century phraseology is most observable in his "Apprentice" series. The strong, spicy dialects and gutter language of the streets are complemented by the beauty and grace of his imagery. He always gives the feeling of a tale being told now, even when he gives his characters the voice of their own time and class; he makes clear an archaic word usually by means of a synonym:

> Sure enough, next day Larkins came out in tetters all over his face; and Hobby rejoiced. . . . Although it was a well-known fact that Larkins often came out in tetters and black spots on the side of his nose and boils on the back of his neck, the coincidence this time was too great for Hobby not to feel that he had friends in dark places.
>
> ——*The Enemy*, p. 7

Of all major writers, Alan Garner yields least in the use of dialect:

> "It's Stewart Allman," said William. "He took me sledge and wrecked it."
> "And good riddance," said Grandad. "I never saw such a codge."
>
> ——*Tom Fobble's Day*, p. 41

Still, although the language is what gives Garner's books much of their feeling of authenticity, it may prove a stumbling block to many North American children.

Rosemary Sutcliff may be the greatest alchemist of all with period dialogue. Most of her books, being set in prehistoric times or in Roman Britain, are beyond the knowledge of recorded speech, but it is part of her magic that she can make the past so real without, as it were, the tools of the speech of the time. The Druid priest in *Outcast* speaks without archaic words and yet the mythic tone comes through:

> 'Nonetheless, evil will come of it, evil and the wrath of the Gods, if you bring the thing among us! It is a Roman whelp, and what have we to do with such—we, the Free People beyond the frontier?'

Dr. David Bain, an educational psychologist at the University of British Columbia, has noted that in spoken language a child tends to develop the future tense long before the past tense. Still, for most children when they are in grade three, there comes a point when they are able to identify with other people's times and with their own long-range future. Dr. Bain calls these early gropings for communicating with other times "transtemporal communication."[5] The child, he maintains, is not a whole person until the link is made between past, present, and future.

There is good reason to believe that today's children have a marked tendency to concentrate upon the present, as may be evidenced by the popularity of the realistic novel in general and the "problem" novel in particular. The historical novel makes much greater demands on both the writer and the reader than does realistic fiction; quite aside from the sheer factual knowledge that must be mastered, there are severe problems of vocabulary, phraseology, characterization, and viewpoint.

Even so, *some* knowledge of the past, as Dr. Bain maintains, must

5. David Bain, "Transtemporal Communication," in Sheila A. Egoff, ed., *One Ocean Touching: Papers of the First Pacific Rim Conference on Children's Literature* (Metuchen, NJ: Scarecrow Pr., 1979), p. 3.

187

be inculcated and the historical novel offers a time-proven and genuinely effective means of doing so. The validity and appeal of the genre persist, though inevitably its nature has altered very considerably from the times when Bulwer-Lytton's *The Last Days of Pompeii* and Kingsley's *Hereward the Wake* were popular fare for children. Modern writers are concerned with the same themes as the writers of realistic fiction—growing up; facing difficulties and conflicts, whether large events such as war or the crises of everyday living; resolving such conflicts and deriving enrichment from them. Books of historical fiction have become in many ways problem novels, but in larger perspective. Human nature, modern historical fiction is saying, has changed very little. Everyone has to learn to pick up the pieces.

One may conclude that, in its several ways, historical fiction has changed more than any other genre. The romance and adventure have disappeared; no longer does a Douglas Fairbanks "hit the deck" of history with sword in hand. The new writers see their characters as "apprentices" in life, and the modesty of their station, even amidst high-level events, forbids the kind of glamorization of characters and events that was the trademark of earlier historical novels for children. Except for the works of Rosemary Sutcliff, most of the drama of past events has been muted into social history. Among other benefits derived from this rejection of romance, in addition to an increased historicity, has been the virtual divorce of this almost new form of the genre from the competition of TV historical romance, the comic books, and, especially, from the subgenre of "sword and sorcery," that odd combination of the primitive past and fantasy. Historical fiction for the young at least can no longer be deemed a literature of escape into the past, although this can still be found in much writing for adults.

But when historical romance was no longer considered palatable by writers its demise meant the death of the kind of stories that were described rather loosely as "high adventure," those marvelous fast-paced plots tinged with the exotic, such as Stevenson's *Treasure Island* or the works of Rider Haggard. The happy, carefree view of reading expressed so well by Emily Dickinson:

> There is no frigate like a book
> To take us lands away . . .

has all but disappeared in our critical society.

Also seemingly gone is plain, pedantic history rendered palatable by a sugarcoating of fiction. Since this is an approach to history spurned even by pedagogues, it will hardly be missed. It may be, though, that the disappearance of romance, rather than the pedantic, accounts for the fact that no historical novel of the recent past has attained wide, general readership. Scott O'Dell's *The Island of the Blue Dolphins* (1960) might be considered here as the great candidate for historical popularity, but it falls more readily into the sphere of the desert-island survival story rather than into that of the historical novel in the strict sense. Since Rosemary Sutcliff has written over such a long period she has certainly acquired a following but not particularly for one title. One answer to this rather puzzling situation may be the older age of the reader that historical fiction calls for. It is generally younger children who take a book to their hearts and make it their own.

Today's writers of historical fiction face more difficult challenges than writers of science fiction. Although they do not have to create a new time and place, they have to breathe life into old ones, to recreate a living past. Also, in a scientific and technological age, science fiction writers can count on an in-built interest in their work and therefore an audience for it, if only a specialized one. But the writers of historical fiction face a decline in interest in history, as the lack of general history trade books for children attests. That the presentation of real events has become both difficult and complex can be shown by the series of articles in the *New Yorker* magazine in March 1979 on American history textbooks for children and young people. As in adult writing it seems that history can only be handled by a specialist writing on a special period, a Bruce Catton or a Barbara Tuchman.

If history itself has been rendered arid, this should make historical fiction all the more important in children's reading. The genre has always been and still is the best way to make history come alive and readers will find that writers of "the new wave" employ modern concepts and a modern treatment of them in their works. The portrayal of girls and women is only one example. Perhaps because many of the new writers are women, they give their female characters strong and positive personalities and roles even when they are not center stage. Writers today are not naive enough to attempt a "Berica the Britoness," but they do endeavor to portray their female protagonists as high-spirited, intelligent, and independent beings. If they don't have these attributes to begin with, like Cicely in Barbara Willard's *The Lark and the Laurel*, they acquire them. There is also some reason to suggest that there now is a more deliberate attempt to choose situations where women's roles are both important and natural as Marjorie Darke does in *A Question of Courage*, her book on the women's suffrage movement, and as Rosemary Sutcliff does in *Song for a Dark Queen*, her account of Boducca's magnificent and tragic stand against the Roman legions.

Historical fiction strives mightily for relevance and, as a conse-

quence sometimes becomes too obvious in its messages. Its characteristic tone is too unvaryingly one of high seriousness and it can verge
on the portentous. "Story values" too are often attenuated in favor of
character and atmosphere. Yet all of these generalizations have relatively little significance because contemporary historical ficton is
being written by a Sutcliff, a Burton, a Willard, and a Garfield and
these outstanding talents are by definition beyond compartmentaliza-
tion. The only really safe generalization is that as a genre historical
fiction is very much alive and this may indeed be its Golden Age.

Works Cited

Alcott, Louisa May. *Little Women; or Meg, Jo, Beth and Amy*. Illus. by May
  Alcott. Boston: Roberts Brothers, 1868. 341 pp.

Avery, Gillian. *Ellen's Birthday*. Illus. by Krystyna Turska. London:
  Hamish Hamilton, 1971. 88 pp.

Bawden, Nina. *The Peppermint Pig*. Illus. by Alexy Pendle. London: Gollancz, 1975. 160 pp.

Brink, Carol Ryrie. *Caddie Woodlawn*. Illus. by Kate Seredy. New York:
  Macmillan, 1935. 270 pp.

Burton, Hester. *Castors Away!* Illus. by Victor G. Ambrus. London: Oxford
  Univ. Pr., 1962. 222 pp.

——*No Beat of Drum*. Illus. by Victor G. Ambrus. London: Oxford Univ.
  Pr., 1966. 185 pp.

——*The Rebel*. Illus. by Victor G. Ambrus. London: Oxford Univ. Pr.,
  1971. 136 pp.

——*Riders of the Storm*. Illus. by Victor G. Ambrus. London: Oxford
  Univ. Pr., 1972. 170 pp.

——*Thomas*. Illus. by Victor G. Ambrus. London: Oxford Univ. Pr.,
  1969. 178 pp.

——*Time of Trial*. Illus. by Victor G. Ambrus. London: Oxford Univ. Pr.,
  1963. 216 pp.

——*To Ravensrigg*. Illus. by Victor G. Ambrus. London: Oxford Univ.
  Pr., 1976. 148 pp. New York: Crowell, 1977. 143 pp.

Collier, James Lincoln, and Collier, Christopher. *My Brother Sam Is Dead*.
  New York: Four Winds, 1974. 216 pp.

Cummings, Betty Sue. *Hew Against the Grain*. New York: Atheneum, 1977.
  174 pp.

Darke, Marjorie. *A Question of Courage*. Illus. by Janet Archer. Harmondsworth: Kestrel, 1975. 173 pp.

Finlayson, Anne. *Rebecca's War*. Illus. by Sherry Streeter. New York:
  Warne, 1972. 280 pp.

Fitzgerald, John D. *The Great Brain*. Illus. by Mercer Meyer. New York:
  Dial, 1967. 175 pp.

Forbes, Esther. *Johnny Tremain*. Illus. by Lynd Ward. Boston: Houghton, 1943. 256 pp.

Fox, Paula. *The Slave Dancer*. Illus. by Eros Keith. New York: Bradbury, 1973. 176 pp.

Garfield, Leon. *Black Jack*. Illus. by Antony Maitland. London: Longman Young Books, 1968. 192 pp.

————*The Boy and the Monkey*. Illus. by Trevor Ridley. (Long Ago Books) London: Heinemann, 1976. 47 pp.

————*The Drummer Boy*. Illus. by Antony Maitland. London: Longman Young Books, 1970. 154 pp.

————*The Enemy*. Illus. by Faith Jacques. London: Heinemann, 1978. 47 pp.

————*Jack Holborn*. Illus. by Antony Maitland. London: Constable, 1964. 199 pp.

————*The Lamplighter's Funeral*. Illus. by Antony Maitland. London: Heinemann, 1976. 47 pp.

————*Mirror, Mirror*. Illus. by Antony Maitland. London: Heinemann, 1976. 48 pp.

————*The Prisoners of September*. Harmondsworth: Kestrel, 1975. 280 pp.; New York: Viking, 1975. 279 pp.

————*Smith*. Illus. by Antony Maitland. London: Constable, 1967. 218 pp.

————*The Sound of Coaches*. Engravings by John Lawrence. Harmondsworth: Kestrel, 1974. 261 pp.

Garner, Alan. *The Aimer Gate*. Etchings by Michael Foreman. London: Collins, 1978. 79 pp.

————*Granny Reardun*. Etchings by Michael Foreman. London: Collins, 1977. 58 pp.

————*The Stone Book*. Etchings by Michael Foreman. London: Collins, 1976. 61 pp.

————*Tom Fobble's Day*. Etchings by Michael Foreman. London: Collins, 1977. 72 pp.

Haig-Brown, Roderick L. *The Whale People*. Illus. by Mary Weiler. London: Collins, 1962. 184 pp.

Harnett, Cynthia. *The Wool-Pack*. Illus. by the author. Harmondsworth: Penguin, 1961. 238 pp.

Hodges, C. Walter. *The Namesake: A Story of King Alfred*. Illus. by the author. London: Bell, 1964. 197 pp.

Lively, Penelope. *Going Back*. London: Heinemann, 1975. 122 pp.

Marryat, Frederick. *The Children of the New Forest*. London: H. Hurst, 1847. 2 vols.

Nesbit, Edith. *The Railway Children*. Drawings by C. E. Brock. London: Wells Gardner & Co., 1906. 309 pp.

O'Dell, Scott. *The Island of the Blue Dolphins*. Boston: Houghton, 1960. 184 pp.

————*Sing Down the Moon*. Boston: Houghton, 1970. 135 pp.

Pascal, Francine. *Hangin' Out with Cici*. New York: Viking, 1977. 152 pp.

Paterson, Katherine. *The Master Puppeteer*. Illus. by Haru Wells. New York: Crowell, 1975. 179 pp.

————*Of Nightingales That Weep*. Illus. by Haru Wells. New York: Crowell, 1974. 170 pp.

————*The Sign of the Chrysanthemum*. Illus. by Peter Landa. New York: Crowell, 1973. 132 pp.

Peyton, K. M. *The Edge of the Cloud*. Illus. by Victor G. Ambrus. London: Oxford Univ. Pr., 1969. 166 pp.

————*Flambards*. Illus. by Victor G. Ambrus. London: Oxford Univ. Pr., 1967. 193 pp.

————*Flambards in Summer*. Illus. by Victor G. Ambrus. London: Oxford Univ. Pr., 1969. 165 pp.

Pyle, Howard. *Men of Iron*. New York: Harper, 1891. 327 pp.

————*Otto of the Silver Hand*. New York: Scribner, 1888. 170 pp.

Rayson, Steven. *The Crows of War: A Novel of Maiden Castle*. London: Gollancz, 1974. 269 pp.

Stevenson, Robert Louis. *The Black Arrow: A Tale of the Two Roses*. London: Cassell & Co., 1888. 324 pp.

Sutcliff, Rosemary. *The Eagle of the Ninth*. Illus. by C. Walter Hodges. London: Oxford Univ. Pr., 1954. 256 pp.

————*The Lantern Bearers*. Illus. by Charles Keeping. London: Oxford Univ. Pr., 1959. 248 pp.

————*The Mark of the Horse Lord*. Illus. by Charles Keeping. London: Oxford Univ. Pr., 1965, 245 pp.

————*Outcast*. Illus. by Richard Kennedy. London: Oxford Univ. Pr., 1955. 229 pp.

————*The Shield Ring*. Illus. by C. Walter Hodges. London: Oxford Univ. Pr., 1956. 217 pp.

————*Song for a Dark Queen*. London: Pelham Books, 1978. 176 pp.

————*Sun Horse, Moon Horse*. Decorations by Shirley Felts. London: Bodley Head, 1977. 112 pp.

————*The Truce of the Games*. London: Hamish Hamilton, 1971. 83 pp.

Taylor, Mildred. *Roll of Thunder, Hear My Cry*. New York: Dial, 1976. 276 pp.

Trease, Geoffrey. *Cue for Treason*. Blackwell, 1940. 254 pp.

Walsh, Jill Paton. *The Emperor's Winding Sheet*. London: Macmillan, 1974. 240 pp.

Wilder, Laura Ingalls. "The Little House on the Prairie" series. Harper, 1932–1943.

Willard, Barbara. *The Iron Lily*. Harmondsworth: Longman Young Books, 1973. 175 pp.

————*Harrow and Harvest*. Harmondsworth: Kestrel, 1974. 174 pp.

————*The Lark and the Laurel*. Drawings by Gareth Floyd. London: Longman Young Books, 1970. 170 pp.

————*A Sprig of Broom*. Decorations by Paul Shardlow. London: Longman Young Books, 1971. 185 pp.

Yonge, Charlotte. *The Dove in the Eagle's Nest*. London: Macmillan, 1866. 2 vols.

————*The Little Duke, or, Richard the Fearless*. London: J. W. Parker, 1854. 172 pp.

8. Folklore, Myth, and Legend

> How far is it to fairyland? Nearer by far than Babylon. It intersects our mortal world at every point and at every second. The two of them together make one web woven fine.[1]

Puss in Boots, now most usually a picture book confined to the nursery, once strode a larger stage. When French Academician Charles Perrault included the tale in his *Histoires ou Contes du Temps Passé* (1697), Puss piqued the interest of the sophisticated courtiers of Louis Quatorze. A century and a half later, the Brothers Grimm in Germany and Asbjørnsen and Moe in Norway collected and published their Teutonic and Norse tales because they considered them important to scholarship. Whatever the intent of these academic folklorists, "Cinderella," "Hansel and Gretel," and "The Princess on the Glass Hill" quickly underwent metamorphosis into works for children.

The raw power of the stories, stripped of their collectors' original purposes, survived to speak directly to children. Translations into English came relatively soon after their initial publication, and the tales of Perrault and the Grimms spread in a format that was ready-made to receive them. In England this was the chapbook carried in the packs of the "cheapmen," those peripatetic salesmen of preindustrial Britain. These little books, each containing one tale of English origin, sold for only a penny and flooded the market; the introduction of the first foreign stories was unheralded, and these became equally popular. Later, good translations such as that of Sir George Dasent in *Popular Tales from the Norse* (1859) ensured an audience among children, so that by the middle of the nineteenth century

---

1. Pamela L. Travers, *About the Sleeping Beauty* (New York: McGraw-Hill, 1975), p. 8.

trolls, witches, and giants, as well as princes and princesses were firmly established as kindred of the young.

Today, after centuries of almost purely childhood enjoyment, the circle of interest seems to have come round again. Once more there is a dual audience of both adult and child. Folklorists are now offering meticulously researched works of scholarship and publishers are producing them, complete with the seductive illustrative trappings of the modern book of fine art. A combination of authoritative texts and forewords, afterwords, notes, and essays has replaced (except for very young children) the anonymous versions of the chapbooks and those of the late nineteenth- and early twentieth-century retellers for children from Lucy Crane to Wanda Gág. These people, known or unknown, simply saw the cumulation of folk wisdom as tales, in Sir Philip Sidney's words, "which holdeth children from play and old men from the chimney corner." The early illustrators, George Cruikshank, Walter Crane, Arthur Rackham, who illuminated or extended the incidents in the tales, have been followed by modern artists who seek to penetrate the symbolic messages of folklore through diverse art forms, but chiefly surrealism.

The best-known twentieth-century names in the field of scholarship are Peter and Iona Opie, who have explored the largest territory in the realm of folklore in all its diverse modes.[2] In their most recent expedition, *The Classic Fairy Tales*,[3] they build on the work of the great folklorists by bringing together the texts of twenty-four tales and tracing their first appearance in the English language. This type of literary research is a hallmark of the Opies. Never mere collectors of material, they are brilliant, literate interpreters, indefatigable bibliographical detectives whose love of and skill in their craft transforms it into an art. The tales they have included are truly venerable performers, the successes of the European storytelling world, given in their collection with the freshness, purity, and even horror of their first rendering. It is revealing to compare these vigorous versions with the later and often bowdlerized retellings available today in the majority of mass market fairy-tale editions for children. The plethora of illustrations the Opies included complement the historical track of the text and are carefully chosen to illustrate the visual responses to each tale at various points in its history. They are not pieces of "art for art's sake."

It is love for a particular folktale that inspired Pamela Travers's

2. Iona Opie and Peter Opie, *The Lore and Language of School Children* (London: Oxford Univ. Pr., 1955); *The Oxford Dictionary of Nursery Rhymes* (London: Oxford Univ. Pr., 1951).

3. Iona Opie and Peter Opie, *The Classic Fairy Tales* (London: Oxford Univ. Pr., 1974).

194

About the Sleeping Beauty (1975) in which she brings together five traditional versions from different cultures. These are in every case the first published version in English and so they have the savor of the collected rather than of a recreation. Not so Travers's own retelling in a sixth version, which has the leisurely pace and sentiment of a literary folktale. It is rich in subtle humor, drama, and bittersweet human wisdom, and offers a new perspective on the ancient story. Although her rendition is set in a quasi–Middle Eastern country, it reflects no particular ethnic culture in comparison to the traditional versions, but rather that of the human mind and the author's imagination. She uses a rich, witty, and fluid style, resembling an oral tale in the absorbing storytelling, cumulative phrasing, and sharp folklike imagery. But it is also very much a work of literature, polished in every line, and extremely quotable with its mixture of pithy sayings and lyrical images, as exemplified in the following:

> And then, since a man cannot grieve continually—though the same is not true of women . . .
>
> the lizard lay still, like a scribble on marble.

Unlike many modern compendiums of folktales, *About the Sleeping Beauty* has a single illustrator, Charles Keeping, whose illustrations act as a continuous thread running through the diverse retellings. With their "x-ray" power, they invoke the mystery of the world of legend. Dramatic, intense, theatrical, and focused on precise, single images, the drawings resemble superb costume sketches for a stage production. They are much more lyrical and languid than most of Keeping's work; the visions of erotic, dreaming, and sleeping beauties recall the somnambulistic women of the surrealist painter Paul Delvaux.

Pamela Travers also ponders the secrets of the fairy tale in her stimulating "Afterword," which has the perspicacity and intelligence of her other essays, such as "Only Connect,"[4] and which will form as permanent a piece of literature on the fairy tale as Tolkien's essay "On Fairy Stories."[5] Travers writes of her faith in fairy tales, their power, mystery, and imaginative meaning. She speaks of "the everlasting gift, spotless amid all spotted joys, of love for the fairy tale," which she discovered in her youth. Travers asks the potent,

4. Pamela L. Travers, "Only Connect," in Sheila Egoff, G. T. Stubb, and L. F. Ashley, eds., *Only Connect* (Toronto and New York: Oxford Univ. Pr., 1980), pp. 183–206.
5. J. R. R. Tolkien, "On Fairy Stories," in his *Tree and Leaf* (London: Unwin Books, 1964), pp. 11–102.

unanswerable questions which link the archetypes of the fairy tale to our lives: "What is it in us that at a certain moment suddenly falls asleep? Who lies hidden deep within us? And who will come at last to wake us, what aspect of ourselves?" [6]

In physical format, both *The Classic Fairy Tales* and *About the Sleeping Beauty* are very attractive books, indeed beautiful ones. But the mature sophistication of the artwork (as in Travers) and the scholarly apparatus that surrounds both collections can act as barriers between the tale and the child, for whom "once upon a time" can be magic enough. Also, Travers's passionate questions are addressed to the imaginative adult with a love of the myths, folktales, skipping games, and street songs of childhood, rather than to the children themselves who are unconsciously living them.

In contrast to Travers's dedication to childhood and folklore, Bryan Holme in his *Tales from Times Past* (1977) is neither a scholar nor recreator but a connoisseur and a popularizer. His book is really a collector's pastiche. While the tales themselves would have appeal for children if read or told to them, the surprisingly small type, and the illustrations with their fin-de-siècle tone make it more a book for dabblers and dilettantes in folklore.

Balancing Travers's original recreation and Holme's eclecticism, there has emerged another significant trend, a return to scholarly collecting—Grimm, Perrault, and Asbjørnsen revisited. This style of research is distinct from that of the Opies, being based on what are considered more authentic translations from primary sources in languages other than English. It is characterized by the fanatical respect given to the original text or manuscript source and has produced the new three-in-one folklorist-translator-reteller.

One such is Elizabeth Shub whose *About Wise Men and Simpletons: Twelve Tales from Grimm* (1971) is translated from the first German edition. Her commitment to the original form of the tales in German and her unwillingness to modify or alter language or detail from the primary source result in unusually brief renditions with the immediacy and directness of a peasant's storytelling home entertainment. Adherence to the text in no way means uniform editions though, as is evidenced in *The Juniper Tree and Other Tales from Grimm* (1973), selected, translated, and retold by Lore Segal and Randall Jarrell. These are poetic retellings, quite different in tone from Shub's pithy, ingenuous approach. This may be because twenty-three of the twenty-four tales are "translated from the later texts, as reworked by

6. Travers, *About the Sleeping Beauty*, p. 62.

the Brothers Grimm."[7] Or, it may be that all translations, no matter how faithful to the original source, are filtered through the sensibilities of their retellers. Retellings of literary rather than traditional folktales have different problems and points of view, but here also the strict code of authenticity to source matter prevails. Erik Haugaard retains such a scholarly attention in *Hans Christian Andersen, The Complete Fairy Tales and Stories* (1974).

Many modern retellers, while returning to the original sources, strive valiantly for freshness of language. Brian Alderson, in *The Brothers Grimm* (1978), uses as his copy text the ninth edition of the "Grosse Ausgabe" of 1870. With his scholarship, he also attempts to restore the vital freshness of the oral storytelling voice to the respective tales, feeling that over a century of various retellings and translations the stories have become fixed in outmoded quasi-Victorian mannerisms which do not connect with contemporary life. He dips liberally into British folk colloquialism and vernacular, resulting in substantial modification of the language. He renders the tales as if they are being told and not read, and there is a straightforward freshness and raw humor in his approach that gives primacy to the storyteller over the silent reader. The chattering, laughing, living voice is most marked in his retellings of the droll peasant fables and beast tales, such as "Lazy 'Arry," and "The Fisherman and His Wife," while the more classic, romantic fairy tales such as "The Sleeping Beauty" and "Snow-White" retain a dignified balladic voice, but one that is tempered with a down-to-earth vernacular tone. Sometimes, though, his pungent British colloquialisms leave the reader with the bewildering suspicion that the tale may be a British folktale variant of a Grimm original, as the English "Mr. Fox" is a variant of "Bluebeard." This is particularly noticeable when he uses a British North Country dialect which "is intended to correspond with the North German dialect of the Grimm's tales"—a tenuous connection. At any rate his rendition of "Lazy 'Arry, Sunny Jim, and Skinny Lizzy," a combination of three Grimm tales into one run-on farce, had best be left to those who can "do" dialect:

> 'Arry was lazy—and for 'e'd got nothing to do but lug 'is goat orf to the field every day 'e moaned on when 'e came 'ome in the evenings after work. "Strewth," 'e used to say, "it's an 'ard job, a perishin' weary business, lugging a goat like this orf to the fields every year, from one Michaelmas round to the next."

Michael Foreman's surrealistic illustrations give the Alderson

7. Lore Segal and Randall Jarrell, trs., *The Juniper Tree* (New York: Farrar, 1973), vol. 1. Author's note signed "L. S."

version of these tales a tone of medieval darkness and tormented imagination akin to that found in the work of the fifteenth-century Flemish artist, Hieronymous Bosch. But the ominous surreal distortion is balanced by a zesty humor and romantic dreaming spirit in many stories.

In the same vein, combining scholarship with playful iconoclasm, is Angela Carter's *The Fairy Tales of Charles Perrault* (1977). She returns to the heart of Perrault's work, its elegant cynicism and its ironic morality—including the witty moral tags at the end of each tale—but adds her own idiosyncracies. Her translation of dialogue and descriptive detail has a fresh piquancy that reflects a twentieth-century modernity that at times slips into anachronism, such as the reference to Cinderella's "overalls." Carter also provides an eleven-page foreword that includes an entertaining biographical and critical study of Perrault's life and work, an analysis of the social and cultural milieu of his time, and the historical evolution of folklore from oral to written form.

Martin Ware's illustrations manifest a satirical wit, sophistication, and elegant subtlety that is appropriate to the mode of translation. The Lilac Fairy of "Donkey-Skin" appears as a striking, ironic figure—a Mae West parody in costume, stance, and expression. Not surprisingly, Carter mentions in her foreword the impression that "Perrault's specifically magical beings, the Lilac Fairy, Cinderella's godmother . . . have rather less the air of supernatural beings . . . than that of women of independent means . . . personages as worldly-wise and self-confident as Mae West."

The scholarly approach to folklore is also evident in the many recent reissues of complete academic works. *The Complete Grimm's Fairy Tales* with a commentary by Joseph Campbell was first published in 1944 and republished in 1972; Afanas'ev's *Russian Fairy Tales*, first published in 1945, was republished in 1973 with the original striking illustrations by Alexander Alexeieff. Another revival of classic editions has focused on the aesthetic appeal of the nineteenth century's golden age of illustration, appealing perhaps more to adult nostalgia and art appreciation than to any discernible child interest. Notable in this stream are John Bauer's illustrations in Elsa Olenius's *Great Swedish Fairy Tales*, first published in Sweden in 1966 as a vehicle for Bauer's magnificent troll-pervaded artwork. Other significant illustrators whose volumes of folk- and fairy tales have been reissued include Arthur Rackham, Kay Nielsen, Edmond Dulac, Ivan Bilibin, and Boris Zvorykin. The romantic storytelling illustrations of these books of the past stand in striking contrast to the modern, visually sophisticated, but emotionally restrained work of a Martin Ware or Michael Foreman.

The most significant reissues of all are those of the father of the Victorian fairy tale, Andrew Lang. Generations of children were weaned on his *Colour Fairy Books*, orotund in retelling as they were, and most subsequent editors have treaded lightly in his presence, including the usually decisive Kathleen Lines in her *Fifty Favourite Fairy Tales*, chosen from *The Colour Fairy Books* (1963). But Brian Alderson's new series—to date the *Blue* (1975), *Red* (1976) and *Green* (1978)—takes Lang by the scruff of the neck and shakes him, not into the twentieth century, but back to the folktale's primal time and tone. Lang's sentimentality will not be missed, but one does shed a tear for the loss of H. J. Ford's probing illustrations. Although Alderson's sometimes drastic revisions have punch and power, John Lawrence's new illustrations seem merely ill-conceived decoration as compared to Ford's voyages into enchantment.

While the reissues of Andrew Lang are a reminder that not all research and publishing in folklore is directed toward adults, yet its increasing power on the adult imagination can be seen in these critically acclaimed modern collections. A case in point is Segal's and Jarrell's *The Juniper Tree*, illustrated by Maurice Sendak and referred to as the "Sendak Grimm." The twenty-seven stories chosen from the original two hundred and ten are to a large extent not those generally selected for children's collections, including "The Juniper Tree" itself. A collector's item, it is sought by connoisseurs for its fine book production, poetic retellings, and Sendak's most mature and seductive illustrations—his Rapunzel is a languishing sister of Elizabeth Taylor in "Cat on a Hot Tin Roof." But seven years after its appearance it has not made its way into the hearts and minds of children as, for example, has Wanda Gág's more basic selections (and more lightly told and illustrated) in her *Tales from Grimm* and *More Tales from Grimm*. Wanda Gág was not a scholar. She retold the tales in recollection from her own childhood memories. But she could invest them with an aura of enchantment as with the incantation in "The Fisherman and His Wife" which most retellers strive to keep close to a literal translation. Wanda Gág translates the magic power of the refrain:

> Manye, Manye, Timpie Tee,
> Fishye, Fishye in the sea.

That the deeper interpretations of folklore fascinate adults can also be deduced from its entrance into the works of modern poets and artists: W. S. Merwin's poem "East of the Sun and West of the Moon" from a Norse tale; Anne Sexton's poetic interpretation of the Brothers Grimm in *Transformations*; and David Hockney's etchings for *Six Fairy Tales* from the Grimm Brothers. Heretofore, literature and art

199

had taken the symbolism of myth for its metaphors rather than that of folklore.

This trend, that of collecting, retranslating, rewriting, illustrating folklore of more appeal to adults than children, may be looked at in several ways. First of all it may not be crucial; both texts and illustrations may be enjoyed on several levels and if they are made available to both audiences, they may have a chance to find their own levels. The danger is, of course, that they may simply fall into a limbo between the two; the trend may simply reflect confusion. Authors, editors, and illustrators may be unable to decide upon suitability for, or appeal to, a specific audience or age group, which in turn may be attributed to a general lack of consensus as to what a child *is*. This confusion extends to parents, teachers, librarians, and even to children themselves. It certainly extends to what a children's book is in all other genres as well as the folktale.

However, the folktale is a unique literature in that it has always had a shared audience, especially in its true oral form. This is because of the prime role of the teller, who preceded the tale, and it is the voice of the teller that must somehow break through the tale's transference to the printed page. It is, ironically enough, a voice that is too often stilled for children by modern lavishly visual publications.

In our own time no one has done more than Isaac Bashevis Singer to meld the two audiences and, more importantly, to keep that vital storytelling voice. Singer writes in a number of traditional forms: the retellings and embroiderings upon old fables and folktales, the "slice of life" stories of the Jewish peasantry, and the snippets of autobiographical memoir capturing his life as a boy in Poland. In his *Naftali the Storyteller and His Horse, Sus* (1976) he brings all these strands together, but chiefly he pays homage to the venerable, deeply human and comforting art of the storyteller. "The Lantuch," a tale of a Jewish hobgoblin or friendly house spirit, is subtitled, "from my Aunt Yentl's stories," and is retold as first experienced by the child, Isaac, sitting on a footstool at his aunt's feet. Singer captures the tone of the specific moment of telling, of his aunt's speaking voice, of his emotions as a curious, listening child: "In the summers, my Aunt Yentl liked to tell stories on the Sabbath after the main meal, when my Uncle Joseph lay down for a nap."

The pivotal story in the book is "Naftali the Storyteller and His Horse, Sus." Naftali is a child who believes that storybooks are like bread—you can't live without them. Naftali decides to be a traveling bookseller, storyteller, and writer when he grows up and takes to heart the words of Reb Zebulun, the bookseller, as he expresses Singer's personal creed:

"If stories weren't told or books weren't written, man would live like the beasts, only for the day. . . . Today we live, but by tomorrow, today will be a story. The whole world, all human life, is one long story."

Singer's great achievement is to allow us to follow the transition of the oral tradition into literature, to see its workings as it were. In this sense he outstrips the great collectors of the past and their modern counterparts. Singer is perhaps closest to the great Danish storyteller, Hans Christian Andersen, who used many folktale motifs, couching them in highly sophisticated literary thought and language. Singer, however, is more earthy. Andersen's tales, exemplified by his poignant story of a mermaid who wanted a human soul, may seem to be but are really not far removed from Singer's tales of foolish wisemen, those ludicrous sages who confront nonsensical problems with bizarre, maddening, and perfectly appropriate solutions, such as the rabbi's decision in "Shrewd Todie and Lyzer the Miser" from *When Shlemiel Went to Warsaw* (1968).

Singer, like Andersen, understands and makes use of the deep vein of oral culture that survives through changes in fashion and taste. The telling combination of the storyteller's narrative voice and the writer's literary magic has been the hallmark of such favorite tales as "Molly Whuppie," "The Black Bull of Norroway," and "Puss in Boots," and is, in general, the wellspring as well as the buttress of folklore's extraordinary survival record. Singer's direct, universal, yet literary approach is like that of earlier retellers for children, among them Lucy Crane, Joseph Jacobs, Wanda Gág, George Dasent, M. R. James, and others who will undoubtedly outlast such retellers as Brian Alderson and Angela Carter who, in striving for modernity, may well be outdated in a few years.

The retellings of folktales that are specifically directed at a child audience take three specific forms: the lavishly illustrated nursery tale collections, the single illustrated folktale, and those that are told or retold according to sociological tenets.

The Fairy Tale Treasury (1972) with stories selected by Virginia Haviland and illustrated by Raymond Briggs is typical of these collections in that standard versions of the tales are used, often with unnecessary simplification, and in general the choice is based on the more familiar, less sophisticated stories. In *The Fairy Tale Treasury* there is a visible movement which follows the development of a child's reading interests and age levels from the basic nursery tales, beast fables, and drolleries to the complexities of romantic and literary fairy tales at the book's end. Haviland also provides a representation of tales from various cultures, including those of Japan and Africa, as well as the traditional European ones.

The selection is excellent and thorough, but the great excitement within the book comes from the sweeping tour de force of Brigg's illustrative art. He has with relish, gusto, and panache—any words that describe earthy exuberance and vitality—filled each page with a panoply of zesty detail, so that the book is literally overflowing with images—there are here over three hundred illustrations! The warmth of laughter and the delight in visual puns and anachronistic detail in Briggs's art, his legacy, from Caldecott and Brooke, is welcome at a time when so much illustration in children's books is overly sophisticated and the humor often cynical and adult. His original, childlike perceptions capture the eternal nonsense and drama at the heart of the tales, and his immense talent as draughtsman and colorist gives his perceptions compelling power. The massive size of the book itself is such that there is here an entire universe of folklore characters and actions within its covers, with enough spirited detail to fuel the hungry imaginations of a host of children.

An equally popular book for the young child just learning to read is Anne Rockwell's *The Three Bears and 15 Other Stories* (1975). Her naive illustrations, simple and lively, as are the stories, have a childlike European flavor. *Eric Carle's Story Book; Seven Tales by the Brothers Grimm* (1976) also concentrates on bright, vivacious, full-page illustrations of simply phrased retellings of nursery tales. These three books appear designed for young children to read for themselves. An older, but still useful collection, Kathleen Lines's *The Ten Minute Story Book* (1942), although eminently suitable for the same purpose, was designed for the storyteller—the title is sure proof of that. Then too, the contrast of the overly visual modern books with the restrained black-and-white vignettes in Lines's classic points out the dominance of the illustrator in the last two decades.

But the most notable trend in folklore for children in recent times has been the appearance of a multitude of single, illustrated folktales. Every illustrator of note has seemed compelled to illustrate one of the classic folktales, much as many an actress has yearned to play Lady Macbeth as the peak point in a career.

Since children are highly influenced by illustration, for good or for bad, for fright or delight, it may well be that these illustrators, having read the folktales as children, unconsciously decided to improve upon their first visual experience. Another and a simpler reason may be economic. Folktales are in the public domain, except perhaps for versions still in copyright, such as those retold by Virginia Haviland, and most illustrators use standard versions whose copyright, if any, would have expired. And, of course, since these stories have never belonged to a distinct individual, and because the oral tradition is an ongoing process of reshaping, any slight change in wording constitutes a new version. All of this means, of course, that neither illustrator nor publisher has to share the royalties with an author. At the same time the illustrator inherits almost total responsibility for interpretation. Indeed both collections and single illustrated versions now tend to be identified by the illustrator: the "Sendak" Grimm, "Briggs" *Fairy Tale Treasury*, "Wanda Gág's" *Snow White* (1938), "Nancy Ekholm Burkert's" *Snow White* (1973), "Trina Schart Hyman's" *Snow White* (1974), and so on. Illustrators do, of course, leave their personal signatures on a tale. Gág's earlier *Snow White* provides a warm earthiness and, although in black and white, conveys a childlike simplicity and intimacy resulting in a different reading experience of the tale as compared to that evoked by the sophisticated, subtly allusive symbolism of Burkert or the romantic idealism of Hyman.

The illustrator's power becomes evident as one tries to analyze the impact of the single illustrated folktale on children's reading. It would appear that these are used by young children and by adults working with young children, as picture books rather than as folktales per se. With the advent of nursery schools and day-care centers and with public libraries paying more attention to the preschool child, the simpler folktales have become the preserve of the very young. Middle-aged children, those between 8 and 11 years, traditionally the great readers of collected folktales, seem to have exchanged this interest for light fantasy and science fiction. It may well be that the ubiquity of the lavishly illustrated single tale gives the impression to older children that the folk- and fairy tales are for little kids. At any rate this genre now seems to attract either the very young child or the adult aficionado of illustration.

Those rewriters of folktales according to today's avowed sociological needs are not entirely a new breed. There was, notably, Cruikshank who turned "Puss in Boots," "The Sleeping Beauty," and "Cinderella" into temperance tracts, and so incurred the wrath of Charles Dickens. Today's social reformers are no less adamant and ingenious in their demands for new cultural models for children. Although this is the intent of *Womenfolk and Fairy Tales* (1975), its editor, Rosemary Minard, did not attempt to retell or bowdlerize folktales. She simply sought out tales with vital, independent, active, folk heroines. They, including the redoubtable Molly Whuppie, are drawn from a variety of cultures, and keep the integrity of the standard versions. Because of her sincere interest in folklore and literary merit, and her resistance to uncritical militancy, Minard has produced a fine collection of tales for readers of any age or sex, and in some sense, her very success in discovering so many powerful woman and girl protaganists leaves one questioning the assumption of implicit sexism in folklore. Much more successful and subtle than most books of its kind which carry a political or social message, this is a book that certainly answers what the publishers see as an immediate need or demand on the part of the public.

Another approach to folklore is that of a revisionist such as Julius Lester in his *Black Folktales* (1969). With a satirical eye to white history and an angry eye to black history, he puts together a mélange of traditional African tales, southern tales, ballads, and northern ghetto street lore and humor. These are folktales in a sociological evolution, notable for their double entendres, ironic twists, and antiwhite sentiment, which redresses the balance of the condescending tone of Joel Chandler Harris's introduction to his *Uncle Remus Stories* when he talks of the "quaint humor" of the blacks. Br'er Rabbit and his cohorts, of course, stem from an African tradition and are pure folktale. With his wide variety of themes, Lester has also a wide variety of styles. He ranges from the colloquial street language of Harlem to the dignified classic English of the African-rooted tales. While some of his references are even now anachronistic and some of his incidents very mature in their connotation, he has a strong touch of the parental about him, in a refreshing way, perhaps because he is always on the side of the Lord. In "How God Made the Butterflies," God gets complaints after his first day's work:

> The very *idea* of getting complaints about the world, and it wasn't even a day old. *That* was gratitude, and the Lord had a feeling he was going to be getting complaints about the world from now on. He was so mad he didn't care what he snipped, and he snipped all morning long—snip! snip! snip! And then he went back to bed, because he didn't want to hear any complaining about all the snipping he'd done. He had a good mind to just stay in bed forever and let the world handle its own complaints.

Both Minard, in collecting standard tales to adorn a particular viewpoint, and Lester, in unleashing a pent-up anger through a cool traditional form, are, in a sense, doing folklore an injustice. Since in its basic definition it comes out of the past, with a certain definitive kind of wisdom only slightly changed by the coloration of a geographical milieu, it seems a bit absurd to wrench it out of its general observations on humanity. Folklore transcends time and place, so when it is made too timely and too local it appears less than itself. Yet it is also the nature of the oral tradition to be constantly renewed and refreshened, with the injection of new insights. This is the gift of Pamela Travers in her own version of "The Sleeping Beauty." However, Minard's slant comes chiefly in her introduction and Lester gives his retellings the stamp of the litterateur and both collections are a salute to the changing social patterns of our day.

The worst sins in retelling are committed by those who do not have a deep and primal understanding of the commonality of folk literature and its role in the transmission of humanistic, cultural values. Above all, the stories are about people—wise men and fools, kind people and cruel people, greedy ones and generous ones, silly ones and sensible ones. The early "folk" clothed their wisdom in terms of wonder and enchantment, but actually with minimal use of magic and the supernatural. When magic is present it is usually connected with a veto, as G. K. Chesterton points out:

> The note of the fairy utterance always is, "You may live in a palace of gold and sapphire, *if* you do not say the word 'cow' "; or "You may live happily with the King's daughter, *if* you do not show her an onion." The vision always hangs upon a veto.[8]

Cinderella received a coach out of a pumpkin and a coachman from a rat, but she also received a command, that she should be back by midnight. The early storytellers understood the arbitrary realities of life as well as its wonders and meshed them as Pamela Travers has said "to make one web woven fine." This comprehension of both the power and prohibitions of magic is a far cry from the modern substitution of egotistical self-help for the natural verity of folk wisdom.

One of the saddest modern misinterpretations of folklore can be seen in Richard A. Gardner's collection, *Fairy Tales for To-Day's Children* (1974). Dr. Gardner is not in favor of magic being used to "solve a character's central problem" and has rewritten four tales "that make use of the psychological insights available in the twentieth century." His "Cinderelma" has no fairy godmother, although she wishes for one, but she dresses for the ball by borrowing her stepsisters' clothes. The prince finds her, not through a glass slipper, but through her mother's ruby ring. A ring will of course fit more fingers than a shoe will a foot! Once at the palace Cinderelma becomes educated and decides she does not want to marry the prince. She sets up shop as a seamstress and marries the printer next door. They have children "and lived together until the end of their days." Both text and illustrations are painfully devoid of any aesthetic values, while the basic enchantment of life is reduced to a parody of an existential viewpoint.

Most retellers and illustrators have tended to focus on the more

8. G. K. Chesterton, "The Ethics of Elfland" in *Orthodoxy* (London: John Lane, 1909), p. 97.

familiar of the European legacy—"Cinderella," "Puss in Boots," and the Andersen stories are still popular. But many are leaving the cultural images of their childhood reading far behind, choosing rather to explore and interpret folktales from aboriginal cultures and the Third World such as Betsy Bang's charming *The Old Woman and the Red Pumpkin: A Bengali Folktale* (1975). This interest in the folklore and legends of non-European cultures has been rising steadily in the past two decades. Harold Courlander and George Herzog's *The Cow-Tail Switch and Other West African Stories* was published in 1947, but, despite a discernible trickle in the 1950s, the considerable variety from other cultures, in either collections or single illustrated editions, was not obvious until the 1960s and 1970s.

The awareness of cultural diversity and pluralism of the 1960s has led to a vast number of publications in a remarkably short time, and they fill a void occasioned by neglect and a lack of understanding both of the commonality and specificity of indigenous tales. Such a lack of empathy and appreciation toward them began early and has been long lasting. With a limited knowledge of the true aspect of the new cultures they met, early European explorers were naively blind to the quality and nature of the tales they heard. Marc Lescarbot, who traveled to Canada in the early seventeenth century was probably typical. He gave this account of a tale told by the Indians:

> There is another strange thing worthy of record. . . . It is that to southward, near Chaleur Bay, lies an isle where lives a dreadful monster called by the savages Gougou, which they told me, had a woman's shape, but very terrible, and so tall, said they, that the top of the masts of our vessel would not have reached her waist . . . and that she has often devoured, and still devours, many savages, whom she puts in a great pouch when she can catch them, and then eats them; and those who had escaped the peril of this unchancy beast said that this pouch was so large that she would have put our vessel in it.[9]

Seventeenth-century Europeans found it difficult to separate fact from fiction in a land inhabited by "savages," where anything could happen. Such stories were not recognized for what they were, indigenous myths, which in fact resembled the tales from Greek and Norse mythology to a remarkable degree. The titans who could move mountains, the one-eyed Cyclops, Polyphemus, who could swallow a man whole, the god Thor swinging his gigantic hammer, the goddess Artemis who demanded the sacrifice of a young girl—all these larger-than-life figures of myth could easily have fitted into the Indian

9. Marc Lescarbot, *The History of New France*, tr. by W. L. Grant (Toronto: The Champlain Society, 1911), vol. 2, p. 170.

material that Lescarbot recorded with such wonder. Only the names and cultural context were different.

European stories are now culled from written primary sources, but the fascinating feature of indigenous and Third World stories is that they are the product of a living oral tradition that is still being transmitted and transmuted through the popular imagination. To the European mind trained in Aristotle's dictum of a story with a "beginning, a middle, and an end," the structure of indigenous stories often seems dreamlike and fragmented. But the stories do deal with the same basic, elemental human experiences as their European counterparts which have centuries of literary polish behind them. Also, because they are closer in time to the original tribal experience, they seem more raw and more violent.

The Australian aboriginal tales in *Djugurba: Tales from the Spirit Time* (1974), written and illustrated by a group of young aborigines, have a colloquial, nonliterary flavor, along with many brutal and bloody incidents, such as "The Moon Man and His Family" in which the father kills his two sons because the boys do not share their catch with him. It is taken for granted in most of these tales or incidents that destruction and deceit and blood-letting are a part of life. The Australian aboriginal tales frequently resemble the painful survival and revengeful legends of the Inuit, such as the famous Sedna legend in which Sedna's father and her brothers successively cut off the joints of her fingers as she tries to clamber into their boat. Sedna becomes the remorseless sea goddess to whom all the people must pay allegiance.[10] In such books as *Djugurba* and *Tales from the Igloo* (1972), the latter collected orally by Father Maurice Metayer, it can be seen that native retellings have not yet been expurgated or bowdlerized for children and they are therefore more primal in their violence and sexuality. In the European tales time and history in providing an aesthetic distance have made the violence more conventional, while sexuality has been turned into romance.

In a sense, then, the opportunity to witness myth-making in the process may cloud rather than clarify interpretation. It is well to recall the classic warning of the famous anthropologist Claude Lévi-Strauss: "A primitive people is not a backward or retarded people; indeed it may possess a genius for invention or action that leaves the achievements of civilized peoples far behind."[11] It is highly probable that any non-native person's retellings, effective though many of

10. Helen Caswell, *Shadows from the Singing House: Eskimo Folk Tales* (Edmonton, Alta.: Hurtig, 1968), pp. 26–32.

11. Claude Lévi-Strauss, *Structural Anthropology* (New York: Basic Books, 1963), p. 102.

them are, do not begin to suggest the significance and hidden meanings the stories hold for the indigenous peoples themselves; the legends may be far richer than the versions we know.

Another drawback is that indigenous tales have not yet been broken down into their component parts, as have the European tales with their fairly clear-cut divisions between myth, legend, and folklore. With Indian material, for example, we refer to it all, inaccurately, as legend. Also, up until the present at least, most indigenous peoples have lacked definitive litterateurs who can produce versions that are faithful to native cultural values and yet offer the literary and narrative power of their European counterparts. Their equivalents of Grimm, Perrault, Jacobs, and Asbjørnsen have not yet appeared.

There is encouragement in the fact that in most countries people are at least beginning to collect the lore of their indigenous cultures, as have the young Australian aborigines in *Djugurba* and Maurice Metayer with the Inuit *Tales from the Igloo*, which he recorded from an oral telling, then transcribed, translated, and edited with a light hand. Far from being polished, these tales have retained the feeling of immediacy and authenticity of an oral rendition, while providing a direct look at Inuit customs and beliefs. The best collection, chiefly because the same characters reappear throughout its tales, thereby building familiarity, is the Canadian Indian George Clutesi's *Son of Raven, Son of Deer: Fables of the Tse-Shaht People* (1967). The exploits of foolhardy Son of Deer and greedy and thoughtless Son of Raven are retold in brief, almost Aesop-like, fashion. These fables, which have been handed down in Clutesi's family for almost four hundred years, have an assurance and polish that make them unique among Indian tales of North America.

In presenting to children the traditional indigenous lore of a people, the reteller has a choice of two techniques: to adopt a straightforward, sensitively modified authenticity or to recast the tales completely in the European short-story format similar to that used by Christie Harris in *Once Upon a Totem* (1963). That the artistry of the direct, unadorned approach works best for children and for storytelling can be seen in the ongoing popularity of William Toye's retelling of *How Summer Came to Canada* (1969) and *The Loon's Necklace* (1977), both enhanced with authentic and brilliant collage illustration by Elizabeth Cleaver.

Another workable technique is that of using a single character as a peg on which to hang a cycle of stories, thus creating for the reader a feeling of ease and a sense of familiarity. This approach has been adopted most successfully by such non-native retellers as Dorothy Reid in *Tales of Nanabozho* (1960); Ronald Melzack's *Raven, Creator of the World: Eskimo Legends* (1970); Jane Louise Curry's stories of Coyote entitled *Down from the Lonely Mountain* (1965); and Christie Harris's tales of Canada's West Coast Indians that are linked together by the intriguing and authentic character of Mouse Woman, *Mouse Woman and the Vanished Princesses* (1976).

Much of the difficulty of transmitting and transmuting indigenous literature may be overcome through poetry. The poetic form is closer to the inner meaning of legend; in it we are freer from our distinction between history and story. Natalia Belting's *Whirlwind Is a Ghost Dancing* (1974) is a collection of short poems, based on the lore of Indian tribes from a wide variety of locations throughout all North America, that point up the essential oneness of all Indian peoples. The images used are remarkably similar from one Indian group to another.

> Winter is an old man walking in the woods.
> He raps the trees with his war club,
> And men in their lodges hear the sharp cracking blows.

to the Iroquois of New York state, and to the Bella Coolas of British Columbia, "Icicles are the walking sticks of the winter winds." Other perceptive collections are Richard Lewis's *Out of the Earth I Sing: Poetry and Songs of Primitive Peoples of the World* (1968), Knud Rasmussen's *Beyond The High Hills: A Book of Eskimo Poems* (1961), James Houston's *Songs of the Dream People* (1972), and Hettie Jones's *The Trees Stand Shining: Poetry of the North American Indians* (1971).

As yet, the indigenous tales known to us, whether transmitted by natives or non-natives, merely open the door on the fascinations of a world that is at once alien and strangely familiar. Although there are polished differences between them and their European counterparts, they do take their place in the world commonalty of the oral tradition. The combination of familiarity and strangeness is a characteristic quality of myths, hero stories, and folktales and the basis for their chief appeal to children. They reassure by their naiveté, enthrall by their matchless story qualities, and stretch children imaginatively and emotionally as they discover the fundamental attributes of the human race.

These primordial tales, these stories of the world's beginning that are so remarkably similar from culture to culture, these tales of animals and birds that are indigenous to each culture, yet again so similar one to the other, reveal a world that is in many ways close to that of a child—a world in which "every thunderclap came as a threat and every night as the last." Furthermore, it is a world in which imagination has free reign and society is colorful, independent, and close to nature. Many of the virtues the tales extol are universal: kindness to people and animals, courage and strength in the face of adversity, loyalty to family and tribe, unfailing devotion even unto death. They deal with a physical environment that is familiar to us: the mountains, rivers, and animals are ours, along with the frightening wilderness, the endless prairie, the swift-moving rivers, the fruits of earth and sea. Nor is the strong relationship with nature beyond our understanding: the struggle between human and environment is still a dominant one in many parts of the world.

Although the spectrum of folklore reflects the immense variety of life stories to be told and the subtle cultural variations upon similar themes, most world mythologies appear to share one basic human story—the pattern of humankind's experience through birth, life, and death. In this light, Singer's view that "the whole world, all human life, is one long story" is at the root of the word *mythology*—"mythos," a story. While myth, folklore, and legend are all textures of one fabric, the presumption is that myth, the more universal and primal, came first. The motivations of our ancestors who first created the tales have been lost in the mists of time, although there are theories aplenty to account for them. Plato, Vico, Frazer, Lévi-Strauss, Freud, Jung, and in our own time Mircea Eliade, Joseph Campbell, Northrop Frye, and Susanne Langer are only a few of those thinkers who have tried to explain the radical differences in world view between preliterate and literate man.

Although the making of myths undoubtedly preceded the development of graphic symbols, myths became widely known and available only in written form. In the case of European myths, centuries of rewriting have undoubtedly smoothed away the shapes and textures of the original narratives. Even more important, the development of writing froze or locked in ideas and traditions that were originally fluid and variable. Once the theme had been written down, few variations were possible. All of this is in contrast to folklore in which transformations of character, plot, and cultural background were constantly changed in retelling. There are, for example, about four hundred variants of the Cinderella story, culled from various cultures, but the myths of Psyche and Eros or Oedipus are so fundamental that their very names have become symbols larger than themselves and their variants will be literary rather than ethnic—Sophocles's classic presentation of Antigone and Creon as opposed to the revisionist approach of Jean Anouilh.

It is not surprising then that the Greek myths, emanating from a civilization whose language and thought still influence the modern world, should have been given pride of place. But these stories have come down to us in fragmented form, taken in pieces from Homer, Hesiod, Ovid, and the early Greek dramatists. For children especially they were presented as separate short stories and this isolation has been increased in recent time by the publication of single illustrated myths such as Compton MacKenzie's *Achilles* (1972) and Penelope Farmer's *The Serpent's Tooth: The Story of Cadmus* (1971). But whoever the protagonists, they were undoubtedly chosen for a dramatic story interest rather than for a deeper psychological insight into the traditions of early humanity. Then too, in most retellings the characters are highly stylized and their adventures portrayed chiefly as "sword and sorcery." The erotic escapades of Zeus and the other Olympians or the tragedy of Medea are either lacking or much tempered in children's versions.

This tradition was broken and most dramatically with the interpretation of Greek myths by Leon Garfield and Edward Blishen, coauthors of *The God Beneath the Sea* (1971) and *The Golden Shadow* (1973). Garfield and Blishen have succeeded in what they set out to do —to create "a piece of fresh fiction out of some of the oldest tales in the world." As have many other modern retellers of folktales, they were disturbed by the superficial attitude toward mythology and the watered-down approach of most versions for children. Therefore they determined to tell the tales as they felt they would have liked to have heard them as children—as a whole life story.

The psychological novelistic approach to myth of Garfield and Blishen had been previously explored by writers for adults, among them Mary Renault in her historical novels *The King Must Die* and *The Bull from the Sea*, based on the Theseus myths; John Gardner in *Grendel*, an existential version of Beowulf told from the monster's point of view; Rosemary Sutcliff in her harshly realistic tribal interpretation of Arthur in *Sword at Sunset*; and C. S. Lewis in the tender and passionate extension of the Psyche legend, *Till We Have Faces*. None of these writers had reduced the dignity or dramatic scope of the myths or legends by rendering them to a more human proportion and scale and neither do Garfield and Blishen. They pull no punches; they are true to the passionate spirit of the myths and respectful to the maturity, intelligence, and curiosity of their readers.

Essentially, *The God Beneath the Sea* is the saga of creation and destruction in the cosmos. It is the story of desire and conflict among the pantheon of gods and their involvement with the smaller but more poignant affairs of the frail mortals who tenaciously hold to their brief lives. The structure of the book is balanced on the life of Hephaestus, the hideous but visionary artist-smith who creates great beauty in metal and jewels out of his ugliness, pain, and inspiration. Like a bracketing couplet, the book opens and closes with Hephaestus, the god of artifice. It opens with his fall from Olympus, when as a baby his mother, Hera, threw him from the sky, and ends with his parallel return from a second fall and exile in a painful climb upwards "towards the sky which was his home."

The first part of the book is filled with wonderful vivacious tales of lust and humor; of Zeus's great loves and ubiquitous progeny, Hera's monumental jealousy, and Hermes's zestful trickery. Waiting to be answered is the question, "the earth—the sweet green earth. To whom would it be given?" The tone of raw primitiveness changes to one of almost modern realism when Prometheus creates his mortals to inherit the earth. He "shaped the clay into images of the immortal gods" and sent them to seek their inheritance on the earth. With the mortals come pain and death.

The novelistic structure and the narrative flow is less intricate in *The Golden Shadow*, which deals on a more human scale with the early mortal world. It is the domain of heroes, peasants, and storytellers, and its central protagonists are Heracles and the Homeric Storyteller, both human and mortal, as opposed to the divine central figures of *The God Beneath the Sea* in the gods Hephaestus, Hermes, and Prometheus. Nonetheless, there is a striking link between the two books in the presence of art and artifice—the artist-smith, Hephaestus, and the Homeric Storyteller.

There is a strong sense of time passing, of death and aging in this second book; the passing of mortal life as compared with the glorious eternal youth of the gods in *The God Beneath the Sea*. It is also more of a whole, although closer to the form of a picaresque novel than the first; this because of the presence of the Storyteller, a Homer-like wandering bard traveling throughout Greece, gathering legends, and searching for a revelation of the truth of the gods.

> This traveller, bald and short of sight, was a poet, a storyteller, who collected tales that he wove into ballads for the entertainment of any who'd clothe and feed him.

As a man the Storyteller is dingy and pathetic; but as a poet he is obsessed with truth and illusion, reality and appearance. Like Hephaestus and Hermes in the first book, he is also the creator of artifice, illusion, and dream, but in human form. He questions the legends:

> What was the real truth of it all? Housekeepers' tales and his own longing for the world to be larger and more mysterious than it was. However brightly everything shone in his mind, in his hands it crumbled to dust.

Many of the basic Greek myths are woven into the Storyteller's life through his search for the gods, especially the stories of Heracles. Both books give a sense of immediacy, as if the reader were actually witnessing the events, but hidden and watchful, like the mortal Sisyphus hiding in the wood near Corinth and spying through a "grass keyhole on a divine secret," observing the passion and conflict of the gods. These are not events of the dim and distant past; they have happened only a moment before.

Garfield and Blishen have used a warm, romantic, and poetic style that gives credence to the fact that they wrote it by oral creation, chanting to each other. Far more than any other version of the myths, these books do lend themselves to reading aloud.

The emotional intensity of the two novels is matched and even at times exceeded by the illustrations of Charles Keeping. He does not, perhaps unfortunately, connect with the bawdy humor of the tales but emphasizes their primal aspect. His images convey the monumental energy, passion, and violence of the struggles, aspirations, and desires that set human against god, and the forces of nature. As the retellers have pointed out, Keeping chose to emphasize the modernity of the myths in his stylized abstractions, rescuing them from the overly familiar Victorian depictions. Keeping's work in these two books is associated with the most tumultuous and seething he has created for children; his picture books seem very childlike in comparison. Although Keeping's work may be considered erotic, Zevi Blum, in the American edition of *The God Beneath the Sea*, in trying to illustrate specifically, has managed to make his work appear pornographic.

The central metaphor in *The Golden Shadow*, the Storyteller's unending, painful search for the true experience of the gods behind the myths, can almost be taken as a symbol of the inability of modern retellers (aside from Garfield and Blishen) to enter into the living experience of the myths. They, like the Storyteller, have been unable to invest the tales with the passionate spirit of belief. Most retellers for children have cast them in the prevailing attitudes toward children—Hawthorne's fairy-tale aura, Kingsley's Christian sentiment, and in our time, the simple, straightforward approach without moralizing. But they have all failed to convince by merely providing a familiarity with a plot outline as a substitute for the mythic spirit. Even Garfield and Blishen approach the myths indirectly, tackling them from a psychological interpretation and in an experimental style. They succeed in their approach better than their contemporary, Robert Graves, perhaps because they admit, in the person of the Storyteller, contemporary man's inability to believe fully in the tales.

Graves in his *Myths of Ancient Greece* (1961) at first appears to be a naive, straightforward reteller, but gradually one becomes conscious of his note of irony. He is basically a descendant of Ovid, who also told the Greek myths tongue-in-cheek in his *Metamorphoses*. Graves tells the Daedalus and Icarus myth almost as a prologue to indicate the consummate skill of Daedalus rather than as a tale of human drama that has remained in the consciousness of Western peoples until the present. There is little dignity or tragedy in Graves's versions but rather a self-conscious, off-hand humor, that lets the reader in on the joke, but at the expense of intensity:

> Cocalus . . . invited Minos to take a warm bath in the new bathroom built by Daedalus. But Cocalus's daughters, to save their friend—who had given them a set of beautiful dolls, with moveable arms and legs—poured boiling water down the bathroom pipe instead of warm, and scalded Minos to death. Cocalus pretended that Minos had died by accident: tripping over the bath-mat and falling into the tub before cold water could be added. Fortunately the Cretans believed this story.

In his efforts to show the human qualities of the gods, Graves deliberately abandoned any hint of poetry in his style. Thomas Bulfinch, in his adult work *The Age of Fables*, while retelling the myths as separate stories, could still provide a strong visual imagery. In recounting the story of Pluto and Demeter he wrote, "Pluto urged on his steeds, calling them each by name, and throwing loose over their heads and necks his iron-coloured reins." Graves reduces this image to "(Hades) carried her off in his great hearse of a chariot." He has sought to bring the gods and goddesses down to earth, and succeeds. But, one might ask, who needs down-to-earth gods?

At least Graves has a definite style and approach. Most modern retellers, such as Roger Lancelyn Green in *Tales of Greek Heroes* (1958) and Doris Gates in *The Warrior Goddess: Athena* (1972) are faceless and styleless. The inability of modern retellers, with the exception of Garfield and Blishen, to capture the passionate depths of a primal, chaotic world may be understandable in our age of dependence upon government. It is less understandable why so few can enter the formally ordered, romantic, Christian world of medieval legend.

In terms of grandeur and affinity with the material, no modern writer has approached Howard Pyle's cycle of the Robin Hood or Arthurian tales published in 1883 and 1903 respectively. But while Howard Pyle worked "in large," the finest modern interpreter of the medieval legend and hero tale, Rosemary Sutcliff, works "in small," unlike her approach in her historical novels. She takes either short tales like *Beowulf* (in its original, only 9,000 lines are extant) or certain cohesive episodes from the Arthurian cycle—*Tristan and Iseult* (1971) and *The Light Beyond the Forest* (1979)—but approaches them from different angles. In *Beowulf* (1961) and *The Hound of Ulster* (1963), she keeps close to the primary material, paying attention to dramatic incident and creating highly colored but stylized characters in true heroic style. But in *Tristan and Iseult* (1971) she begins to demythologize, removing the pivotal legendary magic of the love potion and accentuating the human drama of love itself. As she explains in her foreword, nothing exterior is required to bring about love between two human beings. It springs from within and, in her retelling, one feels that she has grasped the true tragedy of this star-crossed pair.

Her interest in human psychology behind the legendary mask increases in *The Light Beyond the Forest: The Quest for the Holy Grail* (1979). Although it adheres to a romantic, chivalric, and medieval setting of the court of King Arthur, far different from her harshly realistic account of Arthur as the Dux Bellorum in her adult novel, *Sword at Sunset*—she nonetheless probes beyond the stylized Malory characterizations to a more psychological exploration of distinct individuals. Lancelot is portrayed as a truly tragic figure:

> But Lancelot knelt there silent, with bowed head. He had made his confession as often as any other man. But he had never made it fully; for the love between himself and the Queen was not his alone to confess. Yet he knew in his heart that it was the thing that was shutting him out from God.

Galahad is not seen as a mere symbol of purity. His Christian virtue is shown as compelling, as personal and as difficult as that of the "good" characters in Charles Williams's adult religious fantasies.

> And the old Knight saw the boy's face that had become a man's; a face that was gravely beautiful, but yet without a soft line in it anywhere, and a look of inner certainty that he had never seen in any man's face before.

In her foreword Sutcliff comments on the medieval Christian story. Although all its elements belong to the oral tradition, the material was collected and written down chiefly between the ninth and twelfth centuries, that is, in Christian times. It is, she notes,

> shot through with shadows and half-light and haunting echoes of much older things; scraps of the mystery religions which the legions carried from end to end of the Roman Empire; above all a mass of Celtic myth and folklore.

In such retellings as *Tristan and Iseult* and *The Light Beyond the Forest*, she demonstrates that she is able to cut through that corpulence of detail a story acquires through countless retellings and pierce the heart of the matter, to those tragic themes common to all heroic myths and legends: the force of destiny, the conflict between love of the Lady and loyalty to the Lord, temporal versus divine love. The purity of style and taut condensation of narrative in all Sutcliff's retellings are striking complements to the shadowy mysteries behind her clean prose.

In contrast to Sutcliff's fictionalization of Arthurian matter, John Steinbeck's uncompleted version, *The Acts of King Arthur and His Noble Knights* (1976), is based, as is much of recent folklore, on a definite source—the Winchester manuscripts—and his main objective is not "to rewrite Malory or reduce him or change him or soften or sentimentalize him." And although he does put his version into modern English, this by no means diminishes its literary ancestor. Steinbeck's aim is to retain the spirit and historicity of the original, Sutcliff's is to provide imaginative characterization strengthened by psychological insight within a historical framework; both are vividly alive to the "Matter of Britain." His work, which remained unfinished at his death—only seven chapters were completed—might well have become a "classic" modern version of Malory for children. That Steinbeck did it for children can be surmised from his Introduction where he speaks of his childhood love of Malory's *Morte d'Arthur*. "It did not," he comments, "outrage my sensibilities as nearly all the children's books did."

That the artistry of Steinbeck and Sutcliff and Garfield and Blishen is nourishing to mind and spirit is undeniable; so too is the realization that they have few peers. Most modern writers attempting to retell the legends of chivalry for children, whether scholarly or amateur, are neither imaginative nor skillful enough interpreters of these tales. Medieval legends retold by such writers as Antonia Fraser, E. M. Almedingen, Roger Lancelyn Green, and Barbara Picard unfortunately are dry and banal. One notable exception is Ian Serraillier, who in a succinct poetic form captures the epic quality of Beowulf in his blank verse rendition, *Beowulf the Warrior* (1954), and the rhythmic, lilting tone of the early ballads in his *Robin and His Merry Men* (1969).

If legends are not the favorite reading of most children today, it may be due largely to the mediocrity and enervated spirit of much of the retelling. Their successful retelling demands love, insight, scholarship, and an empathy for the historical as well as the legendary past, qualities that can be present in a committed amateur's enthusiasm, rather than lifelong scholarship, as is evident in Howard Pyle's vital, artistic, and literary reworkings of *King Arthur* and *Robin Hood*. Unfortunately most contemporary retellers appear amateurish in comparison.

In general, although a few retellings for children of myths and legends are brilliantly innovative, as is Garfield's and Blishen's *The*

Golden Shadow, or movingly conceived, as is Sutcliff's *The Light Beyond the Forest,* the majority are all too forgettable.[12] The folklorists are more successful in their efforts, although less experimental, but most writers working in the area of myth and legend appear to be mere dabblers. Why this is so may be that writers tend to feel more confident about retelling the oral and anonymous works in which all storytellers are linked because these are distinguished only by cultural backgrounds and require mainly a kind of piquancy in the retelling. Myth and legend have also come from an oral tradition, but most of the major tales have definite written sources and are even the property of known literary giants of the past: Chrétien de Troyes and Malory for King Arthur; Sigmund Saemand and Snorri Sturluson for the Norse myths; Homer, Hesiod, Ovid, and the early Greek dramatists for Greek myth and legend; and Charlotte Guest for her translation of the *Mabinogian.* These are specific, articulate, and authoritative voices and in their presence most retellers of children's versions falter, haunted no doubt by an inability to live up to a written version, even in translation. Fortunately the raw energy of the stories themselves can often break through the weakest of versions, compelling attention to the powerful narrative core of early mankind's nature and dramatic life experience.

Works Cited

Afanas'ev, Col. Aleksandr. *Russian Fairy Tales.* Tr. by Norbert Guterman. Illus. by Alexander Alexeieff. New York: Pantheon, 1945. 661 pp.

Andersen, Hans Christian. *The Complete Fairy Tales and Stories.* Tr. from the Danish by Erik Christian Haugaard. New York: Doubleday, 1974. 1101 pp.

Bang, Betsy. *The Old Woman and the Red Pumpkin: A Bengali Folktale.* Illus. by Molly Garrett Bang. New York: Macmillan, 1975. [32] pp.

Belting, Natalia. *Whirlwind Is a Ghost Dancing.* Illus. by Leo and Diane Dillon. New York: Dutton, 1974. [30] pp.

Eric Carle's Story Book: Seven Tales by the Brothers Grimm. Illus. and retold by Eric Carle. New York: Watts, 1976. 93 pp.

Caswell, Helen, ret. *Shadows from the Singing House: Eskimo Folk Tales.* Illus. by Robert Mayokok. Edmonton, Alta.: Hurtig, 1968. 108 pp.

Clutesi, George. *Son of Raven, Son of Deer: Fables of the Tse-Shaht People.* Illus. by the author. Sidney, B.C.: Grays, 1967. 126 pp.

12. In many ways the most successful use of folklore and mythology has been made by such modern fantasists as Susan Cooper and Alan Garner, who meld their modern plots with mythic elements.

Courlander, Harold, and Herzog, George. *The Cow-Tail Switch, and Other West African Stories*. Drawings by Madye Lee Chastain. New York: Holt, 1947. 143 pp.

Curry, Jane Louise. *Down from the Lonely Mountain: California Indian Tales*. Illus. by Enrico Arno. New York: Harcourt, 1965. 128 pp.

Djugurba: Tales from the Spirit Time. Canberra: Australian National Univ. Pr., 1974. 62 pp.

Farmer, Penelope. *The Serpent's Tooth: The Story of Cadmus*. Illus. by Chris Connor. London: Collins, 1971. [48] pp.

Gardner, Richard A. *Dr. Gardner's Fairy Tales for Today's Children*. Illus. by Alfred Lowenheim. Englewood Cliffs, NJ: Prentice-Hall, 1974. 96 pp.

Garfield, Leon, and Blishen, Edward. *The God Beneath the Sea*. Illus. by Charles Keeping. London: Longman Young Books, 1970. 168 pp.; U.S. ed. illus. by Zevi Blum. New York: Pantheon, 1971. 212 pp.

——*The Golden Shadow*. Illus. by Charles Keeping. London: Longman Young Books, 1973. 155 pp.

Gates, Doris. *The Warrior Goddess: Athena*. Illus. by Don Bolognese. New York: Viking, 1972. 121 pp.

Graves, Robert. *Myths of Ancient Greece*. Illus. by Joan Kiddell-Monroe. London: Cassell, 1961. 160 pp.; U.S. title: *Greek Gods and Heroes*. Illus. by Dimitris Davis. New York: Doubleday, 1960.

Green, Roger Lancelyn. *Tales of the Greek Heroes*. Harmondsworth: Penguin, 1958. 205 pp.

Grimm, Jacob, and Grimm, Wilhelm. *About Wise Men and Simpletons: Twelve Tales from Grimm*. Tr. by Elizabeth Shub. Etchings by Nonny Hogrogian. New York: Macmillan, 1971. 118 pp.

——*The Brothers Grimm: Popular Folk Tales*. Newly tr. by Brian Alderson. Illus. by Michael Foreman. London: Gollancz, 1978. 192 pp.

——*The Complete Grimm's Fairy Tales*. Illus. by Josef Scharl. New York: Pantheon, 1944. 863 pp.

——*The Juniper Tree and Other Tales from Grimm*. Sel. by Lore Segal and Maurice Sendak. Tr. by Lore Segal; with four tales tr. by Randall Jarrell. Pictures by Maurice Sendak. New York: Farrar, 1973. 2 vols.

——*More Tales from Grimm*. Freely tr. by Wanda Gág. New York: Coward, 1947. 257 pp.

——*Snow White*. Freely tr. from the German by Paul Heins. Illus. by Trina Schart Hyman. Boston: Little, 1974. [48] pp.

——*Snow-White and the Seven Dwarfs; A Tale from the Brothers Grimm*. Tr. by Randall Jarrell. Pictures by Nancy Ekholm Burkert. New York: Farrar, 1972. [31] pp.

——*Snow-White and the Seven Dwarfs*. Freely tr. and illus. by Wanda Gág. New York: Coward, 1938. 43 pp.

——*Tales from Grimm*. Freely tr. and illus. by Wanda Gág. New York: Coward, 1936. 237 pp.

Harris, Christie. *Mouse Woman and the Vanished Princesses*. Drawings by Douglas Tait. Toronto: McClelland and Stewart, 1976. 155 pp.

——*Once Upon a Totem*. Woodcuts by John Frazer Mills. New York: Atheneum, 1963. 148 pp.

Harris, Joel Chandler. *Uncle Remus: His Songs and His Sayings.* The Folklore of the Old Plantation. Illus. by Frederick S. Church and James H. Moser. New York: D. Appleton and Co., 1881. 231 pp.

Haviland, Virginia, ed. *The Fairy Tale Treasury.* Illus. by Raymond Briggs. New York: Coward, 1972. 190 pp.

Holme, Bryan, ed. *Tales from Times Past.* New York: Viking, 1977. 175 pp.

Houston, James. *Songs of the Dream People: Chants and Images from the Indians and Eskimos of North America.* New York: Atheneum, 1972. 83 pp.

Jones, Hettie, ed. *The Trees Stand Shining; Poetry of the North American Indian.* Paintings by Robert Andrew Parker. New York: Dial, 1971. [32] pp.

Lang, Andrew. *Blue Fairy Book.* rev. ed. by Brian Alderson. Illus. by John Lawrence. Harmondsworth: Kestrel, 1975. 373 pp.

———*Colour Fairy Books.* Illus. by H. J. Ford. London and New York: Longmans, Green, 1889-1919.

———*Fifty Favourite Fairy Tales.* Chosen from Colour Fairy Books by Kathleen Lines. Illus. by Margery Gill. London: Nonesuch, 1963. 363 pp.

———*Green Fairy Book.* rev. ed. by Brian Alderson. Illus. by Antony Maitland. Harmondsworth: Kestrel, 1978. 408 pp.

———*Red Fairy Book.* rev. ed. by Brian Alderson. Illus. by Faith Jacques. Harmondsworth: Kestrel, 1976. 372 pp.

Lester, Julius. *Black Folktales.* Illus. by Tom Feelings. (An Evergreen Black Cat Book) New York: Grove, 1970. 157 pp.

Lewis, Richard, ed. *Out of the Earth I Sing: Poetry and Songs of Primitive Peoples of the World.* New York: Norton, 1968. 144 pp.

Lines, Kathleen, ed. *The Ten Minute Story Book.* Illus. by Winnifred Marks. London: Oxford Univ. Pr., 1942. 80 pp.

MacKenzie, Sir Compton. *Achilles.* Illus. by William Stobbs. London: Aldus Books, 1972. 61 pp.

Melzack, Ronald. *Raven, Creator of the World: Eskimo Legends.* Illus. by Lazlo Gal. Toronto: McClelland and Stewart, 1970. 91 pp.

Metayer, Father Maurice. *Tales from the Igloo.* Illus. by Agnes Namogak. Edmonton: Hurtig, 1972. 127 pp.

Minard, Rosemary, ed. *Womenfolk and Fairy Tales.* Illus. by Suzanna Klein. Boston: Houghton, 1975. 163 pp.

Olenius, Elsa, comp. *Great Swedish Fairy Tales.* Tr. by Holger Lundbergh. Illus. by John Bauer. New York: Delacorte, 1973. 238 pp.

Opie, Iona and Opie, Peter, eds. *The Classic Fairy Tales.* London: Oxford Univ. Pr., 1974. 255 pp.

Perrault, Charles. *The Fairy Tales of Charles Perrault.* Tr. by Angela Carter. Illus. by Martin Ware. London: Gollancz, 1977. 159 pp.

Pyle, Howard. *The Merry Adventures of Robin Hood of Great Renown in Nottinghamshire.* New York: Scribner, 1883. 296 pp.

———*The Story of King Arthur and his Knights.* London and New York: George Newnes, 1903. 312 pp.

Rasmussen, Knud. *Beyond the High Hills: A Book of Eskimo Poems*. Photos. by Guy Mary-Rousselière. Cleveland/New York: World, 1961. 32 pp.

Reid, Dorothy. *Tales of Nanabozho*. Illus. by Donald Grant. Toronto: Oxford Univ. Pr., 1963. 126 pp.

Rockwell, Anne. *The Three Bears and 15 Other Stories*. Illus. by Anne Rockwell. New York: Crowell, 1975. 116 pp.

Serraillier, Ian. *Beowulf the Warrior*. Illus. by Severin. London: Oxford Univ. Pr., 1954. 47 pp.

———*Robin and His Merry Men*. Illus. by Victor G. Ambrus. London: Oxford Univ. Pr., 1969. 60 pp.

Singer, Isaac Bashevis. *Naftali The Storyteller and His Horse, Sus, and Other Stories*. Pictures by Margot Zemach. New York: Farrar, 1976. 129 pp.

———*When Shlemiel Went to Warsaw and Other Stories*. Tr. by the author. Pictures by Margot Zemach. New York: Farrar, 1968. 115 pp.

Steinbeck, John, ad. *The Acts of King Arthur and His Noble Knights from the Winchester MSS of Thomas Malory and Other Sources*. New York: Farrar, 1976. 363 pp.

Sutcliff, Rosemary, retel. *Beowulf*. Drawings by Charles Keeping. London: Bodley Head, 1961. 93 pp.

———*The Hound of Ulster*. Drawings by Victor Ambrus. London: Bodley Head, 1963. 192 pp.

———*The Light Beyond the Forest: The Quest for the Holy Grail*. Decorations by Shirley Felts. London: Bodley Head, 1979. 148 pp.

———*Tristan and Iseult*. Illus. by Victor Ambrus. London: Bodley Head, 1971. 134 pp.

Toye, William. *How Summer Came to Canada*. Pictures by Elizabeth Cleaver. Toronto: Oxford Univ. Pr., 1969. 32 pp.

———*The Loon's Necklace*. Pictures by Elizabeth Cleaver. Toronto: Oxford Univ. Pr., 1977. [24] pp.

Travers, Pamela L. *About the Sleeping Beauty*. Illus. by Charles Keeping. New York: McGraw-Hill, 1975. 111 pp.

9. Poetry

When I began to read the nursery rhymes for myself, and, later, to read other verses and ballads, I knew that I had discovered the most important things, to me, that could be ever. There they were, seemingly lifeless, made only of black and white, but out of them, out of their own being, came love and terror and pity and pain and wonder and all the other vague abstractions that make our ephemeral lives dangerous, great, and bearable . . . though what the words meant was, in its own way, often deliciously funny enough, so much funnier seemed to me, at that almost forgotten time, the shape and shade and size and noise of the words as they hummed, strummed, jugged, and galloped along.[1]

The recollections by Dylan Thomas of his own discovery of poetry express something more fundamental than a poet's awakening to his muse—that childhood and poetry have a natural affinity for one another. Poets have played with language since the dawn of time, carefully choosing words for their quality of sound, meaning, and musical rhythm to create what may loosely be grouped under the name of poetry: mythmaking tribal chants; lullabies; sea chanties; epics, ballads, and folk songs; nursery rhymes; dramatic, nonsense, and lyric verse; and, most recently, free forms including projective and free verse and concrete and found poetry. All these are identifiable through form or content, but poetry itself remains an enigma. No single definition of poetry has ever been found to satisfy readers, poets, or critics. Walter de la Mare writes in the preface to his arresting anthology, *Come Hither* (1923): "That is one of the pleasures of reading—you may make any picture out of the words you can and will; and a poem may have as many different meanings as there are different minds."

This chapter was written by Judith M. Saltman, with editorial assistance from Sheila A. Egoff.

1. Dylan Thomas, "Notes on the Art of Poetry," in Gary Geddes, ed., *20th-Century Poetry and Poetics* (Toronto: Oxford Univ. Pr., 1969), pp. 547-48.

221

Poetry has been described in terms of structure, musicality, concentration of language, intensity of emotion, and the splintering and reshaping of human experience. It has also been suggested that poetry is recognizable by instinct, that it elicits certain primal, physiological responses in the reader. According to Emily Dickinson: "If I read a book and it makes my whole body so cold no fire can ever warm me, I know that is poetry. If I feel physically as if the top of my head were taken off, I know that is poetry. These are the only ways I know it. Is there any other way?" [2] Randall Jarrell's chipmunk in *The Bat-Poet* (1964) brings the question and answer together in his response to poetry: "It makes me shiver. Why do I like it if it makes me shiver?"

In turning to that poetry written specifically for children, one quickly encounters the nagging issue of distinction between adult and children's literature. Is poetry for children a separate territory, or is poetry always simply itself, existing like folklore as a shared ground, held in common by both children and adults? If children's poetry is restricted to that written intentionally for children, does it include adult work chosen and adopted by children as their own? Does children's poetry require a simplification of style and subject matter because of childhood's limitations of experience? Or are such assumptions the result of artificial and patronizing adult attitudes? Despite attempts by adults to construct well-intentioned barricades, children continue to seek out poetry, whether children's or adult, that kindles imagination. Perhaps it is the ongoing development of that imagination and an intuitive response to emotion that enable children to take delight in poetry far beyond their conscious understanding.

It is revealing to consider some definitions of poetry given by children themselves in *Chrysalis* (1968), Harry Behn's lyrical study of childhood and poetry. One child says: "A poem is something else. Something way out. Way out in the woods. Like Robert Frost waiting in a snowstorm with promises to keep." Another feels that "a poem should simply make music with words, that's all. The shorter the better. One . . . is only, *Clink, Clank, Clunk.* It's about a carpenter pounding nails in a new house." These lively, perceptive views suggest that children understand intuitively much that is unfamiliar and beyond their acquaintance. Certainly the full impact of some poetry escapes children when it deals with experiences particular to the adult world; nevertheless, children take what they desire, leaving the rest until some moment of fruition at a later point in their lives.

2. Quoted in May Hill Arbuthnot, *Children and Books*, 3rd ed. (Chicago: Scott, Foresman, 1964), p. 193.

Authentic poetry operates on many levels, offering portions of itself to all readers of whatever age.

Although children can appreciate much mature work, they also respond to poetry that perceives the world with the vibrant curiosity and wonder that is natural to childhood. Indeed, many poets have claimed that the thrust of their work is to recall something left behind in childhood—a sense of direct living, of unity, of the joy in constant discovery that goes far beyond mere nostalgia. Much of the work of William Blake and Walter de la Mare expresses this in vivid and wholly realized poetry deliberately aimed at children. Such work is often the result of a combination of disciplined art and creative play. The poet who keeps alive the intense memories of childhood will create poetry suffused with respect for children's intelligence, imagination, and perceptions. This will be a poetry that is not a nostalgic reminiscence about childhood for adults, but rather a celebration of childhood, as gritty and stimulating as it is, for all children.

There also exists the questionable category of "children's verse," that poor cousin of children's poetry which through sheer quantity and numbing mediocrity has always threatened to drown out the music and delight in authentic children's poetry. Children all too often are given verse that is flawed in language, awkward in rhythm, labored in rhyme, and infused with condescension and sentimentality. This superfluity of doggerel generally is offered them because their capacity for mental and emotional response to fine poetry is underestimated. One of the most common pitfalls in the writing of children's poetry is the choice of a nostalgic, subjective tone which too easily slides into a cheaply sentimental romanticization of childhood. Equally dangerous is the tendency toward bombastic didacticism, patronizing moralism, or simply shoddy entertainment. The notion that certain types of subject matter and tone are universally appropriate to children's poetry has led to the continued survival of antiquarian, outmoded verse based on preconceptions of childhood which were specious even in their own era. This is not to say that children's poetry should contain only lofty, so-called "high poetry" as distinct from popular or light verse. One does not expect the insight and transformation of lyric poetry in a light-hearted jingle, which has its own, quite different, values of humor, drama, and musical fun.

A child's response to poetry is instinctive: young children take delight in repetition, rhythm, and rhyme, and it appears that they respond with their very nerves, confirming the belief that poetry is the natural language of childhood. Echoing the rise and fall of the ocean and human breath, rhythm begins for children in the womb,

223

with the first heartbeat, and continues in mother's arms, with rhythmical rockings, soothing lullabies, and lilting Mother Goose rhymes. It is present in the infant's instinctive patterning of cadenced cries and body movements. As they grow older, children greet musical language with an exhilarating swaying of heads, hands, and feet, marking tempo and measure with their bodies and voices.

Poetry comes first to children through the oral tradition when it is read and sung to them by adults. Generations of adults and children are linked together through the shared literature of the nursery which is universal to all cultures. English nursery or Mother Goose melodies are enduring survivors of the oral tradition. Genuinely meant to be sung or recited aloud, they constitute a potpourri of easeful lullabies, robust jingles for infant dandling, riddles, and the catches of old tunes. Rich in music, drama, and humor, they are the miniature poetry of early childhood. And they also provide for children, as Walter de la Mare points out, "a direct short cut into poetry itself,"[3] as does this traditional lyric crammed with vivid images, one of many in Iona and Peter Opie's *The Oxford Nursery Rhyme Book* (1955):

> I saw a peacock with a fiery tail
> I saw a blazing comet drop down hail
> I saw a cloud with ivy curled around
> I saw a sturdy oak creep on the ground
> I saw an ant swallow up a whale
> I saw a raging sea brim full of ale
> I saw a Venice glass sixteen foot deep
> I saw a well full of men's tears that weep
> I saw their eyes all in a flame of fire
> I saw a house high as the moon and higher
> I saw the sun at twelve o'clock at night
> I saw the man who saw this wondrous sight.

Since John Newbery's edition of *Mother Goose's Melody* (ca. 1765), nursery rhymes have remained a traditional and fertile ground for children's book publication and, most especially, for illustration. In almost every art style, the best illustrators of each succeeding generation, from Randolph Caldecott to Nicola Bayley, have taken a hand at interpreting the ample images of Mother Goose. Since 1960, an extraordinary number of new versions of Mother Goose rhymes has been produced, emphasizing experimental art styles, unusual thematic structures, international variants in translation, feisty street rhymes, folk songs, and single illustrated rhymes. These publications

3. Walter de la Mare, "Introduction." In *Nursery Rhymes for Certain Times* (London: Faber and Faber, 1946, 1956), p. 11.

range in scope and intent from the scholarly analysis and interpretation of Iona and Peter Opie's *The Lore and Language of Schoolchildren* (1959) to Raymond Briggs's resplendently bountiful *Mother Goose Treasury* (1966), and the classic folk song, *The Fox Went Out on a Chilly Night* (1961), suspensefully illustrated by Peter Spier.

The transition for children from folk poetry to the original, literary writings of children's poets generally follows a distinct pattern of development. It begins with the irrational musical play of nonsense verse and the stylistic virtuosity and geniality found in humorous and light verse. Proceeding through the dramatic suspense of narrative poetry, the process finally arrives at lyric poetry's melodic intensity.

This pattern of growth in children's appreciation of poetry is observable also in the brief history of poetry deliberately written for children. Like children's literature in general, it has only existed in any quantity for the last two hundred years. Prior to the seventeenth century, that addressed specifically to children was didactic, offering advice and counsel on earthly behavior until the advent of Puritanism. Then concern for children's spiritual education became evident in any poetry written for them.

Except for some of the best works of early writers, a number of Isaac Watts's hymns, a few poems by the Taylor sisters, and William Blake's joyous lyrics, little poetry of merit survives from earlier eras.

Curiously, it was the staid Victorian period that produced in the lunacy of nonsense verse a canon of memorable work. As a secular and playful poetry, it was a reaction to the sentimental morality of most verse then available to children. Chief among the practitioners of this new poetry were those bachelors of nonsense, Lewis Carroll and Edward Lear. Carroll's mathematical precision and satirical wit and Lear's zestful individuality and remarkable syntactical play come together in their capacity to create nonsensical universes perfectly believable and consistent in every detail of their inner laws. Illustrated with his own quirky, naive artwork, Lear's blithe, sly limericks, silly narratives, and sorrowful lyrics reveal a gaiety of language paradoxically married to a deep underlying melancholy. That this is so is evident in these lines from "Calico Pie" in *Edward Lear's Nonsense Omnibus* (1943):

> Calico Pie,
>   The Little Birds fly
> Down to the calico tree,
> Their wings were blue,
> And they sang "Tilly-loo!"
> Till away they flew,—
>   And they never came back to me!

225

> They never came back!
> They never came back!
> They never came back to me!

A second strain of children's poetry developed in the domestic lyric and light verses of Christina Rossetti, Robert Louis Stevenson, and A. A. Milne. This reflected a new awareness of childhood as an entity apart from the adult world and capitalized on children's interest in their own day-to-day lives and activities. Rossetti's poetry of epigrammatic charm and melodic poise in *Sing Song* (1871) conveys a haiku-like appreciation of the tiny details of nature and emotion which occupy the young child. Her images of warm family comforts are the precursors of those of Stevenson and Milne in their portrayal of a safe, secure childhood while yet conveying the self-absorption of the individual child.

Stevenson's empathy toward children's thoughts and feelings and his ability to recall with swift intensity the immediacy of experience in childhood enrich his energetic and tuneful poetry in *A Child's Garden of Verses* (1885). So pervasive was Stevenson's influence that a host of children's poets copied his mannerisms without capturing his essence. From the work of Eugene Field and James Whitcomb Riley in his own time, to that of innumerable, faceless imitators in the early half of the twentieth century, children's poetry mimicked that of Stevenson. Even Milne's poetry in *When We Were Very Young* (1924) and *Now We Are Six* (1927)—extended by Ernest Shepard's droll pen-and-ink illustrations—is similar to that of Stevenson in the descriptions of nursery life and the use of the natural speaking voice of the egocentric solitary child. Milne's own individual talent, which distinguishes him from Stevenson, lies in a keen-edged, comic delight in excessive word play and witty rhyme and an adroit skill with metric patterns.

Most early twentieth-century children's poets imitated these writers, until the emergence of Walter de la Mare brought forth a fresh, original talent. Here at last was a true poet for children, one who could never be successfully mimicked or replaced. He seemed to appear out of a void, but his roots go back to Blake's intense lyricism. A profound identification with children and a transcendent enchantment illuminate his work. Haunting and mysterious, his poems explore both the dream world of night and faerie, and the daylight flesh-and-blood realm of earthly, transient beauty. In his *Peacock Pie* (1913), the poems range from wry nonsense and brightly colored nursery verse, as in "Alas, Alack" which spiritedly begins: "Ann, Ann!/ Come! quick as you can!/ There's a fish that *talks*/ In the frying-pan." to enigmatic narratives and poignant lyrics, such as the whispering "The Horseman":

I heard a horseman
    Ride over the hill;
The moon shone clear,
    The night was still;
His helm was silver,
    And pale was he;
And the horse he rode
    Was of ivory.

The richly varied forms created by de la Mare form a body of work which provides a touchstone for evaluating all children's poetry.

With the exception of de la Mare's work, children's poetry has been marked by its conservatism in comparison to other, more dramatically changing genres of children's literature, having broken less with tradition than, for example, the children's novel. This limitation applies to the work of those poets in the early half of this century following the appearance of de la Mare. Most are forgettable, although a select few, such as Eleanor Farjeon and Elizabeth Coatsworth, produced memorable work.

The traditional forms of nonsense, fairy lore, nursery life, and nature verse had competent interpreters, but nonetheless poetry for children had slowly fossilized into formulae by the mid-fifties. This rigidity was bolstered by the practice of passing down cherished poetry without re-evaluation from one generation of parents and educators to the children of the next. Despite the varied and individualistic responses of children to diverse forms of poetry, it was all too quickly assumed that they are conservative in poetic taste. Whether from acceptance of the theory that children dislike experimentation in form or from a deep rootedness in tradition itself, many children's poets of the past few decades have continued to write in the modes of preceding generations. The constant awareness of the work of the past and the conscious choice to build on its strengths, are more evident in British children's poetry—in the work of James Reeves, Ian Serraillier, and Robert Graves—than in that of North America.

Indeed, the theory of intrinsic conservatism was exploded by primarily American poets of the sixties and seventies who repudiated such an assumption and set out to explore subjects and styles reflecting the reality of their own era. A new generation of children's poets began claiming that the poetry of the classic "child's world" reflected only a stereotypical white, middle-class, secure, and unquestioning vision of childhood and society in the complacent voice of a superannuated Stevenson or Milne. Their reaction against this sacrosanct subject matter created a new mandate to explore themes of their own time, the social concerns and predicaments of today's children who are no longer secure in a stable world, but who have joined the

227

society of adults living in a harshly realistic, problematic, and volatile world. The new poets arraigned themselves with the beats and such sixties poets as Allen Ginsburg, Lawrence Ferlinghetti, and LeRoi Jones, and so allied themselves to rock music and social protest. As in other genres of children's literature, especially the realistic novel, children's poets now wrote of anxiety, alienation, racial and social injustice, war, technological overload, and the dangers of urban life.

In the best of the sociological poetry, this grim naturalism is tempered with satire and humor, as in the works of Eve Merriam and Robert Froman. In *Finding a Poem* (1970), Eve Merriam's dexterous handling of blank verse, free verse, and verbal nonsense is allied with social satire and a fierce political conscience. Contemporary sociological issues are the subject of ironic, angry, sometimes didactic or simply nonmusical flat verse, as expressed in these lines from "The Wholly Family":

> Baby's got a plastic bottle,
> plastic pacifier to chew;
> plastic pillows on the sofa,
> plastic curtains frame the view;
> plastic curlers do up Mama,
> Mama's hairdo plastic, too. . . .
>
> > Praise of plastic thus we sing,
> > plastic over everything
> > keeps us cool and safe and dry:
> > it may not pain us much to die.

As well as conveying social satire, the images of city life in Robert Froman's concrete poetry in *Street Poems* (1971) present dark, frightening pictures such as that in the question-mark-shaped "The City Question." The man lying face down on the sidewalk may be a junkie, an alcoholic, or a victim, and the poet explores the familiar urban dilemma of moral involvement clashing with fear. Fear of and anger toward oppressive city dangers are expressed in "Scare," in which a noise in the night may be a junkie, burglar, or "hater man," but is ironically the refrigerator. Although the visual play of Froman's concrete poetry is ingenious and his social concerns sincere, in general, his language and ideas never rise above the level of "agit-prop." But his interpretation of a child's city life includes small details of beauty and humor in street-haiku format, and his vision is representative of the sophisticated urban poetry written by such other contemporary children's poets as Merriam, Dennis Lee, Lillian Moore, and Marian Lines.

The new realism is also manifest in cultural pluralism. Numerous poets are writing out of specific ethnic and national focuses, speaking with their own authentic cultural voices. This significant growth of the regional voice—its sense of time and place— and the concommitant involvement with translation of poetry from other languages and cultures into English is shared with adult poets, among whom are James Dickey, James Wright, and W. S. Merwin. Especially absorbing are the numerous poets, typified by June Jordan, Nikki Giovanni, and Lucille Clifton, who articulate the black American experience for the young.

June Jordan's complex poetry is not for young children, but it gains power from the picture-book format in which it is presented. Her single long poem, *Who Look at Me* (1969), is illustrated with twenty-seven paintings of black people reproduced from the works of distinguished artists. In flowing, musical, mostly free verse that uses black English dialect as well as formal and colloquial speech, the poem marks the sorrow, rage, courage, and dignity of the black experience in America. It is unblinking in its testimonial to history:

> Sometimes America the shamescape
> knock-rock territory losing shape
> the Southern earth like blood
> rolls valleys cold gigantic
> weeping willow flood
> that lunatic that lovely land
> that graveyard growing
> trees remark where men
> another black man
> died he died again
> he died

This new realistic poetry possesses at its best a fresh candor, and at its worst, an extreme naturalism and pop-political sociology that is also seen in the American problem novel. But unlike it, realistic poetry has not fallen prey quite as blatantly to the lure of social didacticism; its condensed form seems to favor the cri de coeur over that of polemics. It has certainly altered the face of children's poetry. Although there still exists poetry extolling the traditional in subject matter, it is now treated with a recognition of the social concerns and sophistication of today's children.

For example, the once blithe interpreters of nature have been displaced by those who explore their subject with a greater seriousness, even a probing of the darker side of existence. One such poet is Ted Hughes, who reveals his lyrical but stark vision in *Season Songs* (1976). In his poems of spring, summer, autumn, and winter, he uses carefully measured, musical cadences, common speech, arresting images, and incisive diction. His serious, even grim, philosophic tone is rooted in concrete images. As vividly involved in the natural world as Thoreau, Hughes carefully describes his experiences and observations of the seasons' passings, animals, and the growing earth. But unlike traditional nature lyrics, his work also explores the desperate, predatory side of the wild world with a dispassionately observant eye. His dry humor adds dimension to the poems, as in this description from "A March Calf":

> Right from the start he is dressed in his best—
>   his blacks and his whites.
> Little Fauntleroy—quiffed and glossy,
> A Sunday suit, a wedding natty get-up,
> Standing in dunged straw
>
> Under cobwebby beams, near the mud wall,
> Half of him legs,
> Shining-eyed, requiring nothing more
> But that mother's milk come back often.

The sophistication of his writing is extended by Leonard Baskin's mature illustrations which have a subaqueous, darkly steaming quality well suited to a book that, for all its intrinsic beauty, seems more a collector's item for adults than children.

That mainstay of children's verse, the comic and nonsensical, has continued also, but in a very much altered strain. The cutting edge of Lewis Carroll's and Edward Lear's pointed Victorian wit, somewhat blunted in the gentler light verse of the early twentieth century, has been rehoned in the poetry of Dennis Lee, John Ciardi, and Shel Silverstein. Like the traditional nonsense verse of Lear or Carroll, their work is both a release of pure pleasure and a tool of acerbic social observation. But contemporary nonsense differs in its development of a deeper sophistication; there is in it a touch of surrealism, satire, or irony that was not present in most children's light verse prior to 1960.

In his light burlesque of manners, *The Monster Den, or Look What Happened at My House—and to It* (1966), John Ciardi parodies the traditional cautionary tale and satirizes the spirited mischief of children from the vexed parents' point of view. The collection reads as one long narrative, a satirical family saga. Many of the episodes have a mock epic quality reminiscent of Hilaire Belloc's parodied adult-child battleground, as seen in these lines from "And Here's What Happened Next or Those Three," in which the abandoned parents receive a letter from their runaway children:

> They wrote us from India next to say
> How happy they were they had run away.
> "We are seeing the world! It is good to be rid
> Of all those things we never did—

Minding and manners and baths and bed.
Small Benn has warts. Miss Myra's head
Is full of wool. John L. just said
All the bad words he was never allowed
To use at home. (My, he looks proud!)
And none of us ever mind anymore.
And we drop our things all over the floor.
And we never ever go to bed.
Well, thanks for the shoes."—That's what they said. . . .

Edward Gorey's pen-and-ink illustrations have a satisfyingly grotesque, urbane Victorian aura suited to the poems. Ciardi's other collections of nonsense verse are written with the same piquant candor and jaunty gags. Many of his books such as *I Met a Man* (1961) and *You Read to Me, I'll Read to You* (1962) are innovative experiments with controlled vocabulary designed for beginning readers.

Another group of nonsense poets takes a casual, popular culture stance. The cartoon breeziness of Shel Silverstein's poems and line drawings in *Where the Sidewalk Ends* (1974) are riddled with slang, pugnacious, teasing energy, and wry social commentary, reminiscent of children's street verse. They are as audaciously American as Spike Milligan's slapdash, comic poetry in *Silly Verse for Kids* (1959) is incorrigibly British.

Also exercising the colloquial diction and vernacular of contemporary children's street verse is Dennis Lee, a respected Canadian poet for adults as well as children. His work at times reflects a specifically Canadian physical and emotional geography. His three collections of nonsensical, domestic, and lyric poetry, *Alligator Pie* (1974), *Nicholas Knock* (1974), and *Garbage Delight* (1977), create a poetry of pure play, jumping with puns and molding the oral language and codes of childhood into original verse. He writes with a fluid sweep of language suggestive of Stevenson, Milne, and Mother Goose, whom he acknowledges as his models. His marked rhythms, cumulative phrasing, internal rhyme, and incessant word play are seen in "Alligator Pie,"

Alligator pie, alligator pie,
If I don't get some I think I'm gonna die,
Give away the green grass, give away the sky,
But don't give away my alligator pie.

which has already become legendary in the popular culture of Canadian children.

Two other noted adult poets have turned their attention to children's light verse, but the results are curiously disappointing. Unlike Lee, neither Conrad Aiken nor Ogden Nash reveal the teasing

231

and nonsensical child surviving within the adult poet. Nash is dryly amusing and precise in his most successful collection of poems for children, *The New Nutcracker Suite and Other Innocent Verses* (1962), but he runs the risk of poetic parody, failing to capture any real childlike emotion in his uneasy mixture of sly adult satire and child-song lyrics. His historical understanding is tinged with wicked black humor in "German Song" that feels uncomfortable and incongruous in a poetry collection given a picture-book format:

> The German children march along,
> Heads full of fairy tales and song.
> They read of witches in their reader,
> They sing of angels in their lieder.
> I think their little heads must swim;
> The songs are jolly, the tales are Grimm.

Conrad Aiken's poetry in *Cats and Bats and Things with Wings* (1965) and *A Little Who's Zoo of Mild Animals* (1977) shares with Nash's work the potential for clever satire and surrealism. But unfortunately it degenerates into oddly flat, adult irony with little base in children's responses to poetry or humor and is often contrived in invention and word play. On the whole, contemporary nonsense poetry seems most compelling and convincing the more closely it aligns itself with traditional humorous poetry. Children revel in certain styles of poetic satire, but it appears that the more experimental and surrealistic forms slide too easily into adult indulgence and wry, self-contained witticism, forming long, overextended jokes which often preclude children as an audience.

Of all the traditional poetic forms, narrative verse has changed the least. It continues to attract poets, primarily British, who use it in various ways. Ian Serraillier, in retelling such medieval ballads and romances as *The Challenge of the Green Knight* (1966) and *Robin in the Greenwood* (1967), retains a vigorous pace, and with dramatic character and costume captures an authentic medieval tone in modern diction.

Also writing with a contemporary nakedness of speech is Charles Causley, whose incantatory literary ballad *The Hill of the Fairy Calf* (1976) is a piece of modern folk art:

> And when the harvest moon was white
> Above the heavy hill,
> The sky a-quake with beating stars,
> The night-herd soft and still,
> The herdsman laid aside his staff,
> And leaned upon a stone,
> And smiled and said, 'The moon and stars
> Are mine and mine alone.'

Causley's rich diction, clean imagery, tight rhyme scheme, and meter are underpinned in this and other works by more metaphor at the heart of the story than in earlier narrative verse for children. And his herdsman's quest for power over the faery queen is, of course, humanity's search for meaning in life. The poetry's magical, fairy-tale quality is matched by the primitive, dreamlike illustrations of Robine Clignett which recall the paintings of Chagall.

Like Serraillier and Causley, Robert Graves emphasizes formal structure and stylistic technique in his narrative verse. But his poetry has a wider range of themes including folklike narrative romances that resemble literary fairy tales, nursery-rhyme lyrics, and nonsense jingles. His short set pieces of dialogue-oriented dramatic poetry are unlike any found in the work of modern children's poets. The poems in his collections, *Ann at Highwood Hall: Poems for Children* (1964) and *The Penny Fiddle: Poems for Children* (1960), evoke the atmosphere of an earlier century. Self-consciously old-fashioned, exotic-sounding diction and cadenced melodies are evident in the nursery jingle, "The Sewing Basket":

> Needles and ribbons
> And packets of pins,
> Prints
> And chintz
> And little bodkins—
> They'd never mind whether
> You laid them together
> Or each from the other
> In pockets and tins.
>
> For packets of pins
> And needles and ribbons
> Or little bodkins
> And chintz
> And prints,
> Being birds of a feather
> Will gather together
> Like minnows on billows
> Or pennies in Mints.

Graves's period pieces have distant companions in the poetry of childlife. There are still poets writing of the child's immediate world, but they now encompass a broader range of life experiences and portray diverse social and cultural groups of children. But, despite attempts at contemporary relevance, they are closer in spirit to Stevenson or even Graves than to the pop sociology of Merriam or Froman. Various poets follow this tradition, mixing nonsense and light verse with poetry of a more serious lyric and narrative power in

233

an attempt to speak from the center of the child's everyday and imaginative worlds. Such poets as Karla Kuskin, Kaye Starbird, and Myra Cohn Livingston relish evoking the sensibilities of childhood. Livingston's collections, including *The Malibu and Other Poems* (1972), are rich with droll, musical verses which reflect, in a skillful variety of styles, children's active, sensuous lives.

Inevitably, new themes are paralleled by new styles: technical changes in style and form mirror the newfound freedom of subject matter. Children's poets have adopted the stylistic flexibility and experimentation with form of twentieth-century adult poetry, but their work nonetheless remains at least a generation behind contemporary adult writing. On the whole, adult poetry of the sixties and seventies has been less influential in style than in subject matter, compared to that of the preceding half-century. The most innovative adult poetry of the last two decades centers on structuralism and aesthetics, operating in a complex, intellectual, and meditative vein characterized by the works of Samuel Beckett, Paul Eluard, and René Char, as well as that of such "New York School" poets as John Ashbery and Frank O'Hara. Their emphasis on introspective abstraction renders it inappropriate as an influence on children's poetry.

A more fruitful resource has been the poetry of colloquial, idiomatic speech developed by Walt Whitman, W. B. Yeats, W. H. Auden, and William Carlos Williams. Their intense exploration of language is visible also in the work for children by such poets as John Ciardi, June Jordan, Ted Hughes, and Theodore Roethke—all of whom are significantly also writing poetry for adults. They are searching for a natural, illuminating imagery, and an intimate common speech as expressed through free, blank, and projective verse. This quest for a spoken language drawn from both the adult's and child's time and place is accompanied by a return to the oral tradition —to poems made to be spoken and read aloud rather than to remain mute and fixed on the printed page, and to the time-honored role of the poet as bard who recites and sings his work to people assembled at readings or through recordings.

Outstanding among these modern-day bards is Theodore Roethke, whose style is a mixture of free and formal verse. He employs pointed imagery, a modulated tone, and rhythms that embody specific emotional tensions. He has stated that "rhythmically, it's the spring and rush of the child I'm after."[4] As to how well he succeeds in communicating that "spring and rush" can be seen in

4. Theodore Roethke, from "Open Letter," in Geddes, *20th Century Poetry . . .* , p. 539.

"My Papa's Waltz" from *Dirty Dinky and Other Creatures* (1973), familiar to many anthologies:

> The whiskey on your breath
> Could make a small boy dizzy;
> But I hung on like death:
> Such waltzing was not easy.
>
> We romped until the pans
> Slid from the kitchen shelf;
> My mother's countenance
> Could not unfrown itself.
>
> The hand that held my wrist
> Was battered on one knuckle;
> At every step you missed
> My right ear scraped a buckle.
>
> You beat time on my head
> With a palm caked hard by dirt,
> Then waltzed me off to bed
> Still clinging to your shirt.

Its intuitive mix of fear, memory, and love evokes a powerful response, as do others of his mature, affectively memorable poems.

Other practitioners of stylistic change whose work involves a more spontaneous improvisation of forms created by the active imagination include May Swenson, David McCord, Eve Merriam, and Robert Froman. Recognizing that children are not bound rigidly to neat, regular meter and rhyme, they have shared with them delight in the playful visual, aural, and intellectual concepts of shaped verse, concrete poetry, found poetry, and a host of collage and typographical verse forms. May Swenson, in *Poems to Solve* (1969) and *More Poems to Solve* (1971), interprets language through riddle and game poems, visually shaped pattern poems, and word puzzles. Eve Merriam also challenges readers to involve themselves in the fun, accentuating the playful communion between poet and reader. In *Finding a Poem* (1970), she imaginatively explains language terminology, poetic devices, syntax, and grammar, as found in her poem, "Markings: The Semicolon":

> Diver on the board
> lunges toward the edge;
> hedges;
> takes a deep breath;
> hesitates;
>
>   plunges.

She similarly manipulates poetic forms so that they describe themselves, illustrating their structure within the context of the poem itself. Her emphasis on snappy, linguistic wit and clever wordplay is evident in such collections as *It Doesn't Always Have to Rhyme* (1964).

David McCord possesses a quieter, less satiric humor than Merriam, and a deeper base of emotion and theme, ranging from bold nonsense to meditative lyricism. But he shares with Merriam the same attentive care for words and the interest in droll language games and stylish illustration of poetic structure. His concern with technical expertise and rhythmic flair is evident in the antic poem, "Sometimes" from *For Me to Say: Rhymes of the Never Was and Always Is* (1970):

> The clouds are full of new blue sky,
> The water's full of sea;
> The apples full of deep-dish pie,
> And I am full of me.
>
> My money's full of pockets too,
> My teeth are full of jaw;
> The animals are full of zoo,
> The cole is full of slaw.
>
> How full things are of this or that:
> The tea so full of spoon;
> The wurst so very full of brat,
> The shine brimful of moon.

McCord's entire output has been collected in *One at a Time: His Collected Poems for the Young* (1977), a beguiling book of poetry that is predominantly light and playful, but sensitive to childhood's need for wonder, curiosity, and dreaming.

The fascination with verbal play in the poetry of Swenson, Merriam, and McCord is carried one step further in the anarchistic approach to syntax and the visual movement of language of Robert Froman in his concrete and shaped poetry. In *Seeing Things: A Book of Poems* (1974), and *Street Poems* (1971), Froman's simple street-haiku take life from optical tricks with typography and typewriter design; they become visual and verbal puns and acrobatic word arrangements in which the printed shapes support the words by accenting theme.

Influences on modern children's poetry have been eclectic, ranging from the futuristic vision of concrete poetry to the classic control of traditional Japanese haiku. The contemplative tone, compact form, clear humor, empathy with nature, and immediacy of experience of haiku render it inviting to children, and many children's poets have attempted modified nature, street, or nursery haiku. But there is usually lacking the quality of timeless precision and serenity of the

Zen spirit typical of traditional haiku, such as is this poem from Harry Behn's collection called *More Cricket Songs* (1971):

> Hands flat on the ground,
> a dignified prince of frogs
> rumbles a poem.

Stylistic influences also feed back into prose from poetry. The flexibility of contemporary poetry has transformed works of modern children's fiction even more than much of children's poetry. Many prose writers, among them June Jordan in the black English musicality of *His Own Where* (1971), Alan Garner in the extended poetic construction of *The Stone Book* quartet (1976–78), and John Rowe Townsend in the Blakeian allusions of *Forest of the Night* (1974) have made sensitive use of poetic structure, diction, and imagery, along with symbolism and surrealism, transforming their fiction into highly charged verse forms.

Like the modern picture book, poetry for the very young has increased in astonishing quantities since 1960. Recognizing that young children's natural love of rhythm and rhyme make them irresistible targets, poets and illustrators have blended their talents to create a new genre, the poetry picture book. There has always been poetic prose in picture books, but never before have so many skilled poets involved themselves in the picture-book genre as have Elizabeth Coatsworth, Aileen Fisher, Jack Prelutsky, Karla Kuskin, and Norma Faber. The phenomenal growth in the publication of single illustrated poems and collections of poetry in picture-book format follows the trend of the ubiquitous single illustrated song and Mother Goose rhyme. The threat in poetry-picture books of overillustration, stripping the power of children's personal visual imagination and detracting from the poem's innate images is very real, for often the illustrator's interpretation conflicts with the poem's mood. But generally, illustrators have resisted using the format as a mere vehicle or showcase for their artwork.

On the whole, the subject matter and style in these works for younger children remain traditional. An example is *Father Fox's Pennyrhymes* (1971), by Clyde Watson, which is evocative of traditional Mother Goose and game rhymes. A collection of short, spicy verses, it reflects the spirit of American folk culture amid the changing beauty of the Vermont countryside. The wit and musicality of Watson's poetry is effectively matched by the sly details and extended storytelling lines in Wendy Watson's cartoon-strip drawings. The pastiche quality of some of the rhymes is balanced by their charm, as in this verse with its echoes of "Ride a cock-horse to Banbury Cross":

Ride your red horse down Vinegar Lane,
Gallop, oh gallop, oh gallop again!
Thistles & foxholes & fences beware:
I've seventeen children but none I can spare.

Particularly successful as a single illustrated poem is Randall Jarrell's *A Bat Is Born* (1978), a long, lyrical, free verse poem excerpted from his short story, *The Bat-Poet*. In murmuring cadences, darting rhythms, and sharp imagery, the poem describes the beauty of a newborn bat:

A bat is born
Naked and blind and pale.
His mother makes a pocket of her tail
And catches him. He clings to her long fur
By his thumbs and toes and teeth.
And then the mother dances through the night
Doubling and looping, soaring, somersaulting—
Her baby hangs on underneath.

John Schoenherr's sweeping, fluid sketches perfectly illustrate the bat's grace and character in expressive double-page spreads of the night sky. The poetry-picture book form also has been employed as a vehicle for poetry and illustration suitable for older children by such poets as Natalia Belting, Richard Adams, Charles Causley, Robert Frost, and June Jordan.

The presence of so many adult poets such as Jarrell and Causley in the province of children's poetry is strong evidence that it has come of age, that it is now sophisticated and noticeably complex, controversial, and experimental. The distinction between adult and children's poetry is no longer as sharp and separate as it once was. More poetry written primarily for adults is used in children's anthologies, and many books of poetry, among them Ted Hughes's *Season Songs*, may be published for children and yet have an ardent adult audience. Also, innumerable selections from the works of adult poets have been made for children since 1960. A growing faith in the ability of children to appreciate mature poetry has persuaded publishers to issue works of adult poetry edited for children to serve as enticing introductions to the complete works of those poets, among whom Robert Frost is the prime example.

Frost's work has been acknowledged as appealing and provocative to children, not only in picture-book format as exemplified by *Stopping by Woods on a Snowy Evening* (1978), but also in such collections as *You Come Too: Favorite Poems for Young Readers* (1959). His deep, bold lyrics and narratives of country life attract children with their simplicity, easy-flowing idiomatic language, and understated wisdom.

Langston Hughes is another who speaks with immediacy and freshness to children, and his poetry has been selected for them in the collection *Don't You Turn Back* (1969). His work expresses black pride, anger, and courage in the musical rhythms of black speech and the blues. With all their ironic humor, bluntness, and gravity, his poems are still universal in their treatment of elemental human emotions, offering Blake-like nature lyrics, murmuring lullabies, and poignant confessions such as "Mother to Son":

> Well, son, I'll tell you:
> Life for me ain't been no crystal stair.
> It's had tacks in it,
> And splinters,
> And boards torn up,
> And places with no carpet on the floor—
> Bare.
> But all the time
> I'se been a-climbin' on,
> And reachin' landin's,
> And turnin' corners,
> And sometimes goin' in the dark
> Where there ain't been no light.
> So, boy, don't you turn back.
> Don't you set down on the steps
> 'Cause you finds it kinder hard.
> Don't you fall now—
> For I'se still goin', honey,
> I'se still climbin',
> And life for me ain't been no crystal stair.

In earlier days adult poetry was available to children primarily through selections in general anthologies. With the new abundance of poetry publications of all types and formats, it is of some significance that the anthology still retains its prominence and popularity. Anthologies for children today, those "gatherings of flowers," are overwhelming in their sheer number. Some few excellent ones convey distinctive textures, tones, and original points of view, but an even greater number of bland, eclectic collections pad real poetry with the pap production of hacks. Traditional anthologies—general, encyclopedic collections similar in structure to enduring treasuries from the past—still abound. Recognizable by their chronological survey treatment which concentrates on the "high spots" of children's poetry, they are often entertaining, as is Iona and Peter Opie's

The Oxford Book of Children's Verse (1973), but unfortunately most are static, changing little from decade to decade.

In addition to these overviews, there is a glut of anthologies that concentrate on a theme, as does William Cole's collection, *A Book of Animal Poems* (1973); on a poetic genre such as narrative verse in *Rising Early: Story Poems and Ballads of the 20th Century* (1964); on a national identity, *The Wind Has Wings: Poems from Canada* (1968); on a cultural or ethnic identity, *I Am the Darker Brother* (1968); or on a particular age group, *The Faber Book of Nursery Verse* (1958). Then too, paralleling the modern realistic children's novel, many of the collections emphasize bold, colloquial, and experimental language, such as is found in *Reflections on a Gift of Watermelon Pickle . . . and Other Modern Verse* (1967), while others probe the intoxicating and tragic experiences of urban life as depicted in *On City Streets: An Anthology of Poetry* (1968). Like contemporary historical fiction for children which excels in its exploration of prehistoric life, anthologies of primitive poetry for children are abundantly anthologized; one, *Out of the Earth I Sing: Poetry and Songs of Primitive Peoples of the World* (1968), compiled by Richard Lewis, returns children's attention to the primal dream roots of poetry from the often ironic, self-conscious, and overly cerebral verse being written for them today.

These chants and songs from the childhood of the human race find distant music in much of children's own poetry. In a minor key, it echoes the more complex poetic imagery of primitive peoples in such qualities as openness, vulnerability, and intense concentration on living. Children's natural ease in the poetic form has been recognized as never before in the sixties and seventies. There has been as well a growing movement of encouragement in the schools and libraries of the inner-city ghettos and of the suburbs to bring children together not only to read, but also to write, poetry. Beginning with the pioneer work *Miracles: Poems by Children of the English-Speaking World* (1966), compiled by Richard Lewis, voluminous amounts of their work have been enthusiastically published. Although much of that poetry has not been worthy of the acclaim, it definitely holds for children a therapeutic value, providing them with an experience of language enrichment and an insight into the creative joy involved in self-expression. It also is helping to restore the spontaneous and natural connection children develop with poetry in their early years, a connection that is often broken as prose becomes the accepted language of reality and purpose. Poetry is now approached in schools and creative writing workshops in a more spontaneous and oral celebration of the art. The best of the poetry children write reveals a fluid play with language, a depth of emotion and imagination, and an uncanny ability to achieve, without practiced technique, natural poetic effects such as those of the self-taught bat-poet who "just made it like holding your breath."

Much of the poetry written by children today seems a far cry from the fresh, primarily lyric and nature images of *Miracles*, and even farther from the exuberant street and game rhymes invented by children in the oral tradition of childhood's subculture. While still brash and startling in poetic language, the subject matter is likely to be the misery, anger, and courage of ghetto and minority life in the inner city, not surprisingly paralleling that of adult poems for children. Poems in *I Heard a Scream in the Street: Poetry by Young People in the City* (1970), selected by Nancy Larrick, range from those with a musing, introspective tone to those with a stronger, more muscular language and challenging spirit. They vary in poetic craft from the skilled to the naive, but in subject matter they almost invariably speak in anguish of alienation from and despair of their environment. To these children of the ghetto, the city is "full of hate and war"; living in Harlem is "hell"; there may be no chains on their legs but "the chains on my mind are keeping / me from being Free!"; and "if it means a little comfort, / then Hell I must go." There are also notes of cynicism and stoicism; only occasionally do the children admonish the adult world or feel that their city is "full of love." Aside from the numerous flashes of poetic imagination in these works, as opposed to a kind of primal passion, one obvious fact comes through. An urban ghetto limits a child's experience. The book should be required reading for all administrators of large cities.

The emotions of another ghetto are chronicled in *I Never Saw Another Butterfly: Children's Drawings and Poems from Terezin Concentration Camp, 1942-1944* (1964), translated from the Czech. Like Ann Frank's diary, this collection is a gripping testimony of children's capacity for courage, endurance, and compassion in unflinching poetry and shadowy expressionistic drawings that depict the fear, horror, and brief moments of hope or beauty experienced by the condemned Jewish children. The poetry of children is perhaps more interesting to adults than to other children, because it gives them an insight into children's thoughts which are more candidly realistic and colloquial than the artificial, first-person confessional of the problem novel and more authentic and tough in statements of emotional needs than Albert Cullum's disingenuous attempts at a first-person, child lament in the ironic, nihilistic poems of *The Geranium on the Window Sill Just Died, but Teacher You Went Right On* (1971).

Despite the amount of pressure from the adult world, children can still write with a living sense of wonder, as in this six-year-old's poem of a whale's birth in *There's a Sound in the Sea . . . A Child's Eye View of the Whale* (1975):

I have just taken birth out of dark hot mother.
I know I have because I can feel the cool
   water below me.
It is not a nice day because I can feel the
   drops of rain on my back.
My tail was all cramped when I came out.

—————Luisa Kaye, age 6

Richard Lewis, who consciously brought children's poetry to world attention with *Miracles*, speaks of all children when he writes in *Miracles* that it "will serve as a testament to the power and value of the poetic vision that is an integral part of childhood."[5]

Recognizing the spirited continuation of tradition from the past, it is intriguing to speculate on the future of children's poetry. Ian Serraillier discusses its changing role, which he sees as shifting from the printed page in a return to oral tradition through the electronic media of radio and television:

> All art forms, if they are to survive, must adapt to new conditions, and poetry is no exception. If, . . . this is to mean some measure of escape from the printed page, that is no bad thing: it may again come closer to its origins—in song and dance and the spoken word. . . . As for the children's poet, he too has a role to play, a wider one than in the past. If he's still around in the distant future, whatever the outward changes, he will probably still be a curious mixture of creator, interpreter and craftsman.[6]

Poetry written for children at this time in its history has never been so much a part of poetry in general; poets and parents, along with critics and educators have finally put into practice the belief that adult and children's verse are indistinguishable. One may well agree with Naomi Lewis's claim, "Today we think that it is not necessary to write special verses for young or old; a true poem has something for all readers."[7]

Children's poets today work in any or all forms, adapting them to suit their particular mood and intent. Scanning their works one is struck by the sheer number of competent craftsmen in the field. But while competent skills may offer moments of delighted surprise, flashes of beauty, and unity of music, emotion, and thought, they do

5. Richard Lewis, ed., *Miracles: Poems by Children of the English-Speaking World* (New York: Simon & Schuster, 1966), p. 8.

6. Ian Serraillier, "Poetry Mosaic: Some Reflections on Writing Verse for Children," in Edward Blishen, ed., *The Thorny Paradise: Writers on Writing for Children* (Harmondsworth: Kestrel, 1975), p. 102.

7. Naomi Lewis, "Introduction," in Christina Rossetti, *Doves and Pomegranites: Poems for Young Readers*; chosen by David Powell (London: Bodley Head, 1969), p. 12.

not always provide the haunting, quotable memorability which is the hallmark of strong poetry. Despite its various formats, subtlety, and inventiveness, modern children's poetry suffers from an impersonal sameness of style, content, and theme—a lack of distinctive, immediately recognizable voice and vision. Attempting to speak energetically, to articulate the human experience for children in powerful tones and emotions, it often falls short of its goals. It is undercut by its emphasis on the self-consciously relevant subject matter of pop sociology and its tendency to verbal games and jokes that seem condescending toward children's perceptions. Forfeited are the tantalizing original thought and glorious music of language that make poetry memorable and quotable. Ironically, the very freedom of form so vigorously sought has made poetry today more closed; the experiments in style, typography, format, and illustration have fixed poetry to the page, so that its words do not linger to haunt the imagination.

There is a sprinkling of poets, among them Charles Causley, Theodore Roethke, Ted Hughes, and David McCord, whose work is of a caliber far beyond the overwhelming mass of quantity and mediocrity that constitutes contemporary children's poetry. But even these substantial talents do not achieve the universality of childhood vision and musical power that bestowed upon Walter de la Mare the title of "the children's poet." Nonetheless, the best of the modern poetry can awaken in children an awareness of the beauty, sorrow, and wonder in this eternally surprising world. Robert Frost's definition of poetry as a voyage of discovery beginning in delight and ending in wisdom still applies to contemporary children's poetry, although today's voyage may be more turbulent and hazardous than in the past.

In the work of the best children's poets there remains that ineffable property which cannot be explained, which mysteriously slips into the poem, transfiguring a technical structure from a work of merely superior craftsmanship into an intellectual, imaginative, and sensuous unity. Re-entering the charmed circle of Dylan Thomas's images, one realizes that in children's poetry, as in all poetry, "you're back again where you began. You're back with the mystery of having been moved by words. The best craftsmanship always leaves holes and gaps in the works of the poem so that something that is *not* in the poem can creep, crawl, flash, or thunder in." [8]

8. Thomas, in Geddes, *20th Century Poetry . . .* , p. 554.

Works Cited

Aiken, Conrad. *Cats and Bats and Things with Wings: Poems*. Drawings by Milton Glaser. New York: Atheneum, 1965. [32] pp.

――*A Little Who's Zoo of Mild Animals*. Illus. by John Vernon Lord. New York: Atheneum, 1977. [32] pp.

Behn, Harry. *Chrysalis: Concerning Children and Poetry*. New York: Harcourt, 1968. 92 pp.

――, comp. and tr. *More Cricket Songs: Japanese Haiku*. New York: Harcourt, 1971. 64 pp.

Briggs, Raymond, ed. and illus. *The Mother Goose Treasury*. London: Hamish Hamilton, 1966. 217 pp.

Causley, Charles. *The Hill of the Fairy Calf*. Illus. by Robine Clignett. London: Hodder & Stoughton, 1976. (28) pp.

Ciardi, John. *I Met a Man*. Illus. by Robert Osborn. Boston: Houghton, 1961. 74 pp.

――*The Monster Den, or Look What Happened at My House—and To It*. Drawings by Edward Gorey. Philadelphia: Lippincott, 1966. 62 pp.

――*You Read to Me, I'll Read to You*. Drawings by Edward Gorey. Philadelphia: Lippincott, 1962. 64 pp.

Cole, William, comp. *A Book of Animal Poems*. Illus. by Robert Andrew Parker. New York: Viking, 1973. 288 pp.

Cullum, Albert. *The Geranium on the Window Sill Just Died, but Teacher You Went Right On*. New York: Harlin Quist, 1971. 60 pp.

De la Mare, Walter. *Come Hither: A Collection of Rhymes and Poems for the Young of All Ages*. Embellished by Alec Buckels. London: Constable, 1923. 698 pp.

――*Peacock Pie: A Book of Rhymes*. London: Constable, 1913. 122 pp.

The Faber Book of Nursery Verse. Barbara Ireson, ed. Illus. by George Adamson. London: Faber & Faber, 1958. 286 pp.

Froman, Robert. *Seeing Things: A Book of Poems*. Lettering by Ray Barker. New York: Crowell, 1974. 51 pp.

――*Street Poems*. New York: McCall Pub. Co., 1971. 58 pp.

Frost, Robert. *Stopping by Woods on a Snowy Evening*. Illus. by Susan Jeffers. New York: Dutton, 1978. [32] pp.

――*You Come Too: Favorite Poems for Young Readers*. Wood engravings by Thomas W. Nason. New York: Holt, 1959. 94 pp.

Garner, Alan. "The Stone Book" Quartet. London: Collins, 1976–1978.

Graves, Robert. *Ann at Highwood Hall: Poems for Children*. Illus. by Edward Ardizzone. London: Cassell, 1964. 40 pp.

――*The Penny Fiddle: Poems for Children*. Illus. by Edward Ardizzone. London: Cassell, 1960. 62 pp.

Hughes, Langston. *Don't You Turn Back*. Sel. by Lee Bennett Hopkins. Woodcuts by Ann Grifalconi. New York: Knopf, 1969. 78 pp.

Hughes, Ted. *Season Songs*. London: Faber & Faber, 1976. 75 pp.; U.S. ed. Pictures by Leonard Baskin. New York: Viking, 1975. 77 pp.

I Am the Darker Brother: An Anthology of Modern Poems by Negro Americans. Arnold Adoff, comp. Drawings by Benny Andrews. New York: Macmillan, 1968. 128 pp.

I Never Saw Another Butterfly: Children's Drawings and Poems from Terezin Concentration Camp, 1942-1944. New York: McGraw-Hill, 1964. 80 pp.

Jarrell, Randall. *A Bat Is Born: From The Bat-Poet.* Illus. by John Schoenherr. New York: Doubleday, 1978. [31] pp.

——*The Bat-Poet.* Pictures by Maurice Sendak. New York: Macmillan, 1964. 42 pp.

Jordan, June. *His Own Where.* New York: Crowell, 1971. 89 pp.

——*Who Look at Me.* New York: Crowell, 1969. 97 pp.

Larrick, Nancy. *I Heard a Scream in the Street: Poetry by Young People in the City.* New York: Evans, 1970. 141 pp.

Lear, Edward. *Edward Lear's Nonsense Omnibus.* London & New York: Warne, 1943. 480 pp.

Lee, Dennis. *Alligator Pie.* Illus. by Frank Newfeld. Toronto: Macmillan of Canada, 1974. 64 pp.

——*Garbage Delight.* Pictures by Frank Newfeld. Toronto: Macmillan of Canada, 1977. 64 pp.

——*Nicholas Knock and Other People: Poems.* Pictures by Frank Newfeld. Toronto: Macmillan of Canada, 1974. 64 pp.

Lewis, Richard, comp. *Miracles: Poems by Children of the English-Speaking World.* New York: Simon & Schuster, 1966. 215 pp.

——*Out of the Earth I Sing: Poetry and Songs of Primitive Peoples of the World.* New York: Norton, 1968. 144 pp.

Livingston, Myra Cohn. *The Malibu and Other Poems.* Illus. by James J. Sponfeller. New York: Atheneum, 1972. 44 pp.

McCord, David. *For Me to Say: Rhymes of the Never Was and Always Is.* Drawings by Henry B. Kane. Boston: Little, 1970. 100 pp.

——*One at a Time: His Collected Poems for the Young.* Illus. by Henry B. Kane. Boston: Little, 1977. 494 pp.

Merriam, Eve. *Finding a Poem.* Illus. by Seymour Chwast. New York: Atheneum, 1970. 68 pp.

——*It Doesn't Always Have to Rhyme.* Drawings by Malcolm Spooner. New York: Atheneum, 1964. 83 pp.

Milligan, Spike. *Silly Verse for Kids.* London: Dobson, 1959. 61 pp.

Milne, A. A. *Now We Are Six.* Decorations by Ernest H. Shepard. London: Methuen, 1927. 103 pp.

——*When We Were Very Young.* Decorations by Ernest H. Shepard. London: Methuen, 1924. 99 pp.

Nash, Ogden. *The New Nutcracker Suite and Other Innocent Verses.* Designed and illus. by Ivan Chermayeff. Boston: Little, 1962. 47 pp.

Newbery, John. *Mother Goose's Melody.* London: J. Newbery, 1765.

On City Streets: An Anthology of Poetry. Nancy Larrick, comp. Illus. with photos by David Sagarin. New York: Evans, 1968. 158 pp.

Opie, Iona, and Opie, Peter. *The Oxford Book of Children's Verse.* London: Oxford Univ. Pr., 1973. 407 pp.

245

————*The Oxford Nursery Rhyme Book.* Additional illus. by Joan Hassall. Oxford: Clarendon Pr., 1955. 223 pp.

Reflections on a Gift of Watermelon Pickle . . . and Other Modern Verse. ed. by Stephen Dunning, Edward Lueder, and Hugh Smith. New York: Lothrop, 1967. 139 pp.

Rising Early: Story Poems and Ballads of the 20th Century. ed. by Charles Causley. Drawings by Anne Netherwood. Leicester: Brockhampton, 1964. 128 pp.

Roethke, Theodore. *Dirty Dinky and Other Creatures: Poems for Children.* New York: Doubleday, 1973. 48 pp.

Rossetti, Christina. *Sing Song: A Nursery Rhyme Book.* Illus. by A. Hughes. London: G. Routledge & Sons, 1871. 130 pp.

Serraillier, Ian. *The Challenge of the Green Knight.* Illus. by Victor G. Ambrus. London: Oxford Univ. Pr., 1966. 56 pp.

————*Robin in the Greenwood: Ballads of Robin Hood.* Illus. by Victor G. Ambrus. London: Oxford Univ. Pr., 1967. 76 pp.

Silverstein, Shel. *Where the Sidewalk Ends.* New York: Harper, 1974. 166 pp.

Spier, Peter. *The Fox Went Out on a Chilly Night.* Garden City, NY: Doubleday, 1961. unpaged.

Stevenson, Robert Louis. *A Child's Garden of Verses.* London: Longmans & Co., 1885. 101 pp.

Swenson, May. *More Poems to Solve.* New York: Scribner, 1971. 64 pp.

————*Poems to Solve.* New York: Scribner, 1969. 35 pp.

There's a Sound in the Sea . . . A Child's Eye View of the Whale. Tamar Griggs, comp. San Francisco: Scrimshaw Pr., 1975. 93 pp.

Townsend, John Rowe. *Forest of the Night.* London: Oxford Univ. Pr., 1974. 83 pp.

Watson, Clyde. *Father Fox's Pennyrhymes.* Illus. by Wendy Watson. New York: Crowell, 1971. 56 pp.

The Wind Has Wings: Poems from Canada. Mary Alice Downie and Barbara Robertson, comps. Illus. by Elizabeth Cleaver. Toronto: Oxford Univ. Pr., 1968. 95 pp.

10. *Picture Books*

*A child kicks his legs rhythmically through excess, not absence,
of life. Because children have abounding vitality, because they
are in spirit fierce and free, therefore they want things repeated
and unchanged. They always say, "Do it again"; and the
grown-up person does it again until he is nearly dead. For
grown-up people are not strong enough to exult in monotony.*[1]

It did not take twentieth-century psychology to convince adults that experiences in early childhood may be a major and life-long influence. Adults have thus for several centuries ascribed power and significance to the picture book as a means of reaching and affecting children at their most susceptible age.

Because people believe picture books to be so powerful, they are subjected to closer scrutiny and more judgment than are any other type of children's book. And the scrutiny is all the more penetrating because a picture book offers, so to speak, no place to hide. It has perforce a kind of unvarnished directness and frankness; there can be very little of the vagueness that words are so good at between its covers. What is meant cannot be implied but must be shown and related in the precise, literal terms that very young children can recognize.

This candor and clarity can sometimes have alarming or— depending on the viewpoint—amusing consequences. Because there is no blinking one's eye at the offending material, a single picture may lead to the rejection of an entire book. This could have happened when the Chicago police force objected to William Steig's *Sylvester and the Magic Pebble* (1969) because one of its illustrations portrayed policemen as pigs, had not reason prevailed. Conversely, the "Doctor Dolittle" books, though some parts obviously present a view of white

---

1. G. K. Chesterton, "The Ethics of Elfland," in his *Orthodoxy* (London: John Lane, Bodley Head, 1909), p. 106.

racial superiority, arouse relatively little protest. Adults seem willing to judge a "written" book as a whole where they would not do so for a picture book.

A related factor is that adults cannot avoid responsibility for the selection of their children's picture books. Even the most zealous and watchful of parents are likely to let older children select their own reading material or at the very least leave it to teachers and librarians. But in the case of picture books, concerned parents can claim no such exemption from obligation; they must themselves become involved with sharing a book with their preschool child.

All this results in the intriguing paradox that the picture book, which appears to be the coziest and most gentle of genres, actually produces the greatest social and aesthetic tensions in the whole field of children's literature. Add yet another paradox: the genre which seems to be the simplest actually is the most complex, deploying two art forms, the pictorial and the literary, to engage the interest of two audiences (child and adult). Combine these attributes and it is undeniably arguable that the picture book represents the most diverse, the most didactic, and the most debated of all forms of present-day children's literature.

Of the three qualities mentioned in the preceding discussion, only the last is really recent. Until the late Victorian period, books for the very young followed the general pattern for children's books by combining educational devices and moral instruction in the religious battledores for teaching the alphabet, hieroglyphic Bibles for reading instruction, and chapbooks that introduced a moral tale in the guise of natural history. Occasionally, as in alphabet books of today, there were moments of instructive charm such as the classic "A Apple Pie." But in studying what is still extant of the earlier literature of childhood it can be seen that from the Puritan period through to the Victorian, adults preferred precept to pleasure, even in books for the very young.

The picture book for delight came into its own in the late Victorian era with the works of Kate Greenaway, Randolph Caldecott, and Walter Crane, guided and inspired by their printer and engraver, Edmund Evans. Evans was in the forefront of the new technical advances in printing which made possible better and much less costly reproduction of artwork, especially in color. Thus Caldecott's nursery rhymes, Crane's illustrated folktales, and Greenaway's babies in baskets of roses released the picture book from its rigidly educational formula, although many of these still were being produced. But the work of the "three greats" became a standard of excellence in what could almost be considered a new genre.

As picture books became increasingly more varied and attractive, as well as less expensive and technically superior to those of the past, the power of their content to woo young minds to righteousness, good behavior, and the accumulation of factual information seemed to become less important to its creators and its buyers. With some assurance, one could say that the picture book became recognized chiefly as an instrument to introduce children to the joys of reading, as opposed to "readers," and to the pleasures of literature and art. Styles of illustration in picture books changed, of course, from decade to decade to reflect the inevitable changes that were taking place in aesthetic points of view. So too their contents reflected the shifts in society's mores and attitudes toward children.

The picture books of the first two-thirds of this century, for example, reveal a single vision of a secure childhood and an abiding social order. So sure did the society of the time feel about its values— safe, placid, and hopefully enriching—that creators of books for very young children could depict them implicitly rather than explicitly. The picture books show a gentle control, usually played out with animals as exemplars. H. A. Rey's monkey, *Curious George* (1941), ends up in a zoo because of his pranks, but it is pictured as a pleasant, happy playground where George can indulge in his monkeyshines. Marjorie Flack's duck Ping in *The Story about Ping* (1933) receives a gentle spank on his tail for being late. Both animals have an order to return to after their escapades: George to "the man in the yellow hat" and Ping to "the wise one-eyed boat." The concept of order in Ludwig Bemelmans's *Madeline* (1939)—"twelve little girls in two straight lines"—gives a feeling of reassurance and security rather than regimentation. Such books, and many others of the period, with their taut plot lines and storytelling pictures, are still popular with children. Indeed, if there is one book that has established a commonality among young children, even today, it is certainly *Curious George*. Its illustrations are also fairly typical of the period: bright, humorous line drawings clearly following the text.

It was this era, the 1930s to the 1960s, that gave rise to the classic definition of a picture book: "a perfect balance between text and pictures," a work that evoked a total response. Neither the text nor the pictures worked as well separately as they did together. The illustrations could reinforce the story, as in Marjorie Flack's *Angus* books of the 1930s, or play with it as in Wanda Gág's *Millions of Cats* (1928), but the pictures stayed in their place, as it were, never overshadowing the printed word.

The illustrator's literal fidelity to the text gave an extra dimension to the work in the sense that children could "read" the pictures even when they could not read the words. Moreover, their succinct writing with its emphasis on the classic stages of storytelling—a beginning, a middle, and an end—trained children in the recognition of dramatic tension. One result was their seemingly uncanny ability to know exactly when a page should be turned, or when the adult reader omitted or changed a word.

As well as depicting a social vision of order and security in a delicate coordination of picture and text, earlier picture books above all explored childlike experiences. In Marie Hall Ets's *Play with Me* (1955) a little girl discovers the secret of making friends with small wild creatures; in Robert McCloskey's *One Morning in Maine* (1952) Sal loses her first baby tooth, but her wish nonetheless comes true. Significantly there were fewer child protagonists than child surrogates in the forms of animals and mechanical personalities. But when children did appear, there was no question as to the tone of security, affection, and familial comfort that surrounded them. Above all, children were to be protected, and writers and illustrators, however different their themes and styles, were unanimous on this point.

That these protectors were sincere is unquestionable, but, even more importantly, their views were reinforced by the adult world in general. This consensus was shattered in 1963 with the appearance of Maurice Sendak's *Where the Wild Things Are* and it would appear today that not "all the king's horses and all the king's men" could restore that phalanxed viewpoint. On the surface, *Where the Wild Things Are* seems innocent enough, hardly meriting the controversy that swirled around it at the time. Sendak's simple yet poetic text is accompanied by his sweeping and rhythmic pictures that take a naughty child on a fantasy voyage to a land where he reigns as King, subduing the Wild Things. Then he becomes lonesome and returns to his bedroom (to which he had been banished for his naughtiness) where he finds his supper waiting for him "and it was still hot."

While the illustrations disturbed those adults who saw the "Wild Things" as ferociously threatening rather than humorously subservient to Max's will, the extreme reaction to Sendak's work intimated that there was more at stake than a matter of interpretation of the pictures. As it turned out, this as yet unformulated anxiety was justified. Sendak's underlying theme that a child has unconscious needs, frustrations, and fears unsettled society's hitherto conceived ideals of early childhood and the book itself broke the stereotypic mold that had held for almost a hundred years. And yet, what heresy did Sendak commit? He himself best expresses his own philosophy of childhood:

> Certainly we want to protect our children from new and painful experiences that are beyond their emotional comprehension and that intensify anxiety; and to a point we can

prevent premature exposure to such experiences. That is obvious. But what is just as obvious—and what is too often overlooked—is the fact that from their earliest years children live on familiar terms with disrupting emotions, that fear and anxiety are an intrinsic part of their everyday lives, that they continually cope with frustration as best they can. And it is through fantasy that children achieve catharsis. It is the best means they have for taming Wild Things.[2]

This cathartic view was not new, of course. Folktales, for example, had long been seen as vehicles for the vicarious slaying of dragons within a child's life and consciousness. What made Sendak an innovator was that he expressed this catharsis for the preschool children through their own medium, the picture book. He also caught, early and creatively, a general trend of society which was to rise to the fore over the next two decades: an acceptance that the very young child matures more by sharing in the real and emotional world around it than by being protected from it.

In *Where the Wild Things Are* Sendak also produced a work that bridged two eras. He retained in it the earlier feeling of security while acknowledging the angry and helpless side of a child's nature, and in spite of the fact that several dancing pages of pictures are without words, the total effect is a perfectly balanced picture book in the traditional mode. Most importantly, children themselves responded to his artistry and to his perception of their need to walk safely, but a little fearfully, in the wild, wild wood.

Many picture-book creators of the 1960s and 1970s existed most happily and attracted a following by simply hewing to the older, gentler tradition. Leo Lionni's *Inch By Inch* (1962) shows an inchworm (in true folktale style) using his wits to escape being eaten; Beatrice De Regniers's humorous cumulative story *May I Bring a Friend?* (1964) is based on a childhood guessing game. But most new writers and illustrators chose to go beyond Sendak's tightly controlled interpretation of childhood's common and fundamental dragons and their exorcism. They came to see the picture book as a vehicle for the portrayal of specific and complex aspects of childhood darkness. Generally they explored this uncertain territory with a looser text dominated by the artwork.

A case in point is Alan Garner's *The Breadhorse* (1975), illustrated by Albin Trowski, that concerns the ritualistic side of childhood play. Ned is a young boy who says of himself:

2. Maurice Sendak, "Caldecott Award Acceptance," *Horn Book* 40:384 (Aug., 1964).

I can't whistle.
I can't spit.
That's why I'm always It
For Breadhorses.

In this game he is always forced to carry the older children on his back until "Back home in bed/I wished I was dead." In his dreams he conjures up a huge Rommany horse that becomes part of himself and the Game. The other children sense the change in him the next day and treat him as one of the group.

The differences between Sendak and Garner/Trowski are more than superficial. Max's dream monsters are of his own making and under his control; their behavior personifies his emotional conflicts. One of Sendak's wistful monsters is cunningly portrayed with human feet; it is Max's other self! Ned's dream nightmare comes from beyond the individual, from the archetypes of the racial unconscious, from the memories of Gypsy ritual and myth. Trowski's violent horse on a wordless page is not concerned with Ned's security and stability as much as with the proper enactment of the myth in the school playground. More powerful than the child, it suggests more terrors than it allays; having solved one problem, it may return in Ned's dream in another violent guise and what will he do then? Max, on the other hand, was himself "the most Wild Thing of all." Garner's ending is open, evocative, and transpersonal; Sendak's is complete, personal, and yet universal to childhood.

In a conceptual sense many of the picture books since Sendak have shattered the emotional equilibrium of childhood by leaving open-ended the problems raised. There have also been changes in form. The past unity of words and pictures has frequently been broken to suit the jarring new themes, while the pictures themselves have leaped into unprecedented importance, frequently carrying a different message from the words. Almost all of these approaches—artistic experimentation, disparity between text and illustration, and thematic ambiguity—are embodied in Charles Keeping's *Through the Window* (1970). "The street was all Jacob knew of the world, so it was the whole world to him." He looks at what is going on in his street in a poor part of London and he sees events there as "through a glass darkly." The text supplies Jacob's limited view, while the pictures show what is actually happening—a poor woman's dog being killed by runaway horses. But the last image, the boy's own picture which he draws on the window, shows the woman holding a live dog and smiling. Does Keeping suggest that the window has literally limited Jacob's vision, or that he is not yet ready to accept death? Or deeper still, does the curtain symbolize a child's innate distancing from unpleasant reality?

This fascination with structural division as well as open-ended narrative is apparent even in the work of a fairly traditional picture-book creator such as John Burningham. In his Shirley books—*Time to Get Out of the Bath, Shirley* (1978) and *Come Away from the Water, Shirley* (1977)—he fractures the unity of text and pictures for a quite different purpose. The left-hand pictures and brief text carry the mother's adjurations, while the right-hand wordless pictures show Shirley's imagination at work as she ignores her mother's "do's" and "don'ts," lost as she is in a classic pirate fantasy adventure. In a light-hearted but ironic manner Burningham thus expresses simultaneously a too frequent adults' view of children—they have no real sense of the child mind—as opposed to children's own secret desires. The last two wordless pictures are indicative of the long road the picture book has traveled even since Sendak. While his King Max sails happily home in his little boat to his supper, Burningham's Shirley is shown in her boat as a pirate queen blithely departing from reality. In the final left-hand realistic picture she is a child again, but one being dragged home (as her back shows) by her parents.

The conviction grows that many of the profound alterations in the picture book's concept and structure are due in large measure to an excessive emphasis on the pictorial. Where once a single picture was deemed worth a thousand words, it now appears that one thousand pictures are needed to interpret a few words—a prodigal feast of artwork that can be linked to the visual explosion of the 1960s, when images and symbols appeared ready to obliterate other forms of communication. This cultural emphasis on the visual released much hitherto latent talent that expressed itself in many popular art forms, including posters and murals.

Almost every medium sympathetic to visual interpretation was seen as an outlet for artistic experimentation and the picture book was a ready-made format for this pictorial deluge. Along with it came a more advanced technology for reproducing illustration and the publishers, riding on the economic crest of the 1960s, were able to give their artists and illustrators a wonderful new freedom of artistic expression and experimentation, leaving behind the representational style children had been given for decades. There was, after all, only so much ingenuity to be used in realistically portraying dogs and cats. The new illustrators used every possible modern art style: geometric, cubist, hard-edge, pop, op, expressionist, impressionist, surrealist, collage, pointillist, folk, native, cartoon, psychedelic, dada, photographic, magic realism.

So intent have been some picture-book artists upon art for art's

253

sake that much of their work pays direct homage to individual styles and artists. Mitsumasa Anno in *Topsy-Turvies* (1970) created several pictures based on the work of the Dutch artist M. C. Escher; John Steptoe has been greatly influenced by Georges Rouault; Ruth Craft has reproduced Pieter Brueghel's *The Fair* (1976); Sendak acknowledges influences from Dürer to W. MacKay's "Little Nemo" comic strips of the 1920s and illustrator after illustrator imitates Rousseau. The vehicle of picture books has provided a showcase for artists.

So important did the pictures become that many could stand on their own as individual works of art, as do Alan Aldridge's illustrations for *The Butterfly Ball* (1973), airbrushed in the style of magic realism. Fleur Cowles's illustrations for *The Tiger Flower* (1968) existed as paintings before they were put together with a text by Robert Vavra. In these two cases, and in many others, the illustrations overwhelm an often mediocre text.

The emphasis on artwork has, at times, led not only to a lesser feeling for words but often to such single-line or one-word picture books as Brian Wildsmith's *Fishes* (1968), Leo Lionni's *Swimmy* (1963), Uri Shulevitz's *Rain, Rain Rivers* (1969) and *Dawn* (1974), books in which the story is carried by the pictures. It is worth recalling that Sendak's *Where the Wild Things Are*, in spite of its visual impact, has 338 words that perfectly match the pictures.

It was perhaps predictable that the minimalization of language should have led eventually to the wordless picture book. It can be assumed that the illustrators of such books have a greater freedom of artistic expression than those limited by a prepared text and that the result will stretch the child's visual perceptiveness and conceptual imagination. However, some educators claim that such books actually harm children, retarding the development of their reading skills, and are especially troublesome at a time when they are already subjected to the impact of television. The orientation in these books to visual detail only eliminates the traditional linear eye movement that develops reading skill.

Many wordless picture books, among them Shirley Hughes's *Up and Up* (1979), a little girl's imaginary flying adventures, are tied to a plot. But the fact remains that words are better at plot than pictures. For one thing, it is hard to picture a punch line, one of the most charming attributes of the picture book, and one which adds immeasurably to such books as Sendak's *Where the Wild Things Are*, wherein Max's dinner was "still hot," and Leo Lionni's *Inch by Inch*, wherein the little inchworm "inched out of sight." As John Burningham proves in *Come Away from the Water, Shirley*, even a few negative words can inspire a conventional story. It may be, too, that many of the wordless picture books are for the tutored child.

Certainly Mitsumasa Anno's marvelous journey through time and space (*Anno's Journey*, 1978) would be enhanced by some adult guidance. Very young children are hardly apt to recognize the beginning notes of Beethoven's Ninth Symphony.

The wordless picture book is equally strongly defended as an opportunity for the extension of a child's imagination and visual stimulation in an often depressingly mediocre pictorial age. The best offer opportunities for visual puns and the humor of incongruity. And of course, new as they are in the children's book world, they come from the tradition of the pictograph, humanity's primal form of literacy.

Wordless picture books are apt to be more controversial than traditional picture books since pictures by themselves do not allow scope for the "principle of rejection." If a child cannot understand what it is reading, or does not want to, words provide an opportunity for a barrier to be raised between an idea and the expression of it. With pictures there is no place for the mind to hide. Earlier generations of children were frightened by the illustrations in Fox's *Book of Martyrs*. Similarly, many a modern child has reacted with terror to Walt Disney's filmic portrayal of the wicked queen in "Snow White and the Seven Dwarfs," even after having read the story with perfect equanimity. One of the most controversial wordless picture books has been *The Inspector* (1970), created by George Mendoza with illustrations by Peter Parnall. Here an Inspector Clouseau-type detective is finally, one presumes, eaten by his dog who has become monstrous by feeding on other monsters. In spite of the fine line drawings, many adults reacted in horror over its use with children.

But all pros and cons aside, the wordless picture book at present lacks shining examples by which it may be judged. Many have been used with great success by imaginative teachers and librarians, but there has been little evidence to show that children have taken any one of them to their hearts. Raymond Briggs's *The Snow Man* (1978), with its bittersweet depiction of friendship between a child and a snowman who must eventually melt, may win the day. Yet it is so tightly controlled in its cartoon-strip visual images which resemble animation stills as to almost negate the interjection of the viewer's imagination that the proponents of the wordless picture book so extol.

The development of children's aesthetic sensibilities and visual perceptiveness does, in all likelihood, benefit from the emphasis that today is being placed on picture-book art. Since the frame of the television set encloses few, if any, aesthetic stimuli, it may be that for small children the only escape from the medium's banality and crudeness is the picture book. While there is a distinction between illustrators who are stylists and those who are primarily storytellers, both are valid and initiate the young into good book illustration, typography, and design. But a fear remains that the oversophistication of artwork and concept is becoming more important than the artist's ability to connect with children, that the capacity to see and feel with the eyes and heart of a child is being lost.

It may be all for the best that the economic recession of the 1970s has resulted, in many instances, in simpler art styles, both in color and form. There has been a return to an effective use of black and white, as well as two-color artwork rather than three or four, of photography, and of the pen- and pencilwork characteristic of the representational draftsmanship of such illustrators as Ed Emberly, Frank Asch, Barry Miller, and Shirley Hughes. Such simplification has some advantages in forcing both illustrators and writers to be more ingenious within narrower limits that may result in books of more childlike simplicity.

Any childlike simplicity, however, is still noticeably and somehow surprisingly absent from the pages of the fantasy picture books for little children. It is in this subgenre that the new illustrators have found the greatest release for their imaginations. It is here, too, that the new, darker aspects of the picture-book world exist most significantly. In responding to Sendak's call for "the rough edge of fantasy," the new fantasists more often than not have honed it to the knife-edge of violence. In earlier picture books there was less distinction between fantasy and realism. In many cases realism blended into fantasy or was lightly touched with it, as in the larger-than-life stories of Virginia Lee Burton, exemplified by *Mike Mulligan and His Steam Shovel* (1939). Before 1960 there was a stronger feeling that fantasy was not suitable for very young children who needed, first of all, to become conscious of the world around them—to know "the butcher, the baker, the candle-stick maker" before they met a unicorn. Today there is less certainty that young children need that grounding in everyday reality before they encounter a world of fantasy, and the creators of picture books have in general responded to this altered perception of child psychology.

However, many forays into fantasy unleash violent, unbridled thrusts of imagination against an adult world that is portrayed, particularly in the pictures, as unsupportive and oftentimes dangerous. Beni Montresor, whose earlier picture books possessed a warm ambience supported by lively, modern pictures, has, in *Bedtime* (1978), succumbed to the pretentious parable and visual threat inherent in the modern fantasy picture book. In *Bedtime*, a bed awaits the child, but he has to go through a symbolic quest of terrifying experiences to reach it, including crawling through a forest of appallingly huge adult legs. Is the bed symbolic of sexual knowledge or night terrors? It is certainly surrounded by sufficient devils and angels (in violent colors) to populate Blake's vision of Heaven and Hell.

This symbolic interpretation of childhood continues into an abstraction of terrors that can surround the adult world as well. Trinka's terrifying adult film, "The Hand," recurs in theme and image. Kay Saari's *The Kidnapping of the Coffee Pot* (1974), with Trinka-like pictures by Henri Galeron, is a modern fable about junk— bizzare, personified figures who are threatened in the dark world of the junkyard. After a tense kidnapping, the pieces of junk and the junkman-kidnapper find comfort together: "all they have is one another." But the journey to this existential ending is menacing, a far cry from the happy anthropomorphized machine child surrogates of *Little Toot* and *Mike Mulligan and His Steam Shovel* which, in a pictorial sense, are bathed in as much sunshine as *The Kidnapping of the Coffee Pot* is in darkness. Actually, in earlier children's books, especially picture books, even the mention of kidnapping would have been taboo.

The new fantasists have little use for the playful imagination and representational line drawings of a Leslie Brooke or a Robert Lawson. They play out their visual dramas chiefly in surrealism that is nightmarish in atmosphere and content. The use of the dream motif is quite common. Garner's *The Breadhorse*, Cheli Duran Ryan's *Hildilid's Night* (1971), illustrated by Arnold Lobel, and Beni Montresor's *Bedtime*, among many others, are dreams in a serious Freudian and Jungian sense. Hildilid, the old woman in *Hildilid's Night*, wants to kill the night. She tries and tries fiercely to do so by every means at her command, even spitting at it in a scene which children particularly enjoy. She does not succeed, of course, for only the dawn can dispel the night. In spite of its ending the book has dark and violent qualities generally found only in the most symbolic of folktales.

Earlier picture-book creators sought to dispel the dark in works that set a gentle, joyful mood. In Margaret Wise Brown's *Goodnight Moon* (1947), illustrated by Clement Hurd, a child says good night gently and graciously to things of the night; in Janice Udry's *The Moon Jumpers* (1959), illustrated by Maurice Sendak, the children, caught in a luminous glow, dance in the moonlight.

Books of animal fantasy are, on the other hand, less extreme and experimental. Most are similar to those produced before the 1960s— often straightforward, realistic tales of anthropomorphized animals living like people or representing small children. The only fantastic element is that the animals talk. Some are used as "message" books on the idea (as old as Aesop) that these are more palatable in animal

257

form. Russell Hoban's appealing "Frances" books with their huggable badgers play out the simple trials of children who do not want to go to bed or who wish to run away. Robert Kraus's *Whose Mouse Are You?* (1970), illustrated by Jose Aruego, is a charming variation on the question adults have posed to children for generations—"whose little girl are you?" Some are simply for fun. In Manus Pinkwater's *The Terrible Roar* (1970), every time the little lion roars, something in the world disappears until he is all alone. So he simply roars himself to where his world has gone.

In general it is the fantasy picture books that provide the greatest variety in text and illustration. They can vary from Sendak's playful dream *In the Night Kitchen* (1970) with its comic-book flavor to Donald Barthelme's *The Slightly Irregular Fire Engine: or The Hithering Thithering Djinn* (1971), a sophisticated spoof on Victorian ideals and customs that is illustrated with collage pictures of art, artifacts, and industry of the time. It is books of fantasy with their ironic texts and stunning artwork that make the picture book so much the province of adults as to become a cult. Such illustrators as Nicola Bayley in Richard Adams's *The Tyger Voyage* (1976) and Alan Aldridge in Adams's *The Ship's Cat* (1977), both using airbrushed magic realism, Felix Vincent in his *Catlands/Pays des Chats* (1977) with his Rousseau-like paintings, and, of course, Sendak, have all joined to make the picture book a work of art chiefly collected by adults.

There has also been an artistic explosion in the most traditional of picture books—the alphabet books, counting books, and nursery rhymes. There are among them books illustrated for every taste. The books of illustrated nursery rhymes range from the childlike exuberance of Raymond Briggs's *The Mother Goose Treasury* (1966) to the static brilliance of Brian Wildsmith's *Mother Goose's Nursery Rhymes* (1964). Barbara Cooney's illustrations for *Mother Goose in French* (1964) present sturdy peasant characters bathed in luminous colors, while Nicola Bayley in her *Book of Nursery Rhymes* (1975) and *One Old Oxford Ox* (1977) uses framed pictures in airbrushed magic realism. Alphabet and counting books show the same tremendous variety and vitality. Color predominates to such an extent that many a charming, quieter book is overlooked. One such is *Alphabet Book* (1968) prepared by a group of Indian children on a reserve in southwestern Ontario who seem instinctively to have created it out of their own environment. While most alphabet books start with "A," either for "Apple Pie" or for "Ardvaark," these children rather sensibly started with "Airplane" and went on to such practicalities as "P" for "Plants," and "Y," usually for Yak, takes a nice twist with "Lesser Yellow Bird." The children's drawings are in black and white and somehow are more appealing than many lavishly colored alphabet books published in Great Britain and the United States.

Such radical changes in artistic style and experiments in the relationship of words and images still do not reflect the most fundamental changes in the picture book. These are more clearly seen in those books that explore the child's everyday world, the realistic picture book. In these it can be seen, in the simplest combination of words and pictures, that children are not secure, but sad or alarmed. And although the little children portrayed in these books have access to the adult world, that world is shown as fragmented.

In the past, even the most ordinary experiences of childhood were bathed in a rosy glow that included any adult activities, although the details were realistic enough. Fireman Small, in Lois Lenski's *The Little Fire Engine* (1946), is both a little boy and a miniature adult who drives a fire-engine. In capitalizing on the dreams of most little boys who are at exactly the right age, Lenski gives a matter-of-fact picture of the work of firefighters. Robert McCloskey's *Time of Wonder* (1957) is a vacation mood piece in which two children explore on their own the wonders of nature until a mild but common threat to the idyll—"we're going to have some weather" —returns them to the soothing security of their parents. The drawings for *The Little Fire Engine* are representational but cunningly childlike. McCloskey's watercolors capture the seasonal change as summer moves toward autumn on an island off the coast of Maine, a real island. Each in its own way is a piece of perfection in terms of what their creators set out to do: to provide a happy picture of childhood together with the subtle imparting of information.

The picture-book realists of today overwhelm the young child with relentless information about the distressing world of adults as it affects children, information that is reinforced by rigidly literal pictures. Their books are best described as therapeutic—an attempt to help young children cope with their feelings about such adult-oriented problems as moving, making new friends, sibling rivalry, toilet training, thumb-sucking, going to the hospital or the dentist, and the like. They are, in essence, "kid-sized" problem novels, most of which give the impression that they are conceived as a result of adult demands for help with "parenting," rather than rising from the creative urge of either writer or illustrator.

Basically the realistic picture book is now seen as an adjunct to books on childrearing. Since these are by intent "message" books, their words have a greater significance than the artwork which for the most part is humdrum, a reversal of the fantasy picture book. But if separated by philosophy of illustration, both types are joined in one significant aspect: the open-endedness of the text, its lack of resolu-

259

tion. In fantasy this can be seen as a weakness or a misunderstanding of its innate laws. A fantasist, even in a picture book, creates a secondary reality, one that must be controlled to be credible, a story with a beginning, a middle, and an end. The open-endedness of the new realistic picture book makes more sense, since life cannot be blocked off, even for a young child.

Such use of naturalistic open-endedness, with no resolution for the little lament, can be seen in Paul Zindel's *I Love My Mother* (1975), illustrated by John Melo. The little boy says:

> If I see her crying,
> She says, "It's just something in my eye."
> She tells me secrets
> like she's lonely. . . .
>
> I love my mother. I really do.

The mother is crying because the father is missing, but there is no indication of the reason. Is he dead, divorced, or simply absent? At any rate, the child "takes on so" about loving his mother that we know he is saying that he too misses his father and will continue to do so. The banal pictures are literal interpretations of the text.

While the lack of resolution is realistic enough, what is most noticeable in these books that attempt to interpret a problem, such as that of the single-parent family as does Zindel's book, is the consistent note of sadness. It is as if their creators, in spite of divorce statistics, cannot really bring themselves to acknowledge that the single-parent family is now a way of life. In Susan E. Mark's *Please Michael, That's My Daddy's Chair* (1976), illustrated by Winnie Mertons, a little girl becomes reconciled after a tremendous struggle with her feelings, to another man sitting in her father's chair. Here open-endedness, sadness, and listless illustrations combine only to make one see the vulnerability of a young child's life and the insensitivity of the adult world.

With all these reservations about the therapeutic picture book, it must be acknowledged that some do succeed in an artistic sense. John Steptoe's *My Special Best Words* (1974) is almost the epitome of the picture book as a vehicle for depicting social and cultural change. Its text gives a small slice-of-life picture of a motherless, single-parent family in which the little girl has to take on the role of mother for her younger brother. Steptoe writes with panache and humor, and his use of familiar child words for toilet training is a bold step, even in this enlightened age. His pictures of the black family have the dark gleam of stained glass. Nonetheless, this little family saga has the same note of sadness as *I Love My Mother*. "I love you"—the little girl's "special, best words" are for her father, but the responsibility that is thrust upon her ensures that she will miss her mother. Sincerity is evident in the presentation of the young child's problems in today's picture books, just as, with equal sincerity, yesterday's seem almost unconsciously to have hidden them.

But the question remains whether the picture-book format can really support the serious themes that are being attempted. The task is formidable, very like trying to explain the comédie humaine in forty words of one syllable. Death is one such subject that is handled generally in a personal and direct manner. A grandfather dies in Charlotte Zolotow's *My Grandson Lew* (1974); a grandmother and a great-grandmother in Tomie DePaola's *Nana Upstairs and Nana Downstairs* (1973), and a beloved cat in Judith Viorst's *The Tenth Good Thing about Barney* (1971), all situations where death can realistically be expected to enter a child's experience. Lew's grandfather, who used to come by airplane to baby-sit and play with him, dies when Lew is two years old. In one of those strange feats of memory that do occur with children, Lew, now six, awakens one night and thinks of his grandfather. His mother explains that because Lew has remembered him, his grandfather will always be present and that Lew has also given her the gift of memory. It is a calm little book, hardly calculated to disturb a child. Nana, who lives "upstairs," comes "downstairs" in the form of a shooting star, while the tenth good thing about Barney is that his body will make the grass grow.

Long before the ascendancy of the picture book as we know it, death was both frequent and realistically portrayed in children's books, functioning as a triggering incident which could give rise to purposeful didacticism. Turning it into some fanciful, almost neutral event, as has been done in some recent picture books, may be objectively no worse than outright moralizing, but in either case the picture book is too frail a medium to bear the burden of such a mysterious and irrevocable fact of life.

Zolotow is both grandmother and doyenne of the therapeutic picture book. She has written a wee one to cure almost every childhood ailment: *The Hating Book* (1969), for the child who has a falling out with a friend; *It's Not Fair* (1976), for those little girls discontented with their lot in life; *William's Doll* (1972), for the boy who wants a doll (it has to have blue eyes and curly lashes). Since most such offerings do not have a story line, they have the tone of nonfiction but without the depth that a factual book can give.

Many picture books now also attempt to reverse the conventional in sexual roles. In Norma Klein's *A Train for Jane* (1974), Jane finally does get a train and William is given the doll he longs for in *William's Doll*. But such books are really only defining the sexes by outward social mores and the cultural values placed on sexual roles.

261

This is an area where a book on simple, sexual identity may work best if handled as a fact of life rather than as a cause. Stephanie Waxman's *What Is a Girl? What Is a Boy?* (1976) shows the naked bodies of babies, children, and adolescents at the different stages in their development, in clothes and roles that are not traditional, to which are added cultural differences, all in a picture-book format. It shows, most importantly, that sexual roles are defined by the body and not whether a boy plays with dolls rather than trains.

Many picture book creators do try for a larger expression of reality than a simple message, but a similar note of alarm and sadness manages to creep in. Margaret Mahy's *The Ultra-Violet Catastrophe* (1975), illustrated by Brian Froud, provides a joyful splurge of pictures that puts it far beyond the ordinary therapeutic offerings. But while the story line is more original than most, the inspiration for it is provided by uncaring, unthinking adults. In a modern version of the cross-generational story, the old man is treated as a child by his daughter and the little girl is constantly adjured by her mother to "keep clean." Old man and little girl, sent out to walk together because they are in the way of the "real" adults, have a glorious time together in a making-mud-pie fashion. The old man teaches the little girl his means of protection against being treated like a plant: he makes up long words and phrases—ultra-violet catastrophe—"No plant can say that." But in spite of the joie-de-vivre of their few hours together and the feeling the child is now armed with a sense of her own uniqueness and value, the deeper implication is that both will return to a world where they are not respected. The mother's slight softening toward dirty clothes at the end is not a page-turning surprise, but simply unbelievable, given her first presentation.

In concentrating upon problems such as death, children's rights, absentee parents, and sexual adjustments, the realistic picture book, especially in its illustrative aspects, has lost almost all of its charm and force as a window on the world for little children. Bemelmans's Notre Dame cathedral in *Madeline*, McCloskey's New England islands in *Time of Wonder*, the changing pattern of countryside to city in Virginia Lee Burton's *The Little House*, all images that made the world a familiar yet magical place, have been, if not eroded, at least diminished. The excitement of curiosity and discovery directed to the external world has been replaced by a calming, down-to-earth exploration of children's feelings in a closed, domestic environment.

This emphasis on domestic realism is due, in part, to the rise of the small presses, one of the most significant publishing phenomena of the 1960s and 1970s. The fact that many such presses are devoted almost exclusively to the publishing of books for young children expresses perhaps more than any other factor the adult concern to mold young children through their books. The power of the book as a teaching vehicle—a new-old discovery—has regained its former luster. For every group of adult social, political and cultural values there now appears to be a small publishing house to support it. Many were started because of a feeling that certain viewpoints were ignored by the larger but more conservative publishing houses. An obvious example are those small presses concerned with promoting a positive image of girls and women in an area where male protagonists appeared to dominate. Because of lack of funds, the small press books were generally published in paperback with black and white illustrations. In their inception, the proseletyzing urge was overwhelming. But as they became more firmly established, writers and illustrators paid more attention to literary and artistic values and to lightheartedness, having learned the lesson that unless they held the child's interest, their message was of little value. The small presses also opened up a new avenue for talent. The title of Sue Ann Alderson's *Bonnie McSmithers You're Driving Me Dithers* (1974), published by a small Canadian press, is now almost a household phrase in Canada. It is very much in the modern mode as, in controlled humorous verse, the mother finally admits that she can drive her daughter "dithers."

Along with the small presses dedicated to changing society are the experimental avant-garde presses that were established also in the 1960s. Many took an intense interest in picture books as an expression of fantasy, an interest possibly deriving from the counterculture of the period. Harlin Quist Books, a publishing house in New York is a prime example. Quist's books arouse extreme responses; they are either loved or hated. He publishes imaginative, even "freaky" texts with surrealistic illustrations that offer psychological insights into childhood and sly commentaries on the adult world. If they are to be taken as children's picture books, they certainly explore to the limit the potential of visual and linguistic symbolism. These "new wave" publications helped to establish the picture book as an art form for adults.

Significantly, one of Harlin Quist's most prominent writers is the Romanian dramatist, Eugene Ionesco, whose plays depict the absurdity of bourgeois values and the part that chance plays in life. His four story books, entitled *Story Number 1, 2, 3, and 4,* are satiric, brilliant expressions of a young child's mind. In *Story Number 4* (1973), first published in French in 1967, Josette has dreamed that her mother is away. Ionesco cannot resist adult throwaway lines:

"Write to Mama," says Josette.
"Telephone Mama," says Josette.
Papa says, "We must not phone."

263

And Papa says to himself:
"Who knows? She might be somewhere else."

Harlin Quist can also be credited with publishing the apotheosis to date of adult uncaring toward children in Albert Cullum's two diatribes againt the adult world: *You Think Just Because You're Big You're Right* (1976) and *The Geranium On The Window Sill Just Died, but Teacher You Went Right On* (1971). The following extract from the former,

They're fighting again!
They say all the words
they tell me never to say.
Mean, *real mean* words!
I wish it wasn't Saturday
so I could be in school.

and that from the latter,

You're so proud of your shiny new car.
You're so proud of your new color hair,
   your vacation tan,
and your nice clean blackboards.
I sit in the third row last seat.
Teacher, are you ever proud of me?

together with his illustrations, aptly present Cullum's point of view.

The Harlin Quist publications may have pushed the picture book about as far as it can go in representing what a child has to contend with. But these books are symptoms of change rather than cause and they cannot be taken as representing the picture book world in general. The basic and fundamental changes initiated by the small, alternate and avant-garde presses have been absorbed and furthered by the large, traditional publishers who have, as it were, stolen their thunder. All the mainstream houses now do pay more attention to cultural and social change in the individual lives of children.

It must also be noted that multiculturalism also has entered the picture-book world. Where once it was a rare event to find a picture book with a text other than English, now there are dozens with English accompanied by languages ranging from French and Spanish to Punjabi. Not only have the major publishers absorbed the artistic and stylistic experiments from the more risk-taking, imaginative, avant-garde presses and the sociological concerns from the alternative presses, they are now producing smoother, more humorous and more humane versions of the new zeitgeist. Two examples are Shirley Hughes's *Helpers* (1975), an amusing interaction between children and their male teenage babysitter, published by a major English firm, and Judith Viorst's *My Mama Says There Aren't Any Zombies, Ghosts, Vampires, Creatures, Demons, Monsters, Fiends, Goblins, or Things* (1973), by a major American house, a wryly humorous, but at the end comforting, depiction of a child's fears.

As well as experiments in content and illustration, there also have been experiments in physical structure and format. Many picture books, especially the standard ones, are now available in paperback, a happy development for the purse, even if some of the vibrant color of the original hardcover edition is lost in this second-generation printing. Then too there are miniature boxed sets, such as Sendak's "Nutshell Library." Interestingly enough though, the trend is toward a large-size format that perhaps is dictated by the needs of the illustrator for a large canvas. Beatrix Potter's dictum of "little books for little hands to hold" seems not to be of major importance today. A return to the nineteenth-century "gimmick" books has also occurred and there are now available pop ups, like Nicola Bayley's *Puss in Boots* (1976), pull outs, flip books, and, of course, friezes.

Nostalgia is also evident in the reprinting of the classic illustrators of the late nineteenth and early twentieth centuries: Walter Crane, Kate Greenaway, Kay Nielsen, Edmund Dulac, Maxfield Parrish, John Bauer, Elsa Beskow, and Carl Larsson. This is due to a rediscovery of earlier art forms, evolving in the 1960s from an interest in art nouveau and in the 1970s from an interest in the Pre-Raphaelites, both of which were direct antecedents and influences on the children's book illustrators of the turn of the century. The reissuing of these classic illustrators has not only been in the form of picture books, but also in books of folktales, in compendiums of their best work, and in posters and note paper. Perhaps this renaissance of representational romanticism is occurring as a reaction to, or a balance for, much of the abstract, stylized art forms now used in picture books.

The floodgates opened about twenty years ago. The sands that defied Lewis Carroll's "seven maids with seven mops" who swept them "for half a year" are as nothing to the current outpouring of picture books and so they are difficult to treat in any cohesive way. Such numbers have brought a remarkable artistic and conceptual diversity, which give an aura of richness. With this "numbers game" has also come the great democratization of the picture-book scene. Theoretically, every adult point of view in terms of educating the young child can now be satisfied, at least to a certain extent. This in turn indicates that adult views are not as homogeneous as they were in the past. While one parent may want a book with a girl character or one that depicts the single-parent family or one that depicts an older child's acceptance of a new baby, another may simply want a book for delight.

An even stronger partisanship is aroused by the visual arts in picture-book form: while one adult may respond to the sophistication of magic realism, another may reject it altogether. Variety appears only to have elicited a greater variety of reactions for or against an individual work.

Literary criticism in general has declined due to the rise of sociological concerns, salutary though they may be. The picture book is even more buffeted by contending judgments. When the Bratislava Biennale Committee on Picture Books insists upon "the submission, not of printed books, but of original art work," to ensure "that the illustrations shall be judged by . . . 'original, creative' impressiveness,"[3] the classic criteria of the unity of words and pictures falls apart. Are there any surviving criteria for picture books which are not thematically or stylistically subjective? Who guards the guardians?

In all this upheaval it cannot be proven that, book by book, the contemporary picture book is more successful aesthetically, or that it has a greater child appeal, than that of the past. To paraphrase Sir Henry Wotton's observation on the stars, modern picture books frequently satisfy more by their numbers than by their light.

It is impossible to judge the ineffable bonding that can occur when a particular book, child, and adult are brought together. However, some evidence as to what appeals generally to children may be garnered from those picture books that have lasted from the past and that form close to half the picture-book stock in school and public libraries. Other evidence can be deduced from the newer books that are used successfully with groups of children; those that hold the attention of children of diverse backgrounds and interests. Here the children speak for themselves. And it is quite noticeable that they show a steady, conservative taste for books with a strong story line, repetition, cumulation, nursery rhymes, numbers and alphabets, and books in which they can participate by chanting.

A commonality surfaces in the texts. The most successful have a delicate mingling of reality and fantasy, a slightly didactic air, and an integrity of spirit or mood, whether liveliness or quietude. Overriding qualities that such interests suggest are energy, rhythm, and unity of text and pictures. Ultimately, what counts is the expectation —almost the demand—on the child's part that the page be turned. That essential quality of page-turning at just the right time is created

3. Lee Kingman, and others, *Illustrators of Children's Books, 1967-1976* (Boston: The Horn Book, 1978), p. 31.

by the unity of text and pictures and the significance of the pause when they are skillfully combined.

There seems to be a high correlation in content and visual image between the still-living books of the past that are beloved by children and those new ones that appeal today. The creators of such works are indubitably contemporary, but they are also storytellers whose artwork and text match, at least to some degree, the suspense and the representational art style of earlier periods. Such figures include Maurice Sendak, John Burningham, Ezra Jack Keats, Helen Oxenbury, Raymond Briggs, Mercer Mayer, and Leo Lionni, at least in some of their work.

The British author-illustrator John Burningham exhibits most of these qualities. He is not concerned with the dark and complex aspects of childhood, bibliotherapy, or social adjustment. But neither is he simplistic. He offers the profound pleasure of comedy, rather than mere humor, and a deep understanding of a child's imagination, particularly in his "Shirley" books which show how well he is able to penetrate a child's imagination. In his "Mr. Gumpy" books, *Mr. Gumpy's Outing* (1970) and *Mr. Gumpy's Motor Car* (1973), he uses the classic comic genre in miniature form, taking a combined society of children and animals through a free-form chaos to a harmonious resolution. In *Mr. Gumpy's Outing* the children and animals squabble and fight, upsetting the boat; then they happily return home to the symbolic tea table. In *Mr. Gumpy's Motor Car* Burningham makes use of the traditional folktale's artful cumulation, but then comes the slowing down. When the children and animals suddenly decide to push the car, stuck in the mud,

> They pushed and shoved and heaved
> and strained and gasped and slipped
> and slithered and squelched.

Burningham uses a variety of themes and techniques of art, but he always keeps them within a child's comprehension. Many modern picture-book creators begin simply enough but gradually seem determined to push the genre to its utmost limits. A barometer of this approach is Tomi Ungerer who has moved from the playfulness of *Crictor* (1958) to the satiric urbanity of *Allumette* (1974), a parody of Andersen's "The Little Match Girl." Burningham's "Mr. Gumpy" books were preceded by his tales of anthropomorphized animals in natural surroundings: *Borka, the Adventures of a Goose with No Feathers* (1963); *Trubloff, the Mouse Who Wanted to Play the Balalaika* (1964), and *Harquin, the Fox* (1967). These are strongly plotted little tales reminiscent of the best animal fantasy picture books of the 1940s and 1950s. His art style for the most part is best described as a combination of

267

the representational and the impressionistic. His *Harquin, the Fox* owes much to Caldecott in its rhythmic sweep of the English countryside, as does its unsophisticated and good-natured humor.

In his "Little Books," Burningham has taken the picture book to its utmost simplicity, but with the "art that conceals art." His children, busy about their homely little affairs, are a cross between Schultz's Charlie Brown and Sendak's Brooklyn children, but they have an appeal all their own. These are for *very* young children and are true to G. K. Chesterton's observation that, "A child of seven is excited by being told that Tommy opened a door and saw a dragon. But a child of three is excited by being told that Tommy opened a door."[4] Burningham does not give a three-year-old a dragon in the books *The Blanket, The Cupboard, The Dog, The Friend.* In them he depicts a little boy playing with pots and pans in his mother's kitchen, or losing his blanket, or quarreling and then making up with a friend. They are so true to life as to take an adult aback with a wry appreciation of the small, but nailed-down details of infant life, while a very young child can recognize its own activities on the pages of a book without adult commentary. Perhaps Burningham's greatest contribution to the picture book in both words and art is to remind us that children can still be charmed by simple things.

They are also charmed by humor in all its forms. A Lear-like nonsense pervades Ivor Cutler's *Elephant Girl* (1976). Even the little girl's name, Balooky Klujypop—"it's the best name in the world"—recalls the British tradition of linguistic nonsense. Helen Oxenbury's illustrations, which very literally depict Balooky's friendship with an elephant who has been pulled by his trunk from the garden, add to the absurdity.

Oxenbury writes her own version of the incongruous in her picture-storybook *The Queen and Rosie Randall* (1978). Both story and pictures revel in the child's position of dominant authority over imposing adults. Its theme, like that of *May I Bring a Friend?* by Beatrice Schenk De Regniers is modern enough, the giving of stature to a child, but both books are actually an extension of the old nursery rhyme, "I've been to London to look at the Queen."

It is obvious too that the theme of humorous friendship, but with animals as surrogate children, still has popularity and appeal. James Marshall's *George and Martha* (1972) and its sequels, Bernard Waber's *Lyle, Lyle Crocodile* (1973) and its sequels, and Arnold Lobel's *Frog and Toad Are Friends* (1970) take children through domestic details, not grand adventures, as well as showing affection and childlike play. As contrasted to the one-dimensional, single-minded mis-

4. G. K. Chesterton, "The Ethics of Elfland," p. 94.

chievousness of *Curious George*, these modern books reflect a deep humanity and tenderness that touch on sentiment as well as humor. These books with their socializing experiences also present a palatable didacticism that simply reflects the natural and age-old adult urge to broaden children's sensibilities.

The literary folktale so masterfully presented by Wanda Gág during the 1920s and 1930s, and exemplified by her *Millions of Cats* and *Gone is Gone*, is another trend that thankfully has continued into the present. Tomie De Paola's *Strega Nona* (1975) too has bubbled over into children's hearts with the same speed that the pasta spreads throughout his freshly delineated town of Calabria. And Elfrida Vipont's *The Elephant and the Bad Baby* (1969), illustrated by Raymond Briggs, has a chanting voice in the "Gingerbread Boy" style as the elephant and the baby are chased by a growing body of very British tradespeople and shopkeepers. Although British in its detail, this book has found a wide audience perhaps because, like *Strega Nona* it deals with, to paraphrase Lewis Carroll, "Beau-ootiful Foo-ood"; but in the American edition the kinds of food and types of shops were changed.

All these picture books are touched with fantasy of a nonsensical kind and are lightly iconoclastic; theirs are topsy-turvy worlds where children have power and control. However, the completely realistic picture book can offer, in an artistic way, a sense of a child's exploration of its own personal world with a slow but organically developed understanding of that world and some achievement in it. John Burningham's "Little Books" accomplish this as does Ezra Jack Keats's *The Snowy Day* (1962). With its authentic portrayal of a city child's first experience with snow it speaks for all the first discoveries of young childhood. The understated excitement so perfectly conveyed in Keats's subtle collage illustrations have made this a classic among modern picture books.

Burningham, Marshall, Waber, Oxenbury, Cutler, and many others have produced works that by and large fulfill the requisite criteria for a picture book to achieve success. Yet many an individual work manages to break all the rules and still succeed, its author or illustrator or the two together having created something unique, a tour de force. Thus Maurice Sendak in *Some Swell Pup* (1976) pleases with a deliberately didactic message on how to raise a dog; and Arnold Lobel in his books about Frog and Toad brings artistry to the "reader" format; and Raymond Briggs in his *Father Christmas* (1973) and *Fungus the Bogeyman* (1977) bridges the gap between a child audience and an adult audience on two distinctly different levels, children responding to their slapstick humor and adults to their ironic views of life. Alice and Martin Provensen too have given a new

269

dimension to the informational picture book in *Our Animal Friends at Maple Hill Farm* (1974). It is explosive with nonlinear vitality and humor, and unlike farm books of the past, it also indicates the realities of farm life: "This dog killed sheep and had to be put away (as the saying goes)."

It is not surprising that the picture book has been buffeted by the winds of change; it always has been a miniature of the larger world of children's books. But in our own time it may well be leading the changes seen in present-day children's literature. Much in the new trends—experimentation, candor, visual and textual sophistication, social conscience—are admirable and even praiseworthy. But success in an absolute sense seems to elude most practitioners. The failure of many picture books may be attributed to their adult content and emphasis, such as that in Raymond Briggs's *Gentleman Jim* (1980) who begins as a toilet cleaner and ends as one in jail, his desire to play "highwayman" thwarted by bureaucracy.

The modern picture-book world in general raises the question: Is the picture book any longer only the preserve of the little child? It would seem not. A new market is already commercially viable—adults, teenagers, older children. Perhaps the greatest success of the "new-wave" picture books is the realization that in format and artistry, they are books for everybody. But if more than lip service is to be given to the young child as its ideal audience, authors, illustrators, and publishers should consider to a greater extent the children's own interests rather than those of child psychology. Although the adult may wish to expand a child's imagination or develop social values, the child, caveat emptor, may still prefer *Curious George*.

While the 1960s and 1970s seem to have brought plentitude, the very plethora may work to the disadvantage of those artists who need time and encouragement to develop their talent. In the early quieter world of publishing, as Sendak points out, "there was time for young (artists) to grow quietly . . . but now as books come pouring out of the publishing meat grinder . . . the quality has dropped severely."[5] Now a picture-book artist has to be an immediate success, at least with an adult audience—as were Nicola Bayley and Alan Aldridge—before being given another chance.

Children also need time to become intimate with a small number of picture books, to form friendships with favorite characters as they do with their own families and peers. It is this intimacy that forms a

5. *Questions to an Artist Who Is Also an Author: A Conversation between Maurice Sendak and Virginia Haviland* (Washington, DC: Govt. Print. Off., 1972). Reprinted from *Quarterly Journal of the Library of Congress* 28, 4:279 (Oct. 1971).

child's stepping-stone to future worthwhile literary and artistic experiences.

Works Cited

Adams, Richard. *The Adventures and Brave Deeds of the Ship's Cat on the Spanish Maine*. Illus. by Alan Aldridge. London: Jonathan Cape, 1977. 32 pp.

Adams, Richard. *The Tyger Voyage*. Illus. by Nicola Bayley. London: Jonathan Cape, 1976. 30 pp.

Alderson, Sue Ann. *Bonnie McSmithers You're Driving Me Dithers*. Illus. by Fiona Garrick. Edmonton, Alta.: Tree Frog Press, 1974. 53 pp.

Aldridge, Alan. *The Butterfly Ball and the Grasshopper's Feast*. With verses by William Plomer. London: Jonathan Cape, 1973. 76 pp.

Alphabet Book. Toronto: Univ. of Toronto Pr., 1968. 60 pp.

Anno, Mitsumasa. *Anno's Journey*. London: Bodley Head, 1978, 1977. 47 pp. (Original title, *My Journey*, 1977)

———*Topsy-Turvies: Pictures to Stretch the Imagination*. New York: Waler/Weatherhill, 1970. 27 pp.

Barthelme, Donald. *The Slightly Irregular Fire Engine; or, The Hithering Thithering Djinn*. New York: Farrar, 1971. 32 pp.

Bayley, Nicola. *Nicola Bayley's Book of Nursery Rhymes*. London: Jonathan Cape, 1975. 15 pp.

———*One Old Oxford Ox*. London: Jonathan Cape, 1977. 28 pp.

———*Puss in Boots*. Ret. by Christopher Logue. London: Jonathan Cape, 1976. 14 pp.

Bemelmans, Ludwig. *Madeline*. New York: Simon & Schuster, 1939. 48 pp.

Briggs, Raymond. *Father Christmas*. London: Hamish Hamilton, 1973. 28 pp.

———*Fungus the Bogeyman*. London: Hamish Hamilton, 1977. 41 pp.

———*Gentleman Jim*. London: Hamish Hamilton, 1980. 32 pp.

———*The Mother Goose Treasury*. London: Hamish Hamilton, 1966. 220 pp.

———*The Snow Man*. London: Hamish Hamilton, 1978. 32 pp.

Brown, Margaret Wise. *Goodnight Moon*. Pictures by Clement Hurd. New York: Harper, 1947. 31 pp.

Burningham, John. *The Blanket*. (Little Book) London: Jonathan Cape, 1975. 19 pp.

———*Borka, the Adventures of a Goose with No Feathers*. London: Jonathan Cape, 1963. 32 pp.

———*Come Away from the Water, Shirley*. London: Jonathan Cape, 1977. 24 pp.

———*The Cupboard*. (Little Book) London: Jonathan Cape, 1975. 19 pp.

———*The Dog*. (Little Book) London: Jonathan Cape, 1975. 19 pp.

———*The Friend*. (Little Book) London: Jonathan Cape, 1975. 19 pp.

————*Harquin, the Fox Who Went Down to the Valley*. London: Jonathan Cape, 1967. 32 pp.

————*Mr. Gumpy's Motor Car*. London: Jonathan Cape, 1973. 32 pp.

————*Mr. Gumpy's Outing*. London: Jonathan Cape, 1970. 32 pp.

————*Time to Get Out of the Bath, Shirley*. New York: Crowell, 1978. 24 pp.

————*Trubloff, the Mouse Who Wanted to Play the Balalaika*. London: Jonathan Cape, 1964. 36 pp.

Burton, Virginia Lee. *The Little House*. Boston: Houghton, 1942. 40 pp.

————*Mike Mulligan and His Steam Shovel*. Boston: Houghton, 1939. 48 pp.

Cooney, Barbara. *Mother Goose in French: Poesies de la Vraie Meere Oie*. Tr. by Hugh Latham. New York: Crowell, 1964. 44 pp.

Craft, Ruth. *Pieter Brueghel's The Fair*. London: Collins, 1975. 32 pp.

Cullum, Albert. *The Geranium on the Window Sill Just Died, but Teacher You Went Right On*. New York: Harlin Quist, 1971. 60 pp.

————*You Think Just Because You're Big You're Right*. New York: Harlin Quist, 1976. 60 pp.

Cutler, Ivor. *Elephant Girl*. Pictures by Helen Oxenbury. New York: Morrow, 1976. 24 pp.; title of British ed.: *Balooky Klujypop*. London: Heinemann, 1975. 24 pp.

De Paola, Tomie. *Nana Upstairs and Nana Downstairs*. New York: Putnam, 1973. 32 pp.

————*Strega Nona: An Old Tale*. Englewood Cliffs, NJ: Prentice-Hall, 1975. 32 pp.

De Regniers, Beatrice Schenk. *May I Bring a Friend?* Illus. by Beni Montressor. New York: Atheneum, 1964. 46 pp.

Ets, Marie Hall. *Play with Me*. New York: Viking, 1955. 32 pp.

Flack, Marjorie. "Angus" series. New York: Doubleday, 1930-1932.

————, and Wiese, Kurt. *The Story about Ping*. New York: Viking, 1933. 32 pp.

Gág, Wanda. *Gone Is Gone*. New York: Coward, 1935. 63 pp.

————*Millions of Cats*. New York: Coward, 1928. 32 pp.

Garner, Alan. *The Breadhorse*. Illus. by Albin Trowski. London: Collins, 1975. 32 pp.

Gramatky, Hardie. *Little Toot*. New York: Putnam, 1939. 93 pp.

Hoban, Russell. The "Frances" books. New York: Harper, 1960-1970.

Hughes, Shirley. *Helpers*. London: Bodley Head, 1975. 31 pp.

————*Up and Up*. London: Bodley Head, 1979. 32 pp.

Ionesco, Eugene. *Story Number Four*. Tr. by Ciba Vaughan. Illus. by Jean-Michel Nicollet. New York: Harlin Quist, 1973. 20 pp.

————*Story Number One, for Children under Three Years of Age*. Pictures by Etienne Delessert. New York: Harlin Quist, 1968. 32 pp.

————*Story Number Three, for Children over Three Years of Age*. Pictures by Philippe Corentin. Tr. by Ciba Vaughan. New York: Harlin Quist, 1971. 31 pp.

————*Story Number Two, for Children under Three Years of Age*. Tr. by Calvin K. Towle. Pictures by Etienne Delessert. New York: Harlin Quist, 1970. 20 pp.

Keeping, Charles. *Through the Window*. London: Oxford Univ. Pr., 1970. 32 pp.

Klein, Norma. *A Train for Jane*. Illus. by Miriam Schottland. Old Westbury, NY: Feminist Press, 1974. 30 pp.

Kraus, Robert. *Whose Mouse Are You?* Pictures by Jose Aruego. New York: Macmillan, 1970. 36 pp.

Lenski, Lois. *The Little Fire Engine*. New York: Oxford Univ. Pr., 1946. 48 pp.

Lionni, Leo. *Inch by Inch*. New York: I. Obolensky, 1960. 28 pp.

———*Swimmy*. New York: Pantheon, 1963. 31 pp.

Lobel, Arnold. *Frog and Toad Are Friends*. New York: Harper, 1970. 64 pp.

McCloskey, Robert. *One Morning in Maine*. New York: Viking, 1952. 64 pp.

———*Time of Wonder*. New York: Viking, 1957. 63 pp.

Mahy, Margaret. *The Ultra-Violet Catastrophe! The Unexpected Walk with Great-Uncle Magnus Pringle*. Pictures by Brian Froud. London: Dent, 1975. 31 pp.

Mark, Susan E. *Please Michael, That's My Daddy's Chair*. Illus. by Winnie Mertons. Waterloo, Ont.: Before We Are Six, 1976. 36 pp.

Marshall, James. *George and Martha*. Boston: Houghton, 1972. 46 pp.

Mendoza, George. *The Inspector*. Illus. by Peter Parnall. Garden City, NY: Doubleday, 1970. 48 pp.

Montresor, Beni. *Bedtime*. New York: Harper, 1978. 32 pp.

Oxenbury, Helen. *The Queen and Rosie Randall*. London: Heinemann, 1978. 32 pp.

Pinkwater, Daniel Manus. *The Terrible Roar*. New York: Knopf, 1970. 35 pp.

Provensen, Alice, and Provensen, Martin. *Our Animal Friends at Maple Hill Farm*. New York: Random, 1974. 57 pp.

Rey, H. A. *Curious George*. Boston: Houghton, 1941. 55 pp.

Ryan, Cheli Duran. *Hildilid's Night*. Illus. by Arnold Lobel. New York: Macmillan, 1971. 30 pp.

Saari, Kay. *The Kidnapping of the Coffee Pot*. Illus. by Henri Galeron. New York: Harlin Quist, 1974. 32 pp.

Sendak, Maurice. *In the Night Kitchen*. New York: Harper, 1970. 40 pp.

———, and Margolis, Matthew. *Some Swell Pup: or, Are You Sure You Want a Dog?* New York: Farrar, 1976. 32 pp.

———*Where the Wild Things Are*. New York: Harper, 1963. 40 pp.

Shulevitz, Uri. *Dawn*. New York: Farrar, 1974. 32 pp.

———*Rain Rain Rivers*. New York: Farrar, 1969. 32 pp.

Steig, William. *Sylvester and the Magic Pebble*. New York: Simon & Schuster, 1969. 32 pp.

Steptoe, John. *My Special Best Words*. New York: Viking, 1974. 32 pp.

Udry, Janice. *The Moon Jumpers*. Pictures by Maurice Sendak. New York: Harper, 1959. 31 pp.

Ungerer, Tomi. *Allumette: A Fable with Due Respect to Hans Christian Andersen, the Grimm Brothers, and the Honorable Ambrose Bierce*. New York: Parents' Magazine Pr., 1974. 32 pp.

———*Crictor*. New York: Harper, 1958. 32 pp.

Vavra, Robert. *The Tiger Flower*. Illus. by Fleur Cowles. London: Collins, 1968. 44 pp.

Vincent, Felix. *Catlands/Pays Des Chats*. Montreal: Tundra Pr., 1977. 44 pp.

Vipont, Elfrida. *The Elephant and the Bad Baby*. Illus. by Raymond Briggs. London: Hamish Hamilton, 1969. 32 pp.

Viorst, Judith. *My Mamma Says There Aren't Any Zombies, Ghosts, Vampires, Creatures, Demons, Monsters, Fiends, Goblins, or Things*. Illus. by Kay Chorao. New York: Atheneum, 1973. 44 pp.

——*The Tenth Good Thing about Barney*. Illus. by Erik Blegvad. New York: Atheneum, 1971. 25 pp.

Waber, Bernard. *Lyle, Lyle Crocodile*. Edinburgh: Oliver & Boyd, 1966. 48 pp.

Waxman, Stephanie. *What is a Girl? What is a Boy?* Culver City, Calif.: Peace Press, 1976. 45 pp.

Wildsmith, Brian. *Fishes*. London: Oxford Univ. Pr., 1968. 32 pp.

——*Brian Wildsmith's Mother Goose; A Collection of Nursery Rhymes*. London: Oxford Univ. Pr., 1964. 80 pp.

Zindel, Paul. *I Love My Mother*. Illus. by John Melo. New York: Harper, 1975. 31 pp.

Zolotow, Charlotte. *The Hating Book*. Pictures by Ben Shecter. New York: Harper, 1969. 32 pp.

——*It's Not Fair*. Pictures by William Pène Du Bois. New York: Harper, 1976. 32 pp.

——*My Grandson Lew*. Pictures by William Pène Du Bois. New York: Harper, 1974. 30 pp.

——*William's Doll*. Pictures by William Pène Du Bois. New York: Harper, 1972. 30 pp.

11. *The European Children's Novel In Translation*

There is no frigate like a book
To take us lands away.[1]

Translations should need no apology, since important ideas and great literature have never been the exclusive property of any one culture. We have all been shaped by books that were not originally written in English, the Bible and the Greek classics being conspicuous examples. Indeed, the need for translation exists even within the confines of a single language and culture. We read the early books of the English language in translation; *Beowulf* and Chaucer's *Canterbury Tales* have to be rendered into modern English from their Anglo-Saxon and Middle English originals which, to most of us, are as indecipherable as Swahili.

Yet in spite of the obvious importance of translations, they often tend to be derogated; one English writer, George Burrows, described them as "but best an echo." Translations are looked down on, somewhat as are abridgements for not being "the real thing." It is true that even in the best translations nuances and shadings of language may be forfeited. Even more importantly, the social milieu which the original author took for granted may be so ill conveyed as to be lost on the reader. Yet despite these limitations, translation appears to be a useful, even essential literary mode, one that helps to satisfy our insatiable curiosity toward other cultures and their view of themselves. We accept the flaws of translation for the enrichment it brings and because it is, for most of us, our only avenue of escape from cultural isolation. The ultimate proof of the value of translations is, of course, their sheer quantity. They have always been and con-

1. Emily Dickinson, [poem no.] 99, in *The Poems of Emily Dickinson*, ed. by M. D. Bianchi and A. L. Hampson (Boston: Little, 1938), p. 46.

tinue to be published in large numbers because they are at the least valuable and at the most indispensable.

For children, the worth of translations is even less disputable. In the first place, they come to translation naturally since much of their early acquaintance with literature does not stem from English-language originals at all. The folktales, the myths, the legends, even the North American Indian tales come via translation. So do many of childhood's best-loved individual works—France's *Babar*, Switzerland's *Heidi*, Italy's *Pinocchio*, and Sweden's *Pippi Longstocking*.[2]

In the second place, children neither know, nor, if they knew, would they care about the national origins of their book friends; it is adults who know whether a book is translated and add the national tag. In the listening and reading repertoire of the English-speaking child, the French "Cinderella" and the English "Molly Whuppie" are equally stories to delight; Grimm's folktales are simply well named; the French elephant Babar and the American monkey Curious George are cousins under the skin; and the Swedish Pippi Longstocking is an enviable peer with the kind of freedom children of almost any nationality would like to have, at least for a time. When, as has happened, some enterprising teacher decides to read *Heidi* as part of the Social Studies unit on Switzerland, we can be sure that it is Heidi herself who holds the children's interest and not the description of the Swiss Alps.

What matters to children, in translations, as in all their other literature, is simply that the content and characters be recognizable to them. Collodi's *Pinocchio* is not only an Italian book; it is a universal story of mischief, adventure, and childlike repentance, a combination no other writer has ever captured quite so well. It may well be more stylishly translated into German or Swedish than into English, its Italian milieu may move more easily into Spanish than into English, but these are details that are of no concern to children. In their natural egotism they assume that the entire world consists of replicas of themselves. So, in reading any book from another culture, provided only that the familiar elements take precedence over the foreign, they simply translate the translation into their own terms.

Will the foreign element, then, offer no stumbling block to the child reader? Probably no more so than the effort required to move into the "other worlds" of fantasy or into the past of historical fiction. E. M. Forster spoke of requiring the reader to "pay a little extra" to enter a fantasy world. There is also the "payment" for reading a translated novel, but it is an even smaller amount because children

2. Dates given in the text are those of the first translation into the English language.

today will have already received a great deal of exposure to cultures other than their own. English-speaking societies are far more heterogeneous than they were in the past. Informational books on other countries abound. School curricula now frequently present comparisons of cultural differences. And, of course, television brings into view the most alien societies right in the family living room.

Under these circumstances, it is easy to see why children's librarians do not even trouble to segregate translated children's books from those originally written in English. Translations constitute an integral part of the corpus of children's literature as it is read and studied in the English-speaking world and no account of contemporary trends, issues, and achievements in writing for children can be complete without some consideration of translations.

What is important to assess is thus precisely the same as with works written originally in English: what books have survived from the past to form part of the present stock of children's reading and what accounts for their continuing persistence?

Viewed in historical perspective, the impact of translations on our children's reading begins rather late. The first children's novel in translation, still notable for its readership and influence, was Johann Wyss's *The Swiss Family Robinson*, translated from the German in 1814. This is a most intriguing instance of a plot, originally derived from an English-language book, being reworked and given back to English-language readers with a fresh vision and a new appeal. *The Swiss Family Robinson*, as the title acknowledges, stems from Daniel Defoe's *Robinson Crusoe*. But while Defoe's protagonist was an adult, Wyss's characters were children romping through an island of marvels. It was the first time that English-speaking children had a novel that took them out of their everyday home environment. No doubt Wyss's morality, which at times was heavier even than that of Defoe's, and his delight in instruction—in the very act of escaping from the shipwreck, the father pauses to explain the principle of the lever "as well as I could in a hurry"—soothed parental concerns over the suitability of such exotic material for children. Still, children's affinity with the desert island theme and their love of adventure became known facts that hundreds of writers, from Ballantyne to Scott O'Dell, have since used.

While Wyss capitalized on an already popular theme in adult literature, Heinrich Hoffman's *Struwwelpeter* (1848), sometimes translated as *Shock-headed Peter*, gave a new form to the cautionary tale, one of the oldest genres in children's literature. The cautionary tale, a story intended to convey a moral, still held all but universal sway in the first half of the nineteenth century. Hoffman had written *Struwwelpeter* for the *amusement* of his children and by putting into verse

277

the dire consequences that befell little boys who did not eat their soup and little girls who played with matches, he broke the pattern of the humorless moral tale. With his wildly exaggerated look at disobedience, Hoffman directly influenced Hilaire Belloc to write his *Cautionary Tales for Children* (1918). In turn, Belloc's larger-than-life look at children's faults can be viewed as a forebear of *Charlie and the Chocolate Factory* (1964), the popular novel for children by Roald Dahl. There would have been no Charlie had not the Fredericks and Alberts gone before. The trend to verse also continues in direct imitation of Hoffman and Belloc in Maurice Sendak's *Pierre* (1962) and in the Harlin Quist book *From Bad to Worse* (1972) by Geraldine Richelson.

Popular though *Struwwelpeter* was and to some extent still is, it was a little Italian puppet and a little Swiss girl who completely conquered the child reading world, gaining fame not enjoyed by any English-language book of the period and rarely since. Both Collodi's *Pinocchio* (1892) and Spyri's *Heidi* (1884) appeared in their own languages in 1880. Since the children's novel has been relatively insignificant as a literary development in either Italy or Switzerland prior to and since the publication of *Pinocchio* and *Heidi*, the two works seem to have been one-of-a-kind phenomena. Both are of lasting interest in pointing up the qualities that allow a book to leap the boundaries of space and time.

Pinocchio is a character immediately recognizable to children. His naughtiness has the broad humor of a child's joke and the consequences that follow upon his misdeeds evince the simple justice of the folktale, so understandable to children. Pinocchio behaves like an ass and becomes one; he lies and his nose grows longer. He is continually undone by his own selfishness and thoughtlessness, but he has a good heart which enables him to win through. And the tale of his winning through offers the child reader of today a good deal of fun and excitement.

But when *Pinocchio* appeared in its English translation in 1892, it had an effect that went beyond mere delight. At that time English children's literature had reached its First Golden Age and was almost beginning its descent into the age of sentimentality. With the exception of Edward Lear's nonsense verses (1846) and the sophisticated humor of *Alice's Adventures in Wonderland* (1865), the best literature, especially fantasy, was very serious stuff indeed. *Pinocchio* certainly did not throw out the moral tradition in children's literature, but it did something of almost greater consequence; it lightened it with childlike humor rather than with the parody of a Lewis Carroll or the allegory of a George MacDonald. *Pinocchio* represented a breakdown in the strict rules of conduct and order so dominant in English and American children's books of the day.

In Italy, and the other southern countries, less distinction was made between child and adult than in northern countries. Yet children have to be instructed and it was Collodi's genius that he found such a holdable middle ground between didacticism and pleasure. *Pinocchio* has taken on an almost legendary quality and he still would be more easily recognized by children today than most characters in modern fiction. One must here acknowledge the influence of the Walt Disney film and, of course, the pervasiveness of the Disney illustrations in most available editions. However, the recent reissue of the first English edition with the original illustrations may well restore *Pinocchio* to the status he deserves—literature and art rather than cartoon.

When Johanna Spyri's *Heidi* was translated into English in 1884, the English realistic novel for children, and particularly for girls, was barely struggling out of its cocoon of home and hearth, and the narrow settings of gloomy Victorian houses and dingy London streets. Heidi brought a breath of fresh air into children's literature which had been lacking since *Little Women* had been published almost twenty years before. Its freshness lay not only in its physical setting of the Swiss Alps but also in its portrayal of believing, loving relationships between the old and the young, the whole and the maimed. In tune with the prevailing ideas of childhood, Heidi conquers her problems through her innate, childlike qualities of simple goodness and perception. Yet Heidi's feeling of aloneness as she leaves her grandfather's mountain cottage for a wealthy town life is equally movingly described. The sense of alienation that she suffers has now become a major trend in modern children's literature but, unlike the modern writers, Spyri developed her theme without showing the traumatic effects on a child's life of such a disruption. But then Spyri and her contemporaries probably ascribed a tougher quality to children than do their modern counterparts.

The long lapse of time between the 1880s and the 1920s, when the next outstanding foreign stars appear, is not surprising, considering the First World War years. *Bambi*, by the Austrian writer Felix Salten, was translated from the German in 1928. Bambi was a highly anthropomorphized, sentimentalized deer, whose adventures, from infancy to maturity, were played out in a middle-European forest. Children of the period, and a long time after, loved him. Their affection was due in large part to their natural affinity for animals but probably also to Salten's moving attribution of human relationships to animals. His pictures of the loving mother, the aloof, austere father, sisterly and brotherly love, sweetheart relations and intimations of sexuality quite natually piqued their interest.

Bambi's initial success was reinforced in 1942 by the appearance of the Walt Disney color cartoon. Salten's work now seems coy and even cloying, but it has also a peculiarly modern ring. His view of humans as tawdry and evil in their persecution of animals and his theosophical approach to wild creatures has resurfaced in the recent talking animal stories of Richard Adams.

While Salten carried on an established genre, Erich Kästner's *Emil and the Detectives*, translated from the German in 1929, broke new ground. Kästner's achievement was not only to introduce the detective-suspense story into children's literature but to give it its classic form, a form that has held right up into the present. Before Kästner, mystery and detection had been confined to the sensational boys' magazines of the late nineteenth and early twentieth centuries, with their stock creations of adult superdetectives such as Sexton Blake. Emil and the other children he meets in Berlin organize themselves into a team to defeat the villain, who has stolen Emil's money, without the help of adults and by childlike means, chiefly embarrassment, although based on the best police procedures. All in all, the book was a refreshing picture of urban childhood, written with the simplicity, skill, and humor notable in Kästner's novels for adults. Quite rightly he was the recipient of the first Mildred Batchelder award (1966) which honors each year the best book in translation.

The pattern established by Kästner, that of happy, resourceful, independent children acting in concert, continued in the mystery stories of the French writer Paul Berna, most notably in *A Hundred Million Francs* (1957) and its sequel *The Street Musician* (1960). Nowadays the omniscient detective has returned in the persons of the Swedish adult Agaton Sax and the American boy wonder, Encyclopedia Brown. And certainly in the newer American thrillers such as Ellen Raskin's *The Westing Game* (1978) and Paul Zindel's *The Undertaker's Gone Bananas* (1978), the childlike quality has completely disappeared as the writers seem to aim for a "made for TV" theatricality.

Probably no book in translation has achieved the popularity of Astrid Lindgren's *Pippi Longstocking* or held it for so long. When the book first appeared in 1950 it startled and upset many adults, but it became a surefire success with children. Pippi broke all the rules of conventional child behavior. Her manners were atrocious, she was strong enough to lift a horse, which was a good thing because she kept one on her verandah, and she refused to go to school. But above all, she *lied*, even if with a perfectly good excuse:

> "Yes, it's very wicked to lie," said Pippi even more sadly. "But I forget it now and then. And how can you expect a little child whose mother is an angel and whose father is king of a cannibal island and who herself has sailed on the ocean all her life—how can you expect her to tell the truth always?"

But her next-door friends, the "normal" Tommy and Annika, recognize her for what she is, a staunch friend and comrade in every situation. And children around the world feel the same.

For a variety of reasons, no recent novel in translation has reached the popular peak of these earlier stories. Certainly no one book stands out by reason of constant demand by child readers in general. The most obvious cause for this, of course, is the sheer numbers of books now available in the English language. Perhaps more significant is the strong competition and compelling influence exercised by the pervasive "problem novel." The problem novel's emphasis on realism places a premium on familiarity and its simplistic style may make its readers unwilling or unable to cope with more difficult material. Under these circumstances, many children are ill-prepared for the often lengthy and complex foreign novels, especially when the setting is remote from their own environment.

Two excellent foreign novels that have not fared well in terms of general popularity are Fritz Mühlenweg's *Big Tiger and Christian* (1952) and Herbert Kaufmann's *Red Moon and High Summer* (1960), both translated from the German. *Big Tiger and Christian* is a marvelous story of friendship and adventure in which two boys, one a Chinese and one a missionary's son, cross the Gobi Desert in the early 1920s during the time of the generals' wars. It is a lengthy, picaresque novel, filled with dramatic incident and colorful characters. *Red Moon and High Summer* is an equally complex and lengthy story of the Tamashek people who live in the Sahara Desert. A people's way of life is unfolded through the story of Mid-e-Mid, the maker of songs, the girl he loves, Tiu'elen (Red Moon); and the young man she marries, Ajor (High Summer), a prince of his tribe. Like *Big Tiger and Christian* it has a host of characters and a multitude of events played out against a minutely described landscape. The young people struggle with their personal lives and problems as do the young everywhere. The difference between this novel of present-day life in the Sahara Desert and most English-language contemporary scene novels that deal with a growth of understanding toward the self is the delicacy of the relationships among the three protagonists and the unselfishness they exhibit that finally puts their personal worlds into a mature tranquility. The scene in which Red Moon confesses to Ajor that she has loved Mid-e-Mid, and only married Ajor (whom she has now come to love) through obedience to her father's will may in all likelihood be the most moving love passage in children's literature:

> Red Moon thought for a long time. He knew that this was the moment of decision for them both. . . . Right and custom, time and place, all heaped the burden of decision on Ajor's shoulders. . . .
> And in that hour and that night, a young man fought a great battle and won a mighty victory over himself. It was a conquest as outstanding and as painful as the one with which the girl had sacrificed herself to her father's wishes. And in that hour and that night, High Summer and Red Moon were worthy of each other.

Both *Big Tiger and Christian* and *Red Moon and High Summer* are representative of all the best books in translation in the way they impart a strong flavor of a different culture while speaking to universal experience. A translated book's foreignness is often observable in more than the setting; it comes through as well in a discernable difference in the social fabric of a society. Modern Russian society and its emphasis on striving for excellence is thus adeptly suggested in Anatolii Aleksin's *My Brother Plays the Clarinet*, translated from the Russian in 1975. The story is told in diary form by a young girl who professes her determination to sacrifice her life for her brother's career. Although the theme sounds serious, it is presented in a warm and funny way. The girl unconsciously reveals her motivation—that she really hopes to ride to glory on her brother's efforts. But the chief cultural difference between this and most American novels is that an acceptance of excellence permeates the narrative. If the brother, Dema, becomes a fine classical clarinetist, his peers will look up to and admire him. In contrast, the peer pressures in American stories seem to be toward "normality," even mediocrity. In the second story in this book, "The Secret of the Yellow House," both Sergei's parents are engineers but this is a statement of fact; it in no way makes the boy feel "different." It is simply that in the USSR it is customary for a woman to have a career. Nor does the fact that his parents are "perfect"—they enjoy cold showers, jogging, and healthful foods—send Sergei into a trauma which would be the expected reaction in a current American "problem" novel. The story is simply one of a delicate and moving friendship between Sergei and his grandmother, who takes him to restricted movies, and between Sergei and his father's first wife.

The working mother is also taken for granted in most modern

Swedish books. In an ordinary mystery story, *The Riddle of the Ring* (1966), by Karen Anckarsvard, where the father is a minister and the mother a dentist, the only comment is a joking one about the marriage between religion and science. A few interesting details about the running of a household with a working mother are given, but both these and the mother's profession do have a bearing upon the plot.

Since the writers of the American problem novel purport to be honestly translating into print the lives of everyday American children, they offer their books for an obvious comparison to books in translation. In general, the books that come to us from abroad are happier and more optimistic in tone and less poundingly social than their American counterparts. This can be seen from two works strongly similar in basic theme—the relationship of a retarded boy with a normal one—as in Bo Carpelan's *Bow Island* (translated from the Finnish in 1971) and in the American Kin Platt's *Hey, Dummy* (1971). In the former book the boys share some happy excursions, while in the latter the main thrust is the cruelty and indifference of the adult world toward a retarded child.

The differences in outlook often come across to the reader through small, seemingly unimportant details. The American Norma Klein in *Mom, the Wolf Man and Me* (1972) refers several times to the fact that Brett's mother wears blue jeans. She sees this all-pervasive uniform as a symbol of independence and nonconformity. In Carpelan's *Bow Island* the boy simply observes how much more suitably his mother is dressed for a boating picnic in her blue jeans than is a neighbor in a flowery, fragile dress. So too, judging by Maria Gripe's *The Night Daddy* (1971) and *Julia's House* (1975), the single-parent family is more taken for granted in Swedish than in American books. For Gripe, the single parent is simply one of the elements in her setting, not the raison d'être.

Not surprisingly, the greatest difference between English-language novels and those from Europe are seen when they treat of the more momentous themes, such as war. British and American writers such as Jill Paton Walsh, Alan Garner, Nina Bawden, Penelope Lively, Bette Greene, and T. Degens have all used World War II as a setting and a means. They probe deeply into the personal lives of their children, but one senses that the war itself does not matter that much; *any* traumatic interruption in the children's lives would have served just as well to portray their writers' main intent—an insight into the minds of their protagonists and whether maturation results.

Conversely, the European novels tend to stem from a more immediate, everyday connection with war. They are in every sense war novels, being at once more concerned with actual events—the German writer Hans Richter, for example, includes a chronology of events in an appendix to both *Friedrich* and *I Was There*—and yet more mythically charged, mythic in the sense of a larger story enveloping the immediate tale. The major power in these German novels arises from the fact that we know the ending to the actual events. They therefore create both a catharsis and an irony that is lacking in the more personal war stories in English literature.

It is a revealing fact that in adult literature, with the exception of Stephen Crane's *The Red Badge of Courage* (an American Civil War tale), the two most memorable books about war have come from Europe: Erich Maria Remarque's *All Quiet on the Western Front* (about World War I) and Ignazio Silone's *Bread and Wine* (concerned with Italy under Mussolini). War is an experience of which Europeans have acquired all too close a knowledge. At the same time the sheer magnitude of the theme lends itself particularly well to translation. Not surprisingly then, war novels figure largely among translations for both adult and juvenile audiences.

While all the finest war novels are really antiwar stories, those written for children—indeed, *because* they are written for children— also make clear statements about tyranny. So most of them have a sweeping, timeless quality, the ideas seeming somehow larger and more universal than the tragedies of civil life.

Alki Zei's *Wildcat under Glass* (1968) and *Petros' War* (1972), two of the finest children's novels in translation, exhibit almost all the features commonly found in the European war novels. The setting of the former is Greece under the dictatorship of General Metaxas in 1936 and the latter concerns the occupation of Athens by the Germans in World War II. There are in both books underground movements, as in most of the stories set in conquered countries, and the children are participants in the resistance as the "go-betweens." Thus physical danger is close and terrifying.

In British books such as *The Machine-Gunners*, by Robert Westall, and *Tom Fobble's Day*, by Alan Garner, the children are mostly affected by the change in their everyday living conditions; excitement and terror intervene only occasionally when bombs rain from the sky. But in Europe the children have experience of war from the ground up, so to speak. They are enmeshed in the events and cannot stand apart from war's destruction and death. They also want only what war has taken away, their families, or, less dramatically, the ease, physical comfort, and security that a loving, stable family life once had given them. They cannot be concerned with "growing up" or "coming to terms with themselves." They are, in a sense, already there. War has already made them wise beyond their years, even when, as in the Zei books, they are shown to retain some childlike attributes when the war comes to an end.

But whether wise or naive, the children in the European books are children, that is, nine, ten, or eleven years old when the story begins, as opposed to the young adolescents in most of the British and American books. And they are much more unsophisticated. *Wildcat under Glass* begins:

> Sunday, in winter, is the dreariest day of the week. I would like to know if all the children in the world have such a boring time as my sister Myrto and I do.

Melia's perceptive but childlike style continues as the events are seen through her eyes: the difficulties that arise in a close family after Myrto joins the children's legionnaire group and Melia and her young friends help Uncle Niko, who is in the resistance movement. A mythic feeling permeates the story. Greece's past and present are linked through Grandfather's retellings of the ancient Greek tales and Uncle Niko's stories of "the wildcat under glass" that lives in the parlor and that becomes a symbol of freedom. And as the story ends the children are still children, Uncle Niko has escaped to Spain, and

> Then—you would think we had agreed to do it ahead of time —we all stood on top of the rocks and cupped our hands and called:
> "Stay well, Nikoooo! Can you hear us? Stay well, Nikoooo!"
> The wind bore our voices far away over the sea. Alexis called too, even though he had never known Niko and the wildcat in the glass case.

The warmth of feeling evinced in *Wildcat under Glass*, particularly in the depiction of family life, is characteristic enough of European war novels but such warmth does not negate or erase the presence of higher feelings and tragic events. The children in European war fiction are by no means as sure of being physically "safe survivors" as are their English-speaking counterparts. Thus in Alki Zei's *Petros' War*, a child is shot by a German officer in a last, frustrated gesture as the Germans flee Athens. In the German novels, particularly those of Hans Peter Richter, outright bitterness is frequently the dominant tone.

Richter's *Friedrich* (1970) and *I Was There* (1972) tell of the effects of the Nazi regime on the children of the Third Reich. Both books could also be described as stories of friendship and World War II in Germany, but the main protagonist is really the Nazi Party and the events roll on to their inexorable conclusion. Like the child in Jerzy Kosinski's adult novel *The Painted Bird*, Richter's protagonists are helpless before "the man on horseback." They are the children of a thousand years of oppression and war. As in the Zei books, the children are very young when the realities of their situation are brought to their attention. But for a while, they are very ordinary children. In *I Was There* the nameless narrator and his friend Gunther, whose father does not approve of Hitler, are only eight years old as the book opens and they sing the "Internationale" without realizing its implications in Nazi Germany. The first part of *Friedrich* shows the Schneiders, a Jewish family, living a warm, happy life:

> Frau Schneider crouched down. Laughing, she hugged Fried-
> rich against her and knocked the snow off his coat. Then she
> took hold of his shoulders and danced around him in the snow.

But by 1942 the family has been destroyed and, as the bombs fall, Friedrich, denied entrance to an air raid shelter, is killed. Death is also the ending for two of the three protagonists in *I Was There* whose story moves from childhood to service in Hitler's army.

The consequences of political tyranny are constant motifs in these European war novels, serving, as in the Zei and Richter books, as springboards for personal events. It is not a theme particularly noticeable in English and American realism, probably because it is not seen as part of the social fabric. Tyranny does surface, however, and constantly in the works of modern British epic fantasists, such as Susan Cooper's "The Dark Is Rising" quintet and in Joy Chant's *Black Moon and Red Mountain* where it is translated into the universal concept of evil. Such books have an epic proportion and differ from European fantasies that portray tyranny with a folktale-like direct-ness and allegorical moralizing such as do Otfried Preussler's *The Satanic Mill* (1972), translated from the German, and Vaclav Ctvrtek's *The Little Chalk Man* (1970) from Czechoslovakia. Both these books have the unescapable directness of Jan Trinka's famous film on tyranny, "The Hand."

Even a more introspective book such as Anne Holm's *I Am David* (1965), translated from the Danish, attempts a large statement. David escapes from an internment camp in Greece and makes his way to his home in Denmark. As a captive child, he has learned none of the practical details of the real world. After he stows away on a ship bound for Italy, he is discovered by a sailor:

> The Italian shook his curly black head. Never had he met
> such a child! "First he swigs my wine without knowing what it
> is, and then he thanks me for it as if it weren't sheer robbery!"
> And he was so quiet. A boy caught when he was up to mischief
> usually made off as fast as his legs would carry him.

But David also has a wisdom beyond his years. He does not want to play war because he knows it is "horrible and evil." This wisdom frightens the mother of Maria, the child whose life David has saved. The mother says:

> "He tells her about such things so that she can take care of herself and so that she may know how fortunate she is. But I'll not have Maria's innocent, carefree childhood spoilt by a knowledge of evil she has no idea of. Children have their own troubles—they mustn't be expected to bear the miseries and sorrows of the grown-up world."

No matter how harrowing the events in European novels this is a viewpoint to which most of their writers implicitly subscribe.

I Am David has been one of the more popular recent books in translation possibly because Anne Holm's stance is close to that of many of her English-language contemporaries. Like them, she does not spare her readers the more personal cruelties that society wreaks and allows. And David does come to a self-awareness, one that leaves him tainted; he has moved from Blake's *Songs of Innocence* to *Songs of Experience*. But for all he learns about himself, David is still more of a symbol than the children are apt to be in English-language books—a watching symbol, ruthlessly surveying the adult corruption and evil in which he has been enveloped.

This feeling of envelopment is apparent most of all in Erik Haugaard's *The Little Fishes* (1967). Although actually written in English, it has the feeling of a translation because it is the work of a Dane, is set in Italy, and so carries the eye-witness feeling of an European war novel. Gino, like David, is the child made wise beyond his years. Again, unlike the protagonists in the British war stories, the "little fishes" do not experience war as a distant, personal excitement staged for their development and ambivalent thrill. They recognize their insignificance as they struggle for the basic needs of physical survival, for food and shelter in a world of desperate insanity. Much of the realism of the book comes from the remarkable depiction of the subculture of these cunning and loyal waifs. Though Chas's gang in Westall's *The Machine-Gunners* and Bill and Julie in Jill Paton Walsh's *Fireweed* provide some British counterparts, their experiences cannot match the compelling harshness of Haugaard's look at war. His children realize so clearly and sadly how adults, out of negligence or fallibility, will not provide them with love or security. In *The Little Fishes* it is not just an enemy army that is the threat but the whole adult world.

Paradoxically enough the European war novel is almost matched, for quality and number of contributions by the "literary folk tale." This form of light, humorous fantasy is not a strong part of the English-language tradition any more. Such books as Wilhelm Hauff's *Dwarf Long-Nose* (1960), Otfried Preussler's *Robber Hotzenplotz* (1964), and *The Little Ghost* (1967) offer a kind of gentle parody of the folk tradition, done up in simple, almost cartoonlike fashion. In probably the best example of the genre, Preussler's *The Little Ghost* lives in the town museum of Eulenberg, but he has never seen the town by daylight. When he gets his wish to do so, his reversed black figure in the daytime frightens the townspeople; after all, a white ghost at night is much more normal. He is finally restored to his night hauntings by two resourceful children.

These lighter books for younger children, built on fantasy and humor, continue in the extravaganza-like vein of a *Pippi Longstocking*. The cultural flavor in them is almost nonexistent, but in the midst of the now more serious English-language books they provide islands of fun. And in their lighthearted way they offer a reversal of the child-adult relationship; the normal world is turned upside-down for a change. The Norwegian Alf Prøsen in the *Mrs. Pepperpot* series (from 1959) has an old lady as his main character who, although unexpectedly and without reason shrinks to the size of a child, uses her wits to overcome all the ensuing difficulties. The Austrian Christine Nostlinger in *Conrad* (1976) plays a trick on the adult world by having her factory-made child a model of what adults would consider perfection. Conrad has to be taught to be naughty. All in all Europeans seem less worried about childhood than their English-speaking counterparts and less inclined to push their characters into adulthood. Swedish Maria Gripe's delicate fantasy, *The Glassblower's Children*, has two doll-like children who are just as charmingly wooden at the end of the story as at the beginning. But in its sophisticated portrayal of adult human needs and desires it is reminiscent of the literary fairy tales of Hans Christian Andersen and Oscar Wilde.

But while European novelists still hold to the traditional view of childhood as a separate state from adulthood, they usually add to that view the modern understanding of the basic need for a child's sense of self. Both these concepts are prominent in the works of Maria Gripe, who is deservedly considered a "classic" writer in her own time. In her childhood trilogy *Josephine, Hugo,* and *Hugo and Josephine* (1960-70), Gripe remembers the simple anxieties and uncertainties of childhood as well as the great flashes of joy. She remembers her own reactions to colors, tastes, and sounds, and the intensity of all feeling:

> It's blazing hot today. Mama hasn't time to take Josephine down to the lake and swim. No one has time for her. . . .

What on earth can she do today?

Go to the village, maybe, and chew gum? That will show the other children!

First she must practice her chewing in front of the mirror.

While Josephine is the loved and protected child who still has problems—she lacks self-assurance—Hugo is the personification of self-knowledge and personal satisfaction with oneself. He is, in a sense, a Pippi Longstocking without the fantasy. And while one can read into Pippi a longing for a father and a mother, Hugo knows exactly what he is about. "Hugo is Hugo. And no one else. The rest is unimportant." Being at one with himself gives him a maturity uncommon for his years. When his mother dies, he does not need comforting. "Yes. She's dead—but that's my business," and he sends his grieving father away for a rest because it "does everyone good, a change of air."

Hugo does not have to work at his independence. He is one of those delightful, rare beings who seem to be born with self-confidence and a sense of who he is and what he is doing. In fact, after some time at school he wistfully admits that he is beginning to miss himself. Hugo's assurance gives him an inner strength to make his own way in the world and he is not confused nor awed by other people's differing ideas. Because of his strength of character he unintentionally becomes something of a problem for his schoolteacher. "Hugo never meant to interfere—just felt he had to follow his own ideas on how to behave with people, as with animals." He causes disruption because he has reasoned opinions about everything he does and believes and his natural wisdom contrasts with the empty answers which are the teacher's only defense. In *Hugo and Josephine*, he explains: "There's no sense in our answering, when we don't know anything. We're the ones who ought to ask the questions."

Child readers, however, may well have more empathy with Josephine simply because she lacks self-confidence. "Deep down, Josephine really admired her. Gunnel was her Enemy Number One. ... I'm no good, she thinks, even as an enemy." She learns something about the nature of independence from Hugo, even though she does not altogether understand it. "Either you must be exactly like all the others. Or you must be completely different from them—as Hugo is. You mustn't ever be nearly like everyone else. As Josephine is."

Maria Gripe's subtle art in these books lies in her style. With utter simplicity and restraint she evokes the interior thoughts of the child Josephine—her earnest sensitivity and clear common sense—as she gropes toward an intellectual understanding of herself, her friends, and the adults around her. Somehow, in a gentler, purer manner, she recalls the musings of Salinger's Holden Caulfield. Gripe's is the greater triumph, for a child's mind is more closed from this kind of keen comprehension than is that of a teenager. In both her allegorical fantasies and realistic tales, her human relationships are handled in a delicate, almost ritualistic way and the very writing about them suggests a ceremonial act.

The *Hugo* and *Josephine* books are unique in modern children's literature because they deal so perceptively with such *young* children and because, although both Hugo and Josephine are individual characters, Gripe still manages to convey through them a quality of universal childhood. There are few English-language writers today who share either of these qualities with Gripe, even though their writing may be every bit as literary and sensitive. Most explore their concepts with older children or young teenagers as the protagonists, and the coloration given to the traumatic and specific events of the stories lessen the attention paid to the nature of the child's reactions —the commonality of childhood.

Gripe's books are not laden with either national or local color. The King does come to Josephine's town; her life as a parsonage child does set her off from other children; but there is no overt quality of foreignness in Gripe's books. She translates well in this respect, and if her popularity does not equal that of Astrid Lindgren with *Pippi Longstocking*, she is still a favorite among English-speaking children.

But most novels gain from some cultural additive, particularly those that are not otherwise outstanding. This quality is seen at its best in the European variants of the problem novel. Whereas the American writers of problem novels take their own culture so much for granted that their backgrounds and settings become homogeneous and ultimately invisible, most European writers define their physical and cultural setting a little more specifically, as they define the problems with a little more adult humaneness.

Norwegian Babbis Friis-Baastad, in her *Don't Take Teddy* (1967), and Russian Vadim Frolov in his *What It's All About* (1968), like their American counterparts, are concerned with problems that stem from a mistrust of the adult world. Teddy does not trust his parents enough to tell them of his retarded brother's act of violence and flees with him. The Russian boy, Sasha, is alienated from the adults in his family because they have not told him the truth about his mother who has left his father, is happily living with another man, and pursuing her career as an actress.

While the background in *Don't Take Teddy* is neither outstandingly rich nor colorful, still the presence of a Danish mother, the depiction of a rural family and its difficult economic position, and

290

Teddy's flight with his brother to the mountainous countryside all add up to a feeling of reading a novel rather than analyzing a problem. The Frolov book contains far more references to Soviet culture, economics, and general way of life:

> Then Olga pitched in. She explained very clearly that both Yurka and I had to go to the village or we would be considered parasites and spongers, and if we didn't go somewhere and find work for ourselves, we'd be sent out of Leningrad, just as simple as that. We would find work in the village because people were always needed there, and if we were real Soviet citizens, then it was our duty to help out in the country's agriculture.

The endings are more conclusive, at least in these two novels, than in most of their American counterparts. They leave the feeling that the protagonists will not be deeply scarred because of their experiences. Teddy, through his parents' efforts, is finally convinced that his brother will be happier in a home for retarded children, and Sasha's uncle is there to support him as he decides that probably no one understands what life is all about.

Neither of these books is outstanding in a literary sense, at least in their English translations. This may reflect the difficulty of translation or simply the fact that it is not only the best books that are translated. But the chief point remains that translations are valuable additions to a nation's literary stock, not only because of the individual author's style and plot, but also because they can bring an entirely different viewpoint to a literary genre.

Another example of this can be seen in the historical novel. In the recent English-language historical novel the events, however accurately and faithfully reconstructed, are generally but a backdrop for the creative development of characterization. Even minor figures in such novels as Betty Sue Cummings's *Hew against the Grain* and K. M. Paterson's *Of Nightingales that Weep* are carefully developed. European historical fiction, on the other hand, tends more toward the imaginative reconstruction of events at the expense of a deep treatment of characters. Who is to say which is the better way to treat history in fiction? We are enriched by being able to read in English the best authors of both styles.

The German writer, Hans Baumann, with versatility, conviction, and skill has moved from the nomadic life of the Mongols and the establishment of the Chinese empire of Kublai Khan in *Sons of the Steppe* (1957), to Hannibal's invasion of Italy in *I Marched with Hannibal* (1962). Bartos-Höppner, in books also translated from the German, writes about *The Cossacks* (1962), and the aspirations of the Muslim tribes in the face of Russian domination in *Storm over the*

Caucasus (1968). More recent books in translation have continued to enlarge our world view. Moving out a step from Europe, there is Zvi Livne's *The Children of the Cave* (1969), translated from the Yiddish. Set in Palestine in 70 A.D., it describes with vivid simplicity the daily survival of a group of Jewish children against the tremendous odds of Roman oppression.

The struggle of one people against another for territorial and cultural dominance on the one hand, and survival on the other, is a common theme, one that in English-language historical fiction is the prime domain of Rosemary Sutcliff, who also describes the varied cultures that melded with pain and violence to form the British nation. In a more recent European novel, *An Old Tale Carved Out of Stone* (1973), by Russian anthropologist A. Linevski, there is a more moderate solution to tribal conflict in neolithic Siberia than one finds in most historical novels, particularly the European ones. Liok and his brother learn from a more advanced tribe the crafts of making utensils and forging weapons and are allowed to return home with their new-found knowledge. Although there is violence in the book, as in most historical fiction, here it is balanced by a Homeric detail of craftsmanship:

> Liok could not tear his eyes away from the skillful, sure movements of the master's fingers. Now Kibu was finished and looked his handiwork over with satisfaction. The spearhead seemed to have grown out of the wood.

These writers all offer a convincing glimpse into the irrevocable, rushing forces of history or, conversely, a quiet, leisurely look at the everyday life of the past.

A sensation of world citizenship is also experienced when reading novels in translation that are set in cultures other than the author's own. Both Cecil Bødker, who is translated from the Danish, and Signy Van Iterson, from the Dutch, write with a bifocular dimension, that is, in their own language and from the perspectives of their own culture about other ways of life of which they have personal knowledge.

Van Iterson in *Pulga* (1971), writes of the life of a waif in Colombia, a child who suffers the worst indignities of an uncaring and impoverished society, but who makes the best of it without whining and complaint and who wiggles his way into a better situation, after a series of adventures, by his childlike trust, optimism, courage, and resourcefulness. Bødker's *The Leopard* (1975), is set in Ethiopia and has all the ingredients of a first-rate thriller on a child's scale. It has chases, dangers, disguises, support, and friendship between two children. It is also a refreshing look at childhood in another culture. In a situation where the everyday need for food is of prime importance, Tibeso, the child protagonist, has no concern with self-introspection or even consideration for himself. The leopard has killed one of his family's few cattle while it was in his care and he must prevent a repetition. There is a touch of symbolism too in that the head of the gang of thieves and murderers is also designated "The Leopard." But for the most part this is a rousing and appealing adventure story made plausible by its background. These two books in particular seem to call out for a child audience around the world.

In the day-to-day world of English-language children's books, the fine novels in translation are frequently looked upon as a minority group which, despite having all the right attributes, are not really in the mainstream. Often they are praised critically and aesthetically, but are nonetheless ignored in the daily use of books with children. This seeming slight against books in translation comes at a time when their quality has never been better.

Yet one can find hope for the acceptance and survival of books emanating from other cultures in the success of Isaac Bashevis Singer. In his literary folktales, exemplified by *When Shlemiel Went to Warsaw* (1968), written in Yiddish and translated into English, he opens up to English-language children a lost world. In it are the turn-of-the-century Jewish shtetles of Poland, populated with wise men and fools, lovers, and storytellers. His art superbly evokes a single time and place, but transcends in its deep humanity any boundaries or divisions between cultures. Singer may be a supreme example of the writer whose works must be rendered into English for children, but the other fine books in translation echo, if they do not attain, his universality. Their undidactic message is clear and important—human nature is the same the world over.

Works Cited

Aleksin, Anatolii. *My Brother Plays the Clarinet.* [Two stories] Tr. by Fainna Glagoleva. Illus. by Judith Gwyn Brown. New York: Walck, 1975. 114 pp.

Anckarsvard, Karin. *The Riddle of the Ring.* Illus. by Michael A. Hampshire. Tr. from the Swedish by Annabelle MacMillan. New York: Harcourt, 1966. 188 pp. (First published in Swedish, 1964)

Bartos-Höppner, Barbara. *The Cossacks.* Tr. by Stella Humphries; Illus. by Victor G. Ambrus. London: Oxford Univ. Pr., 1962. 249 pp.

——*Storm Over the Caucasus.* Tr. by Anthea Bell. New York: Walck, 1968. 272 pp. (Originally published in German, 1963)

Baumann, Hans. *I Marched with Hannibal.* Tr. by Katharine Potts; illus. by

Ulrik Schramm. New York: Walck, 1962. 225 pp. (First published in German, 1960)

————*Sons of the Steppe.* Tr. by Isabel and Florence McHugh; illus. by Heiner Rothfuchs. London: Oxford Univ. Pr., 1957. 273 pp. (First published in German, 1954)

Belloc, Hilaire. *Cautionary Tales for Children.* Pictures by B. T. B. London: Duckworth, 1918. 79 pp.

Berna, Paul. *A Hundred Million Francs.* Tr. from the French by John Buchanan-Brown; illus. by Richard Kennedy. London: Bodley Head, 1957. 174 pp.; U.S. title, *The Horse without a Head.* New York: Pantheon, 1958. 180 pp. (First published in French, 1955)

————*The Street Musician.* Tr. from the French by John Buchanan-Brown; illus. by Richard Kennedy. London: Bodley Head, 1960. 164 pp. (First published in French, 1956)

Bødker, Cecil. *The Leopard.* Tr. by Gunnar Poulsen. New York: Atheneum, 1975. 186 pp.

Brunhoff, Jean de. *The Story of Babar, the Little Elephant.* Tr. from the French by Merle S. Haas. New York: Random, 1933. 47 pp.

Carpelan, Bo. *Bow Island.* Tr. from the Swedish by Sheila La Farge. New York: Delacorte, 1971. 140 pp. (First published in Swedish, 1968)

Carroll, Lewis. *Alice's Adventures in Wonderland.* Illus. by John Tenniel. London: Macmillan & Co., 1865. 192 pp.

Collodi, Carlo, pseud. *The Adventures of Pinocchio.* Tr. from the Italian by M. A. Murray. London: T. Fisher Unwin, 1892. 232 pp. (First published in Italian, 1880)

Ctvrtek, Vaclav. *The Little Chalk Man.* Illus. by Muriel Bathermann; tr. from the Czech. New York: Knopf, 1970. 81 pp.

Cummings, Betty Sue. *Hew Against the Grain.* New York: Atheneum, 1978. 174 pp.

Dahl, Roald. *Charlie and the Chocolate Factory.* Illus. by Joseph Schindelman. New York: Knopf, 1964. 162 pp.

Friis-Baastad, Babbis. *Don't Take Teddy.* Tr. from the Norwegian by Lise Sømme McKinnon. New York: Scribner, 1967. 218 pp.

Frolov, Vadim. *What It's All About.* Tr. by Joseph Barnes. New York: Doubleday, 1968. 254 pp.

Garner, Alan. *Tom Fobble's Day.* Etchings by Michael Foreman. London: Collins, 1977. 72 pp.

Gripe, Maria. *The Glassblower's Children.* Drawings by Harald Gripe. New York: Delacorte, 1973. 170 pp. (First published in Swedish, 1964)

————*Hugo.* Tr. from the Swedish by Paul Britten Austin. Drawings by Harald Gripe. New York: Delacorte, 1970. 153 pp. (First published in Swedish, 1966)

————*Hugo and Josephine.* Tr. from the Swedish by Paul Britten Austin. Drawings by Harald Gripe. New York: Delacorte, 1969. 168 pp.

————*Josephine.* Tr. from the Swedish by Paul Britten Austin. Drawings by Harald Gripe. New York: Delacorte, 1970. 132 pp.

————*Julia's House.* Drawings by Harald Gripe. New York: Delacorte, 1975. 182 pp. (First published in Swedish, 1971)

——The Night Daddy. Tr. from the Swedish by Gerry Bothmer. Drawings by Harald Gripe. New York: Delacorte, 1971. 150 pp.

Hauff, Wilhelm. Dwarf Long-Nose. Tr. by Doris Orgel; illus. by Maurice Sendak. New York: Random, 1960. 60 pp.

Haugaard, Erik Christian. The Little Fishes. Illus. by Milton Johnson. Boston: Houghton, 1967. 215 pp.

Hoffman, Heinrich. The English Struwwelpeter; or Pretty Stories and Funny Pictures. Leipzig: Rütten and Loening, 1848. (First published in German, 1845)

Holm, Anne. I Am David. Tr. from the Danish by L. W. Kingsland. London: Methuen & Co., 1965. 190 pp.; US title: North to Freedom. New York: Harcourt, 1965. 190 pp.

Kästner, Erich. Emile and the Detectives: A Story for Children. Tr. by May Massee. Illus. by Walter Trier. New York: Doubleday, 1929. 224 pp. (First published in German, 1929)

Kaufmann, Herbert. Red Moon and High Summer. Tr. by Stella Humphries. London: Methuen & Co., 1960. 209 pp. (First published in German, 1957)

Klein, Norma. Mom, the Wolf Man and Me. New York: Pantheon, 1972. 128 pp.

Lear, Edward. Book of Nonsense. London: Thos. McLean, 1846. 2 vols.

Lindgren, Astrid. Pippi Longstocking. Tr. from the Swedish by Florence Lamborn; illus. by Louis S. Glanzman. New York: Viking, 1950. 158 pp.

Linevski, A. An Old Tale Carved Out of Stone. Tr. from the Russian by Maria Polushkin. New York: Crown, 1973. 230 pp.

Linne, Zvi. The Children of the Cave: A Tale of Israel and of Rome. Tr. by Zipora Raphael. Illus. by Victor G. Ambrus. London: Oxford Univ. Pr., 1969. 168 pp.

Mühlenweg, Fritz. Big Tiger and Christian. Illus. by Rafaello Busoni. New York: Pantheon, 1952. 593 pp.

Nils-Olaf, Franzen. Agaton Sax and the Criminal Doubles. Illus. by Quentin Blake. London: Andre Deutsch, 1971. 128 pp. (First published in Swedish, 1963)

Nostlinger, Christine. Conrad. Tr. by Anthea Bell. Illus. by Franz Wittkamp. London: Andersen Press/Hutchinson, 1976. (First published in German, 1975)

Paterson, K. M. Of Nightingales That Weep. Illus. by Haru Wells. New York: Crowell, 1974. 170 pp.

Platt, Kin. Hey, Dummy. Philadelphia: Chilton, 1971. 169 pp.

Preussler, Otfried. The Little Ghost. Tr. from the German by Anthea Bell. Illus. by F. J. Tripp. London: Abelard-Schuman, 1967. 126 pp.

——The Robber Hotzenplotz. London: Abelard-Schuman, 1964. 126 pp.

——The Satanic Mill. Tr. by Anthea Bell. New York: Macmillan, 1972. 250 pp. (First published in German, 1971)

Prøsen, Alf. Mrs. Pepperpot's Outing and Other Stories. Tr. by Marianne Helweg. Illus. by Bjorn Berg. London: Hutchinson Junior Books, 1971. 123 pp.

Raskin, Ellen. *The Westing Game.* New York: Dutton, 1978. 185 pp.

Rey, H. A. *Curious George.* Boston: Houghton, 1941. [55] pp.

Richelson, Geraldine. *From Bad to Worse.* New York: Harlin Quist, 1972. 38 pp.

Richter, Hans. *Friedrich.* Tr. from the German by Edite Kroll. New York: Holt, 1970. 149 pp. (First published in German, 1961)

————*I Was There.* Tr. from the German by Edite Kroll. New York: Holt, 1972. 205 pp.

Salten, Felix. *Bambi: A Life in the Woods.* Tr. by Whittaker Chambers. Foreword by John Galsworthy. London: Jonathan Cape, 1928. 209 pp.

Sendak, Maurice. *Pierre: A Cautionary Tale in Five Chapters and a Prologue.* New York: Harper, 1962. 48 pp.

Singer, Isaac Bashevis. *When Shlemiel Went to Warsaw and Other Stories.* Tr. by the author and Elizabeth Shub. Pictures by Margot Zemach. New York: Farrar, 1968. 116 pp.

Sobol, Donald J. *Encyclopedia Brown, Boy Detective.* Illus. by Leonard Shortall. New York: T. Nelson, 1963. 88 pp.

Spyri, Johanna. *Heidi; Her Years of Wandering and Learning: A Story for Children and Those Who Love Children.* Tr. from the German by Louise Brooks. Boston: DeWolfe, Fiske & Co., 1884. 2 vols. (First published in German, 1880)

Van Iterson, S. R. *Pulga.* Tr. from the Dutch by Alexander and Alison Gode. New York: Morrow, 1971. 240 pp.

Walsh, Jill Paton. *Fireweed.* London: Macmillan, 1969. 140 pp.

Westall, Robert. *The Machine-Gunners.* London: Macmillan, 1975. 189 pp.

Wyss, Johann. *The Swiss Family Robinson.* London: M. J. Goodwin, 1814. 2 vols. (Originally published as *The Family Robinson Crusoe*)

Zei, Alki. *Petros' War.* Tr. from the Greek by Edward Fenton. New York: Dutton, 1972. 236 pp. (First published in Greek, 1971)

————*Wildcat under Glass.* Tr. from the Greek by Edward Fenton. New York: (Laurel-Leaf Library) Dell, 1968. 175 pp. (First published in Greek, 1963)

Zindel, Paul. *The Undertaker's Gone Bananas.* New York: Harper, 1978. 239 pp.

Epilogue

It has always been possible to perceive the patterns that characterize the literature of a previous generation and synthesize them into an aesthetic and societal logic. The literature of the last twenty years is no exception. At first glance, the unprecedented number of publications seems to hamper the emergence of a clear image of the literature of the 1960s and 1970s. A tug at any one of the loose ends of its fabric will release innumerable mediocre books that mirror the time but provide no insights into it. Their writers are akin to the forgotten Mary Howitts of the nineteenth century, rather than to the Maria Edgeworths or the George MacDonalds.

There is an equally sizeable group of meritorious books, written with inventive spirit, but which have failed to achieve any popular or critical acclaim. The fate of this group prompts the suspicion that many a worthwhile work is simply rendered invisible through the power of numbers. It is somewhat ironic that while individual books may disappear under this deluge, the patterns of modern children's literature can be documented as clearly and as strongly as in earlier times. The very scale and swiftness of social change and its immediate absorption into books for the young have made the characteristics of the literature distinctive from those of the past. Contemplating each book in its own right may support Saint Exupéry's thesis in *The Little Prince* that each rose is unique. Still, only a single step backwards reveals that the garden is filled with flowers of the same species.

It is the elements of recent social change which have created the new style, content, and even intention of the books which reflect them. Literature continues today to fulfill its ancient and most important role, that of reflecting society's view of the young and the young person's view of society. The initial confused reactions of the 1960s have settled down to a fairly consistent theme: that the process of growing up is something difficult, if not fearful. The best of modern writers are not concerned, as were their predecessors, with a state called childhood, either distinct from or in tandem with adulthood, but rather with an investigation of those conundrums of life most evident in the psychological transition from childhood to adulthood. Whether the plot consists of the probing of character and incident, or the unveiling of the cosmic forces—life, death, time, good and evil—in either case the young protagonists bear their own burdens of self-awareness and responsibility. They are the children of the old nursery rhyme, those born on Thursday who have "far to go." Every genre, from picture book to epic fantasy, addresses itself in some degree to these large philosophical issues. From Maurice Sendak's *In the Night Kitchen* to Susan Cooper's *The Dark Is Rising* quintet, the young wrestle with the secrets of themselves and the universe. Thus *In the Night Kitchen* the infant Mickey crows in an egotistical revelation:

> I'm not the
> milk and the
> milk's not me!
> I'm Mickey!

And Merriman in Cooper's *Silver on the Tree* warns the children that:

> "We have delivered you from evil, but the evil that is inside men is at the last a matter for men to control. The responsibility and the hope and the promise are in your hands—your hands and the hands of the children of all men on this earth."

Revelation and revolution hover in the air. If the young are not always actually at the barricades, they are at least depicted in an adversary position toward either an individual or a situation that represents the world at large—a world that is disillusioning, ominous, and threatening. In an increasing number of instances, despair itself forms the major theme. Writers such as Robert Cormier in *The Chocolate War*, William Corlett in *The Dark Side of the Moon*, Robert Westall in *The Machine-Gunners*, Simon Watson in *No Man's Land* and some of the writers of the problem novel have pushed it into seemingly nonredeemable proportions.

Fortunately, despair is usually not the final state, but a stage in the process of optimistic self-discovery. Madge, in Jill Paton Walsh's *Goldengrove*, has had her compassionate but fumbling attentions to a blind man rejected. He has seen her as a temporary relief from his despair rather than as a person in her own right. At the end Madge says:

> 'Ralph said some things couldn't be mended, some things were too late to be put right. And I just thought that sounded sick and wicked, I didn't understand what he meant at all. But now I see.'

Madge's optimism, and that of countless other modern protagonists, comes finally through her own inner strength. She may not like the world, but ultimately she finds the courage to face it as it is. As compensation there is the constant surprise of discovering both the inner self and the outer world of human behavior. The short-term despair is situational and eventually appeased by the deeply human interplay which merges the trauma with understanding. The deep shocks of perception that threaten to change life for the worse also lead to emotional growth: a clear change for the better.

Almost all great literature contains elements of the metaphorical journey toward integration of the self. Until recently these were not a notable part of children's literature, since children, from the faithful Puritans to the self-sufficient Ransome families, were assumed to be whole beings, much more so than adults. Modern writers tend to assume that children are every bit as fragmented as adults and place them on the dangerous road toward selfhood. The emphasis on the code of the self—courage, stamina, freedom of choice, responsibility, constant awareness of life's absurdity, and how the resulting complexities affect personal morality—forms the common currency of existentialism and is fully present in most modern books. Today's fictional children are more apt to be junior Kierkegaards or Sartres than "Swallows or Amazons."

In their constant and determined expression of "going it alone," however, modern writers have brought their own brand of rigidity to children's literature, one that is as noticeable as that of the early writers of the Moral Tale. Whether the "pearls of wisdom" come in the measured tones of an enlightened adult—or of their animal or mythic surrogates—or in the less snappy, nannyish outlook of a Mary Poppins, the result is similar. Writers may intend "wisdom" to replace "authoritarianism" but they still propound a single rule for the conduct of life. In keeping with the spirit of the present age, the rule is now self-determination through self-discovery.

The new literature is also characterized by its pace and style. Although an actual count of days, weeks, and years covered in individual books would probably show that the time spans are no shorter than in earlier books, the impression left with the reader is quite different. Earlier writers conveyed a sense of slow, easy, organic time in dealing with childhood and its concerns. Nowadays the pace is more frenetic—like microwave cooking as opposed to the long stew. This is conveyed in the compact, conversational, somewhat cinematic style. Often the use of explicit language, the graphic portrayal of violent scenes, and an overall show of sophistication suggests that writers hope to equip children for the real world by denying them nothing except imagination.

First-person narrative dominates the scene, at least in realistic fiction, giving the book a one-dimensional vision. Even most third-person narratives have the same effect, since events are sifted through the feelings of the main character. It is only when writers deal with a group of the young interacting that the effect is different. There is in such books as Ivan Southall's *To the Wild Sky*, Elisabeth Mace's *Ransome Revisited*, Rosemary Harris's *Quest for Orion* and Virginia Hamilton's *Justice and Her Brothers* a broader outlook, one encompassing John Donne's belief that "no man is an island." When each character's actions and expressed emotions affect another, or others, they all seem closer to real life. These books are also, of necessity, more strongly plotted than the one-person introspective novels, whether written in the first or the third person.

At the beginning of Aidan Chambers's brilliant, iconoclastic, young adult novel *Breaktime*, Morgan takes the role of devil's advocate, charging that literature is "outmoded," "a lie," "neat and tidy" as opposed to life which is not, "a game played for fun."[1] Morgan's friend Ditto, the book's chief protagonist, undertakes an experiment to prove his thesis that literature is related to life, that "literature offers us images to think with," that its "unreality has nothing to do with untruth."[2] Ditto's experiment, the keeping of a journal which will either document the authentic events of half-term, "breaktime," or be his fictional invention, is a challenge to Morgan's cynicism. It can also be taken as an apologia for the best of modern children's literature.

Like Ditto's story, the best of the new literature constitutes an authentic reality. It does not speak with an outmoded voice; it does not deal with emotional fabrications; it does not impose an artificially consistent set of conventions upon the chaos of life; and it most certainly does not game-play for mere entertainment. It reflects today's life. Its frankness; its open-endedness; its themes of struggle, alienation, and personal courage; its shocks all are certainly the outward manifestations of our time. But is it any longer *children's* literature in any sense other than the physical ages of the characters?

1. Aidan Chambers, *Breaktime* (London: Bodley Head, 1978).
2. Ibid., p. 8.

While the protagonists, usually "old children" or young teenagers, frequently make very perceptive remarks about themselves and their feelings at a level of sophistication which makes the earlier literature seem very old-fashioned indeed, one misses the unflinching, yet childlike perceptions of the past. As Oswald Bastable begins the story of *The Treasure Seekers* (1899), he says, "Our Mother is dead, and if you think we don't care because I don't tell you much about her you only show that you do not understand people at all." The boy Hugh's musings in *A Castle of Bone* (1972) are epistemological: "If time melted, had no force, then space, the whole physical world could easily melt as well."

There are little children aplenty in the modern picture book but they too bear the burden and are expected to figure things out for themselves. In Robert McCloskey's *Blueberries for Sal* (1948), when both Sal and the little bear frighten one another, each runs to mother for a resolution. The little children in John Steptoe's 1980 book come themselves to the conclusion that *Daddy Is a Monster Sometimes*.

The adult style, outlook, and ideas do not, however, make it "adult" literature either, because adult characters are rarely shown as engaging in adult preoccupations. In the pages of these books they are chiefly shown as in positions of control in the world of the young, or as guides and mentors. Frequently, then, the impression is left of a watered-down adult book rather than a genuine children's book. In this sense the merging of the child's world with that of the adult does a disservice to both. The source of energy in earlier books also may now seem naive, since it stemmed from a happy and optimistic feeling about childhood in itself. The source of energy in the new literature can equally be charged with one-sidedness since it stems almost entirely from confusion and unhappiness, suggesting only childhood's end.

It should be remembered, with some comfort, that the shift in outlook that took place in the late nineteenth century with such works as *Alice in Wonderland*, *The Princess and the Goblin*, *Little Women*, *Tom Sawyer* and *Huckleberry Finn* was far more cataclysmic than that which has taken place since the 1960s. The idea of children's literature as literature in its own right was not only a courageous and original literary innovation, it helped generations to recognize and appreciate the personality of childhood.

Does the new literature call for different standards of judgment from the past? At first glance its characteristics may seem to call for a new approach. But any such attempt turns out to be illusory. The best books stand up to objective scrutiny according to age-old literary standards, while the poorer ones do not. However, it does take more time, knowledge, understanding, and courage than ever before to

301

separate the best from the poor or mediocre. This is chiefly because standards in any walk of life now tend to be deemed authoritarian. As modern society espouses the viewpoint, "if I do it, it must be right," so with literature, "if I like it, it must be good."

The principal barrier to easy evaluation is sheer numbers. The huge market simply makes it more difficult and time-consuming to sort out true originality from invention or mere imitation. The reviewing media are far less helpful than is *Consumer Reports* if one wants to buy a food processing machine, even if one accedes to the unfortunately common view of children's books as "products" rather than as works of art. In fact, this very notion of an item to be produced, sold, and forgotten, which increasingly characterizes trade publishing in general, makes possible the phenomenon mentioned earlier whereby the merely "good" book tends to get lost in the glut of mediocre-to-poor books. It takes the exceptional writer to overcome the economics of today's book marketing practices, which encourage one of the strongest characteristics of the new literature: the imitative "bandwagon" effect. Sensationalism and shock value may pass for originality on first appearance, but its effects are short-lived indeed. Dealing with the trendy issues of divorce, premarital sex, cruelty to children, and the like may sell out a first printing, but, as in the past, only the power of language well used and the insight which finds the timeless significance of these problems creates a book which will not be treated as just another instantly forgettable, and disposable, newspaper story or television drama.

Contemporary writers have changed the face of children's literature and there is little doubt that another generation will change it again. It will also be up to this generation to sift out what it wants from the books of the last twenty years. Judging from the past, one can expect that what is truly literature will keep its place—those books that are central to a cultural heritage, those that present the coherent and unifying power of human sympathy in vivid images.

Index

Designed by Jim Billingsley

Frontispiece art by Kevin Royt

Composed by Chas. P. Young–Chicago Ticomp System
   on Autologic APS-5 in Palatino

Printed on 55-pound Glatfelter Natural, a
   p-H neutral stock, and bound in B-grade
   Holliston Roxite cloth by Edwards Brothers, Inc.